NATURAL SCIENCES IN AMERICA

MAMMALS OF INDIANA

Marcus Ward Lyon, Jr.

ARNO PRESS
A New York Times Company
New York, N. Y. • 1974

Reprint Edition 1974 by Arno Press Inc.

Reprinted from a copy in the University
    of Illinois Library

NATURAL SCIENCES IN AMERICA
ISBN for complete set: 0-405-05700-8
See last pages of this volume for titles.

Manufactured in the United States of America

Publisher's Note: The illustrations in this
book have been enlarged by 5%.

———————————◆———————————

Library of Congress Cataloging in Publication Data

Lyon, Marcus Ward, 1875-
    Mammals of Indiana.

    (Natural sciences in America)
    Reprint of the 1936 ed. published by The University
Press, Notre Dame, Ind.
    Bibliography: p.
    1. Mammals--Indiana.   I. Title.   II. Series.
QL719.I6L9   1974   599'.09'772   73-17829
ISBN 0-405-05747-4

The American Midland Naturalist

Published Bi-Monthly by The University of Notre Dame, Notre Dame, Indiana

VOL. 17   JANUARY, 1936   No. 1

MAMMALS OF INDIANA

Marcus Ward Lyon, Jr.

CONTENTS

Introduction _____ 5
Acknowledgements _____ 9
Indiana as Type Locality for Species of Mammals_____ 9
Physiographic Features and Ecologic Areas_____ 10
Life Zones in Indiana _____ 12
Class Mammalia, Mammals _____ 14
  Order Marsupialia, Marsupials _____ 18
    Family Didelphiidae, Opossums _____ 19
      Genus *Didelphis* Linnaeus, Opossums _____ 19
        Didelphis virginiana Kerr_____ 19
  Order Insectivora, Insectivorous Mammals _____ 25
    Family Talpidae, Moles _____ 25
      Genus *Parascalops* True, Hairy-tailed Mole _____ 26
        Parascalops breweri (Bachman) _____ 27
      Genus *Scalopus* Geoffroy, Common Mole _____ 28
        Scalopus aquaticus machrinus (Rafinesque) _____ 28
      Genus *Condylura* Illiger, Star-nosed Mole _____ 34
        Condylura cristata (Linnaeus) _____ 35
    Family Soricidae, Shrews _____ 37
      Genus *Sorex* Linnaeus. Shrews _____ 39
        Sorex cinereus cinereus Kerr _____ 39
        Sorex longirostris longirostris Bachman _____ 43
        Sorex fumeus fumeus Miller _____ 44
      Genus *Microsorex* Coues, Pigmy Shrews _____ 45
        Microsorex hoyi hoyi (Baird) _____ 45
      Genus *Cryptotis* Pomel, Small Short-tailed Shrew _____ 45
        Cryptotis parva (Say) _____ 45
      Genus *Blarina* Gray, Large Short-tailed Shrew _____ 47
        Blarina brevicauda (Say) _____ 47
  Order Chiroptera, Bats _____ 53
    Family Vespertilionidae, Common Bats _____ 56
      Genus *Myotis* Kaup, Mouse-eared Bats _____ 57
        Myotis lucifugus lucifugus (LeConte)_____ 60
        Myotis austroriparius (Rhoads) _____ 63
        Myotis grisescens A. H. Howell _____ 63
        Myotis keenii septentrionalis (Trouessart) _____ 64
        Myotis sodalis Miller and Allen _____ 66
        Myotis subulatus leibii (Audubon and Bachman) _____ 67
      Genus *Lasionycteris* Peters, Silver-haired Bat_____ 68
        Lasionycteris noctivagans (LeConte)_____ 68
      Genus *Pipistrellus* Kaup, Pipistrelles_____ 71
        Pipistrellus subflavus F. Cuvier _____ 71
      Genus *Eptesicus* Rafinesque, Serotine Bats_____ 74
        Eptesicus fuscus (Beauvois) _____ 74
      Genus *Lasiurus* Gray, Hairy-tailed Bats_____ 78
        Lasiurus borealis (Müller) _____ 78

Lasiurus cinereus (Beauvois) _____ 80
Genus Nycticeius Rafinesque, Rafinesque's Bats_____ 83
Nycticeius humeralis (Rafinesque) _____ 84
Genus Corynorhinus H. Allen, Big-eared Bats _____ 85
Corynorhinus rafinesquii (Lesson) _____ 86
Order Carnivora, Carnivorous Mammals _____ 88
Family Ursidae, Bears _____ 89
Genus Euarctos Gray, Black Bears _____ 89
Euarctos americanus (Pallas) _____ 89
Family Procyonidae, Raccoons _____ 95
Genus Procyon Storr, Raccoons _____ 95
Procyon lotor lotor (Linnaeus) _____ 95
Family Mustelidae, Mustelids _____ 98
Genus Martes Pinel, Martens _____ 99
Martes americana (Turton) _____ 99
Martes pennanti (Erxleben) _____100
Genus Mustela Linnaeus, Weasels _____101
Mustela rixosa allegheniensis (Rhoads) _____103
Mustela noveboracensis (Emmons) _____104
Mustela cicognanii Bonaparte _____109
Mustela vison mink (Peale and Beauvois) _____109
Genus Gulo Pallas, Wolverines _____113
Gulo luscus (Linnaeus) _____113
Genus Lutra Brisson, Otters _____115
Lutra canadensis lataxina (F. Cuvier) _____117
Genus Spilogale Gray, Spotted Skunks _____119
Spilogale putorius (Linnaeus) _____121
Genus Mephitis Geoffroy and Cuvier, Common Skunks _____123
Mephitis nigra Peale and Beauvois _____127
Mephitis mesomelas avia Bangs _____129
Genus Taxidea Waterhouse, Badgers _____131
Taxidea taxus (Schreber) _____131
Family Canidae, Dogs, Foxes, Wolves _____134
Genus Vulpes, Oken, Red Foxes_____135
Vulpes fulva (Desmarest) _____136
Genus Urocyon Baird, Gray Foxes _____140
Urocyon cinereoargenteus (Schreber)_____141
Genus Canis Linnaeus, Wolves_____143
Canis latrans Say, _____143
Canis nubilus Say _____150
†Genus Aenocyon J. C. Merriam, Dire Wolves _____155
†Aenocyon dirus (Leidy) _____156
Family Felidae, Cats and Allies _____157
Genus Felis Linnaeus, Cats _____157
Felis couguar Kerr _____158
Genus Lynx Kerr, Lynxes _____161
Lynx canadensis Kerr _____162
Lynx rufus (Schreber) _____164
Order Primates, Lemurs, Monkeys, Apes, Men _____167
Family Hominidae, Men_____167
Genus Homo Linnaeus, Men_____168
Homo sapiens Linnaeus_____168
Order Rodentia, Rodents or Gnawing Mammals _____169
Superfamily Sciuroidea, Squirrel-like Rodents _____171
Family Sciuridae, Squirrels _____171
Genus Marmota Blumenbach, Marmots_____172
Marmota monax (Linnaeus) _____172
Genus Citellus Oken, Ground Squirrels _____178
Citellus tridecemlineatus (Mitchill) _____179

Citellus franklinii (Sabine) _____182
Genus *Tamias* Illiger, Chipmunks _____187
    Tamias striatus fisheri Howell _____187
    Tamias striatus griseus Mearns _____191
Genus *Sciurus* Linnaeus, Tree Squirrels _____194
    Sciurus hudsonicus loquax Bangs _____195
    Sciurus carolinensis Gmelin _____199
    Sciurus niger rufiventer (Geoffroy) _____205
Genus *Glaucomys* Thomas, Flying Squirrels _____210
    Glaucomys volans volans (Linnaeus) _____211
Family Geomyidae, Pocket Gophers _____214
Genus *Geomys* Rafinesque, Pocket Gophers _____215
    Geomys illinoensis Komarek and Spencer ____216
Family Castoridae, Beavers_____220
Genus *Castor* Linnaeus, Beavers _____220
    Castor canadensis carolinensis Rhoads _____220
†Family Castoroididae, Giant Beavers _____226
 †Genus *Castoroides* Foster _____228
    †*Castoroides ohioensis* Foster _____230
Superfamily Muroidae, Mouse-and Rat-like Rodents _____231
Family Cricetidae, Cricetine Rodents _____231
Subfamily Cricetinae, Cricetine Rodents _____231
Genus *Reithrodontomys* Giglioli, Harvest Mice _____231
    Reithrodomtomys humulis merriami (Allen) ___231
Genus *Peromyscus* Gloger, White-footed Mice _____233
    Peromyscus maniculatus bairdii (Hoy and Kennicott) __236
    Peromyscus leucopus noveboracensis (Fischer) _____238
    Peromyscus leucopus leucopus (Rafinesque) _____239
    Peromyscus gossypinus megacephalus (Rhoads) _____241
    Peromyscus nuttalli aureolus (Audubon and Bachman)__241
Genus *Oryzomys* Baird, Rice Rats _____241
    Oryzomys palustris palustris Harlan _____241
Genus *Neotoma* Say and Ord, Cave Rats _____242
    Neotoma pennsylvanica Stone _____243
    Neotoma floridana illinoensis Howell _____247
Subfamily Microtinae, Microtine Rodents _____247
Genus *Synaptomys* Baird. Lemming Mice _____251
    Synaptomys cooperi stonei (Rhoads) _____251
Genus *Microtus* Schrank, Meadow Mice _____254
 Subgenus *Microtus* Schrank _____254
    Microtus pennsylvanicus (Ord) _____254
 Subgenus *Pedomys* Baird _____257
    Microtus ochrogaster (Wagner) _____257
Genus *Pitymys* McMurtrie, Pine Mice _____259
    Pitymus pinetorum (LeConte)_____259
    Pitymys pinetorum scalopsoides (Aud. and Bach.)__261
    Pitymys pinetorum auricularis (Bailey)_____262
Genus *Ondatra* Link, Muskrats _____262
    Ondatra zibethica zibethica (Linnaeus) _____264
Family Muridae, Rats and Mice _____270
Genus *Rattus* G. Fischer, Common Rats _____270
    Rattus norvegicus (Erxleben) _____271
    Rattus rattus rattus (Linnaeus) _____272
Genus *Mus* Linnaeus, House Mice _____274
    Mus musculus Linnaeus _____274
Superfamily Dipodoidae, Leaping Rodents _____276
Family Zapodidae, Jumping Mice _____276
Genus *Zapus* Coues, Jumping Mice _____276
    Zapus hudsonius (Zimmermann) _____277

Superfamily Hystricoidae, Hystricomorph Rodents _____281
Family Erethizontidae, Porcupines _____281
Genus *Erethizon* F. Cuvier, Porcupines _____281
Erethizon dorsatum (Linnaeus) _____281
Order Lagomorpha, Hares, Rabbits and Allies _____286
Family Leporidae, Hares and Rabbits _____287
Genus *Lepus* Linnaeus, Hares _____287
Lepus americanus phaeonotus Allen _____288
Genus *Sylvilagus* Gray, Rabbits_____289
Subgenus *Sylvilagus* Gray, Cottontail Rabbits _____289
Sylvilagus floridanus mearnsii (Allen)_____290
Subgenus *Tapeti* Gray, Swamp Rabbits _____293
Sylvilagus aquaticus aquaticus (Bachman)_____295
Order Artiodactyla, Even-toed Ungulates _____296
†Family Tayassuidae, Peccaries _____297
†Genus *Tayassu* Fischer _____297
†*Tayassu lenis* (Leidy) _____297
†Genus *Mylohyus* Cope _____298
†*Mylohyus nasutus* (Leidy) _____299
†Genus *Platygonus* LeConte_____300
†*Platygonus vetus* Leidy _____301
†*Platygonus compressus* LeConte_____301
Family Cervidae, Deer and Allies _____302
Genus *Cervus* Linnaeus, Elks _____303
Cervus canadensis (Erxleben) _____303
Genus *Odocoileus* Rafinesque, Deer_____307
Odocoileus virginianus (Boddaert) _____307
†*Odocoileus dolichopsis* (Cope) _____313
Family Bovidae, Cattle_____315
Genus *Bison* Hamilton Smith, Bisons or Buffaloes _____315
Bison bison bison (Linnaeus) _____317
†*Bison antiquus* Leidy _____321
†*Bison latifrons* (Harlan) _____322
†Genus *Ovibos* De Blainville, Muskoxen _____324
†*Ovibos moschatus* (Zimmermann) _____325
†Genus *Symbos* Osgood, Muskoxen _____326
†*Symbos cavifrons* (Leidy) _____329
Order Perissodactyla, Odd-toed Ungulates _____330
†Family Tapiridae, Tapirs _____330
†Genus *Tapirus* Cuvier, Tapirs _____330
†*Tapirus haysii* Leidy _____330
†Family Equidae, Horses and Allies _____332
†Genus *Equus* Linnaeus, Horses _____332
†*Equus* sp. indet. _____332
†Order Proboscidea, Proboscideans _____334
†Family Elephantidae, Elephants and Mastodons _____335
†Genus *Mammut* Blumenbach, Mastodons _____335
†*Mammut americanum* (Kerr)_____338
†Genus *Elephas* Linnaeus, Elephants and Mammoths _____341
†*Elephas boreus* Hay _____342
†*Elephas roosevelti* Hay_____343
†*Elephas jeffersonii* Osborn _____343
†*Elephas columbi* Falconer _____348
†Order Xenarthra, Sloths Anteaters, Armadilloes and Allies _____349
†Suborder Gravigrada _____349
†Family Megalonychidae, Ground Sloths _____349
†Genus *Megalonyx* Jefferson, Ground Sloths _____349
†*Megalonyx jeffersonii* (Desmarest) _____350
Bibliography _____352

INTRODUCTION

This work is an attempt to bring up to date the main facts of the mammalian fauna of Indiana and make them available in a single volume without recourse to the published writings of others more or less hidden away in serial publications containing other matters. The first serious observations on Indiana mammals were made 100 years ago by the Prince of Wied who spent the winter of 1832 to 1833 in the vicinity of New Harmony, the results appearing in print in 1839-41 and later again in 1861 to 1862. The next naturalist to write of the mammals of the State was Plummer who in 1844 published a list of those occurring in Wayne County. The first list of the mammals of the state as a whole was that of Evermann and Butler appearing in 1894, followed by another list the next year by Butler alone. In 1909 Hahn published a descriptive catalogue of the mammals of Indiana in one of the reports of the geological survey of the state. This last work is so complete that but little can be added to it. A few species suspected to be in the state by Hahn (1909) as well as by Evermann and Butler, (1894) and by Butler (1895) have been definitely added to Indiana's fauna and the range of many species widely extended either by the actual collection of specimens or by fairly trustworthy records. In the years since Hahn's publication many changes in the nomenclature of North American mammals have taken place all of which are incorporated in the present volume. My own interest in Indiana mammals began in 1922, in the autumn of which year I made a small collection of the mammals of the dunes region of Porter County. The study of this region was continued during the next two years. Since then I have secured occasional specimens from various parts of the state and have visited most of the ecological habitats in Indiana.

Like the lists of the authors preceding me this list includes not only the mammals actually living within Indiana today but also those forms that have been exterminated since the state was claimed by the white man. Three exotic mammals have actually been taken within or reported from Indiana's boundaries. They are so obviously accidental introductions that never could survive, that no mention of them is made in the text below. These are a rat, *Nyctomys* (Hahn 1909), a species of *Nasua* (Lyon 1923), and some sort of armadillo (newspaper reports). They are all tropical or subtropical forms. The present list like its predecessors also includes, printed in smaller type, several species of mammals which ought to be taken in Indiana but for whose presence in the state there is no satisfactory evidence.

As the Pleistocene mammalian fauna of Indiana is even of greater interest than the recent fauna and many of the larger forms excite great curiosity when found, all these that have actually been found in or reported for the state are included in the present list. They have mainly been taken from the publications of Hay (1912, 1923). No attempt has been made to include the Pleistocene forms that theoretically should occur in the state. For such the reader is referred to Hay's 1912 publication. But one zoological sequence is

followed in the list and the Pleistocene forms are placed in their regular taxonomic order, each extinct name being preceded by a dagger, †.

This descriptive list has been prepared largely with the idea of stimulating
a more active interest in the study of one of the most important groups of
animals known, the group to which man and most of his domestic animals
belong. Taxonomic study, that is classification and naming, can only be done
by means of well prepared study skins and skulls. The appearance of such
skins and skulls is well illustrated in several of the plates beyond. Two
excellent pamphlets on the preparation of such material are available at
nominal cost to the serious student. The directions prepared by Gerrit S.
Miller, Jr., constituting part N of Bulletin 39, United States National Museum, Government Printing Office, Washington, D. C.; and H. E. Anthony's
The Capture and Preservation of Small Mammals for Study, Guide Leaflet
No. 61, American Museum of Natural History, New York, N. Y. With a
little practice any school boy with a bent for natural history can learn to make
satisfactory skins and clean skulls for study purposes. There is no reason
why the largest high school in each county should not have its own little
collection of local mammals. In the course of a few years, with little effort,
each such collection would soon acquire all the common forms and some of
the rarities and in this manner make substantial contributions to our knowledge
of Indiana mammals and their distribution. The most important things to
know about any specimen are its actual place and environment of capture or
finding, the date, its sex indicated by these signs, ♂ male, ♀ female, its
total length, tip of nose to tip of tail (exclusive of hair); length of tail from
its root to its tip (exclusive of hair); length of hind foot, from end of heel
to end of longest toe, including claw. To these may be added its weight
(there are very few exact records of the weights of most of our small mammals), and length of ear. Notes may be made of such things as kind and
quantity of food in stomach or cheek pouches, number of mammae, number
of embryos in pregnant females, etc.

Unlike birds, mammals, with a few exceptions such as the squirrels, do not
appeal to man's esthetic sense. The majority of the smaller forms are seldom
seen in the wild state and many persons scarcely know of their existence.
They live on or under the ground, and are only secured by the use of traps
placed in suitable situations. It is often surprising to see what a line of small
mouse traps will yield. To determine the small forms in any locality it is
necessary to work with not less than 50 traps and twice that number is desir-
able. The best trapping that I have done in Indiana seldom yielded more
than a 10% catch, and sometimes not that. There are no legal restrictions on
trapping such small forms as mice and shrews and moles, and it is among
such small forms that our exact knowledge of distribution is lacking. Instead
of using traps that kill, all these small forms may be taken in traps that
catch them alive. The specimens may then be placed in suitable vivaria and
valuable observations may be made on their habits. Field observations and
records of mammals except on the larger more conspicuous forms are largely
unknown in marked contrast to such observations in birds.

Although descriptions and keys to all the Indiana species of mammals are included in the text and most of the forms are illustrated to show the external form of the animal and the appearance of the skull, yet the most earnest student will find difficulty in making satisfactory identifications in some of the groups, especially the bats and shrews. The larger museums, at Washington, New York, Chicago, Ann Arbor, etc., will always be ready to identify such difficult material, but as a matter of courtesy the museum consulted should be offered part of the material in exchange for the information given.

In addition to the description, a brief account of the life history of each is given. I have drawn freely from standard works and special articles, quoting frequently and in nearly every instance giving reference to the source of information, using Indiana material as much as possible. Historical references to the larger species have been taken from various sources, some authentic and some questionable. The most questionable are county history records. These histories were often published without name of author or compiler, and whoever prepared the brief mention of wild life in them I fear frequently did so on general principles rather than from exact knowledge. For the sake of completeness I have included all that I found containing reference to mammals. I scanned all the county histories and related works in the stacks of the Library of Congress. Hahn went through all the county histories presumably in the State Library, Indianapolis. It is interesting that we each found material overlooked or not available to the other. In addition to these there are many references to Indiana mammals in various sporting and outdoor magazines. Most of these references were given to me by Mr. E. A. Preble of the United States Biological Survey and I personally verified them.

The material on which this list is based is found in the larger museums where collections of mammals are maintained. By far the greatest number of Indiana specimens is found in the United States National Museum due to collections made by Hahn and by me. The Field Museum of Natural History, Chicago, and the Museum of Zoology, University of Michigan, also contain many specimens of Indiana mammals. Smaller numbers are to be found in the American Museum of Natural History, New York, the Museum of Comparative Zoology, Cambridge, Mass., and in the Museum of the Academy of Natural Sciences, Philadelphia, the Chicago Academy of Sciences and the Milwaukee Public Museum. There are collections of local mammals in the University of Notre Dame and in Indiana University. I have examined all this material. A few are recorded by Hahn as in the State Museum. These have been moved about in the State House so many times that their labels have become lost and they are of little scientific value. Unfortunately I have not had the opportunity of assembling it in one place and studying it as a whole. Most of the identifications have been made by others who have revised groups from time to time and have given complete lists of specimens examined by them. I have made free use of these descriptions and observations. In the case of the Pleistocene forms I have had to be content in large part

with the published records given by Hay (1912, 1923), though I have seen
much of the Pleistocene material in the United States National Museum
the American Museum of Natural History, the Carnegie Museum and some
in local collections. At the time I had opportunity to visit Earlham University the Pleistocene material in its possession was not available for examination,
being packed in storage boxes, following the salvaging of most of it from a
fire in the former museum building.

In the maps illlustrating the distribution of each species in Indiana, the
location of specimens, recent and historical observations the following symbols
are used:

A.—American Museum of Natural History, New York.
C.—Chicago Academy of Sciences, Chicago, Illinois.
D.—Department of Conservation, State Museum, Indianapolis.
E.   Earlham University, Earlham, Indiana.
F.—Field Museum of Natural History, Chicago, Illinois.
I.—Indiana University, Bloomington, Indiana.
M.—Museum of Zoology, University of Michigan, Ann Arbor, Michigan.
N.—University of Notre Dame, Notre Dame, Indiana.
O.—Recent observation, hitherto unpublished, mainly from questionnaire sent by the
Department of Conservation to game wardens and county agricultural agents.
P.—Academy of Natural Sciences, Philadelphia, Pennsylvania.
R.—Published record without specimen or place of specimen unknown, frequently
accompanied by the year when last seen.
U.—United States National Museum, Washington, D. C.
Z.—Museum of Comparative Zoology, Cambridge, Massachusetts.
1, 2, 3, etc., explained in the legend of the map.
The county has been made the unit of distribution.

The nomenclature and systematic sequence is that employed by Gerrit S.
Miller, Jr., in List of North American Recent Mammals, 1923, Bulletin 128,
United States National Museum 1924, unless groups have been revised or
other changes made since that date. Common names have been given for all
species, including the extinct forms, even though these names are often nothing more than an attempted translation of the scientific name, and frequently
they are longer. Following the current name is a brief synonymy in which
are given the names used by Wied, Plummer, Evermann and Butler, and
Hahn, and occasionally other names that have been applied by various authors
to Indiana specimens. The original place of publication of each species and
sub-species, together with its type locality are also given. In these cases the
author's name appears in small capital letters, and unless the original description is based on Indiana material the work is not included in the bibliography.

Measurements and weights are given almost entirely in the metric system,
the one actually employed in scientific work. In some old original descriptions
quoted and in the case of many of the larger forms the measurements are
given in inches and feet and the weights in pounds, followed by the approximate metric equivalents. One inch equals 25.4 mm., one pound equals 11/5
kilograms, or 1000 grams equals 2.2 pounds. Millimeters may be converted to
inches for all practical purposes by multiplying by .04. The three standard
measurements are given, total length excluding terminal tuft of hairs of tail;
length of tail or tail vertebrae, from root of tail to end of bone in tail; hind
foot, heel to most distant claw point. In most cases the approximate length

of skull between perpendiculars and its greatest width between perpendiculars are also given.

ACKNOWLEDGEMENTS

One of the pleasures in compiling this volume has been the uniform cordiality and generosity of the several institutions having Indiana mammals in their collections and of those in charge of them. These are: United States National Museum, Washington, D.C., U. S. Biological Survey; American Museum of Natural History, New York, University of Michigan, Field Museum of Natural History, Chicago Academy of Sciences, Academy of Natural Sciences, Philadelphia; Museum of Comparative Zoology, Cambridge; Carnegie Museum, Pittsburgh; University of Notre Dame; and Indiana University. Among those who have contributed notes, records, photographs, or bibliographic material are: American Museum of Natural History, United States National Museum, New York Zoological Society, Milwaukee Zoological Garden, University of Michigan, University of California, Chas. C. Deam, A. W. Butler, Frederick Test, Mrs. Grace Osterhus, Miss Louise Husband and a host of other friends and correspondents. All have my sincere thanks. My wife, Dr. Martha Brewer Lyon, has aided me in numerous ways and accompanied me on all collecting trips. Lastly I have to thank that brilliant Indiana naturalist, the late E. B. Williamson, for his enthusiastic support of the project. Through his efforts the State Department of Conservation made it possible to do some field work in the summer of 1930 in various parts of the state. This Department also procured several photographs, prepared a questionnaire and did other favors, hereby gratefully acknowledged. Dr. Remington Kellogg very kindly read the entire manuscript.

The descriptions, geographic distributions and life histories have been drawn from a great variety of sources. Among the older authors may be mentioned Audubon and Bachman, Baird, Coues and Allen. Among more recent authors may be mentioned Merriam, Mammals of the Adirondacks; a host of authors in the North American Faunas and in the Journal of Mammalogy, which are veritable mines of information; Stone and Cram, American Animals, Doubleday, Page & Company, New York 1904; H. E. Anthony, Field Book of North American Mammals, G. P. Putnam's Sons, New York and London 1928; and Ernest Thompson Seton, his well known and valuable Lives of Game Animals, volumes 1 to 4 (each volume in 2 parts), Doubleday, Doran & Company, Garden City, New York 1929. Much material regarding the characters and geographic distribution of the orders, families and genera has been taken from the Catalogue of the Mammals of Western Europe in the Collection of the British Museum by Gerrit S. Miller, Jr., 1912. All of these and many more are specifically referred to in their appropriate places and listed in the bibliography. As far as possible incidents in life histories have been taken from accounts relating specifically to Indiana mammals, such accounts all too few in number. Some have been taken from accounts of the same species in nearby states. It is probable that many such have escaped my notice.

INDIANA AS THE TYPE LOCALITY FOR SPECIES OF MAMMALS

Every scientific name is based primarily on the description of a single specimen which is designated as the type, at least all modern scientific names. Frequently the older taxonomists based names on descriptions without designated specimens or localities which in many instances has led to confusion. The locality from which the type came is known as the type locality. Indiana is the type locality of nine species of mammals, four of them being currently recognized species, three of them synonyms of other species, and two of them held bona fide species by one authority and held as synonymous by another authority. These species are:

Amphisorex lesueurii Duvernoy, Posey County, synonym of *Sorex cinereus* Kerr, See p. 39.

Sorex (Brachysorex) harlani Duvernoy, Posey County, Synonym of *Cryptotis parva* (Say) See p. 45.

Myotis sodalis Miller and Allen, Crawford County, Wyandotte Cave. See p. 66.

†*Aenocyon dirus* (Leidy), Vanderburg County. See p. 155.

Hesperomys indianus Wied, Posey County, synonym of *Mus musculus* Linnaeus. See p. 274.

†*Mylohyus nasutus* (Leidy), Gibson County. See p. 299.

†*Odocoileus dolichopsis* (Cope), Vanderburg County. See p. 313.

†*Parelephas jeffersonii* (Osborn), Grant County, considered by Hay as a synonym of *Elephas boreus* Hay. See p. 343.

†*Mammonteus primigenius compressus* Osborn, Fulton County, considered by Hay as a synonym of *Elephas roosevelti* Hay. See p. 343.

PHYSIOGRAPHIC FEATURES AND ECOLOGIC AREAS OF INDIANA

Indiana is a comparatively small state and without marked physiographic features or difference in temperature,[1] which accounts for the comparative paucity of its mammalian fauna. It contains or did contain no more than 69 living species and subspecies of known modern indigenous mammals. More intensive collecting and study might raise the number to 75. Fourteen additional species are known from the Pleistocene deposits. The highest point in the state is in Randolph County about 1285 feet, and the lowest at the mouth of the Wabash, only 313 feet above sea level, less than 1000 feet in extremes of elevation. The whole state was profoundly influenced by the glaciers that once spread over most of it.

Twice in the Pleistocene Period, Indiana was more or less covered by great ice sheets coming down from the north. The more extensive and older of these was the ice of the Illinoian Glacial Stage whose southern limits are shown on map, p. 13. This was probably a half million years ago. The second of these was less extensive and was the most recent of the Glacial Stages known in North America and is termed the Wisconsin. The southern boundaries of this ice sheet and its principal morainal deposits are shown on map, p. 13. It is probably not more than 10,000 years ago since this ice sheet retreated from the southern end of Lake Michigan. As a result of these ice sheets most of Indiana is covered with glacial drift, although a considerable area in the south central portion of the state was unaffected by these movements. The presence of these ice sheets had a profound effect upon the ancient mammalian fauna and accounts for the presence of the remains of such boreal forms as the Mammoth, the Mastodon, and the two genera of Muskoxen. Probably a host of smaller boreal forms were living in the state at the same time, but no remains of them are known. At some time in the past, either preceding or in the interval between the two known glacial stages, the climate of the state was in general much warmer than now, for remains of Peccaries

---

[1] The average temperature in the northern part in January is 25° F. and in the southern part 33° F; in July the corresponding figures are 75° and 79°.

F------- The "Flats."
K------- The "knob" area.
L——— The lake area.
P-----·- The prairie area.
L.W.V.----- The lower Wabash Valley

Fig. 1. Map of Indiana showing the prairie area, the lake area, the Lower Wabash Valley area, the unglaciated or "knob" area and the so-called flats, as based mainly on a study of the trees and shrubs. After Charles C. Deam, Trees of Indiana, ed. 2, 1931, p. 316, also Shrubs of Indiana, 1932, p. 368.

are known from Gibson and Wabash Counties and in Vanderburg County have been found a fragment each of the Dire Wolf, of a Tapir and of a Ground Sloth, animals so far as known requiring a warm climate. See also Origins of Indiana's Mammals (Lyon 1934).

Several physiographic and ecologic areas are recognized in Indiana which have had an important influence on the distribution of plant life in the state, but they have not had so much influence on the mammalian fauna. These areas are shown on map, page 11, taken from Deam's Trees of Indiana, 1931. This brief mention of these areas is taken from the same work. The northern third of Indiana is characterized by moraines and glacial lakes and bogs which are fast disappearing through artificial drainage. At the southern end of Lake Michigan the Lake Region is marked by conspicuous sand dunes, which are also topographic features farther east about Pigeon River. Thrusting itself into the northwest portion are irregular extensions of the western prairies which here reach their eastern limit. The middle portion of the state is occupied by the Tipton till plain, a ground moraine with little variety in topography. The unglaciated part of the state (See also glacial map after Hay, p. 13) essentially coincides with the Knob area, containing small steep hills and important limestone caverns. The Flats in the southeast are the eroded peneplain of the Illinoian drift. The lower Wabash Valley includes the valley of the Wabash from the lower end of Vigo County to the Ohio River.

Only three of these areas have mammals peculiar to them. Prairie Area: Pocket Gopher, Franklin's Ground Squirrel, Thirteen-lined Ground Squirrel, Prairie White-footed Mouse, Illinois Skunk and Mearns' Chipmunk. Wabash Valley: Swamp Rabbit, Spotted Skunk and perhaps Rice Rat. The Knob area with its caves: Most of the bats and Wood Rat.

LIFE ZONES IN INDIANA

In 1892, Dr. C. Hart Merriam brought out an important paper and map on "The Geographic Distribution of Life in North America with special reference to the Mammalia" (Proc. Biol. Soc. Washington, vol. 7, pp. 1-64, and 1 map, April 13, 1892). Essentially the same map with slightly different terminology employed by Merriam and his associates in later publications of the life zones is given by Anthony (1928). The whole of North America is divided into three chief regions limited largely by the average annual temperature.

1. The Boreal Region comprising three zones, Arctic, Hudsonian and Canadian. The Boreal Region is circumpolar in extent and quite similar in its animal and plant life to the northern portions of Europe and Asia and this region of both North America and Eurasia have aptly been united to constitute the Holarctic Region.

2. The Austral (or Sonoran) Region with three zones, the Transition, the Upper Austral and Lower Austral. The Austral Zones constitute a well marked zoogeographic region termed by some students the Sonoran Region. The Transition Zone as may be inferred from its name is an area in which there is a mixture of both Boreal and Sonoran forms of life.

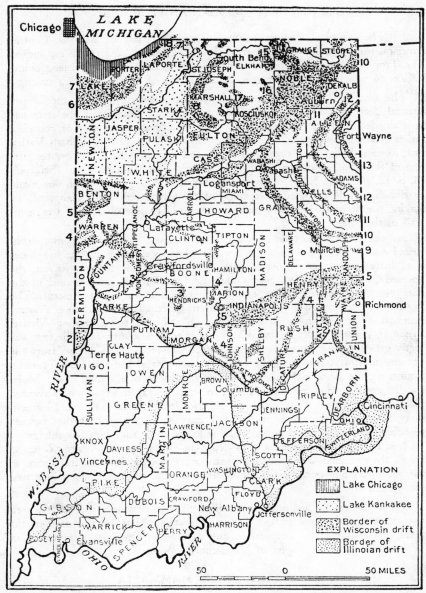

Fig. 2. Glacial Geology of Indiana. After O. P. Hay, the Pleistocene of North America and its Vertebrated Animals from the States east of the Mississippi and from the Canadian Provinces east of longitude 95°, Carnegie Institution of Washington, Publ. 322, 1923, p. 473. The southern limit of the Illinoian drift, from Cincinnati to Jeffersonville, thence north to Brown County, thence southeast to Posey County, is shown by a wavy line limiting a stippled border. The southern limit of the Wisconsin drift is represented by a smooth line and a coarser stippling. North of this terminal moraine are represented important moraines developed during the recession of the Wisconsin ice sheet.

3. The Tropical Region, confined to either coast of Mexico, Central America, the tip of Lower California, the tip of Florida and the West Indies. The Tropical Region is essentially the northern extension of the Neo-tropical Region to which the peculiar mammalian fauna of South America belongs.

The whole of Indiana is assigned by most mammalogists to the Upper Austral Zone of the Austral (or Sonoran) Region. Botanically the state has been divided into the Transition Zone in the upper tier or two of counties, Lower Austral along its southern border especially, the Lower Wabash Valley with its cane brakes and cypress swamps, and Upper Austral the greater portion of the state in between. (Chas. C. Deam, Proc. Indiana Acad. Sci., vol. 34, p, 42, 1925.) I fully concur in this division. A similar division was made by Blatchley (1909) based on a study of the Orthoptera and Coleoptera. In making the divisions Blatchley made some use of the distribution of the mammals of the state.

As one studies the recent mammals of Indiana, however, the more convinced one is that their distribution in the state in determining the life zones is of little importance. However, the occurrence of the Swamp Rabbit, the Spotted Skunk, Bachman's Shrew and the Rice Rat (if really found in the state) in the southwest corner show that portion to be Lower Austral. The Big Eared Bat, *Corynorhinus* in the southern caverns is another Lower Austral mammal. The Porcupine, the Cinereous Shrew and the Lemming Mouse, *Synaptomys,* are usually regarded as Transition Zone mammals. The first was pretty generally distributed over Indiana, the Cinereous Shrew ranges from the extreme southwest corner to the northern border, and the last from Franklin County to the northen border. The few specimens of the Star-nosed Mole, usually considered a northern genus, have been taken at widely separated places in the state. The occurrence of the Red Squirrel and the Northern Gray Squirrel in the north of the state may be construed that that portion probably belongs to the Transition Zone as many of the plants would imply. At best one can say that most of Indiana lies in the Upper Austral Zone, so far as the mammals are concerned, with one or two Lower Austral forms in the southwest and certain Transition forms in the north and some scattered throughout the state.

As one traces the mammals of Indiana back in past ages it is clearly seen that all the zones have passed through the state, Arctic in the days of the great glaciers, and the Tropical in the days when Peccaries were found in Wabash County and Tapirs in Vanderburg County.

MAMMALS, CLASS MAMMALIA

The technical term Mammalia was invented by Linnaeus in 1758 when he proposed his now universally used though much modified classification of living organisms, both animal and vegetable. From the technical word Mammalia the English word Mammal is derived. It is not a very popular word, however, and a large number of persons use the word Animal as the equivalent of Mammal, regardless of the fact that any thing that lives and is not a plant is an animal in the broad sense of the word. The word Mammal is derived from the Latin *mamma,* the breast. Other languages than English have words more popular, or at least more expressive, for the Class Mammalia.

Mammals constitute one of the five great groups of vertebrated animals, that is animals with a distinct internal skeleton consisting of a backbone, with a skull articulated to it; and an anterior and a posterior pair of limbs more or less connected or correlated with the backbone. Rarely the limbs have become more or less degenerated and are lacking. The five classes of Vertebrates named in order of their height of development and general time of appearance on the earth are Fishes, Amphibians, Reptiles, Birds, and Mammals. However, Birds and Mammals appeared rather simultaneously, and in many respects Birds form an exceedingly highly developed and specialized type of Vertebrates.

A Mammal may be defined as a warm-blooded Vertebrate, generally covered with hair, (absent in whales), young nourished by means of milk-secreting glands (mammary glands), with non-nucleated and generally round red blood cells. The circulation of the blood is double (also the case in Birds), that is the circulation of the blood through the lungs is entirely distinct from that through the rest of the body. The aortic arch, the large vessel carrying the blood from the heart to the body, turns to the left. In Birds the analogous vessel turns to the right.

Mammals are widely distributed over the Earth, being found practically everywhere from the Arctic to the Antarctic regions, but more abundantly in the warmer regions between. Aside from Man who is a Mammal himself they were not found, or were at least rare, on oceanic islands and also on the large island of New Zealand. They have adapted themselves to heat and cold, and to a variety of habitats, such as strictly terrestrial, like the deer; subterranean, like the mole; arboreal, like the squirrel; aquatic, like the whale; and aerial, like the bat.

Practically our only domestic animals are mammals. As such they constitute an important source of food and clothing. Wild mammals served in the same capacity to early man and today the furs of wild mammals are an important article of clothing and human adornment. Unfortunately the hunting of wild mammals is altogether too common a human sport. This, coupled with destruction of mammals for furs and other products and the obliteration of natural habitats by agriculturalists, bids fair to hasten the day when man and his domestic animals and a few inconspicuous adaptive forms will constitute the sole survivors of one of the most highly organized and most interesting groups of animals.

From the viewpoint of classification the known mammals of the world fall into three well marked groups. The first and most primitive constitutes the subclass Prototheria of which there are but two existing representatives, the Duck-billed Platypus of Australia and Tasmania, and the Spiny Ant-eaters of Australia, Tasmania and New Guinea. These mammals differ from all others by laying eggs, in having a very elementary type of mammary gland, without external mammae and possess certain skeletal peculiarities about the shoulder and breast bone. The second of these great groups constitutes the

Metatheria with the single order Marsupialia. Marsupials are so called because of the marsupium or pouch found in the females of most of the group and in which the young, born living and not in eggs, are suckled and raised. There are three other important characters of the group: The pelvis is provided with a pair of epipubic bones, the angular process of the lower jaw is bent inward, and the molar teeth are typically more than three in the right and left halves of both upper and lower jaws. (See remarks on teeth below). The marsupials are confined mainly to Australia and certain nearby islands, while a few forms are found in South America, and one, the opossum, even ranges into North America and is found throughout Indiana. The third of the great groups constitutes the Eutheria or ordinary mammals. The young are born in a much more mature state; a true placenta aiding in their prenatal development is present. No pouch for carrying them is found in the females; epipubic bones are absent, the angular process of the lower jaw (mandible) is not bent inward, molar teeth are never more than three in each side of upper and lower jaw. The Eutheria comprise most of the mammals of the world, and are widely distributed. Even a few native forms are found in Australia where the bulk of the mammals belongs to the Marsupialia.

The teeth of mammals are of such a nature as to be rather characteristic for the class and are very important from the standpoint of classification.

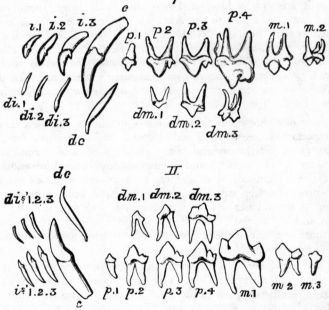

Fig. 3. Milk and permanent dentition of upper and lower jaw of Dog, *Canis familiaris*, with the symbols by which the different teeth are commonly designated. The third upper molar, m3, is the only tooth wanting in this animal to complete the typical heterodont mammalian dentition. After Flower and Lydekker, An Introduction to the Study of Mammals, Living and Extinct, 1891, p. 26.

There are four distinct kinds of teeth in the typical mammal, such as the dog or the opossum. (Note skull of the coyote and of the opossum. Figs. 53 and 5.) 1, the incisor teeth, the three small teeth on both sides in front of the large tushes, both above and below. 2, the canine teeth, the tushes, immediately following the incisors. 3, the premolar teeth, the four teeth behind the canines. 4, the true molar teeth, the last two teeth in each half of the upper jaw and the last three in each half of the lower jaw. The total dentition of a mammal is indicated by a formula and certain obvious abbreviations. In the coyote, which has nearly a full Eutherian dentition the dental formula is

$$i \frac{3\text{-}3}{3\text{-}3}, \ c \frac{1\text{-}1}{1\text{-}1}, \ pm \frac{4\text{-}4}{4\text{-}4}, \ m \frac{2\text{-}2}{3\text{-}3}, = 42.$$

In the opossum the dental formula is

$$i \frac{5\text{-}5}{4\text{-}4}, \ c \frac{1\text{-}1}{1\text{-}1}, \ pm \frac{3\text{-}3}{3\text{-}3}, \ m \frac{4\text{-}4}{4\text{-}4}, = 50.$$

In man the dental formula is

$$i \frac{2\text{-}2}{2\text{-}2}, \ c \frac{1\text{-}1}{1\text{-}1}, \ pm \frac{2\text{-}2}{2\text{-}2}, \ m \frac{3\text{-}3}{3\text{-}3}, = 32.$$

Individual teeth are designated, in man for example, upper jaw i^1, i^2, c^1, pm^3, pm^4, m^1, m^2, m^3; lower jaw i_1, i_2, c_1, pm_3, pm_4, m_1, m_2, m_3, assuming that i^3, i_3, pm^1, pm_1, pm^2, pm_2 have disappeared. The incisors, canines and last three premolars have all been preceded by temporary, deciduous or so-called milk teeth which fall out before the Eutherian mammal reaches maturity and are succeeded by the permanent adult teeth. The molar teeth and the premolars number 1 have no predecessors. The deciduous teeth are designated by similar symbols preceded by d as di^1, di^2, dc^1, dm^1, dm^2, dm^3, dm standing for deciduous molar, for these temporary teeth serve the place of the true molars in the young mammal. Any or all of the teeth may be lacking depending upon the species of mammal involved. There is never more than a total of four canines in any mammal, nor more than a total of twelve molars in Eutherian mammals, nor a total of more than 44 teeth. (Some toothed whales are exceptions.) The premolar teeth are generally smaller and somewhat differently shaped than the molars. The deciduous premolars very often resemble the molars in shape and appear quite different from their permanent successors. In the case of the Proboscidea the premolars are not succeeded by permanent teeth as will be explained in detail when that order is considered. The dental formula for each species will be given in its appropriate place.

In the Marsupials the only deciduous teeth are dm^4, right and left, or to say it somewhat differently pm^4 is the only tooth that has a predecessor.

KEY TO THE LIVING ORDERS OF INDIANA MAMMALS

Upper incisors 5-5 upper premolars 3-3, upper molars 4-4, brain case, small, young born in a very immature condition and carried in a pouch or marsupium by mother. Subclass Metatheria, Marsupialia -------------------------------- 18

Upper incisors never more than 3-3 nor upper molars more than 3-3, brain case well developed, young born in a relatively mature condition, maternal pouch or marsupium lacking. Subclass Eutheria.

Forelimbs modified into wings for true flight. _____CHIROPTERA   53
Forelimbs not modified into wings for true flight.

Teeth in a continuous row from incisors to molars, neither incisors nor canines conspicuously developed, molar teeth usually with distinct W pattern, size small. _____INSECTIVORA   25

Teeth frequently not in a continuous row from incisors to molars, incisors and canines frequently conspicuously developed, molar teeth never with distinct W pattern, size variable.

Canines conspicuously developed adapted for seizing prey, projecting far beyond rest of tooth row, pm3 and m$_1$ usually conspicuously different from other teeth which are adapted for cutting. CARNIVORA   88

Teeth variable, but not as above.

Forelimbs terminating as hands with an opposable thumb, hind limbs adapted for strictly bipedal locomotion. _____PRIMATES 167

Forelimbs not terminating as hands with an opposable thumb, limbs for quadripedal locomotion (partly bipedal in genus *Zapus* of Rodentia).

Incisors $\dfrac{1-1}{1-1}$, chisel-like, adapted for gnawing, a wide dias-

tema between incisors and cheek teeth, canines lacking. _____RODENTIA 169

Incisors $\dfrac{2-2}{1-1}$ or $\dfrac{0-0}{3-3}$

Incisors $\dfrac{2-2}{1-1}$, canines absent, superficially resembling Rodentia, feet with claws. _____LAGOMORPHA 286

Incisors $\dfrac{0-0}{3-3}$, canines variable, fore and hind feet with two functional toes each, encased in hoofs.
_____ARTIODACTYLA 296

OPOSSUMS, KANGAROOS, ETC., ORDER MARSUPIALIA

Mammals characterized by primitive form of brain, epipubic bones on the pelvis, an inturning of the angular process of the jaw, in the females the uterus and vagina are double although they coalesce into a single external opening, in the male the penis is more or less forked or bifid. A placenta is not developed to nourish the embryos. It is from the double uterus that the scientific generic name of the only genus found in North America is derived, *Didelphis* (Greek δι, two; δελφύς, womb). Usually there are four molar teeth. The only deciduous tooth in the dentition is the one on either side of the upper jaw immediately in front of the molar teeth, this particular temporary tooth is molariform in appearance, but when shed is succeeded by a permanent premolar, pm ³, resembling the other premolars in shape. The order is abundantly represented in Australia and neighboring islands, a few forms are found in South America, and one genus extends northward into the United States.

North American Opossums
Family Didelphiidae

Characters, essentially those of the genus below.

Opossums
Genus Didelphis Linnaeus

The only North American representative of the Marsupials, size medium, tail naked and scaly, prehensile; female provided with a marsupium or pouch for care of the young, dental formula:

$$i\frac{5\text{-}5}{4\text{-}4}, \; c\frac{1\text{-}1}{1\text{-}1}, \; pm\frac{3\text{-}3}{3\text{-}3}, \; m\frac{4\text{-}4}{4\text{-}4}, = 50.$$

Five toes on each forefoot, each furnished with a claw, five toes on each hind foot, each furnished with a claw except the first which is nailless and more or less opposable, after the manner of the human thumb, to the other toes. Its geographic distribution is from New York to Florida and from the Atlantic coast westward to southern Wisconsin and Iowa, Texas and into Mexico.

Virginia Opossum
Didelphis virginiana Kerr

Didelphis virginiana KERR. Anim. Kingd., p. 193, 1792.
　　Type locality: Virginia.

Didelphis virginiana Wied. 1839-41. Evermann and Butler, 1894. Hahn 1909.

The opossum is so well known as scarcely to require any description. It is a gray coarse haired animal about the size of a cat, with a whitish face, pointed nose, rather conspicuous naked rounded ears and a long scaly prehensile tail. The pelage is composed of long coarse hairs and short soft under-fur. Normally the underfur is white or whitish and black tipped and the long over hair whitish or grayish. Variations may occur in which the long over hair is black, giving the animal a very dark appearance. Brown opposums are known, in which the underfur is tipped with brown and the long coarse hairs are white or more rarely brown. (Hartman, 1922) The few specimens of Indiana opossums that have come to my notice have been of gray variety, that is with long whitish over hairs and black tipped underfur.

Total length of adults, 24 to 33 inches (600 to 825 mm.), tail 10 to 15 inches (250 to 375 mm.), hind foot 2¼ to 3 inches (70-75 mm.); weight up to 8 pounds (3.6 kgs.).

The range of the Virginia Opossum is the entire eastern United States including eastern Nebraska, Kansas, Oklahoma and northern Texas. (Except Florida and a narrow strip along the Gulf of Mexico occupied by a darker allied form *Didelphis virginiana pigra* Bangs.) It is found in every county of Indiana.

The opossum is nocturnal in its habits and seldom seen except by accident, when caught in traps or chased by dogs. It is both terrestrial and arboreal and seldom found away from woods or other suitable cover. It makes a den in any suitable place such as under roots or stumps, in hollow trees, either standing or fallen. It is sometimes found under woodpiles, or litter about dwellings. Its nest is usually lined with leaves or other suitable material and it is not improbable that the prehensile tail may be used in carrying them. It is said to be a fair digger. It is not a bad tree climber, though not agile. While its tail is prehensile it is not of much service in climbing. It can only support itself by that organ when at least half of the tail is grasping a comparatively thick branch. (Seton, 1929).

The diet of the Opossum is extremely varied and covers a wide range of animal and vegetable matter, such as wild fruits and berries, green corn, nuts, birds, mice, eggs, small reptiles and amphibians, insects and crawfish. It is truly omnivorous. It is known at times to enter poultry houses and destroy hens and eggs. It will even attack, kill and eat its own kind.

Much misinformation regarding reproduction in the Opossum is or has been current. The male organ is forked and as the only double opening visible in the animal is the pair of nostrils it has been thought by the uninformed that intercourse took place by the nose and semen or even embryos were afterwards blown into her vagina or the pouch by the female. As a matter of fact the vagina though opening by a single orifice on the body in conjunction with the anus is double inside and intercourse occurs as in any other mammal. The period of gestation is 12 to 13 days. (Hartman, 1920, 1928) The manner of birth of the young is described by Dr. Carl Hartman, (1920) as follows:

The animal showed signs of restlessness, and soon began cleaning out the pouch, which she did about four times. Then began a short series of spasmodic contractions of the abdominal wall, after which she came to a sitting posture with legs extended. . .

After assuming the sitting posture our specimen bent her body forward, and licked the vulva; however, her position at this time was such that we could not see the embryos, which very likely passed into the pouch with the first licking of the genital opening. Hence, we went to the outside where we could plainly hear her lap up the chorionic fluid; then suddenly a tiny bit of flesh appeared at the vulva, and scampered up over the entanglement of hair into the pouch, to join the other foetuses, which now could be seen to have made the trip without our having observed them. Unerringly, the embryo travelled by its own efforts. Without any assistance on the mother's part, other than to free it of liquid on its first emergence into the world, this 10-day-old embryo, in appearance more like a worm than a mammal, is able, immediately upon release from its liquid medium, to crawl a full 3 inches over a difficult terrain. Indeed it can do more: After it has arrived at the pouch, it is able to find the nipple amid a forest of hair. This it must find—or perish.

. . . . the pouch contained a squirming mass of 18 red embryos, of which 12 were attached, though 13 might have been accommodated. The remainder were, of course, doomed to starvation. Even some of these unfortunates, however, held on with their mouths to a flap of skin, or to the tip of a minute tail, while several continued to move about.

With the mother under the influence of ether, we now gently pulled off a number of embryos from the teats in order to test their reactions. The teats had already been drawn out from about a millimeter in height to double that length, doubtless by the traction of the embryo itself, for the bottom of the pouch certainly presented a busy scene with each member of the close-pressed litter engaged in very active breathing and sucking movements.

Fig. 4. Opossum, *Didelphis virginiana*, photograph by J. C. Allen, West Lafayette.

One detached young, placed near the vulva, crawled readily back into the pouch. Two or three others regained the teats after some delay; and one wanderer, which lost out in the first scramble, found a vacated teat and attached itself even after 20 minutes' delay showing that the instinct to find the teats persists for some time. . . .

For locomotion, the embryo employs a kind of "overhand stroke," as if swimming, the head swaying as far as possible to the side opposite the hand which is taking the propelling stroke. With each turn of the head, the snout is touched to the mother's skin as if to test it out; and if the teat is touched, the embryo stops, and at once takes hold.

Most female Opossums possess 13 teats, of which usually only the posterior 11 are functional. They are arranged in horseshoe form, the open side forward, 6 on either side and the odd teat in the middle opposite the third teats. Rarely there are two in the middle, the total number may be as small as 11 or as great as 17. Hartman says he has often found as many as 11 pouch young attached; but only in 2 cases, as many as 12. Litters consisting of 15, 17, and 18 newly born young in the pouch are found with as few as 7 attached to the teats. As many as 22 normal foetuses near term have been removed from pregnant uteri. Apparently about twice as many embryos are produced as are destined to become young opossums. (Hartman, 1923).

The weight of a new born young is 0.13 gram (Hartman, 1928, p. 178). They are about the size of Navy beans. 10 mm. in length. The young grow rapidly and in the course of a week increase their weight nearly 10 times. The young remain firmly attached between 52 and 74 days to the mother's nipple which becomes much elongated and distended. At that time they are about the size of house mice, weighing about 25 grams. Gradually they relax their hold and occasionally stick their heads out of the pouch. Still later they venture from the pouch, but return to it for safety and nourishment; they are weaned when about 80 days of age. The young remain with the mother for about three and a half or more months. Usually two broods are produced each year in southern states, one in late winter or early spring and one in summer. The female is capable of breeding at one year of age. The longevity of the Opossum is about seven years.

Opossums are quiet and usually solitary animals. They do not seem to pair off except for the brief period of mating and as a rule only one is found at a time except in the case of females with litters. They are slow in their motions and not aggressive, although both before the female comes into heat and after she passes out of that stage she is extremely combative. One of their defense reactions is to roll over and apparently feign death, or in popular parlance, "play 'possum." It is inconceivable that the animal is at all aware what it is doing in the reaction, any more than humans are conscious of their psychologic defense reactions. Probably one great advantage of the reaction is the fact that motionless objects are far less noticeable than those in motion. The gray color of the Opossum renders it inconspicuous in most situations.

Opossums become excessively fat in autumn and probably pass part of the winter in a state of semi-hibernation. Their winter sleep cannot be profound for them for their tracks have been seen abroad even in zero winter weather.

In recent years the Opossum has come into its own as a fur bearer. Its

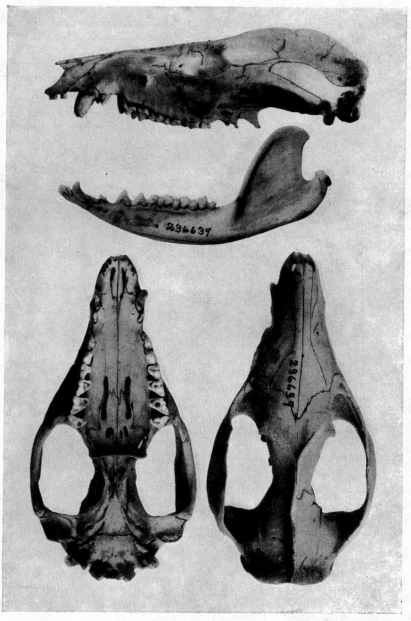

Fig. 5. Photographs courtesy U. S. Nat. Mus. Opossum, *Didelphis virginiana*, lateral, palatal and dorsal views of skull, Cat. No. 236,639, U. S. Nat. Mus., Bicknell, Knox County, July 12, 1920, W. S. Chansler. About 8/11 natural size.

skin is used for trimmings, such as collars and cuffs and made into entire coats, the fur usually being left undyed. Raw skins range in price from 10 to 45 cents; ladies' Opossum coats sell for around $50.00. (1933 prices). Most of the County Agricultural Agents and most of the Game Wardens stated in reply to a questionnaire that opossums are trapped for fur in Indiana to a considerable extent. 332,308 Opossum skins from Indiana were handled by dealers during 1931-32.

Although Opossums are often eaten, they cannot be regarded as a very substantial source of food, as in the case of the rabbit. There are two ways of cooking the Opossum. One is to remove the hair and roast him in his skin like a little pig; the other is to skin him and remove most of the fat layer and cook him like any other animal. The animals are hunted at night with dogs which tree them, and then up comes man, the Opossum's worst enemy. In spite of human persecution and of a few large owls and carnivorous mammals the Opossum holds its own and seems to have extended its geographic range in recent years.

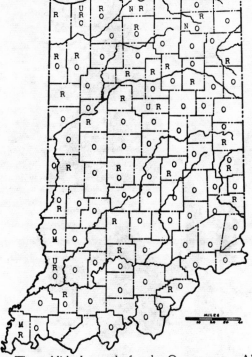

Map 1. Published records, recent observations, and specimens in collections of the Opossum, *Didelphis virginiana*, in Indiana.

The published records for the Opossum are: Allen (Evermann and Clark 1911, 1920), Benton (Evermann and Butler 1894), Carroll (Evermann and Butler 1894), Cass (Evermann and Clark 1911), Franklin (Haymond 1870, Quick and Langdon 1882, Evermann and Butler 1894), Hancock (Binford 1882), Hendricks (Evermann and Butler 1894), Howard (Evermann and Butler 1894), Huntington (Evermann and

Butler 1894), Jasper (Butler 1895), Knox (Butler 1895, Hahn 1909), Lake (Din-widdie 1884, Blatchley 1898, Brennan 1923), Laporte (Anonymous 1880, Brennan 1923), Lawrence (Hahn 1907, 1908), Marshall (Evermann and Clark 1911, 1920), Miami (Evermann and Butler 1894), Monroe (Evermann and Butler 1894, McAtee 1907), Newton (Butler 1895), Noble (Hahn 1909), Parke (Evermann and Butler 1894), Pike (Evermann and Butler 1894), Porter (Butler and Evermann 1894, Blatchley 1898, Brennan 1923, Lyon 1923, 1925), Posey (Wied 1839-41, 1861-62), Randolph (Evermann and Butler 1894, Cox 1893), St. Joseph (Evermann and Butler 1894, Engels 1933), Tippecanoe (Butler 1895), Vigo (Evermann and Butler 1894, Thomas 1819), Wabash (Evermann and Butler 1894), Wayne (Plummer 1844), Kankakee Valley (Hahn 1907, 1909).

MOLES, SHREWS, ETC., ORDER INSECTIVORA
Key to the Families and Genera of Insectivora

Forefeet large and heavy, adapted for digging, habits fossorial _____TALPIDAE   25
    Nostrils surrounded by a fringe of finger-like tentacles _____Condylura   34
    Nostrils not surrounded by a fringe of finger-like tentacles
        Tail short and essentially naked. _____Scalopus   28
        Tail short and well haired _____Parascalops   27
Forefeet normal, habits terrestrial _____SORICIDAE   37
    Tail about one-fourth the length of head and body
        Total teeth 32, size that of a mouse. _____Blarina   47
        Total teeth 30, size smaller than a mouse. _____Cryptotis   45
    Tail at least half as long as head and body
        Third unicuspid not disc-like, nor flattened antero-posteriorly __Sorex   39
        Third unicuspid disc-like, flattened antero-posteriorly _____Microsorex   45

The Insectivora, from the Latin, meaning insect-eaters, comprise a number of small mammals of varied form and habit, all characterized by the possession of five (rarely less) clawed toes on each of the four feet, with a long and pointed snout extending well beyond the end of the skull, with the orbital and temporal portions of the skull not separated from one another, with the zygomatic arch frequently lacking, the teeth with well defined cusps which are generally arranged in the form of a W, canines always present, but inconspicuous and usually simple and shaped like either the nearby incisors or premolars, eyes and ears usually small, anus and vagina usually open by a common orifice, the testes are abdominal. It is frequently impossible to distinguish the sexes except by dissection.

The group contains the smallest mammals known, the Shrews, often no larger than one's little finger. The largest Insectivore is found on some of the Malayan Islands and has nearly the size of the common opossum, and bears a curious superficial resemblance to that animal. Insectivora are widely distributed throughout the world, but none are found in Australia, nor in the southern two-thirds of South America. Two families of them are known in North America and Indiana, the Moles and the Shrews.

Moles
Family Talpidae

Zygomatic arch and auditory bullae present in skull, i 1 with a single cusp, eyes rudimentary, external ear absent, forefeet usually extremely large and heavy, adapted for digging, usually fossorial in habits. The family is composed of some 15 genera found in the temperate regions of the northern hemispheres. Two genera, *Scalopus, Condylura,* and possibly a third, *Parascalops,* are found in Indiana.

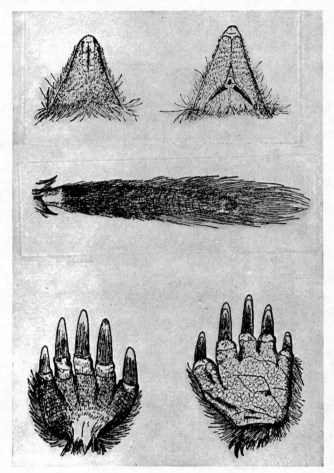

Fig. 6.   Snout, tail, and dorsal and palmar aspects of forefoot of Hairy-tailed Mole, *Parascalops breweri,* about 1½ x.   After Jackson, North American Fauna, No. 38, 1915, pp. 78-79. Not certainly known to occur in Indiana.

Hairy-tailed Moles
Genus **Parascalops** True

Body heavy as in *Scalopus,* (see below) tail short and rounded, but relatively longer, densely covered with long coarse hairs. Forefeet not quite so large as in *Scalopus,* palms about as wide as long, toes of hind feet not webbed. Size rather smaller, total length, about 150 mm.; tail vertebrae, 30 mm.; hind foot, 19 mm., greatest length of skull, about 32 mm., mastoid breadth, 14 mm. Dentition:

$$i \frac{3-3}{3-3}, \; c \frac{1-1}{1-1}, \; pm \frac{4-4}{4-4}, \; m \frac{3-3}{3-3}, = 44.$$

the full Eutherian formula. Skull smaller than that of *Scalopus* and with certain differences in shape. Mammae latero-pectoral, 2-2; latero-abdominal, 1-1; inguinal, 1-1.

HAIRY-TAILED OR BREWER'S MOLE
Parascalops breweri (Bachman)

Scalops breweri BACHMAN. Boston Journ. Nat. Hist., vol. 4, p. 32, 1842.
    Type locality: Marthas Vineyard, Massachusetts.
Scapanus americanus Evermann and Butler, 1894.
Parascalops breweri Hahn 1909, Jackson 1915.

The Hairy-tailed Mole is not known with certainty as an Indiana species of mammal. It was included by Evermann and Butler, 1894; and by Hahn, 1909, in their hypothetical lists. The latter author writes, page 684, "There are two specimens in the Indiana University collection, correctly identified, catalogued and labeled as coming from Bloomington, Indiana. I do not place much credence in these labels and am not willing to record the species as occurring in the State on the basis of these specimens." No reasons are given for discrediting the labels. These specimens were not mentioned by McAtee in his list of two years earlier date. I have seen both of these specimens, only one is labeled as having come from Bloomington, the other is without locality. This

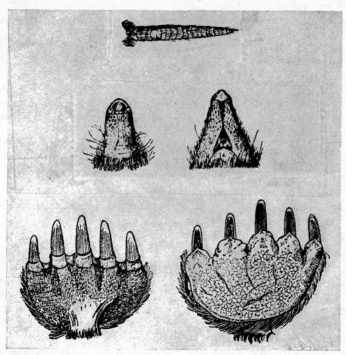

Fig. 7. Tail, snout, and dorsal and palmar aspects of forefoot of common Mole, *Scalopus aquaticus*, about 1½ x. After Jackson, North American Fauna, No. 38, 1915, p. 29.

mole has a much wider range westward than is generally conceded. (Enders, 1930) He speaks of it as more abundant in the Allegheny Plateau, (of Ohio) that is the unglaciated region, and refers to specimens as far west and south as Adams County, not over 60 to 75 miles east of the Indiana line. As Bloomington, Indiana, lies just at the northern edge of a similar unglaciated area there are no reasons why the Hairy-tailed Mole should not find suitable living conditions in Indiana. Instead of referring to every mole taken as "just another mole," it should be carefully examined before being placed in that category. Comparatively few Insectivores of any kind from Indiana are in collections. The maps show how few moles have been preserved. The Hairy-tailed Mole has essentially the same habits as has the common mole.

COMMON MOLES
Genus **Scalopus** Geoffroy

Body heavy, tail short rounded, naked in appearance though scantily haired, palms wider than long, hind toes webbed. Functional adult dentition

$$i\frac{3-3}{2-2}, c\frac{1-1}{0-0}, pm\frac{3-3}{3-3}, m\frac{3-3}{3-3}, = 36.$$

i_3, and c_1 are not persistent and disappear before the mole becomes mature. The genus is distributed among 13 species or subspecies and ranges from Massachusetts to Florida and Nebraska to Texas. One form is found throughout Indiana and in the adjacent states.

The Mole has a peculiar adaptation of the pelvis brought about by its fossorial habits. In the adult animal the pelvic canal is extraordinarily narrow and the urogenital tract and the alimentary canal pass ventral to the symphysis pubis. Hisaw and Zilley (1927) have shown that this is a secondary modification of the pelvis. In embryos of 20 mm. length the pelvic canal is of relative normal diameter and the urogenital and alimentary tracts pass through it. As the embryo advances in age the original pubic symphysis becomes absorbed and later a secondary symphysis is formed from the unabsorbed portion of the pubic bones.

PRAIRIE MOLE
Scalopus aquaticus machrinus (Rafinesque)

[*Sorex*] *aquaticus* LINNAEUS. Syst. Nat., ed. 10, vol. 1 p. 53,
    1758. Type locality: Eastern United States.
Talpa machrina RAFINESQUE. Atlantic Journal, vol. 1, p. 61,
    1832. Type locality: Lexington, Kentucky.
Scalops canadensis Wied 1839-41, Plummer 1844.
Scalops aquaticus Evermann and Butler 1894.
Scalops aquaticus machrinus True 1896, Hahn 1909.
Scalopus aquaticus machrinus Jackson 1915.

Fur soft and velvety; winter coat, above dark brown in color, under parts more grayish; summer coat, lighter in color and usually more grayish. Total length of males about 200 mm., tail 31 to 38 mm., hind foot 22 to 24 mm.; females slightly smaller. Weight about 85 grams. Greatest length of skull, 39 mm., mastoidal breadth 20 mm. Skulls of females slightly smaller; combined length of maxillary teeth, upper premolars and molars, 12.5 mm.; combined length of lower premolars and molars, 12 mm. Mammae: latero-pectoral, 1-1; latero-abdominal, 1-1, and inguinal, 1-1, = 6.

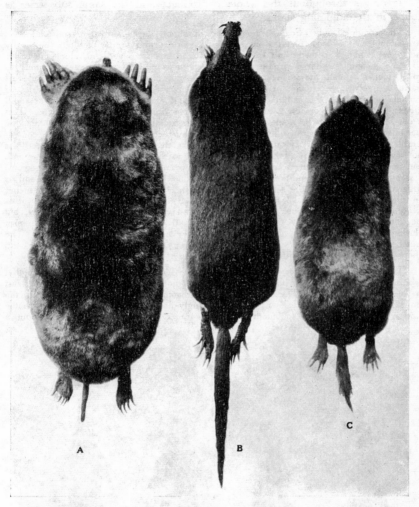

Fig. 8. Photographs courtesy U. S. Nat. Mus. Skins of Moles, all in U. S. Nat. Mus., about 2/3 natural size.

A. Prairie Mole, *Scalopus aquaticus machrinus*, Cat. No. 240,628, Porter County, Oct. 30, 1924, M. W. Lyon, Jr.

B. Star-nosed Mole, *Condylura cristata*, Cat. No. 254,030, Cambridge, Mass., Oct. 10, 1897, Wirt Robinson. Taken a few times in Indiana. No Indiana specimens extant so far as known.

C. Hairy-tailed Mole, *Parascalops breweri*, Cat. No. 86,669, Franklin, West Virginia, June 22, 1899, J. H. Riley. Not certainly known to occur in Indiana.

It ranges throughout the whole of Indiana and the same subspecies is found in the adjoining states.

The common mole *(Scalopus)* is found in almost any area where soil and food are suitable; it is most plentiful in meadows, gardens and similar habitats, but is by no means confined to them, and frequently is found in open woodland, along the banks of streams, and in other environments. It dwells in a series of subterranean tunnels 10 to 18 inches beneath the surface, and from these it forces to the outside small piles of earth, scarcely large enough to be worthy the name "mole hills." A second series of tunnels is made just beneath the surface of the soil and appears as a series of small ridges, usually more or less branching and at times ramifying in all directions. This second series seems to be made chiefly during the animal's hunt for food and may be occupied but once; generally, however, the main surface tunnels are used for a considerable time. During dry weather the mole works deeper and practically deserts the surface ridges. Its change of habit is due in part to the increased hardness of the soil, but undoubtely is more the result of its pursuing worms and insects into moister regions. Essentially the same condition is produced during winter, when the surface soil is frozen. The common mole seldom leaves its tunnels. Its nest is about 5 or 6 inches in diameter and usually 12 to 18 inches beneath the surface; most frequently it is placed under roots of shrubs or pasture grass and is made of grass and rootlets, but occasionally partly of leaves. In the northern half of its range the young are born during March or April, in the southern part they appear earlier in the spring. The number of young in a litter varies from two to five, the usual number being four and there is probably only one litter produced each year.

The young of *Scalopus* are born hairless (Measure about 50 mm. in length). Vibrissae soon appear upon the lips but hair does not show until the animal is at least a week or ten days old. The fresh first pelage remains short and grows little until the animal is nearly one-third grown; it is exceedingly fine and silky, and lies close to the body, giving the animal a smooth sleek appearance. Two young probably about a

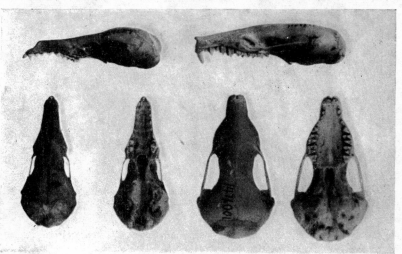

Fig. 9. Phot   'phs courtesy U. S. Nat. Mus. Skulls of Moles, natural size. Left hand group.   ir-nosed Mole, *Condylura cristata*, Cat. No. 234,027, Cambridge, Mass., Oct. 8, 18..., Wirt Robinson. This species has been taken in Indiana less than half a dozen times, and there are no extant Indiana specimens. Right hand group. Common or Prairie Mole, *Scalopus aquaticus machrinus*, Cat. No. 144,001, Lake Maxinkuckee, Marshall County, Sept. 1906, H. W. Clark.

week old . . . . have the general proportions of the body much as in adults. The feet, both fore and hind, have much the same shape as in adults, and are relatively about the same size. . . The external ear appears as a thickening of the dermis into a flat papilla 1.5 mm. in diameter. The center of this is penetrated by a minute auditory opening that seems to be closed by the contact of its sides; as an auditory organ its function is probably exceedingly limited. The rudimentary eye appears as a small pigmented spot covered by dermis; a minute imperfect opening passes through the dermis to the eye proper, and may be sufficiently penetrable for the animal to perceive light from darkness; it seems improbable, however, that the eye is sufficiently developed for form perception, and it is probable that with advanced age the sense of light perception becomes less acute (Jackson 1915).

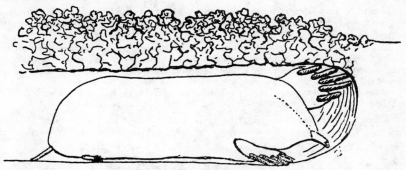

Fig. 10. Construction of superficial tunnel, appearing as surface ridge, by the Mole, *Scalopus aquaticus*. The body is rotated about 45° to right or left and the earth is pushed up by extending the front legs laterally. After Frederick L. Hisaw, Journal of Mammalogy, vol. 4, p. 83, 1923.

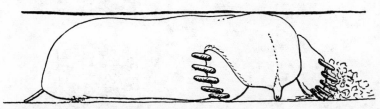

Fig. 11. Transference of earth in a deep tunnel, by the Mole, *Scalopus aquaticus*. The head and shoulders are turned abruptly to the right or left and the loose earth is pushed forward by one of the forepaws. After Frederick L. Hisaw, Journal of Mammalogy, vol. 4, p. 85, 1923.

About 80% of a mole's diet consists of animal matter, and 20% vegetable matter. The preference of animal matter seems to be earthworms followed by white grubs and other insect larvae, then adult insects; the vegetable matter eaten is in the porportion of moist seeds, including corn about 12% and vegetables (potatoes, apples, tomatoes) 8%. It will not eat raisins or turnips and only rarely sweet potatoes and carrots. Six captive moles under suitable laboratory conditions ate a total of 5466.5 grams of food in 208 days, which is an individual average of 26.28 grams. The average weight of these six animals was 84.33 grams, thus giving a daily food consumption of 32.08 percent of the body weight. A mole which had not been fed for 12 hours has been observed to eat 66.6 percent of its body weight in the next 18 hours. Apparently it detects food by contact, perhaps also by smell. Active insects are slammed against the side of its burrow with one of the large forepaws and it may be eaten held in this manner. Objects that are being eaten may or may not be held between the backs of the forepaws; usually they are eaten while resting on the bottom of the burrow. While eating the nose is constantly in motion. Many times when water was allowed to drip on the soil of the observation cage the mole came to the surface and drank from the puddle like a pig. (Hisaw, February, 1923).

The mole excavates its burrow by antero-posterior strokes and lateral thrusts of the front feet, the vertical angle of the movements being regulated by rotating the forepart of the body.

In the excavation of shallow burrows the earth is disposed of by being pushed upward to form a ridge, while in the construction of deep tunnels, from 6 inches to 2 feet below the surface, the earth is loosened with the strong claws of the forefeet and transferred either to the surface or to some vacated part of the burrow.

Loose earth is transferred and pushed to the surface by lateral thrusts of the fore feet (the body being turned sidewise).

When the left foot is digging, the right is held either against the right or upper right side of the burrow, and the soil is loosened by lateral strokes. When the right

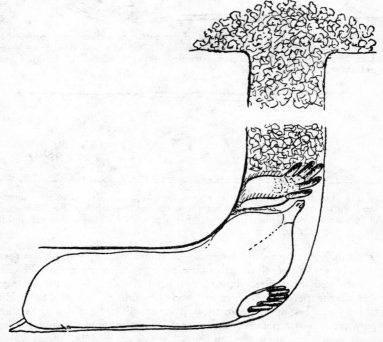

Fig. 12. Formation of mole hill, by excavating dirt from a deep tunnel, by the Mole, *Scalopus aquaticus*. The body is turned at an angle and the earth is pushed to the surface by extending the fore legs laterally. After Frederick L. Hisaw, Journal of Mammalogy, vol. 4, p. 85, 1923.

paw is used, the reverse is true. If the inactive foot is held against the side of the tunnel, the digging strokes are almost horizontal and backward, but if held against the upper right or left sides, the strokes are directed downward and backward. At each stroke the excavated earth is thrown beneath the belly. Periodically one of the hind feet reaches forward under the body and kicks the loose earth to the rear of the animal.

After a quantity of earth is loosened and piled in the tunnel behind the mole, the animal turns about and pushes the dirt out of the burrow with one of the broad front paws. (Hisaw, May 1923.)

The greatest damage done by moles is to make superficial burrows in lawns, gardens and cultivated fields. This probably is more than offset by the large number of immature and adult insects eaten. Moles may be taken in either the so-called spear traps or still better by the Nash trap which crushes the animal from side to side. They cannot be poisoned, but small portions of paradichlorbenzene placed in their burrows will probably cause them to seek less odoriferous feeding grounds.

Moles are about equally active at all hours of the day or night. Superficial tunnels can be made at the rate of about a foot a minute.

Map 2. Published records, recent observations and specimens in collections of the Prairie Mole, *Scalopus aquaticus machrinus*, in Indiana; 1, Milwuakee Public Museum; 2, collection of F. H. Test.

The published records for the Prairie Mole are: Allen (Jackson 1915), Carroll (Evermann and Butler 1894, Hahn 1909), Dekalb (Jackson 1915), Franklin (Haymond 1870, Quick and Langdon 1882, Butler 1886, Evermann and Butler 1894, Hahn

1909), Jefferson (Hahn 1909, Jackson 1915), Knox (Jackson 1915), Kosciusko (Hahn 1909), Lagrange (Evermann and Butler 1894, Hahn 1909), Lake (Brennan 1923), Laporte (Anonymous 1880, Brennan 1923) Lawrence (Hahn 1909), Marshall (Evermann and Clark 1911, 1920, Jackson 1915), Miami (Jackson 1915), Monroe (Evermann and Butler 1894, McAtee 1907, Hahn 1909), Newton (Hahn 1907, Jackson 1915), Ohio (Hahn 1909), Orange (Jackson 1915), Porter (Lyon 1923, 1925, Brennan 1923), Posey (Wied 1839-41, 1861-62, Hahn 1909), Randolph (Cox 1893, Evermann and Butler 1894, Hahn 1909), St. Joseph (Anonymous 1880, Engels 1933), Sullivan (Jackson 1915), Tippecanoe (Evermann and Butler 1894, Hahn 1909), Vigo (Evermann and Butler 1894, Hahn 1909), Wayne (Plummer 1844, Hahn 1909).

STAR-NOSED MOLES
Genus **Condylura** Illiger

Body more slender than other moles, tail rather long, equalling length of body without head, palms about as wide as long, hind toes not webbed; snout moderately elongated, terminating in a naked disc surrounded on its margin by 22 small slender, fleshy, finger-like tentacles, more or less unequal in size, symmetrically arranged, 11 on each half of the snout. Skull slender; dental formula

$$i \frac{3\text{-}3}{3\text{-}3}, \; c \frac{1\text{-}1}{1\text{-}1}, \; pm \frac{4\text{-}4}{4\text{-}4}, \; m \frac{3\text{-}3}{3\text{-}3}, = 44,$$

the full Eutherian number. The genus contains but a single species, ranging

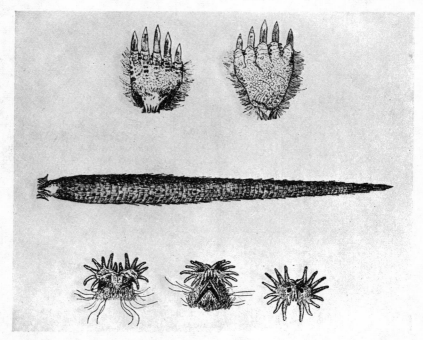

Fig. 13. Dorsum and palm of forefoot; tail; dorsal, ventral and frontal aspects of snout of Star-nosed Mole, *Condylura cristata*, about 1½ x. After Jackson, North American Fauna, No. 38, 1915, pp. 84-85.

throughout the northeastern United States (as far west as Wisconsin and as far south as Georgia) and the adjoining Canadian Provinces.

STAR-NOSED MOLE

Condylura cristata (Linnaeus)

[*Sorex*] *cristatus* LINNAEUS. Syst. Nat. ed. 10. vol. 1, p. 53, 1758.
          Type locality; Pennsylvania.

Condylura cristata Butler 1888, Evermann and Butler 1894, True 1896, Hahn
          1909, Jackson 1915.

The peculiar tentacle-fringed snout distinguishes this mole from all other moles as well as from all other mammals. Fur, mole-like; upper parts dark, almost blackish in color; under parts are more brownish; tail, scaly, moderately haired, in autumn and winter much enlarged. Total length, 185-200 mm.; tail vertebrae, 65-80 mm.; hind foot 26-30 mm. Greatest length of skull, 35 mm.; mastoidal breadth, 13.5 mm.; maxillary tooth row, 11.3 mm.; mandibular premolar-molar row, 11.5 mm. Mammae, 8: latero-pectoral, 2-2; latero-abdominal, 1-1; inguinal, 1-1. Weight: Average of 30 males 53.4 grams, extremes 39-70; of 18 females, 50.3 grams, extremes 35.2-77.

Unlike the common mole the Star-nosed Mole is semi-aquatic and it is an inhabitant of damp and marshy grounds. It is less fossorial than other moles and in addition to underground tunnels uses surface runways under and through the grass in marshes and meadows. The burrows vary in width from 1.3 to 3 inches, and in height from 1.5 to 2 inches. The tunnels usually follow a course undulating in a vertical plane, so they appear as surface ridges alternating with deeper tunnels. At irregular intervals the dirt loosened in making the tunnels is pushed out in rather characteristic mounds which may measure 2 feet in diameter and stand nearly 6 inches above the level ground. An opening to the surface is first prepared and through it the excess dirt closely packed and molded to the form of the burrow is pushed, and the size of the mound depends upon the amount pushed out. Freshly made mounds in wet ground show the characteristic lamellae in the piles thrust out, due to the dirt having been closely packed by the mole in forcing it out. The tunnels in many instances open under water for the Star-nosed Mole is an excellent swimmer and diver. A number of specimens have been taken on or near the bottom of streams or small lakes especially in winter. Unlike other moles *Condylura* frequently leaves its tunnels in winter and burrows in the snow or even runs on top of it.

Nests are composed of dead leaves and grasses and shaped like a depressed sphere. Nests for raising young are about 7 inches in diameter and as many as 10 inches below the surface unless natural cover such as a log is used. Although many passage-ways penetrate to the nest yet no earth is thrown out in its vicinity for an area of several feet. The nest is always placed above the water level of the soil.

The Star-nosed Mole digs not unlike the common mole. When digging the tentacles of the nose are brought together so as to close the openings of the nostrils. In swimming the tentacles are closely pressed together. In water progress is chieflly made by alternate rapid strokes of the hands. The hind legs are kicked alternately. The tail is used only to a slight extent.

The chief food of the Star-nosed Mole consists of aquatic worms and insects. Of all insects eaten scarcely more than 8% were terrestrial forms; of worms eaten 20% were terrestrial. Of the total diet 49% consisted of worms, 33% of insects, 6.5% of crustacea, 2.2 % of mollusks, 1% of minnow, and the rest of extraneous matter. When feeding the backs of the hands are slightly elevated from the substratum and hold the food firmly. The tentacles are firmly drawn together when the animal is feeding. The nose and all the tentacles are immersed while it drinks. The tentacles are in constant motion when the animal is searching for food with the exception of the two median upper ones which are held rigidly forward. Food to the extent of 25% of the weight of the animal is probably needed for daily sustenance.

It is thought that *Condylura* pairs in the autumn and that the sexes remain together until the young are born, April to June. Probably there is only one litter a season. The number of young born at a time seems to be 3 to 5, usually the latter, though females containing 7 embryos have been dissected. No young have been seen at birth. The earliest and smallest known were about 75 mm. long including 20 mm of tail. They were pale pink and no hair was visible. The nasal rays may be seen in embryos half developed.

About Ithaca, New York, sexual activity on the part of males commences in late January. Prior to this the testes are small and not descended. From the middle of March to May they become enormous so they may weigh as much as 8.8% of the total weight of the animal.

As in the common mole the eyes of *Condylura* probably serve little more than to distinguish light from darkness. The eyeball measures 0.9 mm. in diameter. The external opening of the ear (no couch is present) is well developed and the sense of hearing is thought to be good. Its tactile sense is good being mainly confined to the tentacles at the end of the nose. Specialized tactile hairs are found on its hands, as in other moles.

There is a remarkable swelling of the tail of the Star-nosed Mole during the winter and spring. In both sexes it may become enormously enlarged and somewhat flattened and constricted at the base. When greatly swollen the scales covering the tail are pulled apart and the pink skin shows between. The largest tail measured was 14 mm. in diameter through the thickest part. The swelling of the tail is not thought to serve as a food reservoir, nor to be a secondary sexual affair. Adults of like or opposite sex have been taken on the same day, one of which exhibited a remarkable enlargement of the tail, whereas the other was quite normal. (Hamilton 1931).

The Star-nosed Mole is one of the rarest of Indiana animals, known only from four counties. The first specimen was brought in by a cat. There are no known specimens in collections. Northern Indiana with its many marshes and lakes ought to furnish ideal habitats. However the state has not been intensively trapped for small mammals and *Condylura* is difficult to take in traps. The animal appears to be rather colonial in nature and not uniformly spread over wide areas like *Scalopus*.

Map 3. Published records of the Star-nosed Mole, *Condylura cristata*, in Indiana.

The published records for the Star-nosed mole are: Bartholomew (Butler 1895, Hahn 1909), Dearborn (True 1896), Miami (Butler 1888, 1892, Evermann 1888, Evermann and Butler 1894, True 1896, Hahn 1909), Noble (Hahn 1909).

SHREWS

Family **Soricidae**

Zygomatic arch, incomplete; auditory bullae, absent, a tympanic ring present instead; fore and hind feet small, about equal in size, not greatly dissimilar as in the Moles. Small external ears present. First upper incisor projects forward, rather hook-like and bears at its base a blunt but pronounced cusp. There are three upper molar teeth, the third distinctly smaller than the two anterior, their cusps arranged in a distinct W-pattern and anterior to them a large premolar. Between the upper molars and the first incisors is a series of 5 unicuspid teeth, usually classified i^2, i^3, c^1, pm^2, pm^3, though Cabrera (1922) considers the canines lacking. The first lower incisor is slightly hook-like and projects forwards. There are three lower molars with cusps arranged in a reverse W-pattern. Between these and the long forward-pointing incisor are two teeth, the first of which is usually considered the canine and the second a premolar. Teeth in the American forms, all pigmented.

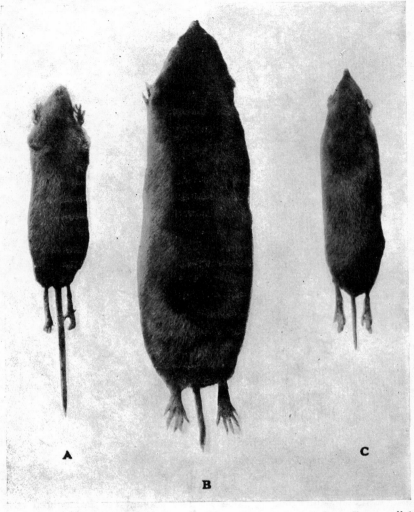

Fig. 14.   Photographs courtesy U. S. Nat. Mus.   Skins of Indiana Shrews, all in U. S. Nat. Mus., natural size.

A.   Cinereous Shrew, *Sorex cinereus*, Cat. No. 239,783, Porter County, 1923, M. W. Lyon, Jr.

B.   Large Short-tailed Shrew, *Blarina brevicauda*, Cat. No. 240,637, Porter County, 1924, M. W. Lyon, Jr.

C.   Small Short-tailed Shrew, *Cryptotis parva*, Cat. No. 240,630, Porter County, 1924, M. W. Lyon, Jr.

The family is distributed throughout tropical and temperate Europe, Asia, Africa, North America and the extreme northern portion of South America. About 15 genera are known, four of which are found in North America and three of these and probably a fourth are found in Indiana. Three of these genera are peculiar to America.

COMMON SHREWS
Genus **Sorex** Linnaeus

Dentition:

$$i\frac{3-3}{1-1}, \ c\frac{1-1}{1-1}, \ pm\frac{3-3}{1-1}, \ m\frac{3-3}{3-3}, = 32.$$

When the skull is viewed from the side the five unicuspid teeth show distinctly as five teeth, although the fifth may be minute and indistinct, the third unicuspid not disc-like, not antero-posteriorly flattened; anterior lobe of primary of the first upper incisor relatively broad, the length less than twice the width and usually less than twice the length of the secondary lobe. Size small and mouse-like, nose long and pointed, hair soft and velvety, tail moderately long and more or less completely covered with hair, ears small and almost concealed by the fur, eyes small; mammae, abdominal, 1-1; inguinal, 2-2 = 6.

"So far as known there is no sexual variation of color, size, or proportions in any of the American long-tailed shrews. The adult males of all species have a relatively long and narrow gland on each flank, which develops conspicuously during the breeding season." (Jackson 1928). It appears to give off a musky odor which probably renders these animals more or less distasteful to cats, which frequently catch but do not eat them.

The genus occurs in the northern portions of both hemispheres.

CINEREOUS SHREW
Sorex cinereus cinereus Kerr

Sorex arcticus cinereus KERR, Anim. Kingd., p. 206, 1792.
   Type locality: Fort Severn, Ontario.

Amphisorex lesueurii DUVERNOY, Mag. de Zool. ser. 2, vol. 4, p. 33, 1842.
   Type locality: Posey County, Indiana.

Amphisorex leseurii (sic) Butler, Proc. Indiana Acad. Sci. 1891, p. 163, 1892.

Blarina platyrhinus Evermann and Butler, Proc. Indiana Acad. Sci. 1893, p. 133, 1894.

Sorex personatus Merriam, North Amer. Fauna, No. 10, p. 60, 1895.

Sorex personatus Hahn 33d Ann. Rep. Dept. Geol. Nat. Res. Indiana 1908, p. 604, 1909.

Sorex personatus Miller, U. S. Nat. Mus. Bull. 128, p. 17, 1924.

Sorex cinereus cinereus Jackson, North Amer. Fauna, No. 51, p. 38, 1928.

The common long-tailed shrew is at once distinguished from all other Indiana mammals by its small size, sharp-pointed nose, small and delicate fore and hind feet and relatively long tail. The color is essentially a uniform

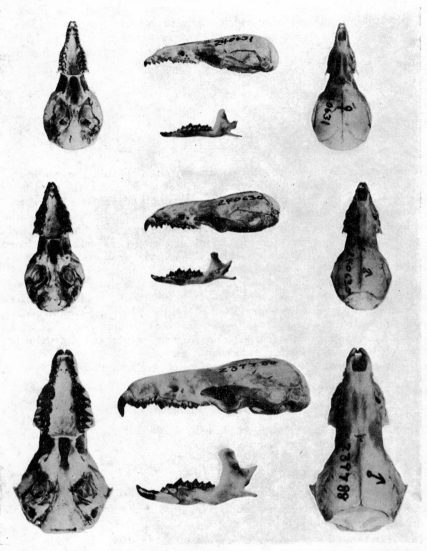

Fig. 15. Photographs courtesy U. S. Nat. Mus. Skulls of Indiana Shrews, all specimens in U. S. Nat. Mus., enlarged twice natural size.

Top series. Cinereous Shrew, *Sorex cinereus*, Cat. No. 240,631, Porter County, Nov. 9, 1924, M. W. Lyon, Jr.

Middle series. Small Short-tailed Shrew, *Cryptotis parva*, Cat. No. 240,630, Porter County, Oct. 31, 1924, M. W. Lyon, Jr.

Bottom series. Large Short-tailed Shrew, *Blarina brevicauda*, Cat. No. 239,788, Porter County, Oct. 30. 1923, M. W. Lyon, Jr.

sepia brown above with a faint sprinkling of lighter and darker hairs. Below, the color is grayish to buffy and on the side blends with the color above. The bases of the hairs are slate colored. In winter the colors are slightly darker and less brown than in summer. Total length, 95-102 mm.; tail vertebrae, 39-43 mm.; hind foot, 11-12.5 mm.; skull: condylo-basal or greatest length, 15.1-16.1 mm.; greatest width, 7.3 to 8.0 mm.; maxillary tooth-row 5.5 mm. Weight about 3.25-5 grams. Flank gland 2-3 mm. long.

The Cinereous Shrew ranges throughout the northeastern United States and Canadian Provinces to central Alaska, the Rocky Mountains, south in the mountains of North Carolina and Tennessee and into southern Indiana. It probably occurs sparingly throughout most of Indiana, but more specimens have been taken in the northern part; none has as yet been taken in the southeastern part of the state.

Shrews are the active, vicious, voracious little imps of the mammal world. They are largely nocturnal, but are not infrequently active during the daytime, particularly under the snow in winter or during cloudy weather at any season of the year. They are apparently active during the entire winter and do not hibernate, although they have small hibernating glands, and it has been erroneously written that they do hibernate. They live for the most part in little burrows or runways underneath logs, rocks, leaves and grass, where they hunt insects and worms. These runways may be made by the shrews themselves or by various species of mice or other shrews. . . They constantly move their long snouts in every direction, apparently depending more on the sense of touch and smell than on sight.

Long-tailed shrews are exceedingly quick and active and move with a queer, jerky, trot-like run, starting and stopping abruptly. They may be considered almost strictly terrestrial, although they occasionally climb small branches of very low bushes, fallen trees, or herbs. . . . Though in no sense aquatic (except the subgenera Neosorex and Atophyrax, they are good swimmers when occasion demands it of them. (Jackson 1928).

Not only are these agile and restless little Shrews voracious and almost insatiable, consuming increditable quantities of raw meat and insects with great eagerness, but they are veritable cannibals withal, and will even slay and devour their own kind. I once confined three of them under an ordinary tumbler. Almost immediately they commenced fighting, and in a few minutes one was slaughtered and eaten by the other two. Before night one of these killed and ate its only surviving companion, and its abdomen was much distended by the meal. Hence in less than eight hours one of these tiny wild beasts had attacked, overcome, and ravenously consumed two of its own species, each as large and heavy as itself! The functions of digestion, assimilation, and the elimination of waste are performed with wonderful rapidity, and it seems incomprehensible that they should be able to procure sufficient animal food to sustain them during our long and severe winters; indeed I incline to believe that their diet is more comprehensive than most writers suppose and that they feed upon beechnuts and a variety of seeds, and possibly roots as well, though I confess that I have no direct evidence to adduce in support of this supposition. (Merriam 1884, pp. 76-77).

I have made 62 stomach examinations of this species, taken in 5 states and in Nova Scotia. Practically all were summer specimens, so little can be said of the food other than at this season. In all probability it is about the same as that of Blarina in winter. The percentage of food by bulk follows: Insects, 65.3 percent; Vertebrates, [mammals, salamanders] 7.1 percent; Centipedes, 6.8 percent; Worms, 4.3 percent; Molluscs, 1.4 percent; Sowbugs, 1.2 percent; Vegetable matter 1.1 percent; Inorganic matter, .9 percent; Arachnida, .9 percent; Undetermined, 10.9 percent. The insects include 5 determined orders: Coleoptera, Diptera, Lepidoptera, Hymenoptera, and Orthoptera, but consisted chiefly of adult beetles and the larvae of all the other orders.

The amount of food eaten is much less than commonly supposed. One half the weight of the animal is a sufficient daily diet. (Hamilton 1930).

Blossom (1932) observed that a captive female ate 3.3 times its own weight every 24 hours during a period of a week.

The specimen recorded on the map from Miami County was caught in a bee-hive where the animal had probably gone to feed upon the larval bees.

Very little is known in regard to the nests and home life of Long-tailed Shrews. They build nests of grass and leaves under logs, in stumps, and similar situations, but few of these have been found much less critically studied. . . Judging from the dates of collection of pregnant specimens, the height of the breeding season is June, July and August.

Only scant information is available on the young. . . . The Cinereous Shrew is born blind, hairless, and relatively speaking, but slightly developed. Following birth however, it would seem that development and growth are comparatively rapid, although they remain in the nest until well along toward maturity. (Jackson 1928).

Litter number 4 to 10. Birth weight of Cinereous Shrew, 0.1 gram. A young of one day measured: total length, 19 mm., tail 3 mm. (Blossom 1932).

Map 4. Published records and specimens in collections of the Cinereous Shrew, *Sorex cinereus cinereus*, in Indiana.

The published records for the eastern Long-tailed Shrew are: Cass (Hahn 1909), Porter (Lyon 1924, Jackson 1928), Posey (Duvernoy 1842, Merriam 1895, Hahn 1909, Jackson 1928), Randolph (Butler 1892), St. Joseph (Engels 1931), Wabash (Butler 1892, Evermann and Butler 1894, Merriam 1895, Hahn 1909).

Shrews are rarely seen by people, and comparatively few persons know of the existence of these smallest of mammals unless they are specially trapped for or accidently brought in by the house cat which seldom eats them probably because of their musky odor. The average person usually calls them young moles regardless of the fact that their hands are anything but molelike. Long-tailed Shrews are not common in Indiana. The few I have taken were in damp situations, similarly with the relatively large series taken by Engels (1931). As a bait for shrews Jackson in a letter recommends a mixture of ground English walnut meat, 3 parts and finely chopped liver 2 parts. Sometimes he adds 1 part apple. The bait is best when 1 to 3 days old.

Jackson (1928) accredited Shrews with making a series of sharp squeaks, and also a weak purr-like grunt. Other observers also note squeaking, especially when fighting. Blossom (1932) noted the same sounds as well as a gritting of the teeth.

The Cinereous Shrew is apparently a rare animal in Indiana. The published records are comparatively few, and not many specimens are in collections, however, they are widely scattered over the state, so that one might expect to find this Shrew anywhere in suitable habitat.

BACHMAN'S SHREW
Sorex longirostris longirostis Bachman

Sorex longirostris BACHMAN, Journ. Acad. Nat. Sci. Philadelphia. vol 7, p. 370, 1837. Type locality: Swamps of Santee River, South Carolina.
Sorex longirostris Hahn, 1909, Jackson 1928.

The distinguishing characters of this rare Indiana shrew are:

Small; with short rostrum and crowded unicuspid tooth row; first and second unicuspids about equal in size, the third and fourth decidedly smaller than first and second, the third somewhat smaller than the fourth; fifth unicuspid very much smaller than fourth almost minute; teeth inextensively pigmented. Differs from the *cinereus* group in its relatively shorter, broader rostrum, shorter and more crowded unicuspid row. (Jackson 1928).

Its external appearance is not strikingly different from the Cinereous Shrew, but is described as more reddish. Only by an examination of the skull and teeth can the two forms be distinguished. Total length 80-90 mm.; tail vertebrae, 27-30 mm.; hind foot 10-10.5 mm.; greatest length of skull 14.6 mm.; greatest width, 7.3 mm.; maxillary tooth row, 5.0 mm.

The distribution of Bachman's Shrew is the Atlantic Plain and Piedmont region from southern Maryland to Florida and central Alabama. It is then found west of the Appalachian Mountains, with a distribution from northeastern to southern Illinois and in southwestern Indiana. It probably has a much wider distribution in the middle west than the few specimens in collections indicate.

Bachman's Shrew probably does not differ in habits from the Cinereous Shrew aside from the fact that it seems to prefer swampy terrain. However, the first specimens of the Cinereous Shrew that I took were in a quaking bog in Porter County. It is not unlikely that intensive trapping in moist situations throughout the state using Jackson's shrew bait will show this shrew to be more common than we now suspect.

Map 5. Published records and specimens in collections of Bachman's Shrew, *Sorex longirostris longirostris*, in Indiana.

The published records of Bachman's Shrew are: Knox (Hahn 1909, A. H. Howell 1909 Apr., Hollister 1911 Apr. 17, Jackson 1928).

SMOKY SHREW
Sorex fumeus fumeus Miller

Sorex fumeus MILLER. North Amer. Fauna, No. 10, p. 50, 1895.
    Type locality: Peterboro, Madison County, New York. Jackson 1928.

The Smoky Shrew is admitted as a possible member of Indiana's fauna on geographic grounds. It ranges from the New England states (except Maine) westward and southward through New York to south central Ohio, and northwestern Georgia. It has also been taken in southeastern Wisconsin, at Racine. It has lately been taken in the entrances to Mammoth Cave, Kentucky (Bailey 1933). It should be sought for in the northern counties of the state as well about the cold entrances of the caves in the southern counties.

The Smoky Shrew is slightly larger than the Cinereous Shrew; total length 115-120 mm.; tail vertebrae, 45-48 mm.; hind foot, 13-15 mm.; greatest length of skull, 18 mm.; greatest width, 8.7-9.0 mm.; maxillary tooth row 6.2-6.6 mm. It is distinctly unicolor (except tail) in appearance, winter pelage deep mouse gray, summer pelage more brownish than in winter; under parts only slightly lighter in color than upper parts; tail indistinctly bicolor, brownish above, yellowish beneath. The skull is decidedly larger and heavier than that of the Cinereous Shrew, with a distinctly heavier rostrum. The unicuspid teeth lack the pigmented ridge extending from apex of tooth to interior edge of cingulum of tooth.

Its food and habits are probably not essentially different from those of its more common relative, the Cinereous Shrew.

PIGMY SHREWS
Genus **Microsorex** Coues

This genus is at once distinguished from the known Indiana Shrews by its small size; total length, 80-82 mm.; tail vertebrae, 30-31 mm.; hind foot, 10-11 mm.; greatest length of skull, 14.3-15.0 mm.; greatest width, 6.4-6.6 mm.; maxillary tooth row, 4.8-4.9. It presents the following technical differences: When the skull is viewed from the side but three unicuspid teeth are seen instead of five as in *Sorex*. "First upper incisor large, elongate, two lobed, the anterior (primary) lobe relatively long and narrow, the length more than twice the width and more than twice the length of the secondary lobe; first and second unicuspid teeth (i 2 and i 3) peglike with distinct ridge from cusp to cingulum, distinctly and sharply curved caudad toward terminus, with a pronounced secondary cusp near terminus of ridge on cingulum; third unicuspid disklike, antero-posteriorly flattened; fourth unicuspid (pm 1) normal, peglike; fifth unicuspid (pm 2) minute; molariform teeth not essentially different from those of *Sorex*." (Jackson 1928). Flank gland prominent about 9 mm. long.

The Pigmy Shrew is one of a half dozen other shrews that vie for the distinction of the smallest known mammal. Weight, 2.5 grams.

Geographic distribution: Northern North America, in the east as far south as Virginia.

HOY'S PIGMY SHREW
Microsorex hoyi hoyi (Baird)

Sorex hoyi BAIRD 1857. Type locality: Racine, Wisconsin.
Microsorex hoyi hoyi Jackson 1928.

This species is provisionally included among Indiana mammals on geographic grounds. It was originally taken near Racine, Wisconsin, and a related species has been found in eastern Ohio. It may be looked for anywhere in the state. Pigmy Shrews are exceedingly rare. In Jackson's recent monograph (1928) he had but 138 examples as against 10,293 specimens of the genus *Sorex*, a proportion of about one *Microsorex* to 70 *Sorex*. Only about 25 specimens of *Sorex* are known from Indiana.

Little is known of the habits of the Pigmy Shrew, but they are probably similar to those of the Shrews of the genus *Sorex*.

SMALL SHORT-TAILED SHREWS
Genus **Cryptotis** Pomel

Head and body about the size of *Sorex*, tail more slender as well as decidedly shorter than in *Sorex*. Dentition:

$$i \frac{3-3}{1-1}, \; c \frac{1-1}{1-1}, \; pm \frac{2-2}{1-1}, \; m \frac{3-3}{3-3}, = 30.$$

Genus is distributed from Central America to the northern portions of about the eastern two-thirds of the United States, and to southern Ontario.

SMALL SHORT-TAILED SHREW
Cryptotis parva (Say)

Sorex parvus SAY. Long's Exped. Rocky Mts. vol. 1, p. 163. 1823.
    Type locality: Blair, Nebraska.
Brachysorex harlani DUVERNOY. Mag. de Zool. ser. 2. vol. 4, p. 37, 1842.
    Type locality: Posey County, Indiana.
Blarina cinerea Butler 1892, Evermann and Butler 1894.
Blarina exilipes Evermann and Butler 1894.
Blarina parva Butler 1892, Evermann and Butler 1894, Merriam 1895, Hahn 1909.
Cryptotis parva, Lyon 1925.

Size small; total length, 75-80 mm.; tail vertebrae 15-16 mm.; hind foot

10-10.5 mm.; greatest length of skull including front incisors 16.5 mm.; greatest width of skull 7.5-8 mm.; maxillary tooth row about 4.5-5 mm.; weight 5-6 grams. Upper parts dark brown, darker in winter than in summer, under parts ashy gray; tail slender, above like back and below like under parts.

The Small Short-tailed Shrew is found from the Atlantic seaboard south of New England west to Colorado, north to southern Ontario and south to the Gulf of Mexico. A related species is found in peninsular Florida. It is probably found throughout Indiana, having been taken in the extreme north and south of the state. It is not a common animal and specimens in collections are not numerous.

Not much has been written concerning its habits. It is usually accredited with living in rather dry open weedy brushy fields, though it has been found in damp meadows. The only one I ever took was in a trap set on the surface

Map 6. Published records and specimens in collections of the Small Short-tailed Shrew, *Cryptotis parva*, in Indiana; 1, Alcoholic specimens in collection of Mr. Raymond J. Fleetwood; 2, Alcoholic specimen in collection of Prof. R. N. McCormick; 3, skin and skull in collection of F. H. Test. Specimen from Franklin County in collection of A. W. Butler.

The published records for the Small Short-tailed Shrew are: Franklin (Langdon 1881, Quick and Langdon 1882, Butler 1892, 1892B, 1893, Evermann and Butler 1894, Merriam 1895, Hahn 1909), Jefferson (Butler 1892, 1892B, Evermann and Butler 1894, Hahn 1909), Knox (Hahn 1909), Lawrence (Hahn 1908, 1909), Marion (Brayton 1882, Merriam 1895, Hahn 1909), Monroe (McAtee 1907), Ohio (Hahn 1909), Porter (Lyon 1923, Sanborn 1925), Posey (Duvernoy 1842), Putnam (Merriam 1895, Hahn 1909), Randolph (Cox 1893, Evermann and Butler 1894, Hahn 1909), Vigo (Butler 1892B, Evermann and Butler 1894, Merriam 1895, Hahn 1909).

of a damp woods not far from a damp meadow. Mr. R. J. Fleetwood found several specimens that had fallen into freshly dug post holes.

Its food habits are probably similar to those of other shrews.

Evermann and Butler (1894) say it is sometimes called the "bee shrew" or " bee mole," because it occasionally gets into bee hives and there builds its nest and feeds upon the brood.

The number of young in a litter appears to vary from three to five. The nest is made of leaves and dried grasses and placed beneath some convenient object or perhaps in a subterranean runway.

SHORT-TAILED SHREWS
Genus Blarina Gray

Short-tailed Shrews are at once characterized by their robust form, short tail, small external ears, short legs, small hands and feet; teeth resembling those of *Sorex,* but dental formula

$$i \frac{3\text{-}3}{1\text{-}1}, c \frac{1\text{-}1}{1\text{-}1}, pm \frac{3\text{-}3}{1\text{-}1}, m \frac{3\text{-}3}{3\text{-}3}, = 32.$$

The unicuspid teeth five in all in each half of the upper jaw are grouped in pairs the first two (i^2 and i^3) largest and subequal in size, followed by another pair (c^1 and pm^2) much smaller and also subequal in size; the fifth unicuspid tooth (pm^3) the smallest and not visible when the skull is viewed from the side. Side gland well developed in the male, about 10 mm. long and 3-4 mm. wide, present but very much smaller in the female. Mammae abdomino-inguinal 3-3 = 6.

Geographic distribution: The eastern half of the United States and adjoining Canadian provinces extending as far west as Nebraska.

The genus contains eight or nine species or subspecies. Two subspecific forms occur in Indiana.

COMMON SHORT-TAILED SHREW
Blarina brevicauda (Say)

General characters already described under the genus. Dark slate colored almost throughout, but under parts lighter, somewhat darker in winter than in summer. Hairs soft and mole-like. Head and body, 100-125 mm.; tail vertebrae, 20-28 mm.; hind foot, 12-17 mm.; greatest length of skull 20-25 mm.; greatest width 10-13 mm. Weight 15-30 grams.

Short-tailed Shrews are active both day and night, summer and winter, spending their lives in runways on or under the ground. They are seldom seen although they are probably among the commonest of Indiana mammals. When seen they are usually classed as "young moles" in spite of their small hands. With their short tail and stockier body they are more mole-like in appearance than the long-tailed shrews. They are very active, never resting for a moment except while eating.

In hunting for food they seemed to depend entirely on their sense of smell, and when thus prospecting they wriggled their long pink snouts continuously and inserted them into every nook and crevice. They appeared to use their eyes merely in avoiding well-lighted situations. (Klugh, 1921).

The runways may be on the surface of the ground, or just beneath it so that the surface is gently pushed up like a small mole surface runway, or the runways may run downward and be several inches beneath the surface. Two types of nest are made, the larger breeding nests and smaller, more frequently found, resting nests. The breeding nests measure 7 to 8 inches long, about 6 inches wide and about as many deep. The inner diameter of the breeding

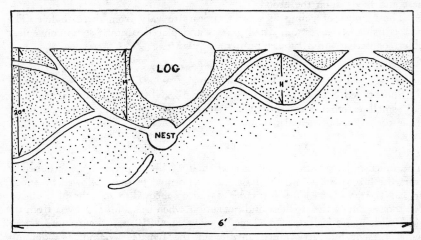

Fig. 16. Nest of Short-tailed Shrew, *Blarina brevicauda*, with adjoining runways. After William J. Hamilton, Jr., Journal of Mammalogy, vol. 10, p. 126, 1929.

nests is about 2 inches. Nests appear to be placed under logs at a depth of a few inches to a foot. They are made of dead leaves or grasses which are not shredded. There are usually about 3 openings to a nest. Nests have been found lined more or less by mouse hair. Dung appears to be deposited in the burrows a few inches away from the nests. No evidences of food are found in the vicinity except a few empty shells of *Polygyra*.

The number of young varies from 5 to 7, though as judged by the number of mammae in the adult 6 would appear to be the normal number. Adult *Blarina* with as many as 10 embryos have been dissected. At birth the young are dark pink all over, wrinkled and about the size of a large honey bee. Weight at 36 hours 1.34 (adult weight about 30 grams), total length, 31 mm.; tail, 4 mm. At four days the total weight of five was 3.8 grams. At about 8 days short hair appears all over the body; previous to that only nine minute vibrissae are to be found on either side of the nose. At about two weeks the young begin to crowd out of the nest. At three weeks the eyes are not yet opened and the Shrew has attained about a third its normal weight. It is thought that at three weeks the young are weaned. At what age they attain the adult size is not known. The side gland in the males is conspicuous at 5 days; the mammae of the females are distinctly visible by 14 days. (From Hamilton 1929).

The side gland is undoubtedly a secondary sexual organ; growth of the sweat glands in it and the preparatory stages toward secretion follow the ripening of the testicles. When the animals are fully in heat all the sweat gland tubules are secreting. A musky odor is given off which apparently renders the animals more or less distasteful to carnivorous beasts. The side glands begin to show more prominently and reach their maximum size about the first of April. Hamilton (1929) thinks that normally the males outnumber the females and that there is much rivalry among them. My own limited experience in Indiana would indicate the sexes about equally divided. There appear to be two reproductive periods a year: first in May or late April, and a second brood late in summer. I have taken specimens in northern Indiana that were evidently nursing in early October. Hamilton's observation led him to believe that the males and females mate and remain together more or less permanently, except when the female has young in the nest. This same observer gives 21 days as the period of gestation.

The most recent observations on the food of Blarina (Hamilton 1930) give these percentages: 88.6 animal food; insects, 47.8; worms, 7.2; crustacea, 6.7; vertebrates (mice 4, birds 2, salamanders 3, stomachs), 4.1; mollusks, 5.4; centipedes, 3.8; arachnids, 2; millipedes, 1.7; undetermined matter, 5.2; inorganic matter, 2.3; empty, 1.7; and plant material 11.4%. An examination of a series of stomachs taken during the winter showed an increase of plant remains to 25.3; vertebrates to 7.6; and insects to 58.6.

It took an adult shrew 6-10 seconds to finish a cutworm which it first bit in the head to kill. The cutworm weighed one-third of a gram. The shrew began at the head end and worked caudally, using the forepaws for assistance in manipulating the insect.

Small slugs and sowbugs were taken into the mouth entire, but chewed well. Four minutes was the average time taken to consume a large night-crawler. Feeding would almost always begin at the head and proceed caudally. (Hamilton 1930)

I had not previously known that the Shrew was a mouse-eater. . . Therefore having caught a vigorous though undersized Shrew, I put him in a large wooden box and provided him with an ample supply of beechnuts, which he ate eagerly. He was also furnished with a saucer of water from which he frequently drank. After he had remained two days in these quarters, I placed in the box with him an uninjured and very active white-footed mouse. The Shrew at the time weighed 11.20 grams while the mouse which was a large adult male weighed just 17 grams. No sooner did the Shrew become aware of the presence of the mouse than he gave chase. The mouse though much larger than the Shrew, showed no disposition to fight, and his superior agility enabled him, for a long time, easily to evade his pursuer, for at a single leap he would pass over the latter's head and to a considerable distance beyond. The Shrew labored at great disadvantage, not only from his inability to keep pace with the mouse, and also to a still greater extent, from his defective eyesight. He frequently passed within two inches of the mouse without knowing of his whereabouts. But he was persistent, and explored over and over again every part of the box, constantly putting the mouse to flight. Indeed, it was by sheer perseverance that he so harassed the mouse, that the latter, fatigued by almost continuous exertion, and also probably weakened by fright, was no longer able to escape. He was first caught by the tail; this proved a temporary stimulant and he bounded several times across the box, dragging his adversary after him. The Shrew did not seem in the least disconcerted at being thus harshly jerked about his domicile, but continued the pursuit with great determination. He next seized the mouse in its side, which resulted in a rough and tumble, the two rolling over and biting each other with much energy. The mouse freed himself, but was so exhausted the Shrew had no difficulty in keeping along side, and soon had him by the ear. The Shrew was evidently much pleased and forthwith began to devour the ear. When he had it about half eaten off the mouse again tore himself free, but his inveterate little foe did not allow him to escape. This time the Shrew clambered up over his back, and was soon at work consuming the remainder of the ear. This being satisfactorily accomplished, he continued to push on in the same direction till he had cut through the skull and eaten the brains, together with the whole side of the head and part of the shoulder. This completed his first meal, which occupied not quite fifteen minutes after the death of the mouse. As soon as he had finished eating I again placed him upon the scales and found he weighed exactly 12 grammes—an increase of .80 gramme.

The Shrew was half an hour in tiring the mouse and another half hour in killing him. (Merriam 1884).

Killing mice placed in a cage and mice in the open are two different things. The rather small number of stomachs containing mouse remains, shows that mouse-eating is a comparatively rare event. Perhaps wild mice are somewhat easily taken when cornered in an underground runway. However the following incident shows they do pursue wild mice.

Bailey (1923) says:

I caught one of these Shrews by the neck and a meadow mouse by the hips. The trap was set across a runway and evidently the shrew was pursuing or had hold of the back part of the mouse when they ran through my trap and both were caught.

My observations with several shrews carried on for an entire spring convinced me that one half of the shrew's weight is ample for it over a 24 hour period, and more often than not, only half of this much is daily eaten. (Hamilton 1930).

In spite of the large food requirement, shrews can fast as long as 24 or 38 hours without actually starving to death.

The habits of captive Shrews would certainly indicate a propensity for storing food. When my Short-tailed Shrews were given more food than suited their appetite at one time, the excess food would be taken into the nest box and stored under the moss in a corner. More often than not, the greater part thus put away would turn bad before the animals were ready to eat it. Both animal and plant food was treated in this manner. Salamanders would be cut into several pieces, but raisins, sowbugs and other small things were stored intact. The storage habit was particularly pronounced in a nursing shrew, which refused to leave her young for a long time. (Hamilton 1930).

The following observations on the Short-tailed Shrew by one of the earliest writers (Plummer) on Indiana mammals are well worth quoting:

In the spring of 1842 I caught another shrew, under a very rotten log, which it had converted into a perfect labyrinth; and in the largest excavation had constructed a bed of dry leaves. . . . I brought him safely home. Turning him out into a glass vessel five inches deep, with perpendicular sides I covered it with a book upon which I laid the vertebra [of a horse,] and supposed my little captive was perfectly secure. In a short time after leaving it, however, he succeeded in pushing the covering to one side, and escaped. The book and bone together weighed on trial upwards of a pound; and, considering the mechanical disadvantage of a smooth glassy surface, and of the rampant position of the Shrew while effecting his liberation, this achievement indicated a degree of strength that surpassed my expectations. Having retaken the little prisoner, I confined him to a box, well provided with masses of rotten wood, paper and other materials. As soon as I turned him into his new habitation, he hastened to the bottom of the box, and commenced making a new arrangement of the smaller pieces of wood and other fragments scattered below, his object appearing more particularly to be, to block up the larger openings around him. This task he accomplished with much skill, first dragging and fitting the larger pieces to the apertures, and then filling up the interstices with fragments of smaller size; after this he crumbled with his teeth the projecting and more accessible parts and the powder falling into the remaining spaces completed a hiding place. . . . [He] appeared to run with great delight, in the most lively manner, through all the windings and irregularities of his new abode, peeping out in rapid succession, and snuffing the air, at the various holes left for egress and ingress. . . . he began to snatch and jerk into the interior such portions of paper and rags as were nearest at hand; these I afterwards found he cut into small pieces, and formed into a neat little bed.

These preparatory employments being over, he began to protrude his body with great caution from a hole which appeared to be a favorite outlet, but started back with the utmost precipitation upon the slightest noise and in a moment afterward he would slyly peep out at some other opening. At length having ventured entirely out, he seized a large earth-worm which I had thrown into the box, the very instant it was perceived, and in spite of all its violent contortions the shrew ate it with avidity, sometimes confining the motions of the worm by pressing it down with its fore feet. . . For days and weeks he received corn, insects and worms from my hand, but always with that sudden snatch that characterized it at the beginning. If I held fast to the worm, he would tug at the other end, and jerk at it till I let go, or the worm was lacerated by his efforts. At such times I have often raised him into the air by means of the worm. . . Flesh of all kinds, fresh fish, coleopterous as well as other insects, slugs, millipeds, corn, oats, and every kind of grain which was tried appeared to be acceptable food. The corcle of the grains of maize was always eaten out, as it is by rats and mice..

When this little quadruped was satiated with food, it never ceased to store away. . . surplus provisions. . . . he had separate storehouses: one for corn, which was neatly packed away, grain upon grain, flatwise; another for his oats; and a third for worms and insects. . . When water was put into the box, he wet his tongue two or three times and went away; but when worms were dropped into the cup, he returned, waded about in the water, snatched up his victim, stored it away and returned repeatedly for more, till all were secured.

By gentle attentions, I had by this time so far subdued his timidity, and instructed him my language, that by night or day and at all times, whether in his hiding places in the box, or running at large in the room, or safely ensconced in secret and inaccessible fissures, he was ready to come at my call, and receive from my hand his accustomed meal. It was curious to observe, that unless he was called into the area of the room, he never approached his box or any other point, except by a circuitous route against the wall.

Farther on Plummer describes placing a mouse with the Shrew, which promptly slew the intruder. A second mouse met with the same fate. A younger Shrew was placed in the box and it in turn was killed. These killings are not described so vividly nor with such detail as those already quoted by Merriam.

The voice of this animal in retreating to its harboring places, is almost precisely that of the ground-squirrel (*Tamias*), being a rapidly uttered chip-chip-chip. Its propensity to gnaw is considerable, but perhaps not so great as that of the mouse. Repeated experiments have convinced me that (unless peculiar odors are an exception) its sight and smell cannot extend beyond the distance of half an inch; but its sense of hearing is extremely acute.

The one in my posession was as cleanly, tidy, and choice in the quality of his food, as any little quadruped I ever knew; always bringing out the putrid worms and decaying grains from his cell, and always preferring the living to the dead: his habitation was as clean as possible, egestation being performed in a concealed corner. I can also say on behalf of my prisoner, that during the two spring months of his dependence on me for subsistence, I never perceived any annoying smell, much less that disgusting odor, which like the Polecat, Shrews are said to stand charged.

(It is not unlikely that Plummer had a female Shrew in which the scent glands are inconspicuous, in spite of the fact that he has referred to his specimen in his account by the masculine pronoun.)

Two races of the Short-tailed Shrew are found in Indiana, distinguished principally by differences in size. They do not differ in appearance or habits as above, and the older writers usually made no distinction between the two forms. In the distributional map both races are included with the probable line of geographic division extending from Vigo to Franklin counties. Near that line specimens will be found to be more or less intermediate between the two forms.

Map 7. Published records and specimens in collections of the Short-tailed Shrew, *Blarina brevicauda*, in Indiana. Specimens from the level of Vigo, Putnam and Franklin Counties southward are referable to the southern race *Blarina brevicauda carolinensis*, those to the northward to the typical form *Blarina brevicauda brevicauda*; 1, Skin and skull in collection of F. H. Test. Specimen from Franklin County in collection of A. W. Butler.

The published records of the Short-tailed Shrew are: Boone (Kennicott 1857), Carroll (Evermann and Butler 1894), Franklin (Quick and Langdon 1882, Evermann and Butler 1894, Merriam 1895, Hahn 1909), Greene (Hahn 1909), Kosciusko (Hahn 1909), Knox (Hahn 1909), Lagrange (Evermann and Butler 1894), Lake (Sanborn 1925), Laporte (Elliot 1907), Lawrence (Hahn 1907, 1908), Marshall (Evermann and Clark 1911, 1920), Monroe (Evermann and Butler 1894, McAtee 1907, Hahn 1909), Newton (Hahn 1907), Ohio (Hahn 1909), Porter (Lyon 1923, Sanborn 1925), Posey (Duvernoy 1842, Evermann and Butler 1894, Merriam 1895, Hahn 1909), Putnam (Merriam 1895, Hahn 1909), Randolph (Cox 1893), Switzerland (Hahn 1909), Tippecanoe (Evermann and Butler 1894), Vigo (Evermann and Butler 1894, Merriam 1895), Wayne (Plummer 1844, Merriam 1895, Hahn 1909).

NORTHERN SHORT-TAILED SHREW
Blarina brevicauda brevicauda (Say)

Sorex brevicaudus SAY. Long's Exped. Rocky Mts., vol. 1, p. 164, 1823.
    Type locality: Near Blair, Nebraska.
Brachysorex brevicaudatus Duvernoy. Mag. de Zool. ser. 2, vol.. 4, p. 36, 1842.
Blarina brevicauda Evermann and Butler 1894, Merriam 1895, Hahn 1909.

Size larger; total length, 115-125 mm.; tail vertebrae about 25 mm.; hind foot, 16 mm.; greatest length of skull 23 mm.; greatest width, 15 mm.

CAROLINA SHORT-TAILED SHREW
Blarina brevicauda carolinensis (Bachman)

Sorex carolinensis BACHMAN. Journ. Acad. Nat. Sci. Philadelphia, vol. 7,
    p. 366, 1837. Type locality: Eastern South Carolina.
Blarina brevicauda carolinensis Merriam 1895, Hahn 1909.

Somewhat more brownish in color than the preceding subspecies, and smaller; total length, 100-105 mm.; tail vertebrae, 22 mm.; hind foot, 12.5 mm.; greatest length of skull, 22 mm.; greatest breadth, 12 mm.

The difference between the two forms are slight and only of importance to the specialist. To designate all the Large Short-tailed Shrews of Indiana by a binomial scientific name, *Blarina brevicauda* is perfectly correct zoologically.

BATS, ORDER CHIROPTERA

Bats are sharply differentiated from all other mammals by the specialization of the anterior limbs into organs adapted for true flight. The forearm consists of a rudimentary ulna, a long curved radius, and a carpus of six small bones supporting a thumb and four greatly elongated fingers. Stretched between them and attached to the sides of the body, the legs and tail, is a delicate skin-like membrane used as an organ of flight. The thumb is not connected with the wing membrane and bears a claw. The second finger in certain Old World groups bears a claw but in all American bats is clawless. The knee is directed backwards, owing to the rotation of the hind limb outwards by the wing membrane. A peculiar elongated cartilaginous process, the calcar, arising from the inner side of the ankle-joint, is directed inwards, and supports part of the posterior margin of an accessory membrane of flight extending from the tail to the hinder limbs, the interfemoral membrane. The mammae are almost universally two, thoracic and generally post-axillary. The external ear is usually large and frequently characterized by the presence of a well developed tragus, a more or less prominent upward-pointed narrow outgrowth from the lower outer margin of the ear canal.

The eyes of most bats are small and probably incapable of vision in the sense that we know it. As many of them spend their daylight hours in the recesses of caves, entering and leaving them at night, it is obvious that bats are endowed with a special and highly developed tactile sense. This sense is of such a nature that the animals appear to be able to detect vibrations

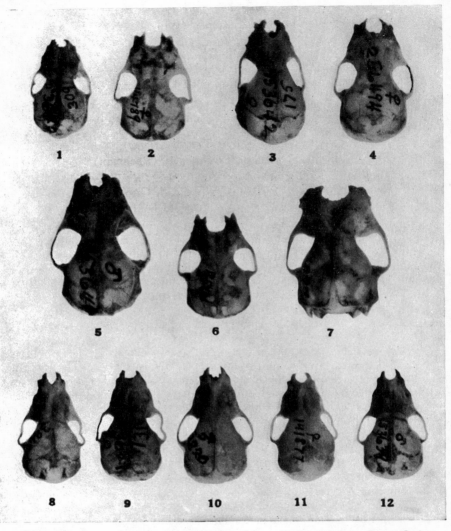

Fig. 17. Photographs courtesy U. S. Nat. Mus. Skulls of Indiana Bats. Owing to lack of satisfactory specimens a few skulls collected in other states were photographed. All specimens in U. S. Nat. Mus. Figures enlarged twice natural size.

1. Georgian Bat, *Pipistrellus subflavus*, Cat. No. 153,645, Mitchell, Lawrence County, Aug. 13, 1907, W. L. Hahn.

2. Rafinesque's Bat, *Nycticeius humeralis*, Cat. No. 114,789, Henderson County, Ill., Aug. 4, 1901, Paul Bartsch. No known Indiana specimen, it has been taken in Chicago.

3. Big-eared Bat, *Corynorhinus rafinesquii*, Cat. No. 153,642, Mitchell, Lawrence County, Dec. 16, 1906, W. L. Hahn.

reflected from a surface which they are approaching. The sensory end-organs of this highly developed sense are probably located in the delicate wing membranes.

Bats are of special interest in Indiana because of the large numbers that spend the winter in a sort of hibernation in the limestone caves of the southern part of the state. An excellent account of the habits, sensory behavior and breeding of several species of bats as observed in these caves is given by Hahn in Biological Bulletin, vol. 15, pages 135-193, 1908.

The teeth are variable according as the diet is of fruit or of insects. The vast majority of bats are insect-eaters and their teeth in general bear a strong resemblance to those of the Insectivora. The insects are captured while the bat is on the wing after the manner of the Swifts and Swallows among the birds. The entire group is nocturnal or crepuscular. Although its members are all of small size the group includes numerous species, distributed among some 175 genera in 15 families. Bats are of world wide distribution but reach their greatest abundance as to number of species and number of individuals in the tropics. Representatives of only one family are found in Indiana and not more than 13 species are supposed to occur in the state.

A careful study of the teeth of bats is essential to proper placing of specimens in genera and often species. Bats should be preserved both as skins and skulls and as specimens preserved in alcohol. In order to study the skull and dentition of alcoholic preserved material, it is necessary to remove the skull. This is usually easily done by taking a sharp scalpel and cutting the skull loose from the lips and other attachments and removing it through the mouth opening. Sometimes a corner of the mouth will be torn but this is easily sewed up by fine thread. It is usually desirable to place a tightly compressed wad of cotton in the skin of the head after the skull is removed. One or two sutures may then be placed in the anterior ends of the lips. An alcoholic specimen may be easily dried for examination by wiping off the excess alcohol with a

---

4. Silver-haired Bat, *Lasionycteris noctivagans*, Cat. No. 256,494, South Bend, St. Joseph County, Aug. 2, 1931, Florence Peck.

5. Brown Bat, *Eptesicus fuscus*, Cat. No. 153,646, Mitchell, Lawrence County, Aug. 2, 1907, W. L. Hahn.

6. Red Bat, *Lasiurus borealis*, Cat. No. 85,111, Burlington, Ia., Sept. 9, 1898, Paul Bartsch.

7. Hoary Bat, *Lasiurus cinereus*, Cat. No. 257,097, Notre Dame, St. Joseph County, A. M. Kirsch.

8. Trouessart's Bat, *Myotis keenii septentrionalis*, Cat. No. 38,674, Wheatland, Knox County, May 1881, R. Ridgway.

9. Little Brown Bat, *Myotis lucifugus*, Cat. No. 153,621, Mitchell, Lawrence County, Nov. 16, 1906, W. L. Hahn.

10. Howell's Bat, *Myotis grisescens*, Cat. No. 52,820, Marble Cave, Stone County, Mo., 1892, T. S. Powell.

11. Indiana Bat, *Myotis sodalis*, Cat. No. 141 877, Wyandotte Cave, Crawford County, A. N. Caudell.

12. Rhoads' Bat, *Myotis austroriparius*, Cat. No. 153,639, Mitchell, Lawrence County, Aug. 9, 1907, W. L. Hahn.

towel and absorbing the rest with frequent changes of dry sawdust.

The feeding habits of bats cannot well be observed in a state of nature. Bats catch larger and smaller insects flying in the air at night like themselves. Many of the insects are moths and of large size. The interfemoral membrane is of much service in holding the captured prey. Some species at least when a large insect is caught fly to the nearest rough object such as a tree trunk, alight in an upright position and make a sort of pouch between the tree trunk, the lower part of the body and the interfemoral membrane which is pressed against the tree trunk. The head is bent downwards and forward and the insect consumed usually head first. (Pittman, Journal of Mammalogy, volume 5, p. 231, 1924). The food requirements of an insectivorous bat in a state of activity are probably about the same as an Insectivore of equal size.

Toward the end of summer most of the Indiana bats put on a heavy layer of fat preparatory to passing the winter in a state of hibernation or semi-hibernation. A few are migratory in their habits.

The breeding habits of the majority of bats that have been carefully studied are rather unique. The sexes usually congregate separately and when males are found roosting with females they are generally immature animals and probably part of the progeny. The sexes cohabit in late summer or early autumn and the uterus is filled with a mass of sperms which remain dormant during the bats' period of hibernation. With the oncoming of spring and bodily activity of the females, ovulation takes place and the ova are then fertilized by the sperms which have now become active. (Hartman 1933). Guthrie (1933) holds that there is a second mating season in spring, at which time fertilization occurs. The young are born in early summer, vary in number from one to two depending upon the species. In the genus *Lasiurus* with a total of four mammae, the females may give birth to as many as four young.

The "natural history" of bats is filled with superstition. One of the most common is that they have a predilection for getting caught in women's hair. I have never heard of an authentic case of such a nature, but as bats in spite of all their sensory adaptations do get snagged occasionally in burdocks, or on wire fences, (Paul B. Johnson, Journ. Mamm., vol. 14, pp. 156-157, 1933) it is possible one might at some time wander into a woman's hair. It could scarcely do any harm and would be glad enough to get away. Another superstition is that they harbor bedbugs and other parasites. They do, but as far as I know these bugs and other parasites are peculiar to certain kind of bats and are of different species from those infesting humans.

COMMON BATS
Family **Vespertilionidae**

The members of this family of bats are distinguished by their simple muzzles and lips, usually separate ears, with well-developed, straight, or slightly curved tragi, long tails extending to the edge of the interfemoral membrane, but never much beyond; presence of only two bony phalanges in third finger. Internally they are distinguished by a highly developed double articulation between scapula and humerus, the very rudimentary ulna, the essentially unmodified shoulder girdle and pelvis, the conspicuous anterior emargination of the bony palate and the essentially normal, insectivorous teeth.

The family is distributed throughout the eastern and western hemispheres between the limits of tree growth and representatives are found on most of the oceanic islands. It contains about 30 genera, seven of which are known to occur in Indiana. (Miller, Gerrit S., Jr. The Families and Genera of Bats, Bull. 57, U. S. Nat. Mus. 1907.)

It is the only family represented in Indiana.

KEY TO THE GENERA OF INDIANA BATS

Ears enormous, much longer than head. _____*Corynorhinus* 85
Ears of normal proportions, not conspicuously if at all longer than head.
   Interfemoral membrane covered with long silky hairs throughout its entire
     dorsal surface. _____*Lasiurus* 78
   Interfemoral membrane covered with hairs only on its basal portion above, or
     almost devoid of hairs.
      Premolars, 3 above and 3 below on each side, size small, general colora-
       tion brownish. _____*Myotis* 57
      Premolars, 2 above and 2 below on each side, size small, general colora-
       tion light brownish. _____*Pipistrellus* 71
      Premolars, 2 above and 3 below, bats of medium size, dark in color with
       silvery tips to the hairs. _____*Lasionycteris* 68
      Premolars 1 above and 2 below on each side.
       Incisors 2 above and 3 below on each side, size large, tail not pro-
        truding beyond interfemoral membrane, which is scantily haired
        on basal fourth. _____*Eptesicus* 74
       Incisors 1 above and 3 below on each side, size medium, tail dis-
        tinctly protruding beyond interfemoral membrane, which is furred
        only at extreme base. _____*Nycticeius* 83

MOUSE-EARED BATS
Genus **Myotis** Kaup

This genus has nearly the geographic range of the family Vespertilionidae. It contains about 80 species making it one of the largest known genera of bats. Five of these species are known to occur in Indiana and a sixth will most certainly be found within the state when its fauna is better known.

Dental formula: $i \frac{2-2}{3-3}$, $c \frac{1-1}{1-1}$, $pm \frac{3-3}{3-3}$, $m \frac{3-3}{3-3}$, $= 38$.

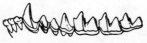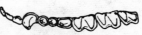

Fig. 18. Teeth of Trouessart's Bat, *Myotis keenii septentrionalis*, enlarged five times. After Miller in North American Fauna, No. 13, 1897, fig. 15, p. 71.

Upper incisors well developed, subequal, closely crowded, the crowns rather higher than long, subterete; the the inner with a distinct posterior secondary cusp, the outer with a well developed concave surface directed toward the can-

Fig. 19. Photographs courtesy U. S. Nat. Mus. Skins of species of Bats occurring in Indiana. All specimens in U. S. Nat. Mus., all 2/3 natural size. As satisfactory skins of Indiana specimens were not always available, three skins from other localities were substituted.

A.—Howell's Bat, *Myotis grisescens*, Cat. No. 157,518, Nickajack Cave, Tenn., Aug. 31, 1908, A. H. Howell.

ine from which it is separated by a space not quite equal to diameter of both incisors together. Lower incisors with crowns about equal in length, forming a continuous convex row between the canines. Skull slender and slightly built, without special peculiarities of form. Ear well developed, slender, tragus slender and nearly or quite straight. Tail about as long as outstretched leg. Interfemoral membrane large, its surface furred at extreme base above. Mammae 2.

The species of the genus *Myotis* are among the commonest of Indiana bats. The habits of all the Indiana species are probably essentially the same, though some species are so rare that practically nothing is known of them. They are typically cave dwellers and in winter collect in the caves of southern Indiana in enormous numbers. They may pack themselves on the walls of caves so closely that as many as two dozen may occupy a single square foot. The temperature of these caves is practically constant throughout the year, average about 56° F. The bats enter the caves in the autumn and when the outside becomes too cold for insect life they move inward and undergo a form of hibernation. They acquire much fat in summer and early autumn and this serves as nourishment during their quiescent period in winter. They usually roost at a considerable distance from the daylight of the cave opening. This location in the cave is changed from time to time during the winter as they seldom remain longer than a week in one spot. Like all other bats their position when roosting is head-downwards. During the summer the bats leave the caves and become scattered, singly or in small groups, over wide areas. By the middle of May the caves that I have been in, in Spring Mill State Park, the bats had left. By the first of September in Marengo and Wyandotte caves a few of the advance guard were just returning. During the summer bats use any suitable dark crannies, or crevices, or dark attics, or towers, or hollow trees during the daylight hours.

Mating occurs in November, but the ova are not fertilized until the bats leave the caves in April. The spermatozoa remain alive, but inactive, in the uterus in the female during the winter. The young are rather well developed when born and cling to the mother's fur and are carried about by her during her quest for insects, at least while the young are very small. The peculiar hook-like teeth of the milk set are probably an adaptation for hanging on to the mother. The strongly developed hind claws are also useful for the same

B.—Indiana Bat, *Myotis sodalis*, Cat. No. 22,028, Center County, Penn., Feb. 7, 1892, B. H. Warren. The apparent inconspicuousness of ears and tail is due to the method of preparing the skin.

C.—Trouessart's Bat, *Myotis keenii septentrionalis*, Cat. No. 173,541, Lake of Bays, Ont., Aug. 20, 1911, T. H. Hungerford.

D.—Rhoads' Bat, *Myotis austroriparius*, Cat. No. 153,630, Mitchell, Lawrence County, Aug. 9, 1907, W. L. Hahn.

E.—Georgian Bat, *Pipistrellus subflavus*, Cat. No. 153,644, Mitchell, Lawrence County, March 7, 1907, W. L. Hahn.

F.—Little Brown Bat, *Myotis lucifugus*, Cat. No. 153,620, Mitchell, Lawrence County, Nov. 6, 1906, W. L. Hahn.

purpose. Female bats able to fly have been captured in which the total weight of the young has exceeded the weight of the parent. As the young become larger and heavier they are probably left in suitable roosting places while the mother is feeding. The number of young in *Myotis* varies from one to two. The young apparently do not reach maturity until late in summer. Immature bats even though of the same size as the adults may be distinguished by an examination of the distal ends of the phalanges of the fingers. In the adults the bone ends in a knob-shaped swelling while in the young there is a gradual swelling of the bone from near the middle of the shaft to the end and epiphyses are plainly visible.

To collect bats when they are half dormant in a cave is an easy matter. In summer their collection is more difficult and largely a matter of chance. A good quick wing shot can shoot them at twilight as they fly over roadways and bodies of water. The summer distribution of the various species of *Myotis* is comparatively little known.

It is easy enough to recognize a bat as a member of the genus *Myotis* usually by external characters and especially by an examination of the teeth. To distinguish the various species is more difficult. The student is advised to collect his material in duplicate and send it all to one of the larger museums for determination. These institutions will be glad to identify material in exchange for part of it.

The following key and descriptions of the Indiana species of *Myotis* has been freely taken from Miller and Allen's (1928) recent revision of the American species.

Key to the Indiana Species of Myotis

Foot small, (6.6-7 mm.) the ratio of its length to that of tibia about .40-.46, belly warm buff, back ochraceous tawny. _____*Myotis subulatus leibii*   67
Foot relatively larger, (8-10 mm.) the ratio of its length to that of tibia from .48-.60.

    Wing membrane attached to tarsus; fur of back without obviously darkened basal area, ratio of foot to tibia about .60 _____*Myotis grisescens*   63
    Wing membrane attached to side of foot; fur of back with obviously darkened basal area; ratio of foot to tibia usually less than .57.

        Hairs on back obviously tricolored; calcar with a small but usually evident keel. _____*Myotis sodalis*   66
        Hairs on back not obviously tricolored; calcar with normally no trace of keel.

            Ear when laid forward extending noticeably beyond tip of muzzle. _____*Myotis keenii septentrionalis*   65
            Ear when laid forward not extending noticeably beyond tip of muzzle.

                Fur above dense woolly; a low but evident sagittal crest always present in adults. _____*Myotis austroriparius*   62
                Fur above, normal; silky, a sagittal crest rarely present. _____*Myotis lucifugus lucifugus*   60

Little Brown Bat,
Myotis lucifugus lucifugus (LeConte)

Vespertilio lucifugus LeConte. McMurtrie's Cuvier, Anim. Kingd., vol. 1, p. 431, 1831. Type locality: Georgia.
Vespertilio gryphus Evermann and Butler 1894.

Myotis lucifugus Hahn 1909, Miller and Allen 1928.

Myotis lucifugus lucifugus is the common little brown bat of Indiana as well as of eastern North America. Its geographic range is from the limits of tree growth in Alaska to Labrador southward to northern Arkansas, Mississippi, Alabama and Georgia. It is found throughout the entire state of Indiana though comparatively few Indiana specimens are in public collections.

Size medium. Head and body, 45-50 mm.; tail, 30-37 mm.; tibia, 16-18 mm.; foot, 9-10 mm.; forearm, 37-40 mm.; length of ear from the meatus, 13-15 mm.; width of ear, 9-10 mm.; greatest length of skull, 14.6-15 mm.; greatest breadth, 9.1-9.4; maxillary tooth row, 5.1-5.6 mm. Weight: Summer, 6 to 7.5 grams; (Mohr 1933).

Ear reaches nostril when laid forward, its anterior edge is convex becoming nearly straight in the upper third to the bluntly rounded tip; below the tip the external or posterior margin is slightly concave or nearly straight in the upper

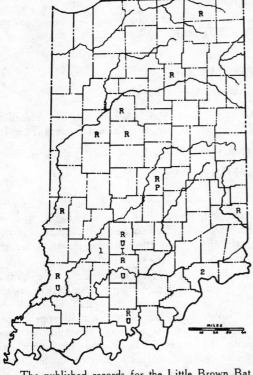

Map 8. Published records and specimens in collections of the Little Brown Bat, *Myotis lucifugus*, in Indiana; 1, Robert Goslin; 2, North Madison High School, Melford Campbell.

The published records for the Little Brown Bat are: Carroll (Evermann and Butler 1894), Clinton (Evermann and Butler 1894), Crawford (Lyon 1931), Franklin (Evermann and Butler 1894), Knox (Miller and Allen 1928), Lagrange (Evermann and Butler 1894), Lawrence (Miller and Allen 1928), Marion (Miller and Allen 1928), Monroe (Evermann and Butler 1894, Banta 1907, Miller and Allen 1928), Tippecanoe (Evermann and Butler 1894), Vigo (Evermann and Butler 1894), Wabash (Evermann and Butler 1894).

half, then convex on the lower half which forms a projecting, but not abrupt, shoulder. The tragus is about half the total height of the ear. At its outer base is a small rounded lobe, marked off by a shallow notch. Above this point and opposite the inner base is the widest region. The inner margin of the tragus is nearly straight, the outer very nearly convex, and faintly crenulate to the narrowly rounded tip.

The extreme tip of the tail is free. The interfemoral membrane has a few scattered inconspicuous hairs along the margin. The calcar is long, exceeding in length the free border of the interfemoral membrane.

Color of upper parts varies from yellowish brown to olive brown, with a dark almost blackish brown spot at the shoulder. Underneath the color is gray with a buffy suffusion. Bases of hairs above and below blackish or dark plumbeous. Wing membranes not pale edged.

One young at a birth seems the rule. They are born as early as June 17 and as late as July 5. Adults do not carry their young with them, but leave them in the breeding cave while they feed. The young are on the wing in from three to four weeks after birth. Summer weight of adults 6 to 7.5 grams, weight of new born young 1.45 to 1.55 grams. (Mohr, 1933.)

RHOADS' BAT

Myotis austroriparius (Rhoads)

Vespertilio lucifugus austroriparius RHOADS. Proc. Acad. Nat. Sci. Philadelphia, 1927, p. 277, 1927 May. Type locality: Tarpon Springs, Florida.

Myotis subulatus Hahn 1909 (part). Four specimens from Mitchell, Indiana.

Myotis austroriparius Miller and Allen 1928.

Rhoads' Bat is only about 1/30 as common as the Little Brown Bat as judged by specimens in collections. It is known from only four localities, Tarpon Springs, Bird Key, and Gainesville, Florida, and Mitchell, Indiana. It undoubtedly has a much wider distribution, and there is one doubtful record from Canada.

Externally like *Myotis lucifugus lucifugus,* except that the fur of the back is shorter, 6-7 mm., instead of 9-10 mm., and more dense, and dark bases of hairs and burnished tips less conspicuous; general color dull yellowish or drabby brown. The hair of the upper parts has a dull woolly appearance. There is an absence of strong contrast in color between the tips and the bases of the hairs. The skull has a more slender general form, narrower interorbital constriction, and in adults, a low sagittal crest, lacking in the Little Brown Bat. Head and body, 51-52 mm.; tail, 34-38 mm.; tibia, 15.2-17 mm.; foot, 9.8-10 mm.; forearm, 37.6-40.2 mm.; ear from meatus, 12-14 mm.; greatest length of skull, 14.5-15 mm.; greatest breadth, 9 mm.; maxilarry tooth row, 10.5-11 mm. Birth weight, 1.10-1.15; adult weight, 7.25 grams (H. B. Sherman, Journ. Mamm., vol. 11, p. 497, 1930).

Map 9. Published record and specimens in collections of Rhoads' Bat, *Myotis austroriparius*, in Indiana.

The published record for Rhoads' Bat, *Myotis austroriparius* is Lawrence (Miller and Allen 1928).

HOWELL'S BAT
Myotis grisescens A. H. Howell

Myotis grisescens A. H. HOWELL 1909 March. Type locality: Nickajack Cave, Marion County, Tennessee.

Myotis grisescens Hahn 1909, Miller and Allen 1928.

Myotis velifer Hahn 1909 (part).

Howell's Bat is distributed throughout the limestone region of the southern Middle West, Tennessee, Alabama, Arkansas, southern Illinois and Indiana. In spite of its rather limited geographic distribution and its comparatively recent introduction to science (A. H. Howell, 1909 March) it is fairly common in collections, Miller and Allen (1928) recording a total of 258 specimens examined as against 744 specimens of *Myotis lucifugus lucifugus*, a proportion of about 1:3. Although it has been recorded by Hahn from Indiana on the basis of specimens examined, no extant specimens from the state are in collections at the present time.

Size decidedly larger than that of *Myotis lucifugus lucifugus*, but general proportions about the same. Head and body, 48.5-52.8 mm.; tail, 38-40 mm.; tibia, 15.6-18.2 mm.; foot, 9.2-10.6 mm.; forearm, 42.0-45.4 mm.; ear from meatus, 13.8-15.2 mm.; greatest length of skull, 15.9-16.2 mm.; greatest width,

10 mm.; maxillary tooth row, 6 mm. The skull has obvious sagittal and lamb-doid crests in adults.

The fur is more velvety than in *Myotis lucifugus lucifugus* and the hairs of the dorsal surface are strikingly characterized by being of essentially the same color throughout instead of conspicuously darker at the base. There are two color phases, dusky and russet.

The ears when laid forward reach the nostrils or slightly beyond, tragus slender, about half the height of the ear, its anterior edge nearly straight, broadest at the base, narrowing in the terminal half to a bluntly pointed tip, a small lobule present at base posteriorly.

The wing membranes arise from the base of the tarsus instead of from the base of the toes as in all the other Indiana species of *Myotis*.

Howell's Bat seems to be a home loving cave bat and it has not been taken at remote distances from its winter caverns. Miller and Allen (1928) conclude from a study of the frequency of the sexes in collected specimens that the males and females are usually segregated except at the period of mating in the autumn, and when the breeding females have immature bats of both sexes with them. The young are probably born early in July.

Usual number of young at birth is one. Birth weight near 2.5 grams. Weight of adults in June 7.64 to 9.1 grams, in January 6.47 to 7.20. Young are born naked and are probably carried by their mothers for about a week, after which they are left in cave while she feeds. (Mohr, 1933 p. 51).

Map 10. Published record of Howell's Bat, *Myotis grisescens*, in Indiana.

The published records for Howell's Bat, *Myotis grisescens* are: Lawrence (H a h n 1908, 1909; A. H. Howell 1909 Mar.)

TROUESSART'S BAT
Myotis keenii septentrionalis (Trouessart)

Vespertilio gryphus var. *septentrionalis* TROUESSART, Catal. Mamm. viv. foss., p. 131, 1897. Type locality: Halifax, Nova Scotia.
Vespertilio gryphus lucifugus Evermann and Butler, 1894.
Myotis subulatus Miller 1897, Hahn 1909. (Not *Vespertilio subulatus* SAY 1823).
Myotis keenii septentrionalis Miller and Allen 1928.

Trouessart's Bat is distributed in eastern North America from Newfoundland and Quebec, south to Tennessee and South Carolina, west to North Dakota and Arkansas. It is about 1/5 as common in collections as *Myotis lucifugus lucifugus*.

In size and general appearance it is much like *Myotis lucifugus lucifugus*, but the tail is relatively longer and the ear actually longer, extending beyond tip of nose when laid forward by about 3 or 4 mm.; tragus more slender, its inner margin straight and tip acute; foot about half as long as tibia instead of more than half as long; skull more slender than that of *Myotis lucifugus lucifugus*.

Size in general like that of the Little Brown Bat. Head and body, 44-47 mm.; tail, 35-40 mm.; tibia, 16.5-17.5 mm.; foot, 8.5-9 mm.; forearm, 35-38 mm.; ear from meatus, 15-16.5 mm.; greatest length of skull, 15-15.3 mm.; greatest width, about 9 mm.; maxillary tooth row, 5.5-6 mm.

Map 11. Published records and specimens in collections of Trouessart's Bat, *Myotis keenii septentrionalis*, in Indiana; 1, collection of Robert Goslin.

The published records of Trouessart's Bat, *Myotis keenii septentrionalis* are: Knox (Miller 1897, Miller and Allen 1928), Lawrence (Miller and Allen 1928), Vigo (Evermann and Butler 1894, Miller and Allen 1928).

Color approximately like that of *Myotis lucifugus lucifugus* but the brown hair tips are not so long nor so glossy.

INDIANA BAT
Myotis sodalis Miller and Allen

Myotis sodalis MILLER and ALLEN 1928. Type locality: Wyandotte Cave, Crawford County, Indiana.

Vespertilio gryphus Evermann and Butler 1894 in part probably.

Myotis lucifugus Hahn 1909 in part.

The Indiana Bat is the only species of existing mammals whose type locality is in Indiana. It ranges from Vermont and Michigan to Arkansas and Alabama. It is probably found throughout Indiana though specimens are known only from the southern part of the state.

General appearance as in *Myotis lucifugus lucifugus*, but with slightly longer tail, less enlarged foot, fur loose in texture and pinkish gray in color. Skull in general as in the Little Brown Bat but usually with a sagittal ridge present. Teeth of the two species indistinguishable.

Ear about as in *Myotis lucifugus lucifugus*, of medium size, reaching nostril when laid forward; lower anterior border convex, then nearly straight in its upper half, with a broadly rounded summit, below which the outer margin is very slightly concave, then passes gradually into the basal shoulder without forming a notch or abrupt transition. Tragus rather short and blunt curving slightly forward, its height a little less than half the height of the ear. Its posterior edge is slightly crenulate.

Size as in the Little Brown Bat. Head and body, 45-48 mm.; tail, 35-50 mm.; tibia, 15.2-16.2 mm.; foot, 8 mm.; forearm, 39-40 mm.; ear from meatus, 13.2-14.8 mm.; greatest length of skull, 14.5-15 mm.; greatest width, 9 mm.; maxillary tooth row, 5.2-5.5 mm.

Texture of fur extremely fine and fluffy, the hairs having a tendency to stand out from each other. On the upper surface the basal two-thirds of the hair is fuscous-black, then comes a narrow grayish band and last of all the cinnamon brown tip. Below, the hair slaty basally, with grayish white tips washed with cinnamon brown. The general effect is a pinkish white below and a dull chestnut gray above, the hairs obviously tricolored when parted.

Concerning its habits Miller and Allen (1928) write:

It is a curious fact that although this bat occurs over much of the eastern United States, nearly all of the known individuals were taken during hibernation. A series was secured in a cave at Proctor, Vt., in early April, when a few *Myotis lucifugus* were found at the same time. A great number annually winter in the Wyandotte Cave, Ind. Two or three lots of bats from this station include this species only. Where the bats go with the coming of spring and in what way their habits differ from those of *Myotis lucifugus* it is impossible to say. Yet it seems probable that some difference in habits exists, for *Myotis sodalis* has not been captured as *M. lucifugus* so often is, either in small colonies in buildings or single individuals shot while flying about the edges of ponds and along streams. [Netting has been more productive, F. L. Osgood, Journ. Mamm., vol. 16, p. 228, 1935].

In collections *Myotis sodalis* ranks about 1/2 in frequency as compared with *Myotis lucifugus*.

Map 12. Published records and specimens in collections of the Indiana Bat, *Myotis sodalis*, in Indiana; 1, collection of Robert Goslin.

The published records for the Indiana Bat, *Myotis sodalis* are: Crawford (Hahn 1909, Cory 1912, Miller and Allen 1928, Mohr 1933), Knox (Miller and Allen 1928).

LEIB'S BAT
Myotis subulatus leibii (Audubon and Bachman)

Vespertilio subulatus SAY. Long's Exped. Rocky Mts., vol. 2, p. 65, 1823.
　　Type locality: Near present town of La Junta, Otero County, Colorado.
Vespertilio leibii AUDUBON and BACHMAN. Journ. Acad. Nat. Sci. Philadelphia, ser. 1, vol. 8, p. 284, 1842. Type locality: Erie County, Ohio.
Myotis subulatus leibii Miller and Allen 1928.

　　Only eight specimens of this bat are known in collections. It ranges from Vermont to West Virginia, Kentucky and Ohio. It will undoubtedly be found in Indiana when more small bats from the state are collected.

　　It is a small animal. Head and body, 43-48 mm.; tail, 30-35 mm.; tibia, 14-15 mm.; foot, 6.6-7 mm.; forearm, 31-34 mm.; ear from meatus, 12.2-13 mm.; greatest length of skull, 13.2-14.2 mm.; greatest width, 8 mm.; maxillary tooth row, 5 mm.

　　Ear when laid forward reaches to tip of nose or extends about 1 mm. beyond. Tragus is slender, tapering, half the height of the ear with a small rounded lobe at the base cut off by a shallow notch. Both its margins are without crenulations.

　　Compared with the Little Brown Bat, Leib's Bat is distinguishable by its smaller size, small foot, and a distinct keel on the calcar. *Myotis subulatus leibii* resembles the darker colored forms of *Myotis lucifugus lucifugus*, but, slightly more golden above and lacks the dark spot at the shoulder. Bases of hairs on body blackish. Face from

nose to base of ears, black; ears, tragus, nose and chin dull blackish. Skull in comparison with the more common species, flattened and distinctly narrower.

Whether Leib's Bat is actually rare or has some peculiar habits that make it escape
collectors is unknown. All small dark colored bats of the genus *Myotis* taken in
Indiana should be critically examined for the characters of Leib's Bat, before being
discarded as "just another bat."

SILVER-HAIRED BAT
Genus **Lasionycteris** Peters

Dental formula: $i \frac{2-2}{3-3}, c \frac{1-1}{1-1}, pm \frac{2-2}{3-3}, m \frac{3-3}{3-3}, = 36.$

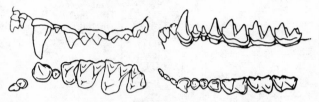

Fig. 20. Teeth of Silver-haired Bat, *Lasionycteris noctivagans*, enlarged five
times. After Miller in North American Fauna, No. 13, 1897, fig. 19, p. 85.

Skull flattened, rostrum broad, dorsal profile of skull nearly straight; ears
short, nearly as broad as long, when laid forward reaching barely to nostril.
Tragus short, straight and bluntly rounded at tip. Back of interfemoral membrane furred on basal half. Mammae 2. The genus is peculiar to North
America and contains but a single species, ranging from the Atlantic to the
Pacific. It probably does not breed south of the Transition Zone. It is known
to migrate southward from the colder parts of its range in the autumn.

SILVER-HAIRED BAT
Lasionycteris noctivagans (LeConte)

V[*espertilio*] *noctivagans* LeConte. McMurtrie's Cuvier. Anim. Kingd., vol.
1, p. 431. Type locality: Eastern United States.
Lasionycteris noctivagans Evermann and Butler 1894, Hahn 1909.

Color deep blackish brown throughout, many of the hairs on the back,
belly, and furred part of the interfemoral membrane tipped with silvery
white. The white tips are most abundant on the middle of the back, and
absent or nearly so about the face and head. Total length, about 100 mm.;
tail, 39-42 mm.; forearm, 41 mm.; ear from meatus, 16 mm.; greatest length
of skull, 16 mm.; greatest width, 10 mm.; maxillary tooth row, 6 mm. Its
peculiar color at once distinguishes it from any other Indiana bat.

It probably occurs throughout Indiana though published records and specimens in museums are rare. There are no records from the southern part of
the state and Hahn never found it in the limestone caves with which he was
so familiar.

Merriam (1882-1884) writes at length concerning its habits:

Fig. 21. Photograph copyright H. H. Pittman. Silver-haired Bat, *Lasionycteris noctivagans*, about natural size.

Like many other bats, it has a decided liking for waterways, coursing up and down streams and rivers, and circling around lakes and ponds. . . Several that were wounded and fell into the water, at a distance of fifteen or twenty feet from the bank, swam ashore. They swam powerfully and swiftly. . . Next to water courses, the borders of hard wood groves are the favorite haunts of the Silver-haired Bat. . . While searching for their insect prey they may be seen to dart in and out among the branches and to penetrate in various directions, the dense mat of foliage overhead.

Merriam is inclined to believe that their feeding is done in the evening and early morning. He refers to their daylight roosting places as caves, hollow trees, and in one instance in an abandoned crow's nest. He refers to a marked dissociation of the sexes similar to that referred to under *Myotis sodalis*. Most of the adult specimens taken by him were females, but of thirty-two young there were nineteen males and thirteen females. The number of young at a birth is usually two and in the Adirondacks they are born about the first of July. They commence to fly when about three weeks old. While only about ten millimeters shorter the first young shot weighed only about half as much as their parents.

The bat hunter has many difficulties to contend with. Night creeps upon him so insidiously that he is only made aware of its presence by the number of shots missed

Map 13. Published records and specimens in collections of the Silver-haired Bat, *Lasionycteris noctivagans*, in Indiana. 1, collection of A. W. Butler.

The published records for the Silver-haired Bat are: Franklin (Evermann and Butler 1894, Hahn 1909), Laporte (Hahn 1907, 1909), Marion (Hahn 1909), St. Joseph (Engels 1933).

(which multiply with painful rapidity with the increasing darkness), and by the great trouble and loss of time experienced in finding the bats that fall to the ground. The temptation to linger as long as the bats can be distinctly seen is very great, but should be resisted if the hunter has any regard for his reputation as a wing shot. When two shot out of three are missed, it is time to go home. Moonlight evenings are also very misleading, but the novice soon learns to avoid such illusions. I believe that I could not average one bat for every dozen shots by the brightest moonlight. The greatest obstacle in bat shooting is the inability to calculate distance after early nightfall, objects invariably appearing much farther off than they really are. . . This deception in distance manifests itself in another embarrassing way, for in searching for the bat in this dim light one is almost certain to over-estimate the distance at which it fell. Hence a well trained dog with a good nose, is of the greatest assistance.

The length of time that the fading light will permit of bat shooting in any single evening varies from a little over half an hour, to less than ten minutes, according to the season. The loss of time, therefore, occasioned by searching for fallen bats can only be overcome by the aid of a dog, or of an associate. In fact the value of a willing assistant can scarcely be exaggerated. He stands a little to one side of the hunter and carefully notes the line in which the bat falls. The hunter likewise marks the direction and as both advance simultaneously, the point of intersection of the two lines shows the exact position of the bat. A lantern with a good reflector is of some service. . . . (Merriam 1882-1884).

PIPISTRELLES
Genus **Pipistrellus** Kaup

The genus *Pipistrellus* is found throughout the greater part of the Eastern Hemisphere, and throughout the southern half of North America. There are five American species one of which is found in Indiana.

Dental formula: $i \frac{2-2}{3-3}$, $c \frac{1-1}{1-1}$, $pm \frac{2-2}{2-2}$, $m \frac{3-3}{3-3}$, $= 34$.

Skull small and lightly built, braincase usually more inflated than in *Lasionycteris*, but rostrum proportionally as broad. Ears distinctly longer than broad and tapering to a narrowly rounded tip. Tragus straight or slightly curved forward. Back of interfemoral membrane sprinkled with hair on basal third. Mammae 2.

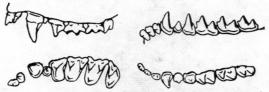

Fig. 22. Teeth of Georgian Bat, *Pipistrellus subflavus*, enlarged five times. After Miller in North American Fauna, No. 13, 1897, fig. 23, p. 92.

GEORGIAN BAT
Pipistrellus subflavus (F. Cuvier) [2]

V[espertilio] subflavus F. CUVIER. Nouv. Ann. Mus. Hist. Nat. Paris, vol. 1, p. 17, 1882. Type locality: Probably Georgia.

---

2 When more is known about Indiana bats the Dusky Georgian Bat, *Pipistrellus subflavus obscurus* Miller will probably be taken in Indiana, especially the northern part of the state.

Vespertilio georgrenus (sic) Quick and Langdon 1882.
Vesperugo carolinensis Evermann and Butler 1894.
Pipistrellus subflavus Hahn 1909.

Probably found throughout the state in summer, though there are no northern records for Indiana. It has been taken as far north as Wisconsin, however. It is a winter resident in the cave region of the state.

Fig. 23. Photographs courtesy Amer. Mus. Nat. Hist. Georgian Bat, *Pipistrellus subflavus*, about natural size.

Distinguished among Indiana bats by its small size and yellowish brown color.

The main body of the fur of the back is made up of short hairs about six millimeters in length, deep plumbeous from base to a little below middle, then yellowish brown to the dark brown tip. Intermixed with these are much longer hairs about ten millimeters in length and clear yellowish brown to extreme tip.

The ears when laid forward reach just beyond nostrils, tragus about half the length of ear. Foot large, slightly more than half as long as tibia, covered with conspicuous light brown hairs on dorsal surface.

Head and body, 85 mm.; tail, 39 mm.; tibia, 15.5 mm.; foot, 8 mm.; forearm, 34 mm.; ear from meatus, 14 mm.; greatest length of skull, 12 mm.; greatest width, 8 mm.; maxillary tooth row, 4.5 mm.

The habits of this species resemble those of the other cave bats. They leave the cave later in the spring and the majority return later in the fall than do the species of *Myotis*.

Mating takes place about the end of November and the young are probably born in July. The single pregnant female which I have examined contained three very small embryos on the 6th of June. [The normal number of young is two].

Map 14. Published records and specimens in collections of the Georgian Bat, *Pipistrellus subflavus*, in Indiana; 1, collection of Robert Goslin; 2, North Madison High School, Melford Campbell.

The published records for the Georgian Bat are: Franklin (Quick and Langdon 1882, Evermann and Butler 1894, Hahn 1909), Lawrence (Hahn 1907, 1908, 1909), Monroe (Banta 1907, McAtee 1907, Hahn 1909).

In flight this species is readily distinguished by its small size and the weak fluttering of its wings which makes it resemble a butterfly rather than a bat. The animals are so small and weak that they certainly cannot capture and eat large beetles or other large insects. Their food probably consists chiefly of small diptera and moths. The species usually flies high over the open fields when feeding. These bats readily learn to eat fresh meat when in captivity.

The Georgian Bat usually clings to the side walls of the higher passages while in the caves. It is less active than the other species of cave bats. Observations in the caves at Mitchell during the winter of 1906-07 showed that *Myotis lucifugus* rarely stayed in one spot more than a week while *Pipistrellus* often slept in one spot for a month. Hibernation is not uninterrupted in either species, however. (Hahn 1909).

SEROTINE BATS
Genus **Eptesicus** Rafinesque

The genus *Eptesicus* is found throughout Africa, Australia, most of Asia and most of America from southern Canada southward. It contains about 45 species, one of which is found in North America.

Dental formula: $i \dfrac{2-2}{3-3}$, $c \dfrac{1-1}{1-1}$, $pm \dfrac{1-1}{2-2}$, $m \dfrac{3-3}{3-3}$, $= 32$.

Fig. 24. Teeth of Brown Bat, *Eptesicus fuscus*, enlarged five times. After Miller in North American Fauna, No. 13, 1897, fig. 26, p. 101.

The skull in general is not essentially different from that of *Pipistrellus*, though because of its large size and angularity the single United States species appears very different. It is one of the largest representatives of the family *Vespertilionidae* in eastern North America. Ears short, narrower than long. Tragus straight, short, directed slightly forward, broadest near the middle and tapering to a moderately sharp point. Back of interfemoral membrane naked except for a sprinkling of hairs on basal fourth. Mammae, 2.

LARGE BROWN BAT
Eptesicus fuscus (Beauvois)

Vespertilio fuscus BEAUVOIS. Cat. Rais. Mus. de Peale, Philadelphia p. 18, 1796. Type locality: Philadelphia.

Vespertilio fuscus Quick and Langdon 1882.

Adelonycteris fuscus Evermann and Butler 1894.

Eptesicus fuscus Hahn 1909.

The Large Brown Bat is found throughout most of the United States and adjoining Canadian provinces, and occurs everywhere in Indiana though specimens and records are comparatively few.

It is at once distinguished from any other Indiana bat by its uniformly dark brown color, large size and thick heavy ears, wings and interfemoral membrane. Total length, 110-115 mm.; tail, about 45 mm.; tibia, 19.5 mm.; foot, 9.7-10.4 mm.; forearm, 45-47 mm.; ear from meatus, 18-19 mm.; greatest length of skull, 20 mm.; greatest width, 12 mm.; maxillary tooth row, about 7.5 mm. Weight, between 14 and 15 grams, males slightly heavier than females.

The Large Brown Bat is domestic in its habits so far as man is concerned. It is one of the common bats to get into dwellings and outhouses. . They are more or less resident throughout the year and hibernate about houses, in hollow trees and in cliffs and caves among rocks. They have even been found hibernating in rolled-up awnings. It is not a common cave bat in Indiana. Among thousands of *Myotis* which Hahn found in Indiana and Kentucky caves, only ten of the Large Brown Bat were observed. All of the ten were near the entrances of the caves where daylight reaches. He is inclined to believe that many individuals migrate in winter. It makes an early appearance in spring and is active until late in the autumn. Its time of emergence in the evening is late. The young vary from one to two and are apparently born in June.

Klugh (1924) has made some recent and interesting observations on a specimen of the large Brown Bat captured in a cellar in midwinter.

At first this bat was very savage, uttering its sharp 'chirring' note when touched and attempting to bite when handled. In four days, during which time it was handled frequently and given food and drink, it became much more tractable, and in a week it was quite tame, never trying to bite nor squeaking, unless suddenly seized. . . . At first when liberated it would always alight as far from me as possible but later it was as likely, and seemingly more likely, to alight near me than elsewhere.

At first it refused everything offered it, though unfortunately I could find no insects to offer, but after a few days it took cooked tongue, which had been moistened with water. Later it ate veal and beef, uncooked and cooked, veal jelly, ham, and cooked haddock, but refused bread or anything of a vegetable nature. It ate only very small pieces of any of these foods, and had great difficulty in handling pieces more than two millimeters in diameter. It used its long flexible tongue with considerable dexterity in getting material into its mouth.

Eptesicus was always ready for a drink of water, and usually would not eat until it had had a drink. The water was given to it in a small shallow dish and it had two methods of drinking. The method most frequently employed was to run its lower jaw under the water, scoop up a little, and suck it down with a biting movement, as if it were 'eating' the water. Bats seem to drink while skimming over the surface of a body of water, and this scooping up method is probably used at such times.

It spent nearly all its time in sleep hanging on a rod I fixed in its box, or hanging from the edge of the box by its hind feet. Usually it woke about seven o'clock in the evening, and if let out then would fly about for some time. When going to sleep it hung itself up and commenced to shiver, its respirations which during activity were about one hundred per minute, became slower and slower, the body relaxed, the tremors ceased and it was fast asleep—all in a period of two minutes. Its sleep was extremely deep—more of a hibernation than an ordinary sleep—and its respirations seemed to occur about once in five minutes and often were so slight as to be undetectable. Even in its deepest sleep auditory stimuli caused a response, a very slight noise being reacted to by a jerk of the head and body.

It cleaned itself by licking and scratching. The alar membrane and the interfemoral membrane came in for a good deal of the washing, during the course of which the former was stretched into all sorts of shapes. The back and sides were scratched with the hind feet, one of these at a time being run from behind forward with a rapid scratching motion.

Fig. 25. Photographs courtesy U. S. Nat. Mus. Skins of species of Bats occurring in Indiana. All specimens in U. S. Nat. Mus., all 2/3 natural size. As skins of Indiana specimens were not always available, two skins from other localities have been substituted.

Map 15. Published records and specimens in collections of the Large Brown Bat, *Eptesicus fuscus*, in Indiana; 1, collection of Robert Goslin; 2, collection of F. H. Test.

The published records for the Brown Bat are: Franklin (Quick and Langdon 1882, Evermann and Butler 1894), Lawrence (Hahn 1908, 1909), Monroe (Banta 1907, McAtee 1907, Hahn 1909), St. Joseph (Engels 1933), Vigo (Evermann and Butler 1894, Hahn 1909).

In alighting it caught with the thumb-hooks while the wings were expanded, took hold with the feet, folded the wings and turned head downwards.

That the guiding sense of bats on the wing is not sight but a superfine sense of touch—a sense which detects the presence of an object by the rebound of air without actually touching the object—seems to be definitely proven by the experiments of Spallanzani and Schöbl and the histological investigations of the latter. Nevertheless I thought it worthwhile to experiment for myself, and I found that Eptesicus was able to avoid

A.—Red Bat, *Lasiurus borealis*, Cat. No. 143,745, Plummer's Island, Md., May 24, 1906, Washington Biologists' Field Club.

B.—Brown Bat, *Eptesicus fuscus*, Cat. No. 221,356, South Bend, St. Joseph County, March 24, 1920, M. W. Lyon, Jr.

C.—Big-eared Bat, *Corynorhinus rafinesquii*, Cat. No. 153,642, Mitchell, Lawrence County, Dec. 16, 1906, W. L. Hahn.

D.—Rafinesque's Bat, *Nycticeius humeralis*, Cat. No. 82,751, Linden, Md. Aug. 11, 1896, N. P. Scudder.

E.—Silver-haired Bat, *Lasionycteris noctivagans*, Cat. No. 256,494, South Bend, St. Joseph County, Aug. 2, 1931, Florence Peck.

objects, and even to dodge objects thrust suddenly in its path of flight, with its eyes sealed up with adhesive plaster as well as with the eyes uncovered.

Engels (1933) says it is easy to catch in a net an *Eptesicus* flying in a room after the animal has passed one, but impossible to capture it approaching head on.

From an examination of 2200 fecal pellets of the Brown Bat, Hamilton (1931) gives the following frequency percentage of insect food:

Coleoptera, 36.1; Hymenoptera, 26.3; Diptera, 13.2; Plecoptera, 6.5; Ephemeridae, 4.6; Hemiptera, 3.4; Trichoptera, 3.2; Neuroptera, 3.2; Mecoptera, 2.7; Orthoptera, 0.6. The absence of Lepidoptera is interesting. Of the beetles, Coleoptera, the family Scarabaeidae (leaf chafers and May beetles) occurred most frequently, next in order occurred the family Elateridae, in which the wire worms are placed. The order Diptera was represented chiefly by muscids, a group embracing the house fly and its allies.

HAIRY-TAILED BATS
Genus **Lasiurus** Gray

This genus ranges throughout the wooded portions of North and South America and West Indies, the Hawaiian and Galapagos Islands.

Dental formula: $i\,\dfrac{1\text{-}1}{3\text{-}3}$, $c\,\dfrac{1\text{-}1}{1\text{-}1}$, $pm\,\dfrac{2\text{-}2}{2\text{-}2}$, $m\,\dfrac{3\text{-}3}{3\text{-}3}$, $= 32$.

Upper incisor in contact with canine; a minute upper premolar at base of

Fig. 26. Teeth of Red Bat, *Lasiurus borealis*, enlarged five times. After Miller in North American Fauna, No. 13, 1897, fig. 30, p. 111.

canine on lingual side. Skull broad, short and deep, quite different from the other species of Vespertilionidae found in Indiana. Ear, broad, blunt and rounded at tip, hairy on most of the dorsal surface. Dorsal surface of interfemoral membrane hairy almost to extreme edge. Mammae 4, an unusual number in bats which almost universally have but 2. The thickly furred interfemoral membrane from which the scientific name is derived and their conspicuous coloring at once distinguishes them from any other North American bats.

It contains two well marked groups, the large Hoary Bat with a long forearm measuring more than 50 mm., and the small Red Bats of wider geographic range with a forearm measuring but 35-45 mm. in length.

RED BAT
Lasiurus borealis (Müller)

Vespertilio borealis MUELLER. Natursyst. Suppl., p. 20, 1776. Type locality: New York.

Vespertilio noveboracensis Plummer 1844. Haymond 1870, Quick and Langdon 1882.

Vespertilio rufus Haymond 1870, Quick and Langdon 1882.

Atalapha noveboracensis Evermann and Butler 1894.

Lasiurus borealis Hahn 1909, Engels 1933.

Nycteris borealis Lyon 1923.

The common Red Bat ranges from Canada to Florida and Texas and westward to Colorado. Related species are found elsewhere.

The ears when laid forward reach a little more than half way from the angle of the mouth to the nostril. Anterior border of ear strongly convex, apex rounded, posterior border also convex; posterior basal lobe strongly developed and deeply notched. Tragus narrowly triangular, anterior border straight, posterior border strongly angled.

Size small, total length, 105-110 mm.; tail, about 50 mm.; tibia, 19.5 mm.; foot, 7.5 mm.; forearm, 39 mm.; ear from meatus, 11.5 mm.; greatest length of skull, about 12.5 mm.; greatest width, about 10 mm.; maxillary tooth row, about 5-5.5 mm.

Very hairy including the entire interfemoral membrane; on middle of back hairs about 7 mm. long and on neck about 10 mm. Upper parts bright rufous red, the hairs blackish at base sprinkled with whitish tips giving a

Map 16. Published records and specimens in collections of the Red Bat, *Lasiurus borealis*, in Indiana; 1, North Madison High School.

The published records for the Red Bat are: Carroll (Evermann and Butler 1894, Hahn 1909), Franklin (Haymond 1870, Quick and Langdon 1882, Evermann and Butler 1894, Hahn 1909), Knox (Hahn 1909), Kosciusko (Hahn 1909), Lawrence (Hahn 1907, 1908, 1909), Miami (Hahn 1909), Monroe (Evermann and Butler 1894, Banta 1907, McAtee 1907, Hahn 1909), Noble (Hahn 1909), Porter (Lyon 1923), St. Joseph (Engels 1933), Vigo (Evermann and Butler 1894, Hahn 1909), Wabash (Evermann and Butler 1894, Hahn 1909), Wayne (Plummer 1844, Hahn 1909).

frosted appearance. There is considerable variation in the intensity of the reddish color, and the amount of frosting. A yellowish white shoulder patch is present. The under parts are paler and less reddish than the upper parts. It is truly a handsome and colorful species.

So far as most observations go the Red Bat is essentially a tree bat, largely or partially solitary, spending the daylight hours suspended in the branches of trees. Less frequently it is found in hollow trees and in caves. Hahn never found it in his extensive experience in the caves of southern Indiana. However, on one occasion he found more than 200 skulls of the Red Bat amid masses of fallen stone on the floor of one cave he explored. He is inclined to believe that it has changed its habits in Indiana in comparatively recent years, from a cave dwelling species to a tree dweller. Merriam (1882-1884) accredits it with hibernating in vast assemblages in rocky caverns or hollow trees, mentioning a cave near Albany, New York, in which the Red Bat was found in large numbers in an extensive cavern, on the authority of Dr. John G. Godman (American Natural History, vol. 1, p. 42, 1842).

There is much evidence that the Red Bat is migratory for it has never been found in northern latitudes in winter and it has been taken in winter in southern localities from which it is absent in summer. It takes to wing early in the evening and is a strong swift flyer evidenced not only by the observations of naturalists but by the fact that it has reached such distant localities as the Hawaiian and Galapagos Islands. The number of young varies from one to four, with perhaps three the more usual number. They are born about the middle of June. Like most bats the young are probably carried about by the mother until they get too heavy for her to carry and are then left during her feeding hours suspended in some trees. They are thought to nurse until at least a month old.

HOARY BAT
Lasiurus cinereus (Beauvois)

Vespertilio linereus (sic) [*cinereus*] BEAUVOIS. Cat. Rais. Mus. de Peale, Philadelphia, p. 18, 1796. Type locality: Philadelphia.

Vespertilio pruinosus Plummer 1844, Haymond 1870, Quick and Langdon 1882.

Atalapha cinerea Evermann and Butler 1894.

Lasiurus cinereus Hahn 1909, Engels 1933.

The Hoary Bat is found throughout most of North America, breeding in the colder portions and in winter migrating south to the southern border of the United States or perhaps farther.

Aside from its much larger size and marked difference in color it closely resembles the Red Bat in general structure. General color, a mixture of light yellowish brown, deep umber and white, the umber brown predominating on the back and dorsal surface of the interfemoral membrane where the hairs are mostly tipped with silvery white. Hairs above, plumbeous at base, light yellowish brown in middle half, umber brown just below the silvery tip. Below, throat yellowish, belly whitish and in between umber brown. Ear is

Fig. 27. Photograph courtesy U. S. Nat. Mus. Hoary Bat, *Lasiurus cinereus*, Cat. No. 21,877, U. S. Nat. Mus., North America, Ward's Natural Science Establishment, natural size. This is the largest species of Bat occurring in the eastern United States.

essentially like that of the Red Bat but larger and basal lobe less developed and without notch on anterior border. Its large size and handsome coloration render it one of our most conspicuous bats and as easily distinguished from all others as is the Red Bat.

Total length, 130-140 mm.; tail, 52-58 mm.; tibia, 23-24 mm.; foot, 9-10 mm.; forearm, 46-55 mm.; ear from meatus, 17-18 mm.; greatest length of skull, about 17 mm.; greatest width, about 12 mm.; maxillary tooth row, about 9.5 mm. Weight, about 35 grams. (Poole, Earl L., Journ. Mamm. vol. 13, p. 365, Nov. 1932).

Although the Hoary Bat is normally a very northern species at least in summer, yet it does breed in Indiana. Hahn (1909) records a female with two half grown young taken as far south as Bloomington, and refers to two specimens taken in Miami County in the latter part of June in which month the young are usually reported as being born. The number of young in a litter most frequently observed is two. Young at least up to five or six grams in weight are carried by the mother on her feeding excursions. They are born with their eyes closed. The Hoary Bat appears late in the evening when the light has about gone.

On hunting this bat in the Adirondacks Merriam (1882-84) writes entertainingly as follows:

The twilight is fast fading into night, and your eyes fairly ache from the constant effort of searching its obscurity, when suddenly a large bat is seen approaching, perhaps high above the tree tops, and has scarcely entered the limited field of vision when, in swooping for a passing insect, he cuts the line of the distant horizon and disappears in the darkness below. In breathless suspense you wait for him to rise. . . when he suddenly shoots by, seemingly as big as an owl, within a few feet of your very eyes. Turning quickly you fire, but too late! He has vanished in the darkness. For more than a week each evening is thus spent, and you almost despair of seeing another Hoary Bat, when, perhaps, on a clear cold night, just as the darkness is becoming too intense to permit you to shoot with accuracy and you are on the point of turning away, something appears above the horizon that sends a thrill of excitement through your whole frame.

There is no mistaking the species—the size, the sharp, narrow wings, and the swift flight serve instantly to distinguish it from its nocturnal comrades. On he comes, but just before arriving within gunshot he makes one of his characteristic zig-zag side shoots and you tremble as he momentarily vanishes from view. Suddenly he reappears, his flight becomes more steady, and now he sweeps swiftly toward you. No time is to be lost, and it is already too dark to aim, so you bring the gun quickly to your shoulder and fire. With a piercing stridulous cry he falls to the earth. In an instant you are stooping to pick him up, but the sharp grating screams, uttered with a tone of intense anger, admonish you to observe discretion. With delight you cautiously take him in your hand and hurry to the light to feast your eyes upon his rich and handsome markings. He who can gaze upon a freshly killed example without feelings of admiration is not worthy to be called a naturalist. From its almost boreal distribution, and extreme rarity in collections, the capture of a specimen of the Hoary Bat must, for some time to come, be regarded as an event worthy of congratulation and record. Although I have been fortunate enough to shoot fourteen, I would rather kill another today than slay a dozen deer.

Merriam farther states that he has not seen this species abroad unless the temperature is under 60° F. However nights as cold as that are uncommon in the lower half of Indiana where Hahn reports it breeding.

Map 17. Published records and specimens in collections of the Hoary Bat, *Lasiurus cinereus*, in Indiana.

The published records for the Hoary Bat are: Franklin (Haymond 1870, Quick and Langdon 1882, Evermann and Butler 1894, Hahn 1909), Jefferson (Hahn 1909), Knox (Langdon 1881 Dec.), Lake (Hahn 1907, 1909), Lawrence (Hahn 1907, 1908, 1909), Miami (Hahn 1909), Monroe (McAtee 1907, Hahn 1909), St. Joseph (Engels 1933), Wayne (Plummer 1844, Hahn 1909), Wells (Hahn 1909), White (Evermann and Butler 1894, Hahn 1909).

RAFINESQUE'S BAT

Genus **Nycticeius** Rafinesque

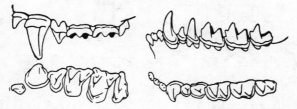

Fig. 28. Teeth of Rafinesque's Bat, *Nycticeius humeralis*, enlarged five times. After Miller in North American Fauna, No. 13, 1897, fig. 36, p. 120.

The genus *Nycticeius* is found in the southeastern United States and in Cuba. It has been taken as far north as Chicago, and occurs as far west as Arkansas and Texas.

Dental formula:

$$i\frac{1-1}{3-3},\ c\frac{1-1}{1-1},\ pm\frac{1-1}{2-2},\ m\frac{3-3}{3-3},=30.$$

Upper incisor distinctly separated from canine.

Skull low and narrow, in general similar to that of *Eptesicus*.

Interfemoral membrane furred at extreme base only; tip of tail free from the membrane. Mammae 2.

RAFINESQUE'S BAT
Nycticeius humeralis Rafinesque

Vespertilio humeralis RAFINESQUE. Amer. Month. Mag. vol. 3, p. 445, 1818.
      Type locality: Kentucky.
Nycticeius humeralis Evermann and Butler 1894.
Nycticeius humeralis Hahn 1909.

Map 18. Published record and specimen in collection of Rafinesque's Bat, *Nycticeius humeralis*, Chicago, Illinois, the nearest it has been taken to Indiana.

Rafinesque's Bat has not yet been taken in Indiana. It was included in both Evermann and Butler's and Hahn's hypothetical lists. A specimen was recently reported from Chicago by Sanborn (1930), so there can be no doubt of its occurrence in Indiana even if the specimens are only stragglers. It should be sought in the southern parts of the state, such as in the cypress swamps.

Rafinesque's Bat is a medium sized species, of a dull umber brown color above, paler below. Fur sparse and short, on middle of back about 6 mm. long. The ears are small, thick and leathery. Tragus short, broad, and blunt bent silghtly forward. Size medium; total length, about 92 mm.; tail, 35-37 mm.; tibia, about 13.5 mm.; foot, about 7.5 mm.; forearm, 34-36 mm.; ear from meatus, 13.5 mm.; greatest length of skull, 14 mm.; greatest width, 10 mm.

Harper (The Mammals of Okefinokee Swamp Region of Georgia. Proc. Boston Soc. Nat. Hist. vol. 38, 1927) says of it,

These bats have been found roosting in a hollow tree in a cypress bay, as mentioned below. They are observed for the most part during the last half hour of daylight, generally at a height of perhaps 40 to 75 feet. As darkness falls, however, they come much closer to the ground so that occasionally specimens may be knocked down with a reed fishing pole.

BIG-EARED BATS
Genus **Corynorhinus** H. Allen

This genus of Big-eared Bats is found throughout the warmer portions of North America from southern British Columbia and the southeastern United States to southern Mexico.

Several closely allied forms comprise the genus. One of these is found in southern Indiana. It is closely related to the Old World Big-eared Bat, *Plecotus*, from which it is distinguished by peculiar glandular masses on the muzzle rising high above the nostrils. On this account the American Big-eared Bats are frequently referred to as Lump-nosed Bats. Ears very long, nearly one-third the total length of the animal.

Dental formula:

$$i \frac{2-2}{3-3}, \ c \frac{1-1}{1-1}, \ pm \frac{2-2}{3-3}, \ m \frac{3-3}{3-3}, = 36.$$

Fig. 29. Teeth of Big-eared Bat, *Corynorhinus rafinesquii*, enlarged five times. After Miller in North American Fauna, No. 13, 1897, fig. 9, p. 52.

Skull slender and highly arched, rostral portion relatively weaker than in any other Indiana bat.

BIG-EARED BAT
Corynorhinus rafinesquii (Lesson)

Plecotus rafinesquii LESSON. Man de Mamm., p. 96, 1827. Type locality:
    Lower parts of Ohio River, probably in southern Indiana or Illinois or
    western Kentucky.
Corynorhinus macrotis Butler 1895, Hahn 1909.
Corynorhinus megalotis G. M. Allen 1916, April.
Corynorhinus rafinesquii Thomas. Proc. Biol. Soc. Washington, vol. 29, p.
    127, 1916 June.

Fig. 30. Photograph courtesy Amer. Mus. Nat. Hist. Big-eared Bat, *Corynorhinus rafinesquii.*

In addition to the striking peculiarities of the Big-eared Bat already described under the genus heading, may be mentioned these additional characteristics. The ears are much longer than the head, joined across the forehead, tips narrow, tragus long and slender. Dark brown above, lighter on the sides, and under parts pale pinkish buff; hairs everywhere gray or slaty gray at base, not strongly contrasted with the color on the tips of the hairs.

Total length, 105 mm.; tail, 50 mm.; tibia, about 22 mm.; foot, 10 mm.; forearm, 43 mm.; ear from meatus, 32 mm.; greatest length of skull, about 15-16 mm.; greatest width, about 9 mm. Adult weight, 9 to 11 grams (Mohr 1933).

The Big-eared Bat is comparatively rare in Indiana, only a relatively few specimens have been taken in the caves in the southern part of the state.

Concerning its habits Hahn (1909) writes:

I can find no published account of the habits of this species and my own acquaintance with it is not sufficiently extensive to permit a detailed description. Those that I have seen in the cave were all in dim twilight near the entrance. They hung head downward on the side walls of high passages; in one instance two of them were directly over the water. When sleeping in this position the long ears are curved backward and flattened against the side of the neck. As far as I know this position of the ears is unique among mammals. The curve is edgewise and the upper or anterior edge of the ear forms a half ellipse. The middle of the posterior edge is formed in a number of small transverse folds. When the animals are awakened from sleep, they slowly straighten the ears, and with them erected, they are truly remarkable looking creatures.

Two of these bats which were seen on February 22, 1907, in Upper Spring Cave at Mitchell, escaped and flew out into the cold air, perching for a few moments on the rocky ledge at the mouth of the cave. The fact that all that have been seen in this region were near the mouth of the cave, may indicate that the species is not truly a cave dweller.

The long ears should make it easy to identify in flight if it comes out in the twilight. I have never seen it flying, and judge that it is a later flyer. [Others report it a twilight flyer.] The flight of those that I have had captive was swift and steady. In

Map 19. Published records and specimens in collections of the Big-eared Bat, *Corynorhinus rafinesquii*, in Indiana.

The published records of the Big-eared Bat are: Putnam (Butler 1895, McAtee 1907, Hahn 1909, Cory 1912, G. M. Allen 1916), Lawrence (Banta 1907, McAtee 1907, Hahn 1908, 1909, Cory 1912, G. M. Allen 1916).

captivity, these bats seem to be delicate. Those that I have kept, refused food and soon died.

The special functions of the extraordinarily long ears and the glandular protruberances of the muzzle of this species are wholly unknown. A careful study of its habits and sensory adaptations, as well as the development and minute structures of these organs, should be well worth while. (Hahn 1909).

The normal number of young at birth appears to be one, born in the latter half of June. Weight of adults, nine to eleven grams, birth weight about three grams. (Mohr 1933).

FLESH-EATERS, ORDER CARNIVORA

The mammals of this order are widely distributed throughout the world, except Australia. Some of them, such as the Least Weasel are of very small size, while others such as the bears are among the largest known land mammals. They possess four extremities, usually with five toes on each foot, each digit being provided with a claw. No digit is opposable to the others. The orbital and temporal cavities are united into a single large cavity. The premolars and frequently also some of the molars are compressed laterally and provided with cutting cusps. The incisors are always small, and the canines are large and pointed, usually projecting much beyond the other teeth and adapted to seizing prey. There is always one tooth in each jaw which is specially modified, and to which the name sectorial or carnassial tooth has been applied. The upper carnassial is the most posterior of the teeth which have predecessors, that is pm ^{4}. It consists essentially of a more or less compressed blade supported on two roots and usually an inner tubercle supported by a distinct root. The blade when fully developed has three cusps or lobes, but the anterior is small and often lacking. The middle lobe is conical, high and pointed; the posterior lobe has a compressed knife-like edge. The inner tubercle varies in extent, but is generally placed near the anterior end of the blade. In the bears, *Ursidae*, this tubercle and root are lacking. The lower carnassial is the most anterior of the teeth without predecessors that is m $_1$. It has two roots supporting a crown, consisting of a bilobed blade, a heel or talon and an inner cusp. In the most specialized Carnivora the blade alone is developed, both talon and inner cusp being absent or rudimentary. Some of the members of the order are omnivorous in their habits, but the great majority, as their name implies, subsist on flesh. Because of this diet the alimentary canal is simple in structure. The brain is highly organized and shows many convolutions. The carnivora are divided into two suborders, the terrestrial or at least only partly aquatic (such as the otters) members with normal paws, termed the Fissipedia, and the strictly aquatic group the seals and sealions, the Pinnepedia which have the extremities modified into flippers.

The Fissipedia embrace nine well marked families, five of which have or have had representatives in Indiana.

KEY TO THE FAMILIES OF LIVING INDIANA CARNIVORA

Larger cheek teeth with crown of a crushing type, without noticeable or conspicuous
cutting edges, feet plantigrade
 Size very large, form heavy, tail short, bears. _____URSIDAE 89
 Size medium, form not so heavy, tail relatively long, racoons. PROCYONIDAE 95

Larger cheek teeth with crowns at least partly of a cutting type, feet mainly
  digitigrade.
    Cheek teeth without crushing surfaces, claws completely retractile, cats.
    _____FELIDAE 157
    Cheek teeth, at least the hindermost with evident crushing surface, claws not
      retractile or only partly so
      Tooth rows relatively long, total teeth 42, dogs. _____CANIDAE 134
      Tooth rows relatively short, total teeth 38 or less, weasels and allies.
      _____MUSTELIDAE 98

BEARS
Family Ursidae

Bears are found in Europe, Asia and both North and South America.
They are usually animals of large size, heavy body and rudimentary tail;
plantigrade feet, five toes on each foot, and claws not retractile.

Dental formula: $i \dfrac{3\text{-}3}{3\text{-}3}, c \dfrac{1\text{-}1}{1\text{-}1}, pm \dfrac{4\text{-}4}{4\text{-}4}, m \dfrac{2\text{-}2}{3\text{-}3}, = 42.$

The teeth are not as trenchant as those of other carnivora but have rather
blunt crowns. The upper carnissial lacks the inner tubercle and its supporting
root, is small and inconspicuous alongside of the large molars. The other
premolar teeth are small single rooted and may be more or less deciduous.
About half a dozen living genera of bears are known, three of which are found
in North America and one genus, *Euarctos,* the Black Bears, was formerly
found throughout the whole of Indiana.

BLACK BEARS
Genus Euarctos Gray

Euarctos differs from other American Bears, by its smaller size and
straighter facial profile; shorter front claws, not much longer than hind ones;
short uniform fur. There are several technical dental characters and the
interested reader is referred to C. Hart Merriam, Proc. Biol. Soc. Washington, vol. 10, p. 78, 1896.

BLACK BEAR
Euarctos americanus (Pallas)

The Black Bear formerly had a range over most of eastern North America
extending west to British Columbia and Yukon. It is still found in the wilder
portions of this range. It is even now seen in the wilder parts of New York,
Pennsylvania and West Virginia, and in northern Michigan and Wisconsin.
Related forms are found in Florida and Louisiana. It is not impossible that
in the early days the Louisiana Bear, *Euarctos luteolus* (Griffith) may have
been found in southern Illinois and Indiana, in correlation with other southern
mammals such as the Swamp Rabbit.

The Black Bear is a medium-sized bear, about 5 to 6 feet (1500-1800
mm. in length; tail, 5 inches (125 mm.), hind foot, 7¼ inches (185 mm.);
height at shoulders, 25-30 inches (635-760 mm.); weight, 200 to 500 pounds
(90-227 kgs.) skull, about 10 inches (255 mm.) long, 7½ inches (190 mm.)

wide. Its general coloration, above and below, is black or dark brown, nose brownish; sometimes there is a white spot on the chest. The hair is longest and glossiest at the time the animals go into winter quarters. The Brown or Cinnamon Bear is only a color phase and does not represent a distinct species. Cubs representing both brown and the more common black phase have been found in the same litter.

Fig. 31. Black Bear, *Euarctos americanus*. Formerly common throughout Indiana. Photograph by J. C. Allen, West Lafayette.

With the oncoming of cool or cold weather the Black Bear hibernates even in southern latitudes. Each bear hibernates singly in such places as hollow trees, hollow logs, about tree trunks, under banks, etc. It is during hibernation that the young are born. The young bears when just born are scarcely larger than rats, measuring about 8 inches long and weighing from

9 to 12 ounces. In relation to small size of offspring to parent the Black Bear is next to the Virginia Opossum. At birth they are blind and covered only with fine close dark hair. The usual number of young at a time is two, but litters may vary from 1 to 4. The mammae are inguinal 1-1, pectoral 2-2 = 6. Seton (1929) ventures the opinion that inguinal mammae are used primarily by the just-born cubs, and that as the cubs grow older they use the pectoral mammae. It seems more probable however, that all the mammae are used simultaneously from the birth of the cubs as the milk stimulating hormones are probably not different in bears than in other mammals. The females apparently breed every other year as they do not seem to mate while they are bringing up the cubs. Mating takes place at three and a half years of age and in Indiana probably occurred late in June. The period of gestation is 7 to 7½ months, the young being born in the latter part of January. A few weeks later in March or early April the mother and young come out of the hibernation den. Bears coming out of winter dens seem to be well nourished and not to have used up all the fat that they have put on in the autumn, before denning up for the winter. The few that have been observed emerging from hibernation have first sought water of which they drank freely and have seemed little concerned about seeking food immediately.

The Black Bear is omnivorous in its diet which consists of fruit, roots, berries, nuts, and other vegetable matter, also meat of any kind, fish and even carrion. They also eat insects and rob bee trees of honey in spite of relentless stinging. They are accredited with killing and eating the young of many of the larger mammals such as deer, sheep and particularly young hogs. In autumn they are particularly fond of nuts and berries, eat ravenously and become excessively fat preparatory to their winter sleep.

Black Bears are expert tree climbers and have been known to fall from goodly heights and run off apparently unharmed. A bear descends a tree hind quarters first. Seton (1929).

Ordinarily Black Bears are harmless creatures and seldom attack a man unless provoked.

Bears have a peculiar habit of standing erect beside a tree or bank and reaching up with their fore claws make scratch marks. Blatchley (1899) records some of these findings in Eller's Cave, as well as bear wallows.

The Black Bear once common throughout the entire state was practically exterminated nearly 100 years ago, although a glance at the map will show many more recent records. The last one was probably killed less than 50 years ago. An idea as to their former abundance is given by Brown (1817) who says: "In traveling seven miles through Dearborn county, I counted two bears and three deer." Indiana contains 36,350 square miles; assuming that Brown saw his two bears in an area of 6 square miles, that would give a bear population of Indiana in the first and second decade of the 19th Century of 12,000. Plummer (1844) writes: "The black bear was killed in the immediate neighborhood of Richmond as late as the year 1824, when some cubs were also taken within a mile of town." Dr. B. W. Rhamy of Fort Wayne recalls as a boy having seen a Black Bear that had been killed in the swamp east of Fort Wayne. He thinks this was about 1888. This confirms the L. H.

Newton account in the History of Allen County (1880, p. 154). "A large marsh known as Bear's Nest covers the northern part of the township [Jackson]. Exterminated elsewhere, this spot was left as their peculiar possession. As recently as four years ago bears were seen and killed in this swamp, and

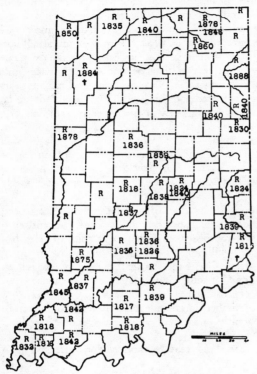

Map 20. Published records with approximate dates when last seen, of the Black Bear, *Euarctos americanus*, in Indiana. †Pleistocene. Specimen from Franklin County in possession of Mr. J. W. Quick, Brookville, Ind.

The published records for the Black Bear are: Adams (Tyndall and Lesh 1918), Allen (Dryer 1889, Hahn 1909), Brown (Blatchley 1899, McAtee 1907, Hahn 1909), Clinton (Hahn 1909), Crawford (Blatchley 1896), Daviess (Butler 1895). Dearborn (Brown 1817), Dekalb (Anonymous 1914), Elkhart (Weaver 1916), Franklin (Haymond 1870, Langdon 1881, Quick and Langdon 1882, Butler 1885, Evermann and Butler 1894, Hahn 1909), Gibson (Birkbeck 1818), Greene (Hahn 1909), Hamilton (Anonymous 1906), Hancock (Binford 1882), Hendricks (Cline and McHaffie 1874), Jackson (Lazenby 1914), Jasper (Collett 1883, Butler 1895), Jay (Montgomery 1864), Johnson (Banta 1888, Harden 1881), Knox (Butler 1895, Hahn 1909), Lake (Ball 1894, Hahn 1909, Brennan 1923), Laporte (Brennan 1923), 1909), Lake (Ball 1894 1894, Hahn 1909, Brennan 1923), Laporte (Brennan 1923), Marion (Anonymous 1906), Monroe (Blatchley 1899, Banta 1907, Goodspeed 1884, McAtee 1907, Hahn 1909), Morgan (Blatchley 1899, McAtee 1907, Hahn 1909), Newton (Butler 1895), Noble (Rerick 1882 Hahn 1909), Orange (Brown 1817), Porter (Brennan 1923), Posey (Wied 1839-41, 1861-62), Putnam (Anonymous 1881), St. Joseph (Anonymous 1880, Engels 1933), Steuben (Anonymous 1888), Vanderburg (Audubon 1926), Vigo (Brown 1817), Warren (Goodspeed 1883), Warrick (Hahn 1909), Washington (Hahn 1909), Wayne (Plummer 1844, Young 1872, Hahn 1909), Wells (Tyndall and Lesh 1918), Kankakee Valley (Reed 1920), Lower Wabash Valley (Croghan 1831).

deer are still present." The bear seen by Rhamy was probably among the last wild ones killed in the state.

Mr. Ferd Mosiman now over 80 years of age knows of several Black Bears that were killed east of Bluffton, Wells County.

J. H. Rerick, M.D., in the history of Lagrange County says that an occasional bear is still seen. The history was printed in 1882.

According to the histories of Counties of Morgan, Monroe and Brown, Indiana, Charles Blanchard, editor, Chicago, F. A. Battey and Co., 1884, bears were extant in those counties as late as 1836. On page 501 is an account of bear tracks being found in light snow near Elletsville. The animal was tracked by a noted bear hunter of his day, 1819, to a large sycamore tree. On cutting down the tree a large female and two cubs, three-fourths grown, were found inside.

Hahn (1909) collected some interesting Indiana bear incidents:

Dr. U. H. Farr, of Paragon, relates two adventures which his mother had with a bear in Morgan County in the period of about 1830. On one occasion she and her sister were hauling maple sap from trees to a camp, with an old mare hitched to a sled. The horse became frightened and on looking for the cause the girls espied a large bear coming into the clearing. They both climbed on the horse and lashing her into a run, made for camp, tearing the sled to pieces on the stumps and hummocks. Their father started in pursuit of the bear which was killed the next day. On another occasion, the same girl was crossing a bayou on a log foot bridge some distance from any habitation; chancing to hear a noise, she looked down the creek just in time to see a large bear rearing up on some logs to look at her from the distance of a few rods. She was much frightened but began to clap her hands and holloo. At first the bear paid no attention but at the third shout he turned around and started slowly away.

Dr. S. C. Richardson also relates several incidents which came within his personal knowledge when a boy in southern Indiana; his experiences reach back to 1828. On one occasion when returning home with his mother at dusk, they came upon a full-grown bear in a path in the woods. Mrs. Richardson . . . began to shout and beat on saplings with a club and the bear slowly got out of the path . . . A few days later near the same place, two brothers and a sister saw a bear lying high up in the forks of a tree.

Not long after . . . a girl . . . in the same neighborhood, while washing clothes beside a creek, was attacked by a bear which got his paws about the girl's throat and injured her so badly that she was confined to bed for a number of weeks. This bear, which was an old female, was killed by the men who rushed to the girl's rescue on hearing her screams, and three cubs were captured.

For illustrations of the skull of an Indiana specimen of the Black Bear see addendum.

PLEISTOCENE BLACK BEAR
† Euractos americanus (Pallas)

Ursus americanus Hay 1902, 1912, 1923.
Euarctos americanus Hay 1930.

There are two records of the Black Bear in Pleistocene deposits in Indiana. No details regarding them are given, and no specimens are in collections. Future finds should be carefully preserved and compared with the living form as well as with *Ursus procerus* MILLER (Proc. Biol. Soc. Washington, vol. 13, p. 55, 1899).

The published records of the Black Bear in Pleistocene deposits are: Dearborn (Warder 1873, Bigney 1892), Jasper (Collett 1883, Hay 1912).

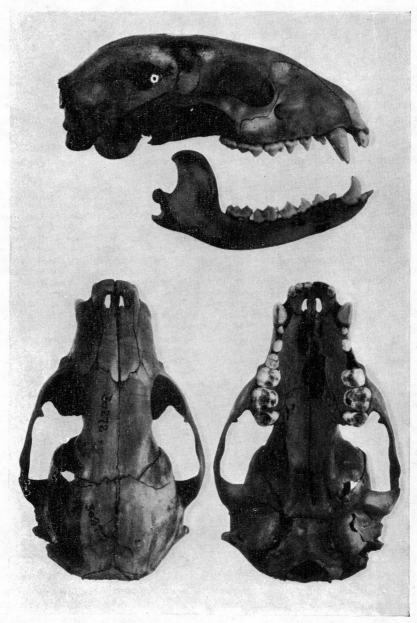

Fig. 32. Photographs courtesy Field Mus. Nat. Hist. Lateral, dorsal, and palatal views of skulls of Raccoon, *Procyon lotor*, about 4/5 natural size. Cat. No. 30,272, Field Mus. Nat. Hist., Porter County. The animal is not fully grown.

RACCOONS AND ALLIES
Family **Procyonidae**

The family Procyonidae is found in both North and South America and the north of India.

Body of medium size, feet plantigrade or semiplantigrade; five toes on each extremity; claws non-retractile; tail relatively long; audital bullae of medium size; penis bone of large size; alimentary canal lacks a cecum. Dentition:

$$i\frac{3\text{-}3}{3\text{-}3},\ c\frac{1\text{-}1}{1\text{-}1},\ pm\frac{3\text{-}3}{3\text{-}3},\ or\ \frac{4\text{-}4}{4\text{-}4}\ (\text{Indiana representative}),\ m\frac{2\text{-}2}{2\text{-}2}.$$

About half a dozen genera are known one of which is found throughout the entire state of Indiana.

RACCOONS
Genus **Procyon** Storr

The genus *Procyon* ranges from Brazil northward throughout the United States and into the adjoining Canadian provinces.

Dental formula:

$$i\frac{3\text{-}3}{3\text{-}3},\ c\frac{1\text{-}1}{1\text{-}1},\ pm\frac{4\text{-}4}{4\text{-}4},\ m\frac{2\text{-}2}{2\text{-}2},\ =40;$$

body stout, head broad, with a pointed nose, legs and tail rather short, the latter well haired, cylindric and ringed with blackish and dull light yellowish, face with a distinct black mask extending backward through the eyes and across the cheeks. The skull is broad and rounded and the rostrum is not as pointed as the external appearance of the animal would indicate.

It contains several closely allied species some of which break up into various geographic races. The so-called typical form, *Procyon lotor lotor* of the eastern United States is found throughout Indiana.

RACCOON
Procyon lotor lotor (Linnaeus)

[*Ursus*] *lotor* LINNAEUS. Syst. Nat. ed. 10, vol. 1, p. 48. 1758. Type locality: Eastern United States.
Procyon lotor Wied 1839-41, Plummer 1844, Evermann and Butler 1894, Hahn 1909.

The Raccoon is so well known through the popularity of "coon skin" coats that scarcely any description of it is needed. The color above is a grizzled gray, brown and black (There is considerable variation in the amount of the black which is sometimes so pronounced as to render the animal melanistic), the soft under fur dull brown; sides lighter than back; and under parts dull brownish, grizzled with yellowish gray. The black band across the forehead and through the eyes and across the cheeks has already been mentioned, otherwise the face is yellowish gray. The tail is alternately banded grayish and blackish, with six or seven dark rings, and terminating in black. Total length, about 2½ feet (750 mm.); tail without the hair, about 10 inches (250 mm.); hind foot, about 4½ inches (115 mm.); greatest length of skull of

Fig. 33.   Photograph courtesy N. Y. Zool. Soc.   Raccoon, *Procyon lotor.*

large animals, about 5 inches (125 mm.); greatest width, about 3 inches (75 mm.). Weight 12-22 pounds (5.5-10 kgs.). There are 8 mammae, 4 on each side, extending from the inguinal region to the anterior pectoral region.

The Raccoon's natural habitat is hardwood forests usually in proximity to water. In its quest for food it is terrestrial but for resting, hibernating and breeding it prefers hollow limbs or trunks of trees, but at times will use holes in banks, or cliffs, and even burrows of other animals. (Seton 1929).

In diet it is omnivorous. Whitney (1931) has found very little meat in the stomachs of animals taken by him between October 15, and February 1. He found corn, oats, nuts, wild cherries, apples, pears, grapes, crickets, white grubs and trout. Other authors describe its fondness for crayfish, frogs, etc. It will capture birds, eat eggs and has been known to enter hen houses. It has been described as washing all its food before eating it, and on this account was given the specific name *lotor* (Latin, washer). The German name for the animal is Waschbär. Whitney inclines to believe that this washing observation was made on captive animals and "in the wild state the Raccoon washes almost nothing that he eats." The Raccoon's fingers are relatively long and he is an adept at handling food in his hands.

Raccoons are nocturnal, spending the daylight hours in suitable dens or nests in hollow limbs. Hahn (1909) says their curiosity is great and as a result they are easily trapped. A steel trap set in shallow water with the pan covered with bright tinfoil will attract them to handle the pan and get caught. Coons are hunted by night through the use of dogs which pick up their scent, follow the trail and finally force the animal up a tree. Peering down from his perch to see what it is all about his eyes are readily "shined" with a flash light and prove a good target for the hunter.

The Raccoon is not a swift, but it is a dextrous runner, and in general when pursued uses good judgment where it has had any experience in the

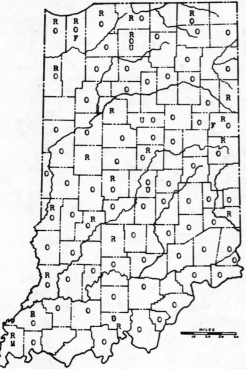

Map 21. Published records, recent observations and specimens in collections of the Raccoon, *Procyon lotor*, in Indiana.

The published records for the Raccoon are: Carroll (Evermann and Butler 1894), Crawford (Blatchley 1896), Franklin (Haymond 1870, Quick and Langdon 1882, Evermann and Butler 1894), Gibson (Audubon and Bachman 1851), Hamilton (Shirts 1901, Anonymous 1906), Hancock (Binford 1882), Jay (Montgomery 1864), Knox (Butler 1895), Lagrange (Evermann and Butler 1894), Lake (Dinwiddie 1884, Ball 1894, Brennan 1923), Laporte (Anonymous 1880, Brennan 1923), Marshall (Evermann and Clark 1911, 1920), Monroe (Evermann and Butler 1894, Banta 1907, McAtee 1907), Montgomery (Cox 1860), Newton (Butler 1895, Ade 1911), Owen (Blatchley 1899), Porter (Brennan 1923, Lyon 1923), Posey (Wied 1839-41, 1861-62), Randolph (Cox 1893, Evermann and Butler 1894), St. Joseph (Anonymous 1880, Engels 1933), Vigo (Evermann and Butler 1894, Thomas 1916), Wabash (Evermann and Butler 1894), Wayne (Plummer 1844, Young 1872), Kankakee Valley (Hahn 1907, Reed 1920), probably in every county (Hahn 1909).

past. It is a fair swimmer. Raccoons are ordinarily not combative, seeking safety in flight and concealment rather than fight, but when cornered with their backs against the wall they are said to be no mean antagonists.

In autumn like bears they eat in excess to provide fat for the winter hibernation. The hibernation is only partial for it retires late and comes out on warm days of winter and very early in the spring. Seton (1929) gives the mating season as February (State of Ohio). Whitney (1931) gives the last week of January as the mating season for Raccoons in New England. "This alone should convince the game and fish commission of any state that no raccoon should be hunted in January." The period of gestation is nine weeks, the young being born in April or early May. The number at a birth varies from 3 to 6, 4 being usual. In June they are about one-third grown and begin to sit outside the den. In July the young accompany the mother in nightly excursions to swamps and streams in search of food.

It is unusual to find a Raccoon alone, for they commonly travel in small companies, consisting of the several members of a single family. They do not return to the same nest every morning, but often make little excursions in various directions, being gone several days at a time, and taking refuge about daylight, in any convenient arbored shelter. Though preferring a hollow limb high up . . . they will put up with almost any kind of hollow trunk. . . . The young remain with the mother about a year. (Merriam 1882-84).

The Raccoon furnishes a valuable fur and care should be exercised that the species is not overtrapped and exterminated. The price of raw Indiana Raccoon skins ranges from $1.50 to $3.00 and a coat costs around $125.00 (1932 prices). According to the records of the Department of Conservation 27,391 Raccoon skins were taken in Indiana during the 1931-32 season.

WEASELS, MINKS, MARTENS, SKUNKS, OTTERS, BADGERS
Family Mustelidae

Carnivores of medium or small size, usually with elongated body, short legs, digitigrade, plantigrade or semi-plantigrade, five digits to a foot, claws non- or semi-retractile. Skull with the rostrum very short, brain case large and depressed, audital bullae generally flattened. Premolars variable in number, molars never more than $\frac{1-1}{2-2}$, m^1 with inner tubercular portion longer in antero-posterior direction than the external secant portion. Cecum absent, scent glands present in the perineal region. Habits terrestrial, arboreal or semi-aquatic.

The family is a large one and widely distributed, especially in the northern temperate regions; it is absent in Australia. It embraces about 18 genera, 11 of which are found in North America, and of these 7 are found or have been found in Indiana. It is divided into several sub-families, based on rather technical characters. An attempt to bring them out in non-technical manner is here made in a synoptic key-like form:

Synopsis of Subfamilies and Genera of Mustelidae

Size large, form stout, tail short, toes not webbed, front claws very strong and heavy, adapted for digging. Skull nearly as wide at posterior plane as at zygomata, premolars $\frac{3-3}{3-3}$, total teeth 34, subfamily *Taxidiinae*, genus *Taxidea*, p. 131.

Size large, form slender, tail long, toes completely webbed for aquatic life, skull nearly as wide at middle of brain-case as at zygomata; premolars $\frac{4-4}{3-3}$, total teeth 36. Subfamily *Lutrinae*, genus *Lutra*, p. 115.

Size small to medium, form slender to stout, tail large and bushy, color black with conspicuous white markings and scent glands remarkably developed; premolars $\frac{3-3}{3-3}$, total teeth 34. Subfamily, *Mephitinae*, p. 119 and p. 123.

Size small, form slender, white markings of more than two longitudinal body stripes and with spots and curving stripes on posterior part of body, genus *Spilogale*, p. 119.

Size moderate, form stout, white markings, mainly of two longitudinal body stripes without spots and curving stripes on posterior portion of body, genus *Mephitis*, p. 123.

Size large, form heavy, not weasel-like, tail short, covered with drooping shaggy hairs, scent glands moderately developed, terrestrial in habits, extinct in Indiana; premolars $\frac{4-4}{4-4}$, total teeth 38. Subfamily *Guloninae*, genus *Gulo*, p. 113.

Size small to medium, form weasel-like, toes united by a short web at base, claws semi-retractile, scent glands moderately to rather highly developed, arboreal, terrestrial or semi-aquatic in habits; premolars variable $\frac{3-3}{3-3}$, or $\frac{4-4}{4-4}$, total teeth 34 or 38. Subfamily *Mustelinae*, p. 99, p. 100 and p. 101.

Premolars $\frac{4-4}{4-4}$, total teeth 38. Size comparatively large, extinct in Indiana, genus *Martes*, p. 99.

Premolars $\frac{3-3}{3-3}$, total teeth 34. Size small or comparatively so, genus *Mustela*, p. 101.

MARTENS AND FISHERS
Genus **Martes** Pinel

The Marten has never been definitely recorded from Indiana. It is found in the northern or temperate regions of both hemispheres. The Fisher is confined to North America and has been noted in Indiana but three times. The dentition, $i\frac{3-3}{3-3}$, $c\frac{1-1}{1-1}$, $pm\frac{4-4}{4-4}$, $m\frac{1-1}{2-2}$, $= 38$, serves to distinguish the genus *Martes* from the other Mustelines in Indiana in which the premolars are $\frac{3-3}{3-3}$, as well as its much larger size. The large upper molar, nearly as large as the carnassial, serves to distinguish the genus *Martes* from *Gulo* which has the upper molar very much smaller than the carnassial.

PINE MARTEN
Martes americana (Turton)

[*Mustela*] *americana* TURTON. Linnaeus, System of Nature, vol. 1, p. 60, 1806. Type locality: Eastern North America.
Mustela americana Hahn 1909.

The Pine Marten was included by Hahn (1909) in the hypothetical list. He reports a skeleton in the museum of the Chicago Academy of Science that was said to have been taken in Illinois many years ago. This same specimen is also listed by Cory (1912). If formerly in Illinois, it probably was found in Indiana. *Mustela martes* is mentioned without comment in Catalogue of Animals observed in Cook County, Illinois, by Kennicott (1855). Seton (1929) brings its former range down to the southern end of Lake Michigan. I have found no other evidence of its former occurrence in Indiana.

The Pine Marten is a relatively large animal, nearly two feet (600 mm.) in length, tail 7 to 8 inches (175-200 mm.), hind foot 3.00-3.50 inches (75-90 mm.). It is of a rich yellowish brown color and with tail rather bushy. It is more or less arboreal in its habits. Seton (1929) gives its haunts as heavy pine or spruce forests. Rhoads (1903) says it prefers hardwood timber.

FISHER OR PEKAN
Martes pennanti (Erxleben)

[*Mustela*] *pennanti* ERXLEBEN. Syst. Regni Anim. vol. 1, p. 470, 1777.

Type locality Eastern Canada.

Mustela canadensis or *pennanti.* Wied 1839-41, Plummer 1844, Hahn 1909.

The Fisher is a large dark colored, almost black, marten. General coloration, grayish to dark brown, darkest or almost black, along the dorsal region; nose, feet and tail blackish; top of head grizzled with gray which extends down neck to shoulders; underparts dark brown. Male distinctly larger than the female. Total length of male about 3 feet, (900 mm.), tail about 14 inches, (350 mm.), hind foot about 4 inches (100 mm.), weight from 8 to 12 pounds (3.6 to 5.5 kgs.).

The Fisher is, or at least was, found throughout the northwestern United States and Canada, westward to the Pacific, where a slightly different colored and larger subspecies is found. It extended southward in the Alleghenies to North Carolina and there is considerable evidence that it formerly occurred in Indiana either as a regular resident or as a wanderer from the north.

Its habits are both terrestrial and arboreal. It is said to be an expert tree climber, and to be able to leap from branch to branch after the manner of a squirrel. On the ground it is swift enough to catch hares and rabbits. Although named Fisher, the animal is not aquatic nor particularly fond of fish. However, it prefers heavy timber near water or in swamps. Its food consists of small mammals, birds, frogs, fishes and some fruit and nuts. It does not hibernate but is active throughout the year. Mating takes place about the first of March and the young usually two to three are born about the first of May. The nest is usually in a hollow tree high above the ground, but it has been found in logs and rocky crevices. It is mainly nocturnal. Seton (1929).

There are but three records of its occurrence in Indiana. Wied (1839-41) says *Mustela canadensis* or *Pennantii* is occasionally observed at New Harmony although he himself had never seen a fresh specimen. Plummer in 1844 writes: "I cannot find that the Fisher has been seen since 1820; at an earlier period it was not uncommon." In the published (Anonymous 1906) records of skins handled by A. B. Cole of Noblesville, who purchased of local trappers, 1859, there is listed one Fisher skin. In the Catalogue of Animals in Cook County, Illinois, Kennicott (1855) says: "The Fisher used frequently to be seen in the heavy timber along Lake Michigan."

R 1855

1859
R

R
1820

R
1833

Map 22. Published records of the Fisher, *Martes pennanti*, in Indiana.

The published records for the Fisher are: Hamilton (Anonymous 1906), Posey (Wied 1839-41, 1861-62, Hahn 1909), Wayne (Plummer 1844, Hahn 1909).

WEASELS AND MINKS
Genus **Mustela** Linnaeus

Size rather small and weasel- or ferret-like. Dentition differs from that of *Martes* in that the premolars are $\frac{3-3}{3-3}$ instead of $\frac{4-4}{4-4}$. It is widely distributed, having representatives in Europe, Asia, North and South America, and northern Africa. Fifty-five named forms are found in North America, three of these being found in Indiana.

KEY TO THE SPECIES OF MUSTELA FOUND IN INDIANA

Size very large, total length well over 500 mm.; color brown except a white spot on chin and frequently on throat but not entire underparts, never turning white in winter; partly aquatic, _____*Mustela vison mink* 109

Size medium or small, total length well under 500 mm.; color brownish above, whitish beneath, frequently turning white in winter; terrestrial.

Size very small, total length not exceeding 200 mm., tail relatively short and not tipped with a tuft of black hairs, _____*Mustela rixosa allegheniensis* 103

Size medium, total length 300 to 400 mm., tail relatively larger, conspicuously tipped with a tuft of black hairs in brown summer and white winter pelages,

_____ *Mustela noveboracensis* 104

Fig. 34. Least Weasel, *Mustela rixosa allegheniensis*, natural size. Mounted specimen owned by Mr. Elmer Baumgartner, Bluffton. Ind. From Amer. Midland Nat. vol. 14, p. 346, 1933.

LEAST WEASEL

Mustela rixosa allegheniensis (Rhoads)

Putorius allegheniensis Rhoads. Proc. Acad. Nat. Sci. Philadelphia, 1900, p. 751, 1901. Type locality: Beallsville, Washington County, Pennsylvania.

Putorius pusillus Kennicott 1858.

Mustela pusilla Plummer 1844 (Probably *Mustela noveboracensis* intended).

Putorius allegeheniensis Hahn 1909, appendix.

Mustela rixosa allegheniensis Dice 1928, Lyon 1933.

The Least Weasel as a whole has a range from North Carolina to Nebraska, northward to Hudson Bay and Alaska. The subspecies *Mustela rixosa allegheniensis* ranges from North Carolina to western Pennsylvania, Ohio, Indiana, Illinois and Wisconsin. It was first reported for northern Indiana by Kennicott (1858) and definitely recorded by a specimen by Dice in 1928. It

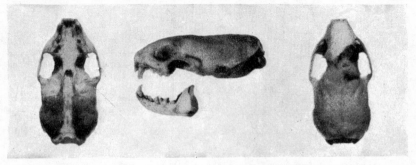

Fig. 35. Palatal, lateral and dorsal views of skull of Least Weasel, *Mustela rixosa allegheniensis*, adult female, about natural size. Medaryville, Pulaski County, autumn 1932, collected by H. P. Cottingham.

will probably be found to occur throughout the northern half of the state.

The Least Weasel is probably the smallest known carnivore. Total length 150 to 200 mm.; tail vertebrae 20 to 35 mm., hind foot 20 to 21 mm., greatest length of skull about 30 mm., greatest width about 15 mm. Males are somewhat larger than females.

Coloration in summer dark brown, except underparts and inside of legs whitish sharply demarked from the brown, and tip of tail with a few blackish hairs, not a distinct blackish tuft. White winter specimens often have the tip of the tail containing a few blackish hairs.

Their food appears to be chiefly mice, though they undoubtedly eat a few birds and some insects. They are probably too small to attack poultry. Their small size readily enables them to follow mice along their runways either above or below the ground. The first Indiana specimen was caught by a dog as it came from beneath a corn shock. Corn shocks seem to be a favorite hunting ground for them. The second Indiana specimen was caught in a gravel pit, Bluffton, the third, turned up by a plow from a shallow hole in the autumn of 1932, Medaryville, Pulaski County.

Their nests are made in holes in banks or other suitable locations.

The young number from 4 to 6 in a litter, the period of gestation is thought to be about six weeks. Mammae: 1-1 inguinal, lower abdominal 2-2 = 6. Whether the young are brought forth at any definite season is unknown. Distinctly immature specimens have been taken in October. The Pulaski County specimen taken in autumn was evidently nursing young. A nest containing very small ones has been dug out in January (T. E. Winecoff, Journal of Mammalogy, vol. 11, pp. 312-313, 1930).

Map 23. Published records and specimens in collections of the Least Weasel, *Mustela rixosa allegheniensis*, in Indiana; 1, mounted skin and skull owned by Elmer Baumgartner of Bluffton; 2, specimen preserved in alcohol owned by H. P. Cottingham, Medaryville, Pulaski County.

The published records of the Least Weasel are: Pulaski (Lyon 1933), Wells (Dice 1928, Lyon 1933), no specific locality (Kennicott 1858), probable in Indiana (Hahn 1909, Henninger 1923).

NEW YORK WEASEL

Mustela noveboracensis (Emmons)

Putorius noveboracensis EMMONS. Rep. Quadr. Massachusetts, p. 45, 1840.
        Type locality: Southern New York.
Mustela erminea Wied 1839-41.
Mustela pusilla Plummer 1844.
Putorius erminea Evermann and Butler 1894.
Putorius noveboracensis Hahn 1909.

The New York Weasel is found throughout most of the northeastern United States from southern Maine nearly to North Carolina, and westward through Illinois. Related forms are found elsewhere in the eastern United States. It is found in every county in Indiana.

Males are much larger than the females. Total length of males 445 to 375 mm., tail vertebrae 150 to 125 mm., hind foot 50 to 42 mm., of females the corresponding figures are 360 to 300, 115 to 95, 40 to 35. Weight of full grown males 265 to 195 grams, of females 125 to 75.

Fig. 36. Photograph courtesy N. Y. Zool. Soc. New York Weasel, *Mustela noveboracensis*, in white winter pelage.

General color of animal in summer rich dark chocolate brown, except chin, throat, belly and inner side of legs, white, more or less washed with yellowish, and except the terminal third of the tail which is blackish. In winter in colder parts of its range the brown hairs are replaced by white ones so that the animal appears uniformly white except for the black end of the tail. When the weather is not cold enough in winter, the fur becomes softer and longer and of a lighter brown color. A trapper in Porter County told me that out of 200 weasels taken in three years only two were white. Ann Arbor (Michigan) naturalists report about 75 per cent of the animals turning white in winter. The change in color is due to an actual shedding of the hairs each spring and autumn. See Hamilton's excellent paper 1933.

Weasels seem to be at home in nearly every environment, however, they are not normally aquatic nor arboreal. They do not hesitate to locate near dwellings. Kennicott in Quadrupeds of Illinois, says:

All the Weasels identified with the *Putorius noveboracensis*, which I have observed,

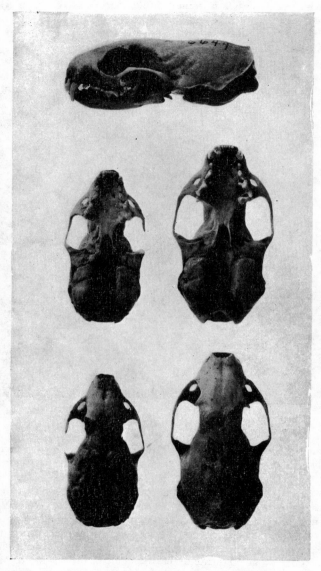

Fig. 37. Photographs courtesy Mus. of Vert. Zool. Univ. of Cal. The American Weasels are being revised by Dr. E. Raymond Hall of the University of California, and all available specimens of such weasels are temporarily in his possession. Skulls of New York Weasel, *Mustela noveboracensis*, lateral, palatal and dorsal views, all natural size.

Upper skull, Cat. No. 236,644, U. S. Nat. Mus. subadult male, Bicknell, Knox County, W. S. Chansler.

were taken in the woods. This species is not a tree climber any more than the Mink, but it has occasionally been seen to ascend trees, and I am informed of a remarkable instance in which one was observed to pursue and overtake a ground squirrel upon a tree.

Mearns quoted by Seton, 1929, vol. 2, p. 620, says:

It is not at all uncommon for this Weasel to take to a tree when surprised in the woods. It does not hesitate to ascend the largest tree, and sometimes ascends to the top, though it more often runs out towards the extremity of one of the larger limbs, and crouches upon it till the danger is past.

Soper, quoted by Seton, 1929, says:

Their life seems an endless roving in search of food, conducted without design, lacking home and apparent destination. This may be regarded as a superficial impression. Having spent many hours on their trails in the snow and cold, unravelling as it seemed, a clue to their very lives and destiny, I have discovered the opposite to be the truth. Although their wanderings seem the most erratic and inconsistent imaginable, there is yet beneath it a species of method. I have never yet been able to connect positively their widely scattered trails with a fixed abode, but I have learned that they habitually return again and again over the same route. The male in particular is perhaps always detached, leading an irregular and nomadic existence. While this may be true, it is seen that a relatively fixed locality is adhered to for their hunting, and is withal, considering their size, of very considerable extent.

One may sometimes be tracked in the snow through a journey of two or three miles, made on a single night. (Kennicott, quoted by Seton 1929).

The young are born blind and essentially naked, and vary from 5 to 8 in a litter. The nests are placed in rock piles, or holes about roots of trees or in usurped burrows of animals about their size. They are lined with dead grass or other vegetable material, and more or less fur from mice. The few reports on nests indicate partially eaten mice or birds in them. The young appear to be born early in spring, and at about six weeks of age, are able to leave the nest. The period of gestation is about 70 days (Hamilton 1933). The mammae are 4-4=8, inguinal and posterior abdominal.

The chief food of weasels appears to be mice, rats and ground squirrels, but they can kill animals the size of a rabbit. They undoubtedly eat a fair number of ground inhabiting birds, and have been known to enter hen houses. Sometimes they are wanton killers and slaughter more than immediate needs demand. In early spring in woods in the Dunes State Park, I once found a pile of seven meadow mice and one white-footed mouse that had probably been collected by a weasel the preceding night. One may well forgive a weasel for an occasional hen killed, because of the immense number of mice and rats it destroys. Instances are reported of weasels living near hen houses and feeding only on rats and mice. As a bird destroyer, the weasel can scarcely equal the domestic cat.

Weasels are a fairly valuable source of fur; 1932 prices for Indiana

---

Lower skulls, Cat. No. 105, Univ. of Notre Dame, adult female, North Liberty, St. Joseph County, June 15, 1931, W. L. Engels; and male, Cat. No. 2679, Mus of Comp. Zool., Cambridge, Mass., Denver, Miami County, Jan. 15, 1895.

The lower skulls show the marked sexual difference in size between the two sexes in this species.

weasels range from 10 to 40 cents. In white pelage the weasel is known as the ermine. However, the true ermine is a European and Asiatic species.

Hamilton (1933) from an examination of 163 specimens gives the frequency of mammalian food as follows: *Microtus* 33.6, *Silvilagus* 17.3, undetermined mice 17.1, *Peromyscus* 11.3, *Rattus* 9.1, *Blarina* 5.9, *Sciurus* 2.7, *Tamias* 1, *Condylura* 0.8, *Ondatra* 0.8%. Weasels consume about one-third of their weight as food in 24 hours.

Weasels have devised a higly successful manner in the securing and killing of their catch. A rapid dash and the bird or mouse is grabbed over the back of the skull, the fore limbs encircle the animal as though hugging it, and the hind limbs are brought up to scratch wildly at the captive. Thus the predator is free from unlikely attacks,

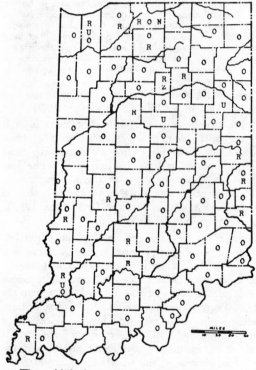

Map 24. Specimens in collections, published records and recent observations of the New York Weasel, *Mustela noveboracensis*, in Indiana.

The published records of the New York weasel are: Carroll (Evermann and Butler 1894), Crawford (Blatchley 1897), Franklin (Haymond 1870, Quick and Langdon 1882, Evermann and Butler 1894), Knox (Hahn 1909), Lagrange (Evermann and Butler 1894), Lake (Dinwiddle 1884), Laporte (Anonymous 1880) Lawrence (Hahn 1908), Marshall (Evermann and Clark 1911, 1920), Miami (Bangs 1896, Hahn 1909), Monroe (Evermann and Butler 1894, Banta 1907, Hahn 1909, McAtee 1907), Porter (Lyon 1923), Posey (Wied 1939-41), Putnam (Anonymous 1881), Randolph (Cox 1893, Evermann and Butler 1894), St. Joseph (Anonymous 1880, Engels 1933), Vigo (Evermann and Butler 1894), Wabash (Evermann and Butler 1894), Wayne (Plummer 1844), Kankakee Valley (Hahn 1907). "Seems to include every county" (Hahn 1909).

and may securely hold the victim, if the grip must be loosened, or changed for one at a better vantage point. If a large animal, as a rat, the weasel usually lies on its side, while the diminishing struggles of the rodent continue; but if a mouse or small bird, the weasel is apt to crouch over its prey. (Hamilton 1933).

BONAPARTE'S WEASEL
Mustela cicognanii Bonaparte

M[ustela] cicognanii [Sic] Bonaparte. Charlesworth's Mag. Nat. Hist. vol. 2, p. 37, January 1838. Type locality: Northwestern North America.
Mustela cicognanii Bonaparte. Iconografia Fauna Italica, vol. 1, part 22, p. 4, 1838.

Bonaparte's Weasel is an inhabitant of the "boreal forest covered parts of North America from New England and Labrador to coast of southeastern Alaska." (Merriam 1896). The most southern record and far from its normal range is New Bremen, Ohio (Henninger 1921).

In general aspect Bonaparte's Weasel resembles the New York Weasel described above. According to Hamilton (1933) it invariably turns white in winter. It is a smaller animal with a tail absolutely and relatively shorter. In the brown summer coat and also in the white winter coat the tail is always tipped with black. Total length of males about 280 to 300 mm., tail vertebrae, 80 to 100; hind foot 36 to 38; greatest length of skull about 43; greatest width 22; of females, the corresponding measurements are about 230, 70, 30, 35 and 18 mm.

There are no records of this weasel for Indiana, but it has been taken at New Bremen, Ohio (Henninger, 1921) not far from the Indiana-Ohio line so that it may come to light any time. The carcasses of all weasels taken by trappers ought to be submitted to some one interested in mammals, not only in the expectation of finding an example of Bonaparte's Weasel but additional examples of the Least Weasel.

MINK
Mustela vison mink (Peale and Beavois)

Mustela mink PEALE and BEAUVOIS, Catal. Peale's Mus., Philadelphia, p. 39, 1796. Type locality: Maryland.
Mustela vison SCHREBER, Säugethiere, pl. 127b, Type locality: Eastern Canada; Wied 1839-41.
Putorius vison Plummer 1844, Evermann and Butler 1894.
Lutreola vison McAtee 1907.
Lutreola vison lutreocephalus Hahn 1909.

The Mink is an inhabitant of the greater portion of North America wherever there are forests and water. The form found throughout Indiana ranges from New England to North Carolina and in the interior to central Georgia and Alabama, westward through southern Pennsylvania, Ohio and Indiana to Missouri. It is probably in every county of Indiana where living conditions for it are suitable.

Mr. S. E. Perkins III, writes that a mink was trapped in a chicken house at Keystone and 56th Sts., Indianapolis, Jan. 11, 1935.

Engels (1933) reports a family living in the St. Joseph River near the Grand Trunk Railroad bridge almost in the heart of South Bend.

The Mink is distinguished from the other Indiana species of the genus Mustela by its large size, bushy tail, and fur modified for aquatic life. There are a few technical differences found in the skull and teeth, so that the Minks are classed in a separate subgenus Lutreola, and many authors in the past have even considered Lutreola as a genus distinct from Mustela. Although it is semi-aquatic, its toes are not webbed.

The general coloration of the Mink is almost uniform umber-brown, darker and glossier on the back and becoming almost black on end of tail. The chin is whitish and there are occasional white spots on the throat, chest or belly. Even in the coldest parts of its range, it remains brown through the winter.

There is considerable variation in size in different individuals and the females are smaller than the males. Total length of males 610 to 640 mm. (about two feet or slightly over), tail vertebrae 175 to 225 mm., hind foot 70 to 80 mm., greatest length of skull about 70 mm. greatest width about 40 mm., weight about 2 pounds (0.9 kgm.).

The Mink is largely nocturnal, and its general behavior is much like a large weasel, except that it is an expert swimmer. It is not so apt a climber.

Fig. 38. Photograph courtesy N. Y. Zool. Soc. Mink, *Mustela vison mink*.

Minks can travel in water at the rate of about two miles per hour. They can swim under water for stretches of nearly 50 feet, and have been seen to make better time than the Muskrat. A Mink's diet consists of any vertebrate from the size of a rabbit down to mice and frogs. All authors say it eats fish which it catches in the water, but most give the impression that it prefers mammals and birds. Muskrats are thought to be one of its favorite foods. Some instances are reported where it has entered hen houses and slaughtered wantonly far beyond its needs, and others where it takes but a single hen per night. Like the Weasel, it kills more than it can eat on the spot and some of the spoils are stored in the nest. Its method of killing prey is essentially the same as that of the New York Weasel. An adult mink requires about 100 grams of rat per day (Svihla 1931).

It makes its den and nest in burrows in banks, under stumps, in hollow logs, or under logs, etc. The nest chamber is about a foot in diameter, lined with grass, feathers, etc. The nest is apparently occupied solely by mother and offspring which are usually five or six in number. The period of gestation is usually stated to be six weeks. The young are born in the spring; hairless, or nearly so, and blind for about 36 days. They grow rather slowly and are about a month and a half to two months old when they leave the nest; weight at birth about 6 grams.

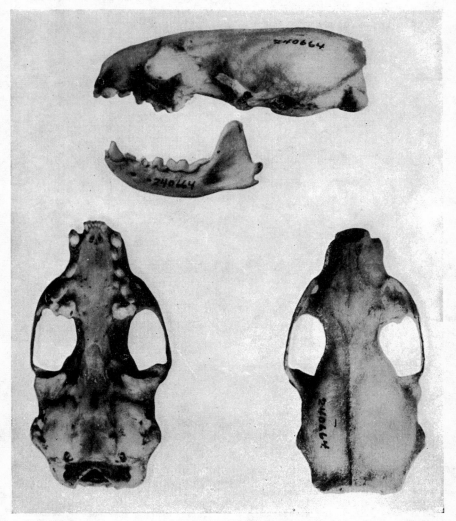

Fig. 39. Photographs courtesy U. S. Nat. Mus. Lateral, palatal and dorsal views of skull of Mink, *Mustela vison mink*, natural size. Cat. No. 240,664, U. S. Nat. Mus., Chesterton, Porter County, Dec. 1924, Elmer Johnson.

The Mink carries a pair of anal glands that secrete a fluid of an extremely fetid and disgusting odor. It cannot be ejected to a distance, like that of the skunk, but is poured out under sexual excitement, and when the animal is enraged. It is commonly emited when the beast is trapped, and sometimes becomes insufferably sickening while removing the skin. It is the most execrable smell with which my nostrils have as yet been offended, and is more powerful and offensive in some individuals than in others —the difference probably depending upon season and age.   Merriam (1882-84).

Anatomically the scent glands are essentially similar to, but smaller than, the scent glands of the skunk. (Coues 1877, p. 174).

Man is the Mink's worst enemy, because of his desire for the fur and to

Map 25. Published records, recent observations and specimens in collections of the Mink, *Mustela vison mink*, in Indiana.

The published records for the Mink are: Carroll (Evermann and Butler 1894), Franklin (Haymond 1870, Quick and Langdon 1882, Evermann and Butler 1894), Fulton (Evermann and Clark 1911, 1920), Hamilton (Shirts 1901, Anonymous 1906) Lagrange (Evermann and Butler 1894), Lake (Dinwiddie 1884, Ball 1884, 1894, Blatchley 1898, Brennan 1932), Laporte (Anonymous 1880, Brennan 1923), Lawrence (Hahn 1908), Marshall (Evermann and Clark 1911), Monroe (Evermann and Butler 1894, Banta 1907, McAtee 1907), Morgan (Major 1915), Newton (Ade 1911), Porter (Blatchley 1898, Brennan 1923, Lyon 1923), Posey (Wied 1839-41, 1861-62), Putnam (Anonymous 1881), Randolph (Wright 1889, Cox 1893, Evermann and Butler 1894), St. Joseph (Anonymous 1880, Engels 1933), Tippecanoe (Evermann and Butler 1894), Vanderburg (Cory 1912), Vigo (Evermann and Butler 1894), Wabash (Evermann and Butler 1894), Wayne (Plummer 1844), Kankakee Valley (Hahn 1907).

be rid of a possible poultry destroyer. They are probably caught now and then by larger carnivores. Mink fur is handsome in its natural state and of excellent wearing quality. The 1932 prices for raw mink pelts range from $1.50 to $3.50, depending on quality. A mink coat costs $500 and up. At the present time, minks are being raised for their fur crop under as natural conditions as possible, but the wild mink will evidently remain for a long time the most important source of this valuable fur.

During the trapping season 1931-32, 18,108 Minks were reported to the Department of Conservation as having been taken by trappers.

WOLVERINES
Genus **Gulo** Pallas

The Wolverine is found in the northern portions of North America, Europe and Asia.

It is a large, heavily built animal, total length 36 to 40 inches (900-1025 mm.); tail vertebrae 7.2 to 8.5 inches (180-210 mm.), hind foot 7 to 8 inches (175-200 mm.), height at shoulder 12 inches (300 mm.); weight 22 to 35 pounds (10-16 kgs.), the larger figure referring to males. Skull heavily built. Dental formula

$$i\frac{3-3}{3-3}, \ c\frac{1-1}{1-1}, \ pm\frac{4-4}{4-4}, \ m\frac{1-1}{2-2}, = 38.$$

Claws large, curved, semi-tractile; feet semi-plantigrade. Tail large and bushy; pelage long, underfur 20 to 30 mm., the longer hairs 50 mm. or more, and thick, the hairs becoming abruptly longer on flank and rump.

Seven species have been described in North America, one of which is supposed to have occurred in Indiana.

WOLVERINE
Gulo luscus (Linnaeus)

[*Ursus*] *luscus* LINNAEUS. Syst. Nat., ed 12, vol. 1, p. 71, 1766.
      Type locality: Hudson Bay.
Gulo luscus Hahn 1909.

Color dark brown above and below, with a broad, light, lateral band, beginning on each shoulder and meeting and stopping on tip of the tail. The general color is paler and grayer on the crown and cheeks. There is much variation in color in different specimens.

The only records of the former occurrence of the Wolverine in Indiana are those of Hahn (1909).

Prof. Van Gorder says: 'In 1840 an animal was shot in Washington Township (Noble County), which at that time was named the Wolverene, the only one reported to have been seen in the county.'

Concerning its occurrence in Knox County, Mr. Chansler writes: 'As strange as it may seem for this animal to be caught this far south, Mr. N. B. Bruce declares that a Mr. Simondson killed one of them near Edwardsport, this county, in 1852. I questioned him and he gave its size, color, form and general makeup all right. What it was doing as far south, I am at a loss to know.'

I have less hesitation in recording the wolverene on the basis of such reports than

I would have for most other species of mammals. Its form, size and color are so different from any other animal that could possibly occur in the State that there seems to be no chance for a mistake. This is the more true because in the days when these animals were reported, the pioneers were familiar with every beast of the woods. Moreover, there is a definiteness about the reports which makes them creditable, the statements in each case being that the animal was *killed* at a certain place in a certain year. The evidence of its occurrence in Indiana is almost exactly parallel to that given by Rhoads for Pennsylvania (1903), and is, I think, quite as strong, although Indiana is somewhat more remote from the known range of the species than the latter State. In its native forests, the wolverine is a great wanderer and the animals found in this state were without doubt strays. (Hahn 1909)

Both Prof. Van Gorder and Mr. Chansler were keen observers and reliable naturalists. That the animal was exceedingly rare in pioneer days is attested by the fact that no mention of it appears to be made in any of the county histories examined by Hahn or by me.

The Wolverine has an interesting life history and way of life, but as it has long been absent from Indiana, even if it ever did form an integral part of its original fauna, it seems better to refer the more interested to such works of those of Seton (1929) and of Coues (1877).

Map 26. Published records of the Wolverine, *Gulo luscus*, in Indiana.

The published records for the Wolverine are: Knox (Hahn 1909) Noble (Hahn 1909).

Otters
Genus **Lutra** Brisson

Otters are essentially cosmopolitan in distribution, but are absent in Australian region.

Skull flattened, rostrum shorter than wide, teeth large, dental formula:

$$i \frac{3\text{-}3}{3\text{-}3}, c \frac{1\text{-}1}{1\text{-}1}, pm \frac{4\text{-}4}{3\text{-}3}, m \frac{1\text{-}1}{2\text{-}2}, = 36.$$

External form highly modified for aquatic life, the body long and of approximately the same width as neck and head, the tail long, very muscular, broad at base, then tapering, legs short, feet broad, toes webbed, short-clawed, the fur dense, and soft, impervious to water, overlaid with longer glistening guard hairs.

About a dozen species make up the genus *Lutra,* six occurring in North America, and one species was formerly found throughout Indiana.

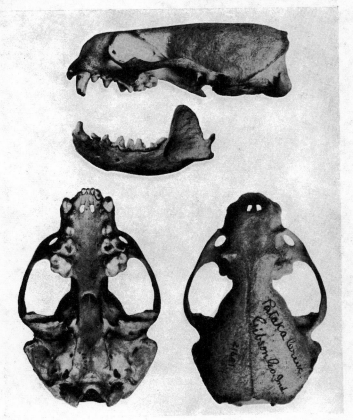

Fig. 40. Photographs courtesy U. S. Nat. Mus. Lateral, palatal and dorsal views of skull of Otter, *Lutra canadensis lataxina,* about ½ natural size. Cat. No. 21,681, U. S. Nat. Mus., Patoka Creek, Gibson County, S. Turner.

Fig. 41. Photograph courtesy N. Y. Zool. Soc. Otter, *Lutra canadensis*, once common in Indiana.

OTTER,
Lutra canadensis lataxina (F. Cuvier)

Lutra canadensis SCHREBER, Säugethiere, pl. 126b, 1776. Type locality: East-
    tern Canada. Wied 1839-41, Plummer 1844, Hahn 1907.
Lutra lataxina F. CUVIER, Dict. des Sci. Nat., vol. 27, p. 242, 1823.
    Type locality: South Carolina.
Lutra hudsonica Evermann and Butler 1894.
Lutra canadensis lataxina Hahn 1909.

The name adopted by Hahn (1909) is here used for the Indiana Otter.
In a general way most of the Indiana mammals are of the same species and
subspecies as those in the eastern United States and for that reason the name
Lutra canadensis lataxina is adopted for the Indiana Otter.

The general color is dark rich brown, the larger so-called guard hairs,
which are longer than and overlie the soft underfur giving it a glossy appearance. The underparts are paler and grayer, and the color of the lips, cheeks,
chin and throat are much paler. There are several records of albinistic Otters
from southwestern Indiana. Hahn reports two such albinistic individuals.
Mr. Sidney Esten writes that a buff colored otter was killed at Hovey's Lake
in February, 1912, and that in the preceding autumn a white one was killed
there.

Length about 40 inches (1025 mm.), tail 12 inches (300 mm.), hind
foot 4 inches (100 mm.), greatest length of skull about 112 mm., greatest
width about 70 mm.; weight 13 to 20 pounds (6 to 9 kgs.) or slightly over.

On account of intensive trapping or hunting for its fur, the Otter has
long been extinct in most counties of Indiana. Baird (1857) mentions an
Otter from "Fort Wayne, Ark." There is no reason to suppose that this
careful author made an error and wrote "Ark." in place of "Ind." Old maps
show that there was once a Fort Wayne in Arkansas and it is much more
probable that Baird had a specimen from there in a general region where
there were Army collectors, than from Fort Wayne, Indiana. Mr. Chas. C.
Deam writes that he met a man in Point township, Posey County who, many
years ago, had killed an Otter in Otter Slough of Half Moon Pond. There
are few positive present day records. Mr. Pat Williams of Evansville, writing
in 1930, says: "In regard to Otter I saw one old one and two young on
Pigeon Creek three years ago this summer, three miles north of Evansville."
Hunters and trappers along Patoka Creek have stated that Otters are still to
be found in that creek in Pike and Gibson counties. None are taken owing to
their being protected by law. Hahn (1909) thought that a few might remain
in the Kankakee region. Mr. Henry Duncker of South Bend, an old hunter
and trapper of the Kankakee, tells me that he saw a dead Otter on the banks
of the Kankakee in Laporte County in 1909, and a live one in the water
which looked at him for some moments, while he cautiously reached for his
gun, but dived out of sight before he had time to shoot it. He thinks they
were among the last otters in the Kankakee valley. Evermann and Clark
(1911, 1920) write "Mr. Anton Meyer, a fur buyer of Plymouth, Ind., tells
us he gets 10 or 12 otter skins each year chiefly from the Tippecanoe and

Yellow Rivers." Dinwiddie (1884) writes: "Otters are still to be seen along the Kankakee." In the list of skins handled in 1859 (Anonymous 1906) at Noblesville, 13 were those of otters. A few additional records may be seen on the map. Hahn (1909) reports an actual Indiana specimen in the State Museum and in the United States National Museum is a beautiful skull of an otter from Patoka Creek, Gibson County. As a rule otters stand civilization fairly well and it is a great pity that an animal whose fur is so valuable should have been virtually exterminated throughout the State.

As may be judged from its specialized aquatic adaptations, the chief food

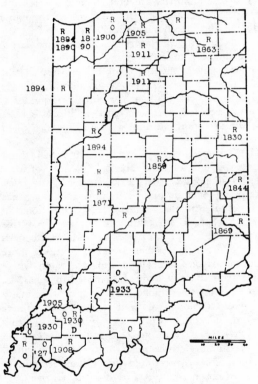

Map 27. Published records, recent occurrences and specimen in collection of the Otter, *Lutra canadensis lataxina*, in Indiana.

The published records for the Otter are: Elkhart (Weaver 1916), Franklin (Haymond 1860, Langdon 1881, Quick and Langdon 1882, Butler 1885, Hahn 1909), Fulton (Evermann and Clark 1911, 1920), Hamilton (Anonymous 1906), Jay (Montgomery 1864), Knox (Butler 1895, Hahn 1909), Lake (Dinwiddie 1884, Ball 1894, Butler 1895, Blatchley 1898), Laporte (Anonymous 1880, Brennan 1923), Marshall (Evermann and Clark 1911, 1920), Montgomery (Cox 1860), Morgan (Major 1915), Newton (Butler 1895, Hahn 1909), Noble (Hahn 1909), Pike (Hahn 1909), Porter (Butler 1895, Blatchley 1898), Posey (Wied 1839-41, 1861-62, Hahn 1909), Putnam (Anonymous 1881, Hahn 1909), St. Joseph (Anonymous 1880, Engels 1933), Tippecanoe (Evermann and Butler 1894), Warrick (Hahn 1909), Wayne (Plummer 1844, Young 1872, Hahn 1909), Kankakee Valley (Hahn 1907, Werich 1920).

of the otter is fish. It also feeds on frogs, crayfish and especially the larger molluscs. Some think it occasionally eats muskrats.

Otters are quick in action. They can do about six miles an hour in open water and can remain under water for more than three or four minutes. Merriam (1882-84) reports them as being able to swim under water for nearly a quarter mile without showing their heads above water.

Otters have a rather extensive range and in winter travel considerable distances over the snow and ice.

Otters never live at any distance from water. Their dens are made in burrows in banks, with the entrance under water as well as an exit inward and on the surface above the water line. Nests are made in enlargements in the burrows and lined with suitable materials such as sticks, leaves, grass, shredded bark, etc.

Young are born in spring and vary from 1 to 3, usually 2. The period of gestation is eight to nine weeks, so that mating must take place in winter or very early in spring. Like other mustelids, the young are born in an immature state, with the eyes closed, and it is nearly two months before they take to the water. The young remain with the mother until the winter following their birth. Many authors are inclined to believe that the male remains with the female and helps care for the young. (Seton 1929)

The otter is said to be a playful animal and one of its chief amusements is the otter slide.

The Otters ascend a bank at a place suitable for their diversion, and sometimes where it is very steep, so that they are obliged to make quite an effort to gain the top, they slide down in rapid succession when there are many at a sliding place. On one occasion, we were resting on the bank of Canoe Creek, a small stream near Henderson [just across the Ohio River from Vanderburg County] which empties into the Ohio, when a pair of Otters made their appearance, and not observing our proximity, began to enjoy their sliding pastime. They glided down the soapy, muddy surface of the slide with the rapidity of an arrow from a bow, and we counted each one making 22 slides before we disturbed their sportive occupation. . . . From the fact that this occurs in most cases during the winter, about the period of the mating season, we are inclined to the belief that this propensity may be traced to those instincts which lead the sexes to their periodical associations. (Audubon and Bachman, vol 2. p. 8).

Others are inclined to the belief that the slides are used at all seasons of the year and that the sport is indulged in by young and old alike.

Spotted Skunks
Genus **Spilogale** Gray

The Spotted Skunks are irregularly distributed from the southeastern United States northwestward to southern British Columbia. They also occur in Mexico. About fourteen species are known, one of which is reported as occurring in extreme southwestern Indiana.

They are medium sized mammals, with conspicuous white stripes and spots on a black background, much more robust than the weasels but not nearly so rubust as the true skunks, genus *Mephitis;* tail long and bushy, feet subplantigrade, front and hind feet with large anterior pad divided into four tubercles, anal scent glands highly developed. Dentition:

$$i \frac{3-3}{3-3}, \; c \frac{1-1}{1-1}, \; pm \frac{3-3}{3-3}, \; m \frac{1-1}{2-2}, = 34.$$

Audital bullae inflated.

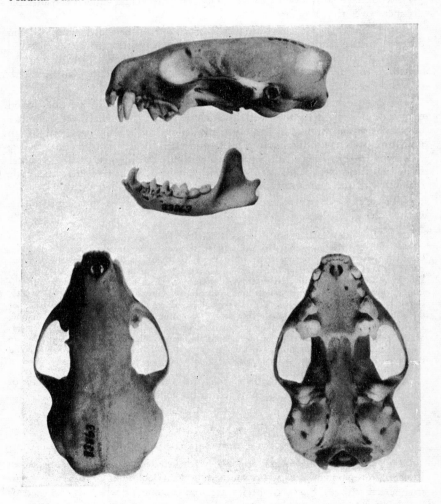

Fig. 42. Photographs courtesy U. S. Nat. Mus. Lateral, dorsal and ventral views of skull of Spotted Skunk, *Spilogale interrupta*, natural size. Cat. No. 83,863, Manhattan, Kansas, Oct. 30, 1896, C. W. Pape. A related species, *Spilogale putorius*, is believed to be of rare occurrence in southern Indiana; no specimens in collections are known.

Spotted Skunk
Spilogale putorius (Linnaeus)

Viverra putorius LINNAEUS, Syst. Nat. ed. 10, vol. 1, p. 44, 1758. Type
    locality: South Carolina.
Mephitis putorius Evermann and Butler 1894, Butler 1895.
Spilogale putorius Hahn 1909, A. H. Howell 1910 March.

The general color of entire animal is black with conspicuous white markings as follows: white spots or irregular areas on forehead between the eyes,
on each side of the rump, and on each side of tail at base, two inner white
parallel stripes running from neck to middle of body, two outer white stripes
running from front of ear to middle of body; a lateral white stripe reaching
from behind foreleg to rump where it curves up onto back; on rump the
white dorsal stripes are continued as spots meeting transverse white bands
passing in front of hips; tip of tail white; underparts and feet blackish. The
strikingly marked fur is sold under the trade name of "Civet Cat" and is
frequently seen made up into coats.

Total length 440 to 560 mm., tail vertebrae 165 to 220 mm., hind foot
38 to 51 mm., (the larger figures referring to males, the smaller to females)
greatest length of skull about 50 mm., greatest width about 35 mm.

The food of the Spotted Skunks is mainly such insects as grasshoppers,
beetles, with occasional mice, lizards, salamanders, small birds and crayfish,
and rarely fruit or other vegetable matter. It practically never attacks
poultry.

The Spotted Skunks are more agile and weasel-like than the true skunks
and often climb bushes and small trees. They live in natural crevices or in
burrows made by themselves or appropriated from other mammals. They are
mainly nocturnal. The mating season is said to be late in winter. The usual
number of young in a litter is four or five. The mammae are usually eight,
two pairs being pectoral, one pair abdominal, and one pair inguinal. (A. H.
Howell, North American Fauna No. 26, p. 9, 1906).

Spilogale putorius.

Fig. 43. Spotted Skunk, *Spilogale putorius*. After Cory, Mammals of Illinois and
Wisconsin, Field Mus. Nat. Hist., 1912.

The evidence for the occurrence of the Spotted Skunk in Indiana is meager and no specimens of it are in collections. It was included in Evermann and Butler's hypothetical list in 1894. Hahn (1909) reports two rather definite instances of its occurrence in Knox County. A. H. Howell (1910 March) reports it as occurring in Posey County, but does not give the evidence. Cory (1912) reports it for southern Indiana but without evidence.

In a letter dated Feb. 5, 1931, Miss Louise M. Husband in the Library of the Workingmen's Institute, New Harmony, writes as follows:

I have asked several old trappers about the Spotted Skunk and they all said they had never seen, bought, nor heard of any in this part of the state. Later I chanced to see a Mr. Byrd of Poseyville, who has a branch produce and junk business here, and asked him. He said he had never seen any, but had heard that there were some caught down below Mt. Vernon ten or twelve yars ago, but if that were true they must have drifted in and were not native. We have an abundance of the common skunks that are very friendly and waddle across the road almost any time one happens to be driving in the country.

H. E. Anthony's 'Field Book of North American Mammals' which is the most useful one we have doesn't list the Spotted Skunk in Indiana. Raymond Conyers who

Map 28. Published records and a comparatively recent observation of the Spotted Skunk, *Spilogale putorius*, in Indiana.

The published records for the Spotted Skunk are: Knox (Hahn 1909), Posey (A. H. Howell 1910 March), southern Indiana (Cory 1912).

killed the fine golden eagle we have in our museum, says that about nine years ago he dug out a skunk that was different from any he had ever seen, down in Lynn Township, this side of Mt. Vernon. The stripes ran around the body, it was smaller and he was told it was a prairie skunk. Anthony's book shows stripes like that on the back of the body, but doesn't locate it in Indiana. He said it was the only one he had ever seen.

Mr. Conyers' observation is the most positive evidence of the occurrence of *Spilogale* in Indiana that I know of.

In October of 1931 Mr. Chas. C. Deam wrote to me that the Mount Vernon Produce Co. have been buying fur for twenty years and that during that time they have bought four or five "Civet Cats" described as smaller than the skunk, black with white and yellow spots. This answers to the Spotted Skunk very well. In addition they say it has no scent sac! Perhaps they handled carefully skinned animals. Anyone who has handled *Spilogale* in the flesh or one alive knows it has well developed and quick working anal scent glands. It is to be hoped that some trapper in southern Indiana will save a few skulls of all kinds of skunks and finally secure in the way of a specimen unquestioned evidence of the presence of the Spotted Skunk in this state.

COMMON SKUNKS
Genus **Mephitis** Geoffroy and Cuvier

The genus is found throughout most of the United States, adjoining Canadian provinces, and northern Mexico. It contains about ten species, two of which are found in Indiana.

Skunks are medium-sized mammals, with long black fur, more or less conspicuously marked with white; tail large and bushy. The general color pattern is uniformly black or blackish above and below with a broad white stripe from back of neck or center of head to shoulders and continued as a lateral stripe on either side to base of tail, a narrow white stripe in center of face, tail black and white in various proportions. There is much individual variation in the amount of white in the color scheme; it may be very extensive and at other times almost suppressed except in the stripe on head and back of neck. Feet semi-plantigrade, large foot pad behind the toes not divided into smaller tubercles. Claws of the forefeet large and heavy, well adapted for digging. Anal scent glands very highly developed. Skull with inconspicuous audital bullae. Dental formula:

$$i\,\frac{3\text{-}3}{3\text{-}3},\ c\,\frac{1\text{-}1}{1\text{-}1},\ pm\,\frac{3\text{-}3}{3\text{-}3},\ m\,\frac{1\text{-}1}{2\text{-}2},\ =34.$$

The anal glands are the skunk's most striking anatomical characteristic; they are two in number, one

on either side of the rectum and are embedded in a dense gizzard-like mass of muscle which serves to compress them so forcibly that the contained fluid [3] may be

---

3 This fluid has nothing whatever to do with urine, nor are the anal glands in any manner connected with the urinary tract. The skunk's bladder and urine are in no wise different from those of other mammals.

ejected to the distance of four or five meters (approximately 13 to 16½ feet). Each sac is furnished with a single duct that leads into a prominent nipple-like papilla that is capable of being protruded from the anus, and by means of which the direction of the jet is governed. The secretion is a clear limpid fluid of an amber or golden color, has an intensely acid reaction, and in the evening, is slightly luminous. . . The fluid

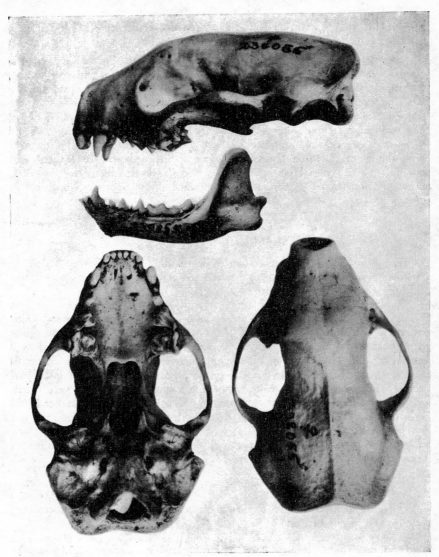

Fig. 44. Photographs courtesy U. S. Nat. Mus. Lateral, palatal and dorsal views of Eastern Skunk, *Mephitis nigra*, natural size. Cat. No. 238,055, Bicknell, Knox County, Aug. 10, 1921, W. S. Chansler.

sometimes shows a decided greenish cast and it always possesses an odor that is characteristic, and in some respects unique. Its all-pervading, penetrating and lasting properties are too well known to require more than passing comment (Merriam 1882-84).

Chemically, the fluid is a mixture of one of the higher mercaptans, that is a sulphur alcohol and other sulphur containing substances. (Aldrich 1896). Like all volatile sulphur compounds it is malodorous. The distance at which the odor may be perceived depends upon the warmth and humidity of atmosphere and direction of the wind. After a full discharge it can probably be detected under favorable conditions at a distance of nearly a mile.

Fig. 45. Photograph courtesy N. Y. Zool. Soc. Skunk, *Mephitis nigra.*

The fluid is credited with various harmful and dire properties, especially if gotten into the eye, but these need scientific confirmation. The fluid is naturally contained in animal tissue and it seems unlikely that it can be decidedly corrosive or injurious to other animal tissues especially if promptly washed off with water; undoubtedly it is highly irritating.

In order to protrude the nipples of the scent gland from the rectum and so expel the fluid it is necessary for the skunk to raise its tail. The only experience that I ever had was with a skunk in a steel trap. The animal watched me intently as I approached cautiously with a club, then with tail raised, made an about face and sent a spray into the atmosphere. I was quicker than the slow moving skunk and made a rapid side-step and escaped the spray Most hunters say the only hope for sprayed clothing is to bury it for a while, but as one is dealing with a volatile compound it would appear more rational to hang the garments in air and sunshine. Seton (1929) says ordinary dry cleaning will remove it.

Many procedures are recommended for handling trapped skunks. As the glands are controlled by motor centers in the spinal cord, any injury at or above the center will prevent their functioning. Merriam advises one to advance cautiously and slowly so as not to alarm the animal and then with a quick sure blow of a club or pole, break the animal's back well above the tail. He reports 6 per cent of failures due to poor technique. Others say that a skunk may be gently approached in a trap and picked up and carried away using the tail as a handle. As long as the tail is on a line with the back the contents of the glands cannot be discharged. The glands are not emptied by one discharge but several shots may be fired before they are entirely drained. How long it takes such a specialized fluid to be formed is unknown. As the discharge is made only under extreme provocation, one is left with the impression that the fluid is considered valuable by its owner and probably slowly reformed. Skunks on fur farms or as pets may be rendered entirely innocuous by a comparatively simple operation of cutting out both scent glands. It is best done when the animal is about a month old, as the operation is more difficult, serious and odorous, the older the animal.

Skunks are slow moving, easy going animals. Although armed with typical musteline carnivorous teeth, they seldom attack other animals or bite persons handling them, depending almost entirely on their powerful scent glands as a means of defense and protection.

Aside from owls, they have essentially no enemies. While occasionally abroad in daylight, their activities are confined mainly to the evening and night hours. They are entirely terrestrial and during the day live in natural cavities, usurped burrows of other mammals, or in burrows of their own making, five to ten feet in length. The den proper is lined with grass which is rolled by the feet to the mouth of the burrow. The grass is then grasped by the teeth and the animal drags it in backwards. They do not avoid habitations and make themselves at home about the farm where they seldom attack poultry. Their food consists mainly of mice, small reptiles, frogs and salamanders, occasionally birds and their eggs. They are particularly fond of insects, especially grasshoppers and other large forms. They readily eat fish, crustaceans and refuse when available. Vegetable matter is sometimes eaten. They are usually well nourished and become excessively fat in autumn. In the severest part of the winter they hibernate in their dens. Frequently many individuals are found in the same den and they are usually thought to be the mother and her offspring of the previous spring which have attained full size by mid-winter.

Mating takes place about March 1. Gestation lasts nine weeks. The young, born blind and naked, are about the size of full grown mice. The adult color pattern is plainly seen on the hairless young. The number in a litter varies from two to ten; six to eight being the most common in full grown animals. The mammae are five or six to a side extending from the inguinal region almost to the axilla. When nursing, the mother squats on her belly and the young lie on either side of her. At about six weeks of age, the young come out into the open and by midsummer they go forth with their mother and apparently remain with her for the rest of the year and all den up together for the winter. The young grow rapidly and by late autumn are practically adult size except for weight. Adult weight four to six pounds (1.75-2.75 kgs.) young of the year not much more than half that. (Seton 1929, Wight 1931).

Skunks are very frequently afflicted with a curious parasitic disease. It is an infestation of the frontal region of the skull by a thread-worm which may result in an unusual swelling of this part of the skull, or actual erosion of the bone, so that the skull as a specimen is considerably disfigured. Of course, skunks have the usual run of intestinal parasites like any other animal, but their effects are not seen in museum specimens.

Skunk fur is long, soft and of good wearing qualities. However, at the present time it is not particularly valuable and one does not see coats made up from it as is so frequently done with *Spilogale*. The dark colored and solid black skins bring the best prices. During the 1931-32 season, 183,234 skunks were taken in Indiana by trappers, according to figures collected by the Department of Conservation. Skins bring from 45 to 90 cents, 1932-33 prices.

Many instances are related of skunks making interesting pets, and safe ones at that, even though the anal scent glands have not been removed.

Skunks are found in every county of Indiana. Two well marked species are recognized in the state, the common Eastern Skunk found throughout most of the state and the Illinois Skunk probably confined to the prairie region. The exact distribution of the two forms in the state must remain in doubt until more material is gathered in museums. Any trapper can add materially to our knowledge of their distribution by saving the skulls of his catches. In habits the two species are essentially alike. The two forms are distinguished as follows:

Tail longer, usually tipped with white, and white markings of neck and body usually more conspicuous. Posterior edge of palate bones terminating in a short spine in the midline, skull relatively wider and heavier _____*Mephitis nigra*.

Tail shorter, usually without any white tip, white markings of neck and body much less conspicuous. Posterior edge of palate bones not terminating in a spine but forming a straight line across, skull relatively narrower and less heavy, *Mephitis mesomelas avia*.

Skulls of females of the two species do not show such pronounced difference as those of males. The exacting student would therefore do well to submit his specimens to a specialist for positive identification.

EASTERN SKUNK
Mephitis nigra (Peale and Beauvois)

Viverra nigra PEALE and BEAUVOIS. Cat. Peale's Mus., Philadelphia, p. 37, 1796. Type locality: Maryland.

Mephitis mesomelas Wied 1839-41.
Mephitis americana Plummer 1844.
Mephitis mephitica Evermann and Butler 1894.
Chincha putida A. H. Howell 1901.
Mephitis putida Hahn 1909.
Mephitis nigra Lyon 1923.

The Common Eastern Skunk ranges throughout New England and the

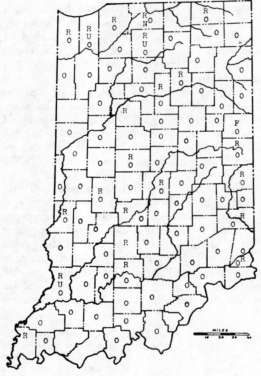

Map 29.   Published records and recent observations and specimens in collections of the Eastern Skunk, *Mephitis nigra*, in Indiana.

The published records for the Eastern Skunk are: Boone (Howell 1901), Carroll (Evermann and Butler 1894), Franklin (Haymond 1870, Evermann and Butler 1894, Hahn 1909), Knox (Howell 1914), Lagrange (Evermann and Butler 1894), Lake (Dinwiddie 1884, Blatchley 1898, Brennan 1923, Sanborn 1925), Laporte (Anonymous 1880, Brennan 1923), Lawrence (Hahn 1908), Marion (Howell 1901), Marshall (Evermann and Clark 1911, 1920, Howell 1914), Miami (Howell 1901), Monroe (Evermann and Butler 1894, McAtee 1907), Morgan (Major 1915), Ohio (Hahn 1909), Porter (Blatchley 1898, Brennan 1923, Lyon 1923, Sanborn 1925), Posey (Wied 1839-41, 1861-62), Putnam (Anonymous 1881), Randolph (Cox 1893, Evermann and Butler 1894), St. Joseph (Anonymous 1880, Engels 1933), Vigo (Evermann and Butler 1894, Thomas 1916), Wabash (Evermann and Butler 1894), Wayne (Plummer 1844), Kankakee Valley (Hahn 1907), probably in every county (Hahn 1909).

Middle Atlantic States, south to Virginia and west to Indiana. It is probably found in every county of Indiana.

It has the usual color pattern of skunks as described under the generic description with considerable variation in the length and width of the white stripes, the tail is usually entirely black with the exception of a white tip.

Total length 575 to 600 mm., tail about 225 mm., hind foot 60 to 62 mm., greatest length of skull 60 to 65 mm., greatest width about 36 to 40 mm., mastoid breadth 37 to 40 mm.

Posterior border of palate with a prominent median spine.

ILLINOIS SKUNK
Mephitis mesomelas avia (Bangs)

Mephitis avia BANGS. Proc. Biol. Soc. Washington, vol. 12, p. 32, Type locality: Mason County, Illinois.

Mephitis mesomelas LICHTENSTEIN. Darstellung neuer oder wenig bekannter Säugethiere, pl. 45, fig. 2, 1832.

Cincha mesomelas avia A. H. Howell 1901.

Mephitis mesomelas avia Hahn 1909.

The Illinois Skunk is found in the prairie region of Illinois, western

Map 30. Published records and specimens in collections of the Illinois Skunk, *Mephitis mesomelas avia*, in Indiana. The occurrence of this species of skunk in Indiana rests on doubtful evidence. Skulls of definitely known sex from the northwestern counties of the state are desiderata in collections.

The published records for the Illinois Skunk are: Benton (A. H. Howell 1901, Hahn 1909), Newton (A. H. Howell 1914), Kankakee Valley (Hahn 1907).

Indiana and eastern Iowa. Its exact distribution in Indiana, owing to lack of specimens, is unknown. It is definitely stated to occur in Newton and Benton Counties. When more material is obtained it will probably be found to have a much wider distribution and perhaps be found to extend its range eastward due to deforestation rendering much of Indiana an essential prairie.

The color pattern is variable. The white stripes may terminate about the middle of the back or reach the root of the tail. The tail is wholly black, sometimes with a white tip.

Total length 600 to 640 mm., tail 185 to 220 mm., hind foot 65 to 68 mm., greatest length of skull about 60 to 65 mm., greatest width 42 to 44 mm., mastoid breadth about 37 mm.

Posterior border of palate straight across and without a median spine.

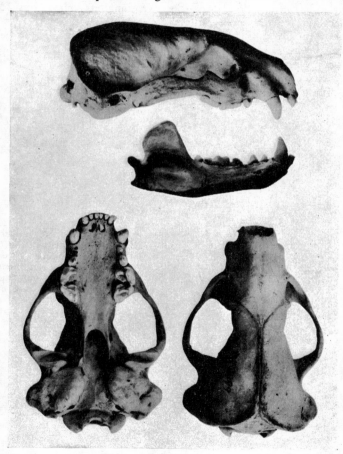

Fig. 46. Photographs courtesy U. S. Nat. Mus. Lateral, palatal and dorsal views of skull of Badger, *Taxidea taxus*, about ½ natural size. Cat. No. 254,999, U. S. Nat. Mus., St. Joseph County, 1929-30, C. S. Robins.

BADGERS
Genus **Taxidea** Waterhouse

Badgers are found in central and western North America from Saskatchewan south through Texas and east into Ohio.

Body large, stout, tail short, legs short, claws of forefeet very large and heavy, adapted for digging. Skull with large audital bullae, wide and squarish in occipital region so that posterior part of skull is nearly as broad as the zygomatic breadth. Dental formula:

$$i \frac{3-3}{3-3}, \ c \frac{1-1}{1-1}, \ pm \frac{3-3}{3-3}, \ m \frac{1-1}{2-2}, = 34.$$

The genus contains but a single species divided into five geographic races, or subspecies, the typical race occurring across northern Indiana.

BADGER
Taxidea taxus taxus (Schreber)

Ursus taxus SCHREBER. Säugethiere, vol. 3, p. 520, 1778.
Taxidea americana Evermann and Butler 1894.
Taxidea taxus Hahn 1909, Lyon 1932.

Taxidea taxus taxus ranges from about 55° latitude in Alberta, Saskatchewan, Manitoba, south to Colorado and Kansas, and east to northern Ohio.

Hairs of the upper parts long and shaggy; general color above silvery gray, each hair yellowish or grayish white at base, then blackish and finally with a white tip; neck, crown, and muzzle brown; cheeks, chin, and stripe from nose to shoulders whitish. Hairs of the underparts shorter, in general yellowish white. Tail yellowish brown. Feet blackish as well as streak on each cheek, and back part of ear.

Total length about 700 to 800 mm., tail 125 to 130 mm., hind foot 95 to 115 mm., greatest length of skull about 115 mm., greatest width about 75 mm., greatest width in posterior plane about 72 mm., weight from 12 to 24 pounds (5.5 to 11 kgs.). Males are somewhat larger and heavier than females.

Badgers are animals of the open country and not woodlands or marsh lands. While they may be seen at any time during the day, yet they are most frequently met from late afternoon on. They are typically fossorial in habit and spend a great deal of time in their large subterranean burrows. Their food consists largely of mice, ground-squirrels and gophers which they usually catch by digging out of their burrows. They also eat rabbits; woodchucks and skunks form part of their fare. One Indiana specimen was caught by placing steel traps at the mouths of woodchuck burrows. Their burrows are large and deep, being from eight to 30 feet in length and going downward for two to six or more feet. There are no reports of their damaging any of man's domestic animals, and the most serious complaint against them is the enormous holes and burrows that they dig. They are reported as able to run backward with ease and when not pursued or harried, often enter their burrows by backing in. Anthony (1928) gives the following graphic account of their digging ability:

Fig. 47.   Young Badgers, dug out of their den, Porter County, about 1927, photograph by J. C. Allen, West Lafayette

A badger that I once came upon as he began digging out a squirrel was only just below the surface and the ejected earth was flying forth in leisurely spurts. The Badger sensed my footsteps as I drew near and immediately changed his tempo. Muttered snarling and rumbling began to pour out of the hole, and a geyser of earth leaped up four or five feet into the air. As I looked on the height of the column dropped almost with the seconds and in a very short time the Badger was so deep that no more earth reached the surface and the sounds of his subterranean rage were only faintly audible.

The time of mating of the Badger is unknown, whether in late autumn or late winter. The young are born in late May or early June and appear to remain in the den until nearly full grown. The number of young in a litter is usually four, varying between one and five. The mammae are two inguinal

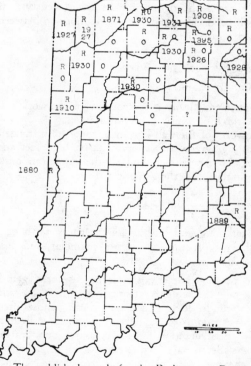

Map 31. Published records with approximate dates of observation and specimens in collections of the Badger, *Taxidea taxus*, in Indiana.

The published reords for the Badger are: Benton (Butler 1895, Hahn 1909, Lyon 1932), Cass (Lyon 1932), Dekalb (Evermann and Butler 1894, Hahn 1909, Lyon 1932), Elkhart (Evermann and Butler 1894, Hahn 1909, Lyon 1932), Franklin (Evermann and Butler 1894, Hahn 1909, Lyon 1932), Grant (Hahn 1909, Lyon 1932), Jasper (Lyon 1932), Kosciusko (Evermann and Butler 1894, Hahn 1909, Lyon 1932), Lagrange (Evermann and Butler 1894, Hahn 1909, Lyon 1932), Lake (Dinwiddie 1884, Lyon 1932), Laporte (Hahn 1909, Lyon 1932), Marshall (Evermann and Clark 1911, 1920, Lyon 1932), Newton (Butler 1895, Hahn 1907, Lyon 1932), Noble (Evermann and Butler 1894, Hahn 1909, Lyon 1932), Porter (Brennan 1923, Lyon 1932), St. Joseph (Anonymous 1880, Lyon 1932, Engels 1933), Steuben (Evermann and Butler 1894, Hahn 1909, Lyon 1932), Vermillion (Evermann and Butler 1894, Hahn 1909, Lyon 1932).

pairs and two abdominal pairs. The breeding den is placed well down in a long burrow with one or perhaps two entrances, and is lined with grass.

During the coldest weather, especially while the ground is frozen, Badgers remain in a state of hibernation, yet even in Minnesota they have been found abroad in every month of the winter.

Badger fur is thick and coarse and not much used by furriers, except for trimmings.   The hair is said to be used in the manufacture of shaving brushes. Skins bring from $3.50 to $8.00. (1932-33)

Badgers are rare in Indiana, but a few are found even at the present time. They extend across the northern portion of the state into northwestern Ohio and southern Michigan.   There are authentic records of their occurring as far south as Franklin County, with a decided gap in their distribution between there and their more accustomed northern range.

WOLVES, COYOTES, AND FOXES
Family Canidae

The family Canidae is found in practically every country of the world. It contains about a dozen genera, three of which occur in Indiana.

They are medium-sized carnivores of the well known dog-like form; muzzle elongated, rather long legs; feet digitigrade with four digits on hind feet and five on the forefeet in most of the genera including all the American ones; claws non-retractile. Dental formula in all the American forms:

$$i \frac{3-3}{3-3}, \ c \frac{1-1}{1-1}, \ pm \frac{4-4}{4-4}, \ m \frac{2-2}{3-3}, = 42.$$

Pelage rather long and thick, tail long and bushy. Larger cheek teeth of a combined trenchant and crushing type, the last upper premolar and first lower molar strongly differentiated as carnassial teeth.

All the American Canidae possess charactertistic sebaceous scent glands on the upper surface of their tails. The hairs arising from them are stiff and mane-like and devoid of soft under fur. The size of these glands differs in the different genera and species and is also subject to marked individual variation. The gland gives off a peculiar odor and serves as an identification mark among its own kind.   As Seton says, with man seeing is believing, but with the dog smelling is believing. The shapes and sizes of these glands are illustrated diagramatically by Seton (1923).

In the Red Fox, genus *Vulpes* the glandular area is at the base of the tail elongated elliptical, 25 mm. long by 5 mm. wide. In the Wolf and Coyote, genus *Canis* it is similarly situated at base of tail, of the same general shape but longer, about 35 mm., 3 mm. wide in the Coyote, and about 5 mm. wide in the Wolf. In the Gray Fox, genus *Urocyon* the glandular area occupies the middle third of the tail. It is 105 mm. long, widest in its basal third and tapering to a point distally.

They are terrestrial in habit.

Key to the Indiana Genera of Canidae

Size large, greatest length of skull about 200 mm. or more. Pupil of eye round,
    Canis --- 143
Size smaller, greatest length of skull 150 mm. or less. Pupil of eye elliptical.
    Temporal ridges of skull uniting to form a sagittal crest posteriorly and enclos-
      ing a narrow V on top of skull, upper incisors lobed. Tail bushy and with-
      out a conspicuous mane of stiff hairs on upper surface, -----------*Vulpes* 135
    Temporal ridges of skull never meeting in the midline, but enclosing a broad
      U-shaped area on top of skull; upper incisors not lobed. Tail bushy and
      with a mane of relatively long stiff hairs on upper surface. ------*Urocyon* 140

Red and Kit Foxes
Genus **Vulpes** Oken

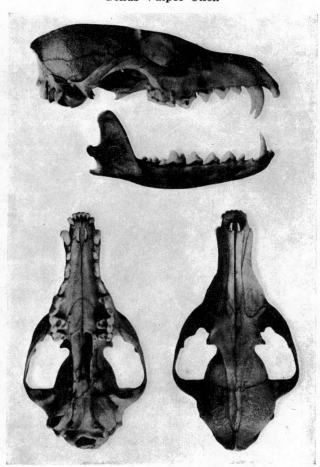

Fig. 48. Photographs courtesy U. S. Nat. Mus. Lateral, palatal and dorsal views
of skulls of Red Fox, *Vulpes fulva*, about ½ natural size. Cat. No. 238,063, U. S.
Nat. Mus., Bicknell, Knox County, Aug. 10, 1921, W. S. Chansler.

The genus *Vulpes* is found from the limit of tree growth in the northern hemisphere south to Morocco, India and Mexico.

The skull is slender and low, interorbital region nearly flat, the frontal sinuses scarcely inflated, the postorbital processes thin, slightly concave above, their edges overhanging and bead-like; dorsal profile of skull rising very slightly and gradually above rostrum; teeth relatively light and small, canines slender and elongated.

About ten species of Red Foxes are found in North America, one of which occurs in Indiana.

RED FOX
Vulpes fulva (Desmarest)

Canis fulvus DESMAREST. Mammalogie, vol. 1, p. 203, 1820. Type locality: Virginia.

Vulpes fulvus Haymond 1870, Hahn 1909.

Vulpes vulpes Evermann and Butler, 1894.

Fig. 49. Photograph courtesy South Bend Park Board and South Bend Tribune. Red Fox, *Vulpes fulva*, about three quarters grown, captured in Illinois not far from the Indiana line.

The Red Fox is found throughout the northeastern United States and probably occurs or has occurred in every county in Indiana.

In general it resembles a small dog with pointed nose, large erect ears, and long bushy tail. The claws are rather long and sharp. The upper parts in the usual specimen are a bright yellowish or reddish yellow, darker in the median line, rump grizzled with whitish; head reddish yellow; feet black; tail yellowish mixed with black, tip white and a black spot on upper surface near base; under parts and cheeks whitish, outer side of ears blackish, inner side whitish. Melanistic forms occur either entirely melanistic or black frosted with white hairs or only partially melanistic with a dark cross on the neck and shoulders and back whence the term, Black, Silver and Cross Fox. All these color phases have been found to occur in the same litter. The hair in general is long and soft and of the two usual sorts, the softer under fur and the longer coarser conspicuous hairs overlying it.

Total length, about 40-41 inches (1000-1025); tail vertebrae, 12.5-15 inches (310-380 mm.); hind foot, 6-7 inches (150-175 mm.); greatest length of skull, about 140 mm.; greatest width, about 72 mm.; weight 8-15 lbs. (3.5-6.5 kgs.). Females are slightly smaller than males.

The Red Fox prefers as its habitat partially settled territory. In the East it does not seem to be an inhabitant of the wilderness, but with partial clearing off of the native forests it has increased in numbers. On the other hand it is ill adapted to complete civilization. Foxes may be seen abroad at all hours of the day or night; they are probably more nocturnal than diurnal.

Foxes live or at least breed in dens or burrows either of their own making or the usurped and enlarged burrows of other mammals. The burrows may be quite extensive, as much as 10 to 15 feet in length and the den at three feet below the surface of the ground. There is usually more than one opening leading to the den. Generally the excavated earth is scattered from the entrance which is left as an inconspicuous hole in the ground or hillside. The burrows are nine to 12 inches in diameter. Their construction must require no little time and skill on the part of the fox for the animal itself is in no wise specialized for digging as is the skunk and badger. The den is an enlargement at one end of the burrow and is occasionally lined with dry grass.

There is much evidence to show that Red Foxes are monogamous and that the male and female remain together throughout the greater part of the year after mating which occurs in late winter. The period of gestation is 51 days so that the pups are born in early April. They number from four to nine and are blind till a week or a week and a half old. At three to four weeks of age they venture forth from their den but use it as a permanent home for about three months. Immediately following their birth the male parent is excluded from the den, but is readmitted after about ten days.

There is one brood to the season. The young are nearly full grown by the end of August, but are still in the old home with the parents. Such quantities of game, dead and alive, have been brought to them during the summer that their front door is now dangerously marked with the bones and feathers of the victims. (Seton, vol. 1, 1929).

The food of the Red Fox is primarily meat of some kind, though at times they are known to eat berries. Most observers concede their chief food to be field mice which are located primarily by their acute sense of hearing. Several observers while off wind report drawing foxes within close range by making noises similar to the squeak of mice. Of their food Dr. A. K. Fisher (1908) writes:

The Fox, from its occasional misdeeds, is looked upon by the majority of mankind as a deep-dyed villain that devotes its entire life to robbery, and derives all its forage from the chicken yard or duck pen. As a matter of fact, even in localities where foxes are abundant, it is comparatively rare that poultry is devoured by them. On all well regulated farms, chickens are housed at night, and the Fox necessarily turns his attention to Field-mice, Rabbits, Ground-squirrels, and insects, such as grasshoppers, crickets, and May beetles, to the great benefit of the farmer. Although it is true that the Fox destroys a considerable number of birds, yet a ruffed grouse has been known to rear its young within 100 feet of a Fox den, and the tracks of the young birds have repeatedly been seen on the fresh earth before the entrance. Among the food brought to this litter and left outside were Rabbits, Mice, and a half-grown Woodchuck, but no birds of any kind.

In an article entitled Food Habits of Mid-West Foxes (Journ. Mamm., vol. 16, pp. 192 to 200, Aug. 1935) Paul L. Errington gives the results of an exhaustive study covering five years in Iowa and Wisconsin. Approximately their food consisted of small pig. 1; rabbit, 40; ground squirrels, 3; meadow mice, 40; white-footed mice, 6; and wild birds, 10%.

It is only fair to say that there are authentic instances of foxes attacking, killing and carrying off young lambs and pigs. The excess of a Fox's kill is buried lightly underground for use at times when hunting is not so good.

The Red Fox is credited with an unusual amount of cunning and sagacity, so characteristically is it true that one might say with "foxiness." Some of its apparent cunning is perhaps mythical, some of it just sheer luck, but a considerable proportion of it is real. The larger works (Seton 1929, Stone and Cram 1904) dealing with habits must be consulted for numerous authentic stories about the manner in which Foxes are able to throw their human and canine pursuers off the scent.

Foxes may be still-hunted, hunted with dogs, caught in carefully placed steel traps or dug out of dens. Hunting them on horseback followed by a few or a whole pack of hounds has been considered great "sport," although it is distinctly a one-side affair with the odds against the Fox. The Fox-drive is another method of hunting down an animal which is popularly disliked. As described, hollow squares several miles across are formed by men and boys who advance at a given time to a common center driving all before them and killing what they can as the square closes up. A recent author of one such account wonders if the few animals obtained on the drive are worth so much effort.

There is some question as to whether the Red Fox is an original native of Indiana or even of northeastern North America, although in the western part of its range it is undoubtedly native.. Most observers in Indiana are inclined to the belief that the Red Fox is a late invader in the state and only appeared when the country became half settled, conditions well suited to its life. There is some question as to whether the Red Fox may not have been imported from England into the eastern United States in Colonial Times for the sport of fox hunting or riding to hounds. (See Seton 1929, vol. 1, p. 472, Hahn 1909, Rhoads 1903, pp. 145-146). Baird in 1857 (p. 100) writes:

It is not a little remarkable that there have as yet been no remains of the red fox detected among the fossils derived from the Carlisle and other bone caves. The gray fox is abundantly represented but not a trace of the other. This would almost give color to the impression somewhat prevalent that the red fox of eastern America is the descendant of individuals of the European red fox imported many years ago, and allowed to run wild and overspread the country. The fact of their present abundance and extent of distribution is no barrier to the reception of this idea, as the same has been the case with horses brought over by the Spaniards, after the discovery of America, and set at liberty.

Fox fur commercially is valuable and is used principally for collars, neckpieces and trimmings. The melanistic variety with white tipped hairs is particularly prized and single skins of such have been sold for very fancy prices running into the hundreds of dollars. Foxes are now artificially raised with more or less success on fur farms for their pelts. The greatest profit on these farms arises from the sale of breeding stock and not from pelts. If fox farming were as simple as some promoters describe it, fox neckpieces ought almost to be a glut on the market. According to reports received by the Department

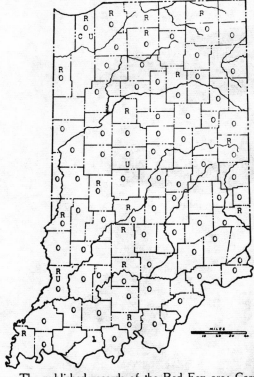

Map 32. Published records, recent observations and specimens in collections of the Red Fox. *Vulpes fulva*, in Indiana; 1, two mounted specimens in the museum at St. Meinrad taken in the vicinity.

The published records of the Red Fox are: Carroll (Evermann and Butler 1894), Crawford (Blatchley 1896), Franklin (Haymond 1870, Quick and Langdon 1882, Butler 1885, Evermann and Butler 1894, Hahn 1909). Knox (Butler 1895, Hahn 1909), Lagrange (Evermann and Butler 1894), Laporte (Anonymous 1880), Lawrence (Hahn 1908), Marshall (Evermann and Clark 1911, 1920), Monroe (Evermann and Butler 1894, McAtee 1907), Morgan (Major 1915), Newton (Butler 1895, Hahn 1907, 1909), Ohio (Hahn 1909), Porter (Hahn 1907, Brennan 1923, Lyon 1923, 1925), Posey (Wied 1839-41), Putnam (Anonymous 1881), Randolph (Cox 1893, Evermann and Butler 1894), St. Joseph (Engels 1933), Vigo (Evermann and Butler 1894), Wabash (Evermann and Butler 1894), dunes region of Lake Michigan (Sanborn 1925), Kankakee valley (Hahn 1907, Reed 1920), Wabash valley (Stuart 1924).

of Conservation 2,964 fox skins were taken in Indiana during the 1931-32 season. The distinction between Red and Gray Foxes is not made. Red Fox skins at that time were worth from $1.75 to $4.00.

GRAY FOXES
Genus **Urocyon** Baird

The Gray Foxes are found throughout most of the United States and extend southward into Central America.

The genus is distinguished externally by a more or less concealed mane of stiff hairs occupying the middle third of the upper surface of the tail. The muzzle is less elongated than in the Red Fox. The skull is distinguished among the American Canidae by the lyrate form of the temporal ridges,

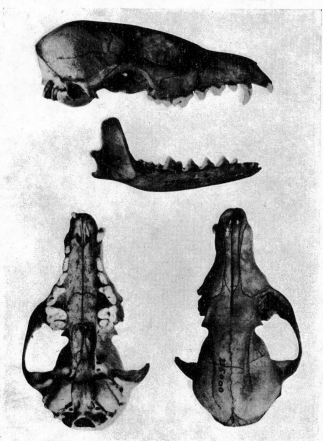

Fig. 50. Photographs courtesy U. S. Nat. Mus. Lateral, palatal and dorsal views of skull of Gray Fox, *Urocyon cinereoargenteus*, about ½ natural size. Cat. No. 255,000, U. S. Nat. Mus., Laporte County, 1929-30, C. S. Robins.

forming a beaded ridge on the outer dorsal surface of the skull, and the rostrum is shorter and blunter. The upper incisors are not lobed.

Urocyon is peculiar to North America and contains about a dozen geographic races, one of which is or was found throughout Indiana.

GRAY FOX
Urocyon cinereoargenteus (Schreber)

Canis cinereo argenteus SCHREBER. Säugethiere, plate 92, 1775. Type locality: Eastern North America. Wied 1839-41.
Canis cinereo-argentatus Plummer 1844.
Vulpes virginianus Haymond 1870.
Urocyon cinereo-argentatus Evermann and Butler 1894, Hahn 1909.

The Gray Fox resembles the Red Fox in general form and structure. It is slightly smaller, however, and of markedly different coloration. Its general color is of a grizzled gray above, lighter on the side, thence passing into a tawny color and on the under parts becoming whitish. The tail contains much black particularly toward the tip whereas in the Red Fox the tip is white.

Fig. 51. Photograph courtesy Milwaukee Zool. Garden. Gray Foxes, Urocyon cinereoargenteus.

The under fur in general is buffy and partly shows through the longer hairs which give the real color to the animal. An ill-defined brownish streak runs from side of nose through eyes; side of muzzle, chin and mane on tail, black. Cheeks, throat, and under parts whitish or light tawny.

Total length, 39-41 inches (1000-1050 mm.); tail vertebrae, 11-12½ inches (275-300 mm.); hind foot, 5-5½ inches (125-140 mm.); greatest length of skull, (not fully adult Indiana specimen) about 120 mm.; greatest width about 72 mm.; weight, about 8 pounds (3.6 kgs.). There are but few definite records of carefully weighed animals.

The Gray Fox is much more omnivorous than the Red Fox, but in general its food habits are essentially the same. In many instances it has been known to feed on vegetable material, such as corn, berries, nuts, acorns. Its chief food is naturally the smaller mammals and ground inhabiting birds, including occasional chickens, also reptiles and amphibians. It also eats young lambs and pigs when they stray from home. It is more an animal of the wildwood than the Red Fox and does not adapt itself to civilization so well. It is an excellent tree climber and can shin a good sized tree and make itself at home on the larger branches or in crotches. It has a cat-like sense of balance and can run along branches or rail fences with perfect ease. It is not as swift of foot as its red cousin and does not possess its endurance and when close pressed by hounds will seek refuge in trees or burrows.

The Gray Fox is said to have a series of refuge dens, sometimes of its own making, more frequently in natural crevices, caves or hollow trees, for

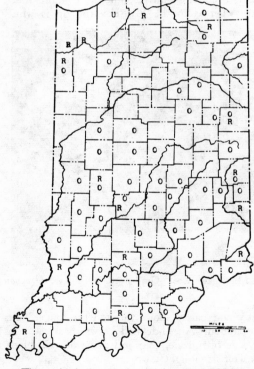

Map 33. Published records, recent observations and specimens in collections of the Gray Fox, *Urocyon cinereoargenteus*, in Indiana.

The published records of the Gray Fox are: Crawford (Cope 1872, 1873, Blatchley 1896), Franklin (Haymond 1870, Quick and Langdon 1882, Butler 1885, Evermann and Butler 1894), Jay (Montgomery 1884), Knox (Butler 1895, Hahn 1909), Lawrence (Hahn 1907, 1909), Morgan (Major 1915), Newton (Hahn 1909), Noble (Hahn 1909), Ohio (Hahn 1909), Posey (Wied 1839-41, 1861-62, Hahn 1909), Putnam (Anonymous 1881), St. Joseph (Anonymous 1880, Engels 1933), Wayne (Plummer 1844), Kankakee valley (Hahn 1909, Reed 1920).

winter use. It is not credited with burying food for future use as in the case of Red Fox. Its breeding habits are much like those of the Red Fox. Three to five young are born in a litter. After the first few days of their life the male helps bring food to the den. It is thought that as in the case of the Red Fox both parents remain together from the time of mating in winter until the young are grown in the following autumn. Seton (1929).

The Gray Fox was the original fox of Indiana and probably is the species referred to by early writers in speaking of "foxes." Even at the present time it is probably found in every county of the state in spite of encroaching civilization and intensive persecution. The specimen whose skull is illustrated was struck by an automobile in Laporte County as late as 1928. In the summer of 1930 two Gray Foxes taken, as small young near Turkey Run State Park, were exhibited there by the Department of Conservation. A glance at the map shows that the State Game Wardens and County Agricultural Agents regard the Gray Fox of not infrequent occurrence throughout most of the state. Mr. Charles Deam tells me he has frequently seen them in some of the southern counties.

While the fur of the Gray Fox is of good wearing quality and not unattractive it is not as highly esteemed as is that of the Red Fox. 1932 prices for Indiana raw skins range from 50 cents to $1.50, those of the Red Fox are somewhat higher.

DOGS, WOLVES, COYOTES
Genus **Canis** Linnaeus

The genus *Canis* has the world wide distribution of the family *Canidae* except South America.

The most obvious character by which it is distinguished from the two preceding genera is its larger size. The American members of the genus *Canis* fall into two well marked groups, recognized technically as subgenera, *Thous* Oken containing the Jackals of the Old World, and the Coyotes of North America, and *Canis* Linnaeus, containing the Dogs and Wolves proper. The subgenus *Thous* contains about 15 North American species or subspecies one of which still occurs in the wild state in Indiana. The subgenus *Canis* contains about 10 species, one of which was once common throughout Indiana but has probably long been extinct.

KEY TO THE INDIANA SPECIES OF CANIS

Size large, total length, 55-60 inches; weight 50-100 lbs.; greatest length of skull well over 200 mm. Wolves, _____*Canis nubilus* 150
Size smaller, total length, 40-48 inches; weight 20-45 lbs.; greatest length of skull about 200 mm. Coyotes, _____*Canis latrans* 143

COYOTE, PRAIRIE WOLF
Canis latrans Say

Canis latrans SAY. Long's Exped. Rocky Mts. vol. 1, p. 168, 1823. Type
    locality: Near Blair, Washington County, Nebraska.
Canis latrans Butler 1895, Hahn 1907, 1909.

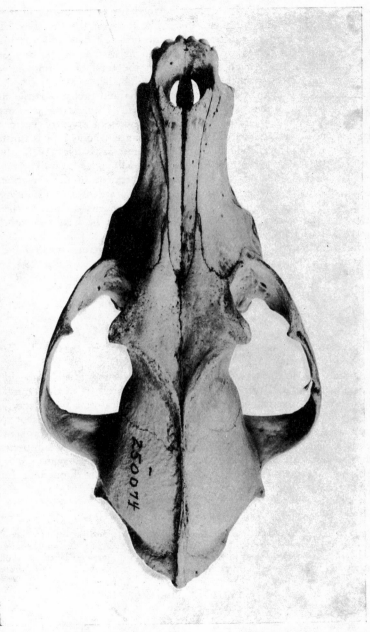

Fig. 52. Photograph courtesy U. S. Nat. Mus. Dorsal view of skull of Coyote, *Canis latrans*, about ⅝ natural size. Cat. No. 250,074, U. S. Nat. Mus., Newton County, 1931, Ned Barker.

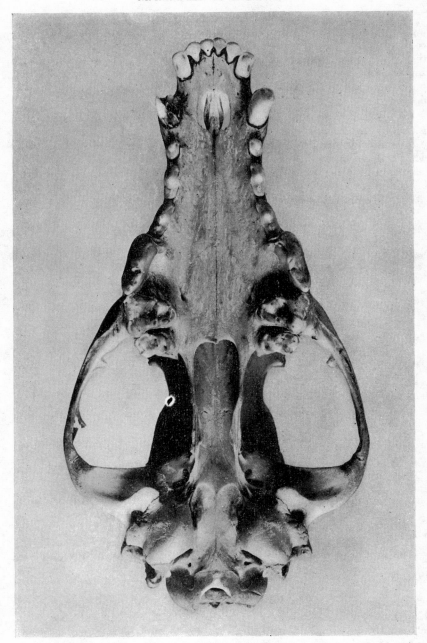

Fig. 53. Photograph courtesy U. S. Nat. Mus. Palatal view of skull of Coyote, *Canis latrans*, about ⅝ natural size. Cat. No. 250,074, U. S. Nat. Mus., Newton County, 1931, Ned Barker.

The common Coyote is found throughout the humid prairies and bordering woodlands of the northern Mississippi Valley, in Iowa, Minnesota, Wisconsin, east to Indiana and westward to the base of the Rocky Mountains in the Province of Alberta. Trustworthy records of its recent occurrence in Indiana are shown on the map. Prior to the settlement of the state the Coyote was probably confined to the natural prairie region in the northwest portion.

The Coyote is a small and slender wolf of a coarsely grizzled buffy, grayish and black color above; below, including inside of legs whitish; muzzle, ears and outer side of legs dull yellowish; tail, above like the back, below whitish or yellowish, tip generally blackish. The fur is coarse and long and composed of the usual softer under fur and the long coarse overlying hairs, heavier in winter than in summer. The skull and teeth are so well illustrated that no descriptions of them are necessary.

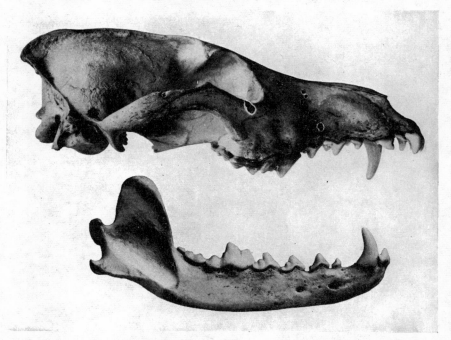

Fig. 54. Photograph courtesy U. S. Nat. Mus. Lateral view of skull of Coyote, *Canis latrans*, ½ natural size. Cat. No. 250,074, U. S. Nat. Mus., Newton County, 1931, Ned Barker.

Total length including the tail to the end of the bone, 40-48 inches (1025-1200 mm.); tail vertebrae, 12-15 inches (300-375 mm.); hind foot, 7¼-8 inches (180-200 mm.); weight 20-45 lbs. (9-20 kgs.) or even more; greatest length of skull (Indiana specimen), about 200 mm.; greatest width, about 105 mm.; premolar-molar series of teeth about 80 mm. A pair of adult

Coyotes from McCoysburg, Jasper County, now in the U. S. National Museum, gave the following measurements as quoted by Hahn (1909), "Adult male, total length 1,095 mm. (43 inches); tail, 165 mm. (6½ in.); hind foot, 195 mm. (7¾ in.); ear from crown, 105 mm. (4-⅛ in.); height at shoulder, 560 mm. (22 in.). Adult female, total length, 1,040 mm. (41 in.); tail, 130 mm. (5⅛ in.); hind foot, 185 mm. (7½ in.); ear, 110 mm. (4⅜ in.); height at shoulder, 500 mm. (20 in.)." This series of measurements brings out well the usual sexual difference in size. The tails of these

Fig. 55. Coyote, *Canis latrans*, photograph by J. C. Allen, West Lafayette. Wisconsin specimen.

two specimens appear to be remarkably short in comparison with measurements made by other authors.

Coyotes are wonderfully adaptive animals and seem to be able to hold their own in spite of advancing civilization. In 1909 Hahn was under the impression that coyotes were more numerous in Indiana than in the preceding few years. They seem to be as numerous now as they were in 1909, showing that they have been able to adapt themselves to an increasing human population. By day they probably hide in dense thickets, woods and swamps or in their dens, though in half a dozen instances that I know of they were seen about in broad daylight. The chief food of Coyotes consists of mice and other small mammals such as rabbits, woodchucks, gophers and ground squirrels. Unfortunately for their own good they wander mainly at night into unprotected chicken yards, and sheepfolds and pig sties. Under the impulse of hunger they can no more resist eating chickens, lambs and young pigs than their cousin the dog. Bounties are paid for their scalps, and the hides of adults in good pelage have some commercial worth.

None of the numerous newspaper accounts of the Coyote in Indiana ever refer to what is described by nearly all naturalists as one of his most distinctive characterists, that is his voice. The specific name bestowed upon him by Say, *latrans,* means the barker or howler. So we presume he has learned that "singing" is dangerous and betrays his presence. Regarding this and some other habits Anthony (1928) writes:

The voice of the Coyote is one of the most characteristic and distinctive mammal calls heard on the North American continent. Singly, or in twos or threes, these small Wolves "tune up" at sunrise or sunset and send a chorus of long howls and yapping barks on the still air. . . [Captive specimens in zoos do the same particularly at the time whistles are blowing and bells ringing.] There is an indescribable quality in the howling of the Coyote which, to me, sets it apart from the obnoxious disturbance of a night howling Dog and makes it a true voice of the wilderness.

It is granted that the stockman, the rancher, and the farmer may call down curses on the head of the Coyote. To many, however, who have heard this ecstatic little Prairie Wolf greet their campfire from out of the dusk, or have arisen at the break of dawn and heard his frenzied hymn to the sun, a West without the Coyote seems colorless and flat.

He quickly learns to avoid ordinary traps and the devices of the average hunter. Instead of retreating before the forces of human occupation, he may merely change his habits and mode of life and remain, in spite of conditions which drive out the less adaptive mammals. Under these circumstances the Coyote will seldom be seen, skulking under cover in the daytime and coming out at night. . .

The Coyote bears enough resemblance to a tawny Shepherd Dog to be easily mistaken for one at a little distance. He can run much faster than the ordinary dog, however, and only the specialized strains of running Dogs can hope to overtake a Coyote in fair chase. And once caught, he is more than a match for any Dog which is near his own size or weight.

Mating occurs in late winter, probably only after the animals are nearly two years old. The young usually 5 to 7 in a litter are born during the first half of April; the period of gestation is nine weeks. As in the case of puppies the young are blind and helpless at birth. They reach adult size in autumn but before that time they have left the den and start shifting for themselves. An underground den, often of considerable length, is dug by the Coyote or an enlargement made of the burrow of some other animal, or it may use some natural cavity among rocks. The den is not used exclusively for breeding, but serves also as a hiding place during the day. The two sexes remain together throughout most of the year if not longer. Seton (1929).

In Indiana today Coyotes are usually hunted with dogs and shot at the round-up. Two killed in St. Joseph County in 1923 were shot by two men who were fox-hunting, using dogs. Two others killed in the same county about five years later were killed by still-hunting without dogs. The skull of one of these latter is in the Field Museum. Another specimen which I have seen as a mounted head and flat rug skin was shot while stalking about an open field by Mr. Roy Teeple of Leesburg, Kosciusko County in the season of 1917-1918. In the Library at New Harmony is a stuffed skin of a Coyote that was killed about five years ago. In the Library at Kokomo in 1931 I saw another stuffed Coyote. This one had been hunted by a posse of men and

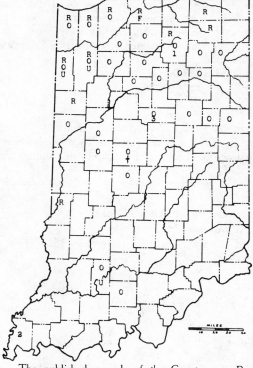

Map 34. Published records, recent observations and specimens in collections of the Coyote, *Canis latrans*, in Indiana; 1, mounted head and rug owned by Mr. Roy Teeple of Leesburg; animal killed in 1917-1918; 2, stuffed skin in Library at New Harmony, killed in vicinity in last 10 years; 3, stuffed skin of animal killed at Vermont in 1930-31, seen in Public Library in Kokomo May 1931. †Pleistocene record.

The published records of the Coyote are: Benton (Evermann and Clark 1911, 1920), Jasper (Battle 1883, Hahn 1907, 1909, Evermann and Clark 1911, 1920), Knox (Hahn 1909), Kosciusko (Hahn 1909, Evermann and Clark 1911, 1920), Lagrange (Hahn 1909), Lake (Dinwiddie 1884, Evermann and Butler 1894, Ball 1894, Blatchley 1898, Hahn 1909, Evermann and Clark 1911, 1920), Laporte (Anonymous 1880, Hahn 1907, 1909), Newton (Butler 1895, Evermann and Clark 1911, 1920), Noble (Hahn 1909), Porter (Lyon 1923), St. Joseph (Lyon 1924, Engels 1933), Vigo (Thomas 1819), Kankakee valley (Evermann and Butler 1894, Reed 1920) boys. A second animal was killed with it. The skin of this was seen in a taxidermist's shop and certainly did not look like a Coyote. The skull of the second specimen is in the University of Notre Dame and is obviously a dog, or at least mostly dog.

In the Indianapolis Star of August 28, 1932, is a rotogravure picture of 14 wolf hides collected by Martin Barker in Jasper, Pulaski and Newton Counties. These all look like Coyotes. Local newspapers frequently contain accounts of wolves being killed in Laporte and Porter Counties, in the present year or last few years. In 1925 the papers reported wolves as being present in a swamp near Leesburg, Kosciusko County, and last year one was reported by the press from Marshall County. None of these have been verified by me either by personal inspection or by correspondence though the latter has been tried without success. They are probably all authentic cases of the present day occurrence of the Coyote in northern Indiana. Frequently the animal is spoken of as the Timber Wolf, but the half dozen instances which I know about have all proved to be Coyotes. The specimen whose skull is figured was killed in Newton County by Ned Barker within the last two years. In the U. S. National Museum is the skull of a specimen from Martin County, showing a rather wide range in the state.

Coyote skins are worth from $1.00 to $3.00, 1932 prices.

PLEISTOCENE COYOTE
†Canis latrans Say

†*Canis latrans* Cope and Wortman 1885, Hay 1902, 1912, 1923, 1930.

A few bones referable to the Coyote have been found in Boone County in association with remains of a mammoth. Hay (1912) thinks the animal in question lived after the passing of the last glacial ice.

The published records of the Coyote in Pleistocene deposits are: Boone (Cope and Wortman 1885; Hay 1912, 1923).

SAY'S WOLF, TIMBER WOLF, GRAY WOLF
Canis nubilus Say.

Canis nubilus SAY, Long's Exped. Rocky Mts., vol. 1, p. 169, 1823. Type locality: Near Blair, Nebraska.

Canis lupus Wied 1839-41, 1861-62. Plummer 1844, Evermann and Butler 1894

Canis lupus var. *ater* Audubon and Bachman, 1851.

Canis nubilis McAtee 1907.

Canis occidentalis Hahn 1909.

Canis lycaon SCHREBER. Säugethiere, pl. 89, 1775. Type locality: Eastern Canada. Lyon 1923.

It is interesting to note that both species of wolves known from Indiana were described by one of Indiana's foremost adopted naturalists, Thomas Say. The same is true of the large and small species of *Blarina* known to inhabit the state. As there is only one authentic specimen of an Indiana wolf extant, one is not entirely certain as to the exact technical name to apply. *Canis lycaon* Schreber originally from eastern Canada may be as appropriate a name as *Canis nubilus* Say. In 1923, I used *Canis lycaon* as the tech-

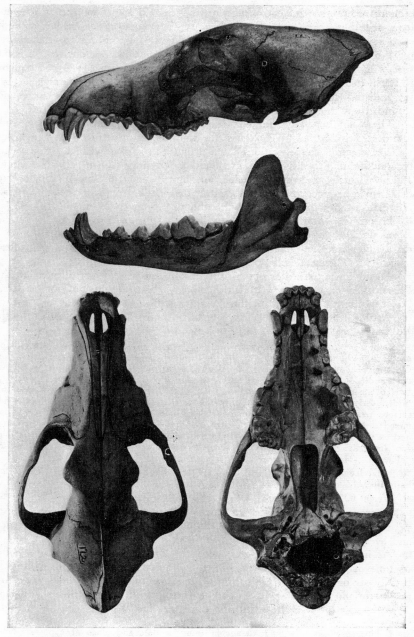

Fig. 56. Photographs courtesy Amer. Mus. Nat. Hist. Lateral, dorsal and palatal views of skull of Say's Wolf, *Canis nubilus*, about 1/3 natural size. Cat. No. 112, Amer. Mus. Nat. Hist., young adult female, collected near New Harmony, Posey County, winter of 1832-33, by the Prince of Wied.

nical name for the Indiana Wolf when I recorded some doubtful fragments from the dunes region of Porter County. It may well be originally both species were found in the state, *Canis nubilus* being confined to the prairie region and *Canis lycaon* to the heavily wooded portions. About ten different species of wolves are recorded from North America from the Arctic regions to northern Mexico and Florida. From the eastern part of this range including Indiana it has been exterminated. The nearest that true wolves are found to Indiana at the present day is in northern Michigan.

The Wolf is a larger, heavier and more thickset animal than the Coyote just described. Seton (1929) gives the following measurements of a male of the species under consideration: Total length, 1575 mm. (62 in.); tail vertebrae, 406 mm. (16 in.); height at shoulders 686 mm. (27 in.); weight, about 100 lbs. Females are slightly smaller and lighter, about 80 lbs. The hind foot of a female is given as 254 mm. (10 in.) Greatest length of the skull of an old male in the Library at New Harmony [4] is given by Hahn (1909) as 8.5 inches (215 mm.) only slightly larger than the Coyote skull figured. Seton (1929) gives the greatest width of a skull as 5¾ in. (146 mm.) decidedly wider than that of the Coyote. Cory (1912) gives the greatest length of a Michigan skull as 254 mm (10 in.) greatest width 127 mm.

The following is a description of a female Indiana Wolf collected by the Prince of Wied in 1832-33 from the lower Wabash presumably not far from New Harmony. The skull of this specimen is now in the American Museum of Natural History, New York, greatest length 233 mm.; greatest width, 120 mm.

Color: In general dull gray-yellowish, everywhere covered with heavy hairs black on the tips. These on the sides of the neck and shoulders are less evident and paler. On the back and on the sides of the body they are longer and blacker, especially is the middle line of the back very strongly marked by these black tipped hairs. . . Side of head dull white-grayish yellow with blackish tipped hairs. . . Lower jaw and throat, dirty white; inner surface of ear covered with long dirty white hairs, outer surface reddish brown. Neck with long heavy hairs, whose tips are black; belly unmixed dirty gray yellowish white. Tail, dull gray-yellow on upper side, on its sides and on the tip on the under half of the tip clothed with heavy black-tipped hairs. The four limbs are dull yellow-reddish. . . Inner side of the four limbs unmixed dull white-yellowish. Claws blackish brown.

Total length 47-9/12 in.; length of tail to end of hairs 18-8/12 in. without the hairs 14-9/12 in. . . . hind foot 9-4/12 in. . . .

Weight 60 American pounds. (Wied 1861-62).

There is no essential difference in color between the Wolf and the Coyote; perhaps the Wolf has more concentration of blackish hairs along the back and over the shoulders.

As in the case of the Coyote the age at mating is nearly two years and its time of occurrence is in late winter. The number of young in a litter is usually six or seven, and the period of gestation nine weeks. The young are not essentially different at birth and in their growth from ordinary puppies. In forested regions such as Indiana once was the Wolf is not so likely to

---

4 This specimen is without data concerning its date and place of capture. Miss Louise Husband of that library says it is thought to have been taken in Indiana very many years ago.

make an underground den for raising its young. It takes advantage of natural cavities, or hollow logs, or cavities under stumps, etc. Unlike the Coyote the Wolf family remains together during the winter and constitutes a pack. Sometimes two or more families make up a pack. (Seton 1929).

The food habits of the Wolf are not essentially different from those of the Coyote. Owing to its larger size it seizes larger prey. Undoubtedly in wilderness days deer was one of its chief sources of food supply in winter. Early settlers refer to loss of live stock by Wolves.

Undoubtedly Wolves were once abundant throughout the whole of Indiana. The first naturalist to write of Indiana mammals, the Prince of Wied says they were not rare in the great forests about the Wabash and in New Harmony one heard their howlings on cold nights (winter of 1832-33). The next writer, Dr. Plummer, says that none had been seen near Richmond since about 1829. Early accounts of the settlement of the state and the accounts in the county histories speak of their former abundance. Many of the stories about them are interesting and no doubt somewhat colored to make the animals appear more savage and destructive than was actually the case in order to make a good story. About the middle of the last century they were practically exterminated although a few fairly authentic records date back as recently as 25 years ago. In the list of skins purchased at Noblesville in 1859 (Anonymous 1906) there are only three Wolf skins as against 1,130 deer skins, showing that the animal was being rapidly killed off though its food supply was still abundant.

The following by S. C. Cox (1860) is a description of the pioneer's method of hunting Wolves, about 1830, in the Wabash Valley:

Black, gray and prairie wolves were quite numerous, and in many localities it was next to impossible to raise sheep or pigs until they had been hunted out. The Legislature enacted laws granting a bounty on wolf scalps, sufficient to stimulate a more active and thorough extermination of these noisy serenaders, who would often approach within a few rods of the cabin, and make night hideous with their prolonged howling. Wolf hunts were then common in which the inhabitants of several neighborhoods, and sometimes of a whole county, took part. They were usually conducted in the following manner: The territory to be hunted over was circumscribed by four lines, sufficiently distant from each other to enclose the proper area. To each line was assigned a captain, with his subaltern officers, whose duty it was to properly station his men along the line, and at the hour agreed upon to cause them to advance in order towards the center of the arena. The lines all charged simultaneously towards the center, on horseback, with dogs, guns and clubs, thus completely investing whatever game was within the lines, and scaring it from the advancing lines toward the center where the excitement of the chase was greatly heightened, and the greatest carnage ensued. Often from two to ten wolves and as many deer were taken in a day at these hunts, and wild cats, foxes and catamounts in abundance. Horses and dogs soon became fond of the sport, and seemed to enter into it with a zest surpassing that of their masters.

Nothing can be added to Hahn's (1909) summary of its occurrence in Indiana the dates for which are all included in the map together with a few other dates obtained from county histories. The Benton County record of 1874 quoted from Mrs. Annie Anderson was probably a true Wolf. The Brown and Lawrence County records of 1902 and 1907 respectively are open to question, no measurements or weights being given. The animals may have been Coyotes. A fairly conclusive recent record quoted from Hahn (1909) is:

December 19, 1908, a wolf was killed near Monroe City in Knox County, Prof.

Max M. Ellis of Vincennes University saw the animal and writes me that it was not a coyote but a timber wolf, measuring about three and one-half feet from tip of nose to root of tail.

About the right size for a small Wolf, but even then the certainty of the record is spoiled when the term "measuring about" is used. Apparently it was not actually "measured." Evermann and Clark (1911, 1920) state that a dealer in skins in Plymouth purchased wolf skins in Starke County, in 1906, at least wolves of two different sizes were purchased, but in the absence of

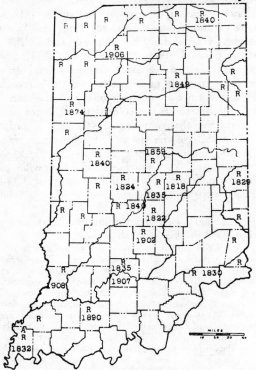

Map 35. Published records and specimen in collection of Say's Wolf, *Canis nubilus*, in Indiana.

The published records for the Wolf are: Adams (Tyndall and Lesh 1918), Allen (Dryer 1889), Benton (Hahn 1909), Brown (McAtee 1907, Hahn 1909), Clay (Evermann and Butler 1894), Dearborn (Anonymous 1885), Elkhart (Weaver 1916), Franklin (Butler 1885, Evermann and Butler 1894), Gibson (Birkbeck 1818, Audubon and Bachman 1851), Hamilton (Anonymous 1906), Hancock (Binford 1882), Hendricks (Cline and McHaffie 1874), Jasper (Battle 1883), Jay (Montgomery 1864), Jefferson (Hahn 1909), Johnson (Cline and McHaffie 1874, Harden 1881), Knox (Audubon and Bachman 1849, Langdon 1881 Dec., Butler 1895, Hahn 1909, Cory 1912), Lagrange (Rerick 1882, Hahn 1909), Lake (Dinwiddie 1884, Ball 1894), Laporte (Anonymous 1880), Lawrence (Hahn 1908, 1909), Marion (Anonymous 1906), Montgomery (Parsons 1920), Morgan (Major 1915), Newton (Butler 1895), Ohio (Anonymous 1885), Porter (Lyon 1923), Posey (Wied 1839-41, 1861-62), Putnam (Anonymous 1881), St. Joseph (Anonymous 1880, Engels 1933), Starke (Evermann and Clark 1911, 1920), Vigo (Brown 1817, Thomas 1819), Wabash (Hahn 1909), Warren (Goodspeed 1883), Wayne (Plummer 1844, Young 1872, Hahn 1909), Wells (Tyndall and Lesh 1918), Kankakee valley (Benton 1903, Hahn 1907, Evermann and Clark 1911, 1920, Reed 1920), lower Wabash (Cox 1860).

actual measurements one cannot be certain that coyotes of two different sizes, due to sex or age, were present. However, their record is placed on the map. Man likes to glory in his deeds and reporters to write good stories, so that the press frequently contains accounts of wolf hunts and wolves killed in northern Indiana at the present day. Like Hahn, all those that I have been able to secure accurate data on refer to the Coyote and not to the Wolf. One specimen of "Wolf" which I have seen among these stories proved to be some sort of a dog or at least mostly dog. The true Wolf is too large and conspicuous an animal and not cunning enough to compete with man in a thickly settled state like Indiana. It is surprising that Coyotes have been able to hold their own so well against the march of civilization.

DIRE WOLVES
† Genus **Aenocyon** J. C. Merriam

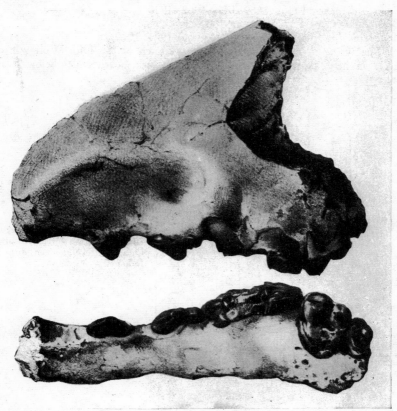

Fig. 57. Dire Wolf, *Aenocyon dirus*, about ¾ natural size. Left lateral and palatal views of the type specimen from Vanderburg County. After the original illustration in the Journal of the Academy of Natural Sciences of Philadelphia, vol. 3, pl. 17, figs. 11 and 12. In the type collection of Mammals, Acad. Nat. Sci. Philadelphia.

The genus *Aenocyon* is a large wolf-like animal distinguished from the genus *Canis* in possessing a narrow brain case, a high posteriorly directed sagittal crest and widely spreading zygomata.

It appears to have been widely distributed in the southern United States especially in southern California, where numerous remains of it occur in the asphalt beds of that state. The best known species is the one that was originally described from Indiana.

DIRE WOLF
†Aenocyon dirus (Leidy)

Canis primaevus LEIDY 1854. Name preoccupied.

Canis dirus LEIDY 1858, J. A. Allen 1876. Hay 1902, 1912, J. C. Merriam 1912.

Canis indianensis LEIDY 1869, Hay 1902, 1930.

Canis lupus Cope and Wortman 1885.

Aenocyon dirus J. C. Merriam 1918, Hay 1923, 1930.

The type and only known Indiana specimen of the Dire Wolf was collected in deposits at the mouth of Pigeon Creek, a few miles below Evans-

Map 36. Published records and specimen in collections of the Dire Wolf, *Aenocyon dirus*, in Indiana.

The published records of the Dire Wolf are: Vanderburg (Leidy 1854, 1856, 1860, 1869, 1873; Allen 1876; Cope and Wortman 1885; Hay 1912, 1914, 1923; J. C. Merriam 1912, 1918).

ville, in Vanderburg County by Mr. Francis A. Linke. Associated with it were portions of *Megalonyx jeffersonii*, *?Bison americanus*, *Cervus* [*Odocoileus*] *virginianus*, *Equus americanus* and *Tapirus* [*haysii*]. The original fragment consists of one side of the upper maxilla with a portion of the teeth in situ. The type is now in the collection of the Philadelphia Academy of Natural Sciences. Leidy's original figure of it is illustrated as figure 57 page 155. It was somewhat larger than the common Wolf of today. It is well known through almost perfect remains from the asphalt deposits of Rancho LaBrea, southern California. The interested student should consult the papers of John C. Merriam (1912, 1918).

Cats and Allies
Family **Felidae**

The family Felidae is distributed throughout the entire continental region of both hemispheres, to the limits of tree growth; and the Malay Archipelago. It is not found in Australia.

The larger cheek teeth are of a cutting type with high compressed crowns and without crushing surfaces. The last upper premolar and the first lower molar show the extreme development of carnassial type of tooth. The skull is short and wide, with much inflated auditory bullae. Size from a small house cat to the largest lion. Feet digitigrade; toes, five on each front foot, and four on each hind. The toes are armed with sharp strong claws which are fully retractile, except in one genus.

The family contains several genera, two of which occur in North America and in early days were found throughout Indiana.

Key to the Indiana Genera and Species

Size large, tail long, coloration of adults unspotted. Dental formula:

$$i \frac{3\text{-}3}{3\text{-}3}, \ c \frac{1\text{-}1}{1\text{-}1}, \ pm \frac{3\text{-}3}{2\text{-}2}, \ m \frac{1\text{-}1}{1\text{-}1}, = 30$$

_____*Felis* 157

_____*Felis couguar* 158

Size medium, tail very short, coloration of adults sometimes spotted, ears tufted. Dental formula:

$$i \frac{3\text{-}3}{3\text{-}3}, \ c \frac{1\text{-}1}{1\text{-}1}, \ pm \frac{2\text{-}2}{2\text{-}2}, \ m \frac{1\text{-}1}{1\text{-}1}, = 28$$

_____*Lynx* 161

Hind feet very large, twice as long as tail; ear tufts very large; fur long and loose, tail black all around the tip, _____*Lynx canadensis* 162

Hind feet not much longer than tail, ear tufts smaller, fur short and close, only upper surface of tail black at tip, _____*Lynx rufus* 164

The True Cats
Genus **Felis** Linnaeus,

The geographic distribution and generic characters are essentially the same as those described under the family *Felidae*. It differs from the genus *Lynx*, the only other North American member of the family in the possession of an extra premolar on each side of the upper jaw, and of a long tail. Several distinct species occur in America but only one of these, the Cougar, or Puma is found in the eastern United States. About ten species or subspecies of the Cougar are recognized in different parts of North America. One species was formerly found over the entire northeastern United States including Indiana. It is barely possible that the Louisiana Cougar, *Felis arundivaga* Hollister, now confined to the cane brakes of that state may have ranged as far north in similar habitats in southern Illinois and Indiana.

PANTHER, PAINTER, COUGAR, PUMA
Felis couguar Kerr

Felis couguar KERR. Anim. Kingd., p. 151, 1792. Type locality: Pennsylvania.

Felis conocolor Wied 1839-41, Evermann and Butler 1894.

Felis cougar (sic) Hahn 1909.

The Cougar is at once distinguished from any other North American mammal by its large size, cat-like form and uniform coloration. Seton (1929, vol. 1) gives these measurements of a male and female: Total length, 7½ feet (2287 mm.); 6½ ft. (1982 mm.); tail 3 ft. (915 mm.); 32 inches (814 mm.). Weight variable, but averages about 150 lbs. (68 kgs.). Greatest length of skull 8-8½ inches (200-250 mm.); greatest width about 5½ inches (140 mm.).

General color dull yellowish brown, much lighter on the under parts and inner sides of legs; tip of tail dark brownish especially in the males; ear blackish on the outside, light colored on the inside. The young are ·spotted until about six months old.

Cougars are active the year round and prey upon whatever meat, bird or mammal, they can find. Probably in Indiana deer was an important source of food. Like all the cats their game is hunted by stalking and not by trailing a scent as in the case of the dogs and wolves.

The Cougar's den or lair is placed in some natural cavity or amid a thick and tangled growth of vines and shrubs. It is generally lined with leaves and grasses.

Mating is supposed to take place in late autumn or early winter. The period of gestation is 13 to 14 weeks and the young are born in late winter or early spring. They vary from one to four in number and like ordinary kittens are blind and helpless at birth. Their eyes open in about a week and a half. At three or four months of age the young are weaned and able to eat meat brought them by the mother. It is at least six months to a year after birth that they are entirely able to care for themselves. Seton (1929.)

Little is known of pioneer methods of hunting Cougars. The present day methods in the west are to trail them with dogs, tree them and shoot them. That they were successfully and easily hunted in the wilds of Indiana is attested by the fact that they were among the first of the larger mammals to be exterminated. Definite detailed records of their occurrence in the state are rare. Many of the county histories refer to their former presence, but the reference is usually not specific and was probably made on general principles.

Fig. 58. Photograph courtesy N. Y. Zool. Soc. Panther, Painter, Puma, or Cougar, *Felis concolor* group, formerly found throughout Indiana.

They were gone from southwestern Indiana at the time of the Prince of Wied's sojourn in 1832-33. They fared slightly better in the northern portion of the state. Brennan (1923) relates that they were common in the Dune region in olden times and there were still some left in the days of the early pioneers. This region, with its varied topography and different kinds of cover, from open pine and oak groves to dense swamps supported numerous deer and other animals that served as prey, was apparently well suited to panthers.

Brennan (1923) further says that two old settlers of the thirties Mr. Monahan, of Michigan City, and Mr. John Morgan, of Chesterton, spoke of large numbers of panthers in the Dunes, the beaches and the woods of the Valparaiso Moraine. Early travelers also mention them.

Evermann and Butler record two young taken east of Brookville in 1838.

Hahn (1909) gathered from Mr. Chansler records for Knox and Daviess Counties: One in 1825; one in 1828; two in 1833, one near Vincennes in 1837.

In Weston A. Goodspeed's History of Brown County it is stated:

The township [Washington] was very wild even in 1836. Deer, bears, wolves and panthers were quite numerous. Green Graham tells that on one occasion at night he had occasion to pass from Jackson's salt works to the eastern part of the township via Weed Patch Knob. He was riding on horseback and was unaccompanied except by a small colt and a cur dog. Just before reaching the summit of the hill he heard what he took to be someone calling him some distance in advance, and he returned the call which was soon repeated, and the person calling seemed each time to be getting nearer. At last just before reaching the top of the knob, he observed that his dog was so frightened that it ran under the side of the mare he was riding and remained cowering there. The mare also began to prick up her ears and sniff the air in fright and shy off to one side of the path. A minute later the leaves rustled to his right, and, looking that way, the already frightened settler saw two cat-like forms skulking through the weeds. He knew that the animals were panthers, and without further parley he put whip to his mare, and regardless of consequences went down the hill at a breakneck pace. [Weed Patch Hill is still a wild place; in the spring of 1930 I saw a large rattlesnake freshly killed by some workmen who were hauling gravel on the summit.]

Three or four other records gathered by Hahn are worth quoting in full:
Dr. U. H. Farr, of Paragon [Morgan County], tells of seeing an animal in 1851 when a child of five, which older people told him was a panther, judging from his description. Mr. Cicero Sims tells of capturing "what was called a mountain lion" in a wolf pen in Clinton County. The exact date is not given, but must have been about 1840. His discription of the animal leaves no doubt that it was a cougar.

Dr. S. C. Richardson, of Indianapolis, tells of going fishing one night in 1851, when he and three companions were threatened [sic] by a panther which they frightened away by rushing toward it with their fish gigs and an ax. It was only seen indistinctly in the moonlight, but its screams were heard as it retreated through the woods. Dr. Richardson's father killed a panther which he discovered crouched in a tree, apparently waiting to spring upon him, sometime previous to 1850. The exact date and place are not given. About the same time one of his steers was attacked in the woods not far from home and horribly lacerated by one of these great cats.

Mrs. George Burgner of Bluffton now 85 years of age says her grand father killed panthers in Wells County.

In the list of skins purchased at Noblesville in 1859 (Anonymous 1906), no panthers are given, although one bear, three wolves and 48 wild cats are recorded.

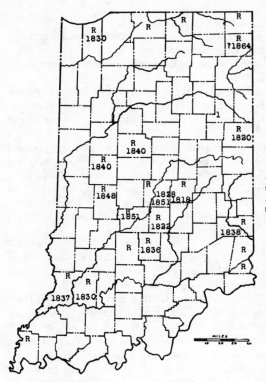

Map 37. Published records and approximate dates when last seen or killed of the Panther, *Felis couguar*, in Indiana; 1, see text.

The published records for the Panther are: Brown (Goodspeed 1884, Hahn 1909), Clinton (Hahn 1909), Daviess (Butler 1895, Hahn 1909, Cory 1912), Dearborn (Anonymous 1885), Dekalb (Anonymous 1914), Elkhart (Weaver 1916), Franklin (Butler 1885, Evermann and Butler 1894, Hahn 1909), Hancock (Binford 1882), Jay (Montgomery 1864), Johnson (Banta 1885, Cline and McHaffie 1874, Harden 1881), Knox (Butler 1895, Hahn 1909, Cory 1912), Marion (Anonymous 1906, Hahn 1909), Montgomery (Parsons 1920), Monroe (Goodspeed 1884), Morgan (Major 1915), Ohio (Anonymous 1885), Porter (Brennan 1923), Posey (Wied 1839-41, 1861-62, Hahn 1909), Putnam (Anonymous 1881), St. Joseph (Anonymous 1880), Steuben (Anonymous 1888), Lower Wabash (Cox 1860), Kankakee Valley (Reed 1920).

LYNXES AND BOB-CATS
Genus **Lynx** Kerr

The genus *Lynx* is found in the northern forested portions of the Old and New Worlds.

In general the genus is similar to *Felis*, but lacks a small upper premolar on each side making the total number of teeth 28 instead of 30. Its general form is heavier, the ears pointed with a more or less conspicuous tuft of hairs; the tail, short. About 16 species or subspecies are known from North America, two of which were once found in Indiana.

CANADA LYNX

Lynx canadensis Kerr

Lynx canadensis KERR. Anim. Kingd. vol. 1: syst. cat. between pp. 32 and 33, and p. 157. Type locality: Eastern Canada.

Lynx canadensis Anonymous 1880, History of Laporte County; Evermann and Butler 1894, Hahn 1909.

The Canada Lynx is found in the colder wooded portions of North America, formerly coming as far south as Pennsylvania, Indiana and northern Illinois. Apparently Indiana was about the southern limit of its range if the published records can be relied on.

The general coloration of the upper parts of the Canada Lynx is a grizzled gray brown and blackish; inside of ears grayish white; tip of the ear tuft and lines down margin of ears black; "ruff" about the throat a mixture of blackish, dark brown and gray; tail brownish with a solid blackish tip; underparts a mixture of grayish and light brown with occasional spots of blackish especially on the inside of the legs. In winter the color is paler than in summer, and the pelage much longer.

Total length 900-1000 mm. (36-39 in.); tail vertebrae, 100-125 mm. (4-5 in.); hind foot, 240-250 mm. (9½-9¾ in.); weight of adults, about 20-30 lbs. Greatest length of skull, about 120 mm. (4¾ in.); greatest width, about 85 mm. (3⅜ in.); Males are somewhat larger than females.

The Canada Lynx lives in dense woods and though mainly terrestrial readily takes to trees and is at home among the branches. From low ones it often pounces on its prey. The large heavily furred hind feet act as sort of snowshoes in winter. Its food consists of any kind of bird or mammal obtainable, but mainly rabbits. It has been known to kill such large game as deer, and the smaller or young domestic animals. It is largely nocturnal in its habits. It is capable of making all the variable, pleasant and unpleasant sounds of the house cat but proportionally louder in accordance with its greater size.

Mating in Indiana probably took place late in winter. The time of gestation is about two months and the young were born in spring. The mother prepares a nest for them much as any cat would do in some hole or hollow log. The number of young varies from one to four. The young are at birth much like ordinary kittens, though some state they are born with open eyes. It is thought they are two or three months old before being weaned and regularly fed food brought by the mother. The mammae are four, one pair inguinal and one pair near by on the abdomen. The young are variously streaked and spotted.

Its fur is valuable and considerably used either in making up whole garments or in trimmings. Its flesh is described as white and tender and in certain of the northwestern parts of its range is highly esteemed. The flesh of the Panther is also highly spoken of as an article of diet by those who have tried it. Seton (1929).

There are no entirely satisfactory records of the occurrence of the Canada Lynx in Indiana, none based on specimens or even measurements of killed animals. Considerable confusion is caused by the popular names bestowed upon the three species of the *Felidae* formerly inhabiting the state. Several terms are used: Panther, Wild-cat, Bobcat, Canada Lynx and Catamount. Panther is self-explanatory; wild-cat undoubtedly refers to the Bay Lynx (discussed below); Canada Lynx may truly mean the Canada Lynx, or be applied to a wrongly identified Bay Lynx. Catamount is an indefinite term and has been used popularly for both the Cougar and the two Lynxes. In county histories and similar works if catamount is used alone I have interpreted as meaning the Bay Lynx. If wild-cats and catamounts are both mentioned I have usually assumed the Wild-cat referred to the Bay Lynx and Catamount to the Cougar. See the account of the wolf hunt in the lower Wabash Valley of about 1830 (page 153). That Catamount was used for the Bay Lynx is clearly shown in Wied's (1862) list of common names for *Felis rufa*.

Evermann and Butler (1894) refer to records of the Canada Lynx in Franklin, Lagrange, Montgomery and Tippecanoe counties in the past. Two species of Lynx are mentioned in the histories of Laporte, St. Joseph and

Map 38. Published records with approximate dates when last seen or killed of the Canada Lynx, *Lynx canadensis*, in Indiana.

The published records for the Canada Lynx are: Dekalb (Anonymous 1914), Franklin (Butler 1885, Evermann and Butler 1894, Hahn 1909), Knox (Hahn 1909), Lagrange (Evermann and Butler 1894, Hahn 1909), Lake (Ball 1894), Laporte (Anonymous 1880), Montgomery (Evermann and Butler 1894, Anonymous 1906, Hahn 1909), Porter (Brennan 1923), Putnam (Anonymous 1881), St. Joseph (Anonymous 1880), Starke (Young 1912), Steuben (Anonymous 1888, Hahn 1909), Tippecanoe (Evermann and Butler 1894, Hahn 1909).

Steuben Counties. In 1912 C. M. Young gives a record of the Canada Lynx in Starke County. Hahn (1909) gives a record by that careful observer Chansler of a Canada Lynx being killed near Bicknell, Knox County in 1832. Brennan (1923) reports one killed in the dunes of Porter County in 1873. The Prince of Wied states very positively that only the Red Lynx was found about New Harmony and that Thomas Say concurred with him. It seems reasonable to assume that some of these numerous reports must truly refer to the Canada Lynx, and that along with the Porcupine, another northern animal, it was at one time a part of Indiana's fauna. The Canada Lynx does not stand civilization and apparently disappeared about the middle of the last century.

BAY LYNX, WILD-CAT, BOBCAT, CATAMOUNT
Lynx rufus (Schreber)

Felis rufa SCHREBER. Säugethiere, Plate 109b, 1777, Type locality: New York.
Felis rufa Wied 1839-41.
Lyncus rufus Plummer 1844.
Lynx rufus Haymond 1870, Evermann and Butler 1894.
Lynx ruffus Hahn 1909.

The Bay Lynx is found in the eastern United States from Maine to southern Georgia and westward as far as North Dakota. It was formerly found throughout Indiana but has been completely exterminated in this state as it has been in much of its former range.

Its general appearance is much like that of *Lynx canadensis* just described, but its feet are smaller, tail longer. The general coloration is brownish and spotted instead of more or less uniform pale grizzled gray. The ear tufts are not nearly so long, nor is the general pelage so long. The color is darkest along the mid-dorsal region. Underparts and inner side of legs whitish, spotted with black. The tail is like the back, above; and the belly, below; except that it is blackish at the tip on the upper surface.

The Bay Lynx is smaller than its more northern and retiring relative. The usual measurements given are: total length, 34-39 inches (850-1000 mm.); tail vertebrae, $5\frac{1}{2}$-7 in. (135-175 mm.); hind foot, $6\frac{1}{2}$-7 in. (165-175mm.); weight about, 15-25 lbs. (7-11 kgs.). Males are larger than females.

A very detailed description of a small female Bay Lynx from the forests of Indiana along the Wabash is given by the Prince of Wied (1862). He records these measurements: Total length to end of hairs on tail, 21 in.; tail, 4-7/12 in.; length of pencil of hairs on tips of ears 3-4 twelfths inch, hind foot 5-8/12 inch, weight 15 lbs. A young female specimen estimated at 10 months old had a total length of 21-11/12 inch. An old male is given the length of three feet.

The Bay Lynx does not differ in its food and habits from the Canada Lynx. It adapts itself to changing conditions better and is not so partial to dense timber. It can survive in partially cleared land and thickets. Owing to its smaller size it probably does not often attack such large prey as sheep or deer as the other species, but confines its diet to mice, squirrels, chipmunks and rabbits as well as ground dwelling birds. The Prince of Wied (1861-62) describes it as catching young domestic pigs running about the forest. Like the other two cats it is strictly carnivorous and never eats vegetable material of any kind.

There are numerous authentic records of the Bay Lynx throughout Indiana in former days, all of which are indicated on the accompanying map.

Fig. 59. Photograph courtesy N. Y. Zool. Soc. Bay Lynx, Wild Cat, or Bobcat, *Lynx rufus*, formerly common in Indiana.

The Prince of Wied found them fairly common about New Harmony in the winter of 1832-33. The two he collected were hunted with dogs, treed and shot. He says they are also taken in traps.

The Noblesville list of 1859 (Anonymous 1906) mentions 48 wild cat skins purchased.

Hahn (1909) gives some interesting relatively recent records:

Wheatland [Knox county] January 10, 1900; adult and two young killed near Montour's Pond in Knox County in 1894 (Chansler).

Mrs. Annie Anderson, of Oxford, relates the following story concerning the occurrence of lynxes in Benton County: "In August, 1870, when I was about ten years old, my brother and I were gathering berries on the banks of Pine Creek, about four miles south of Oxford, when I spied in some hazel brush what I thought to be a maltese cat. I called to the kitty and started to catch it, when my brother stopped me, saying he did not like the looks of its eyes. It was standing still, staring at us, evidently as much surprised as we were. In the following autumn some hunters killed a lynx in the same place, and it proved to be my maltese kitty or one like it. I have not heard of any since until about three years ago (1905) some boys killed a bobcat about a mile from the same place.

Mr. Theo. F. Upson states that he killed a bobcat near Lima, Lagrange County, in the fall of 1857, and knows of none in that vicinity since. Robert S. White, Jr., killed a 'catamount' on Pigeon Creek, Warrick County, in the winter of 1906. This is the latest record that I have been able to obtain. (Hahn 1909).

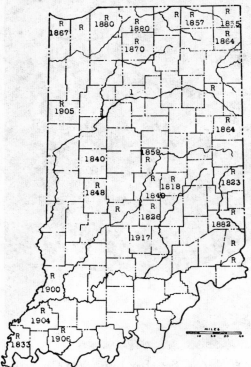

Map 39. Published records and dates of observation of the Bay Lynx, *Lynx rufus*, in Indiana; 1, mounted specimen in a pool room at Royal Center said to have been killed in vicinity about 50 years ago.

The published records for the Wild-cat are: Benton (Hahn 1909, Evermann and Clark 1911, 1920), Dearborn (Anonymous 1885), Dekalb (Anonymous 1914), Elkhart (Weaver 1916), Franklin (Haymond 1870, Langdon 1881, Quick and Langdon 1882, Butler 1885, Evermann and Butler 1894, Hahn 1909, Anonymous 1906), Gibson (Anonymous 1904), Hamilton (Anonymous 1906), Hancock (Binford 1882), Jay (Montgomery 1864), Johnson (Cline and McHaffie 1874, Harden 1881), Knox (Butler 1895, Hahn 1909), Lagrange (Rerick 1882, Hahn 1909), Lake (Dinwiddie 1884, Ball 1894, Hahn 1909, Brennan 1923), Laporte (Anonymous 1880, Brennan 1923), Marion (Anonymous 1906), Marshall (Evermann and Clark 1911, 1920), Montgomery (Parsons 1920), Morgan (Major 1915), Ohio (Anonymous 1885), Porter (Brennan 1923), Posey (Wied 1939-41, 1861-62, Hahn 1909), Putnam (Anonymous 1881), St. Joseph (Anonymous 1880, Engels 1933), Steuben (Anonymous 1888), Warrick (Hahn 1909), Wayne (Plummer 1844, Young 1872, Hahn 1909), Wells (Butler 1895), Kankakee Valley (Reed 1920, Werich 1920), Lower Wabash Valley (Cox 1860).

In a pool room, Royal Center, Cass County is a poorly mounted and much faded specimen of a Bay Lynx. It is said to have been killed in the vicinity about 50 years ago.

The National Union of Nov. 16, 1867, page 3, column 1, tells of a Lynx shot in South Bend. Mr. Frank B. Wade of the Shortridge High school, Indianapolis, says that during the World War he spent a summer in Brown County, near Trevlac, and on two occasions saw a Bay Lynx and one of the kittens.

LEMURS, MONKEYS, APES AND MEN, ORDER PRIMATES

The Primates are of world-wide distribution, but they reach their greatest development in the tropical portions of the New and Old Worlds, especially the latter.

It is difficult to define the order zoologically. It is a primitive generalized group and has certain affinities with the order Insectivora. All members possess two sets of teeth, milk and permanent, and the usual four classes of teeth, incisors, canines, premolars and molars are present. The incisors are generally $\frac{2-2}{2-2}$, and the molars $\frac{3-3}{3-3}$. The molars and premolars are adapted for grinding and crushing food. The molars are more complex than the premolars, and usually possess four main tubercles. The orbit is surrounded by a ring of bone so that the orbital and temporal cavities are distinct from each other. They have two pairs of well developed limbs, radius and ulna always separated; a clavicle always present. Usually there are five digits on the hands and feet. The first digit of the hind foot (except in Man) is opposable to other four, and the same is more or less true of the front foot or hand unless in some rare instance the thumb is wanting. They are mainly arboreal in habit though some members, including Man are terrestrial. The alimentary tract is relatively simple, and the diet largely fruits, or insects, though some, including Man, are omnivorous.

The order is divided into four suborders: Lemuroidea, Chiromyoidea, Tarsioidea, and Pithecoidea, the latter including the monkeys, apes and man. The order as a whole contains between 50 and 60 well recognized genera, divided into many families and subfamilies. Only one genus, *Homo*, occurs in America north of Mexico, and is found throughout the entire state of Indiana.

MEN
Family Hominidae

The family Hominidae is distinguished by having the anterior limbs shorter than the posterior; the first toe of the posterior extremity not opposable to the others; no external tail, no ischial tuberosities; sternum broad and short, dental formula:

$$i \frac{2-2}{2-2}, \ c \frac{1-1}{1-1}, \ pm \frac{2-2}{2-2}, \ m \frac{3-3}{3-3}, = 32.$$

Upper canines in contact with the incisors; canines in the males not more conspicuous than those in the females; hind feet completely plantigrade and the pelvis and hind limbs adapted to bipedal locomotion; leaving the hands with the completely opposable thumb entirely free as an organ of prehension; cranial cavity and brain enormously developed. It contains but a single genus, *Homo*, of world-wide distribution.

MEN
Genus **Homo** Linnaeus

The chief characters of this genus are the same as those of the family Hominidae. The genus has never been adequately studied from the taxinomic standpoint. One species is usually recognized and a few subspecies have been named. Three of these named forms of Man occur or have occurred in Indiana. They are briefly mentioned below in the order of their appearance in the state.

AMERICAN INDIAN
Homo sapiens americanus Linnaeus

[*Homo sapiens*] *americanus* LINNAEUS. Syst. Nat., ed. 10, vol. 1, p. 20, 1758. Type locality: Eastern North America.

The distinguishing characteristics of the American Indian are too well known to require comment. Indians were widely distributed in a wild state everywhere in Indiana The conquering of the country by the Caucasians, *Homo sapiens sapiens* caused a rapid extermination and deportation of the original inhabitants. The dealings and the warfare between these two subspecies of *Homo sapiens* are matters of history, discussed in general, special, and local historical works. They also appear in formal documents or treaties in governmental archives. The balance of nature was undisturbed by the American Indian with his primitive culture and he was just one of the other mammals. The changed aspect of nature only came with the advent of the Caucasian.

WHITE MAN
Homo sapiens sapiens Linnaeus

[*Homo*] *sapiens* LINNAEUS, Syst. Nat. ed. 10, vol. 1: p. 20, 1758. Type locality: Upsala, Sweden.

The occupancy of Indiana by the White Man is subject matter for the historian and not for the zoologist. Suffice it to say that the first White Men entered the state from the north. Then quickly followed a complete occupancy of the southern part of the state and a gradual spreading of the White Man over the whole of Indiana. This invasion in a few years completely displaced the aborigenes, *Homo sapiens americanus*, which is as extinct in a wild condition in the state of Indiana as is the bear and panther. From the published accounts of the travels of the early arrivals of *Homo sapiens sapiens* many facts concerning the former occurrence and distribution of the larger mammals in Indiana have been learned.

COLORED MAN
Homo sapiens afer Linnaeus

[*Homo sapiens*] *afer* LINNAEUS. Syst. Nat. ed. 10, vol. 1, p. 22, 1758. Type locality: Africa.

This subspecies of man was extensively introduced into North America shortly after the discovery of that continent by *Homo sapiens sapiens*, particularly into the southern portions. It has gradually spread northward and there is not a county in Indiana where *Homo sapiens afer* has not become firmly established, but it is nowhere as abundant as *Homo sapiens sapiens*.

RODENTS OR GNAWING MAMMALS, ORDER RODENTIA

Rodents are of world-wide occurrence. They were originally absent from New Zealand and the Antarctic, and some pelagic islands, but through unintentional introduction they are now as widespread as Man himself.

The order *Rodentia* may be defined as follows: Terrestrial and fossorial (occasionally arboreal or semi-aquatic) placental mammals with both brain and placentation generalized in type; feet unquiculate; elbow joint always permitting free rotary motion of forearm; fibula never articulating with calcaneum; masseter muscle highly specialized, divided into three or more distinct portions having slightly different functions; cecum without spiral fold; dental formula not known to exceed

$$i \frac{1-1}{1-1}, \ c \frac{0-0}{0-0}, \ pm \frac{2-2}{1-1}, \ m \frac{3-3}{3-3}, = 22$$

permanent teeth; incisors scalpriform [chisel-like], growing from persistent pulp, the enamel of the upper tooth not extending to posterior surface; distance between mandibular and maxillary toothrows approximately equal, both pairs of rows capable of partial opposition at the same time, the primary motion of the lower jaw in mastication longitudinal or oblique. (Miller and Gidley, 1918).

To which may be added the fibula and tibia are always distinct bones, and the testes are abdominal and only descend periodically at the breeding season into a temporary sessile scrotum; a baculum or os penis is usually present.

The order contains such well known forms as the Beaver, Woodchuck, Squirrel, Gopher, Rat and Mouse. The prominent chisel-like incisors, absence of canines and the wide diastema between incisors and cheek teeth serve to distinguish its members at a glance. They are relatively small mammals, though the extinct *Castoroides* attained the size of a bear. In structure and habits they show great variety and in number of genera and species they far surpass all other groups of mammals. About thirty families are recognized among living rodents, seven of which occur or have occurred in Indiana in recent times, and another in Pleistocene times.

KEY TO FAMILIES, GENERA, AND SPECIES OF RODENTS FOUND IN INDIANA

Body more or less covered with sharp pointed quills, total length of adult about 2 feet, exterminated in Indiana_____ERETHIZONTIDAE, *Erethizon dorsatum* 281

Body covered with ordinary soft hairs or fur.
  Tail broad and flat, scaly, not pointed, total length of adult about 3 feet, exterminated in Indiana_____CASTORIDAE, *Castor canadensis* 220

  Tail not broad and flat, variable, usually rounded and tapering to a point, sometimes laterally flattened, almost naked or covered with long hairs, size usually small, (in *Marmota* and *Fiber* reaching 2 feet)

  Cheek teeth $\frac{5-5}{4-4}$, or $\frac{4-4}{4-4}$, tail rather thickly haired or even bushy,
_____SCIURIDAE 171

Fore and hind limbs connected by a loose fold of skin, adapted for sailing through air, arboreal_____*Glaucomys volans* 211

Fore and hind limbs not connected by a loose fold of skin, arboreal or terrestrial,

Total length about 2 feet of which the tail is less than one quarter, terrestrial _____*Marmota monax* 172

Total length not exceeding 2 feet of which the tail is much more than one quarter, terrestrial or arboreal.

Cheek teeth $\frac{4-4}{4-4}$, back with two pale stripes and three blackish ones, mainly terrestrial _____*Tamias striatus* 187

Cheek teeth $\frac{5-5}{4-4}$ or $\frac{4-4}{4-4}$, coloration variable, arboreal or terrestrial.

Strictly terrestrial, never found in woods or trees, conspicuous internal cheek pouches, hibernate in winter_____*Citellus* 178

Back conspicuously marked with thirteen lines or rows of spots, _____*Citellus tridecemlineatus* 179

General coloration grayish, _____*Citellus franklinii* 182

Arboreal, no conspicuous internal cheek pouches, tail decidedly bushy, do not hibernate, _____*Sciurus* 194

Size large, general coloration clear grayish to blackish,_____ _____ *Sciurus carolinensis* 199

Size large, general coloration reddish gray, ____*Sciurus rufiventer* 205

Size medium, general coloration reddish brown above, whitish beneath, _____*Sciurus hudsonicus* 195

Cheek teeth $\frac{4-4}{3-3}$ or $\frac{4-4}{4-4}$; tail scantily haired or scaly.

Hind feet long and kangaroo-like, tail very much longer than head and body, _____ZAPODIDAE, *Zapus hudsonius* 277

Hind feet normal, front feet with long heavy claws, tail much shorter than head and body, external cheek pouches present,_____ _____GEOMYIDAE, *Geomys illinoensis* 216

Cheek teeth $\frac{3-3}{3-3}$, _____MUROIDAE 231

Upper cheek teeth with tubercles in three longitudinal rows, introduced forms, _____MURIDAE 270

Size small, mice, _____*Mus musculus* 274

Size large, rats _____*Rattus* 270

Head and body longer than tail, upper parts brown, underparts dark grayish, _____*Rattus norvegicus* 271

Head and body shorter than tail, upper parts blackish, underparts yellowish white, _____*Rattus rattus* 272

Upper cheek teeth with tubercles arranged in two longitudinal rows or of prismatic triangles, _____CRICETIDAE 231

Upper cheek teeth with tubercles arranged in two longitudinal rows. Upper incisors with a longitudinal groove. _____ _____*Reithrodontomys humulis merriami* 231

Upper incisors, without a longitudinal groove.

A ridge or bead on upper surface of skull, between eye sockets,
   size of small rat, ----------------------_Oryzomys palustris_ 241
No ridge or bead on upper surface of skull, between eye sock-
      ets, mouse-like, -------------------------_Peromyscus_ 233
   Size larger, tail relatively longer, hind foot 22 mm., tail not
      sharply bicolor, upper parts lighter, -------------------
      -------------------_Peromyscus leucopus noveboracensis_ 238
   Size smaller, tail relatively shorter, hind foot 19 mm., tail
      sharply bicolor, upper parts darker,-------------------
      ------------------------_Peromyscus maniculatus bairdii_ 236
Upper cheek teeth with the enamel in prismatic triangles often grow-
   ing from persistent pulp.
   Total length more than twelve inches, tail relatively long.
      Tail rounded, covered with short hairs, terrestrial,------------
      ---------------------------------------_Neotoma pennsylvanica_ 243
      Tail laterally compressed, mostly naked, semi-aquatic,-----------
      --_Ondatra zibethica_ 264
   Total length less than twelve inches, tail relatively short.
      Upper incisors with distinct groove near outer edge,-----------
      ---_Synaptomys stonei_ 251
      Upper incisors without groove.
         Skull flat, wide, mammae four inguinal, general form modified
            for underground life, -------------_Pitymys pinetorum_, p. 259
         Skull rather high and narrow, mammae four inguinal, and two
            or more pectoral, general form not modified for under-
            ground life, ----------------------------------_Microtus_ 254
         Tubercles on sole of hind foot six, mammae eight, crown of
            m3 with five or more irregular loops, ---------------
            --------------------------- _Microtus pennsylvanicus_ 254
         Tubercles on sole of hind foot five, mammae six, crown of
            m3 with four irregular loops, ----_Microtus ochrogaster_ 257

SQUIRREL-LIKE RODENTS OR RODENTS DERIVED FROM SQUIRREL-LIKE ANCESTORS

Superfamily **Sciuroidae** Miller and Gidley (1918)

This superfamily contains four living families, three of which have representatives in Indiana; the _Sciuridae_ or true Squirrels, the _Geomyidae_ or
Pocket Gophers, and the _Castoridae_ or Beavers. The first two of these families have the teeth developed upon a three-cusped basis, and the third one
on a four-cusped basis. There are many other technical anatomical differences
and the more ambitious student is referred to the original works. The extinct
Castoroididae are a member of this superfamily.

SQUIRRELS, MARMOTS, SPERMOPHILES AND ALLIES
Family **Sciuridae**

The family _Sciuridae_ occurs in the eastern and western hemispheres, except
at the extreme north and south. It is not found on Madagascar, New Guinea,
Australia, New Zealand, or the Pacific Islands.

The form is slender or robust, in accordance with arboreal or terrestrial
habits; tail, densely long haired; skull variable, postorbital processes present;
upper incisor with root in front of anterior cheek teeth; lower incisor with

root not extending conspicuously into ascending portion of ramus; molars rooted, tubercular and transversely ridged, premolars, $\dfrac{2\text{-}2}{1\text{-}1}$ or $\dfrac{1\text{-}1}{1\text{-}1}$.

This is a widely distributed and abundantly represented group of rodents. It contains about 45 genera, about a dozen of which are found in North America, and five in Indiana: *Marmota, Citellus, Tamias, Sciurus* and *Glaucomys*.

The male reproductive tract of the five genera just mentioned has recently been made the careful study of Mossman, Lawlah and Bradley, to whose paper the student interested in anatomy is referred. In one species, *hudson-icus*, which I have included in the genus *Sciurus*, Mossman and his coworkers have found the male reproductive tract so different from all the other *Sciuridae* that they unhesitatingly regard it as generically distinct. A similar course was taken in 1923 by Pocock, who goes so far as to place it in a distinct subfamily, *Tamiasciurinae*.

WOODCHUCKS, GROUND-HOGS OR MARMOTS
Genus **Marmota** Blumenbach

The genus *Marmota* is found in the Northern Hemisphere from the Alps eastward through Asia and North America to the Atlantic seaboard.

It is the largest of the *Sciuridae*, of Badger-like form. The skull is broad and depressed, with conspicuous postorbital processes. The first premolar is nearly as large as the second. Dental formula:

$$i\,\dfrac{1\text{-}1}{1\text{-}1},\ c\,\dfrac{0\text{-}0}{0\text{-}0},\ pm\,\dfrac{2\text{-}2}{1\text{-}1},\ m\,\dfrac{3\text{-}3}{3\text{-}3},=22.$$

The tail is short, not more than one quarter the total length of the animal. Front feet with four well developed toes and a rudimentary thumb; hind feet with five toes. Nearly thirty species or subspecies are recognized in North America, one of which is found throughout the entire state of Indiana.

SOUTHERN WOODCHUCK OR GROUND-HOG
Marmota monax (Linnaeus)

[*Mus*] *monax* LINNAEUS. Syst. Nat., ed. 10, vol. 1, p. 60, 1758. Type locality: Maryland.
Arctomys pruinosus Wied 1839-41.
Arctomys monax Plummer 1844, Wied 1861-62, Evermann and Butler 1894.
Marmota monax Hahn 1909, A. H. Howell 1915.

The Southern Woodchuck occupies the middle eastern United States from Maryland and Pennsylvania, south to northern South Carolina, Georgia and Alabama, west to Iowa, eastern Kansas and Arkansas.

General coloration grayish brown above, underfur blackish brown at base, succeeded by neutral gray; long hairs blackish brown, broadly tipped with white or buffy white; feet and legs blackish brown sparingly grizzled with buffy white; tail dark brown. Underparts similar to upperparts but less abundantly haired. Mammae five pairs extending from inguinal region to the axillary.

It is a large heavy animal with a total length of 550 to 625 mm. (22-25 inches), tail vertebrae 135 to 155 mm. (5¼-6¼ inches), hind foot about 87 mm. (3½ inches); weight of adults 9 to 10 lbs. (4-4.5 kgs.). Greatest length of skull about 95 to 100 mm., greatest width 60 to 65 mm.

The Woodchuck's native habitat was originally the forest but with clear-

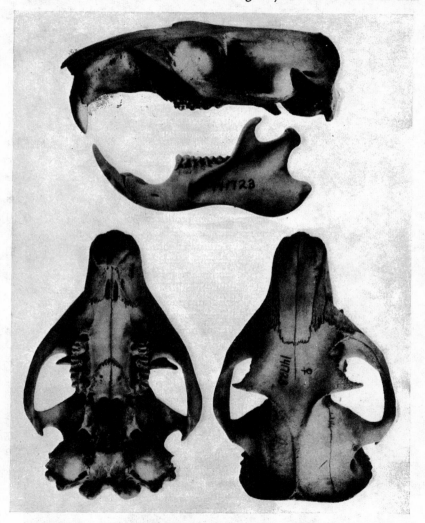

Fig. 60. Photographs courtesy U. S. Nat. Mus. Lateral, palatal and dorsal views of skull of Woodchuck or Ground-hog, *Marmota monax*, about 2/3 natural size. Cat. No. 141,723, U. S. Nat. Mus., Roselawn, Newton County, Aug. 6, 1905, W. L. Hahn.

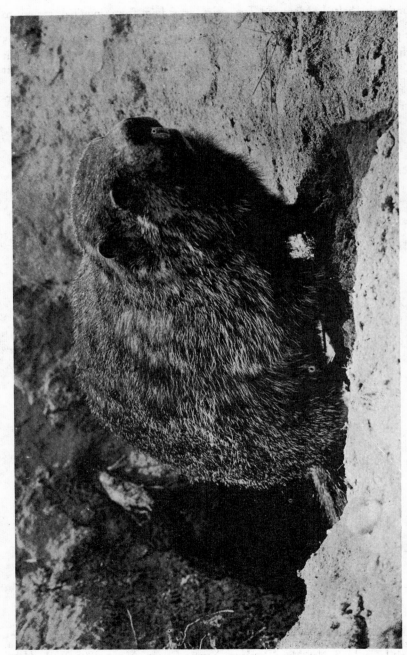

Fig. 61. Woodchuck or Ground-hog, *Marmota monax*, photograph by J. G. Allen, West Lafayette.

ing of the forests, it readily takes to fields, meadows and wasteland and particularly woodland edges. It is one of the commonest large mammals of Indiana and its burrows are seen everywhere. The animal itself, considering its abundance, is not so frequently seen, even though its is largely diurnal in its habits.

It is not afraid of water and is a good swimmer like most squirrels. On this point Col. Wirt Robinson writes (Journ. Mamm. vol. 4, p. 256. 1923):

First as to aquatic habits of the Woodchuck. In front of my home in Nelson County, Virginia, the James River is over 100 yards wide, and, at that particular spot, the river bottom is all on the north side, the south side being a precipitous, rocky bluff. In this bluff there are a number of woodchucks, but the vegetation, laurel thickets and large ferns, does not furnish them with a food supply comparable to that on the cultivated land on the opposite side. They, therefore, frequently swim across, feast on corn, clover, melons, etc., and then swim back. I have several times seen them do this and on June 18, 1899, I overtook one with a boat and captured it in the middle of the river.

Among the best descriptions of Woodchuck burrows are those by W. H. Fisher of Cincinnati, published in the Journal of the Cincinnati Society of Natural History 1893. Fisher investigated nine burrows. The longest (See figure 62) gives a total length, including all its galleries, of 47 feet, 11½ inches. The shortest gives total length of only 6 feet, 8¼ inches. The deepest point reached by any, was 49 inches down. The burrows at the entrance were usually about one foot by six inches, but always they speedily narrowed to a diameter of six or seven by four or five inches. Most had two, some three, entrances; a few had but one. Most had indications of at least one earth pile at the door; a few had no earth pile, though there were signs of its former existence in the increased vegetation. One only had earth piles at both of its two doorways. Some had the entrance concealed under shrubs or in bushes, in each case this seemed to be the original burrow by way of which all the earth had been carried out.

These mounds in front of entrance evidently used as posts of observation, may be four feet in diameter, and as high as nine inches.

Most of the burrows have one enlarged nesting chamber more or less lined.

The time of mating is early spring after awakening from the winter sleep. The young are born about the end of April. The period of gestation is about four weeks. They vary from two to eight in number, but are usually about four. They are blind, naked and helpless at birth. The average birth weight is 26.5 grams (Hamilton 1934). At a month their eyes are open, and about that time they may come forth from the home burrow, and start to feed for themselves shortly after. By late summer they are about full grown and leave their birthplace to make burrows and homes for themselves.

During the active season rectal temperatures of the woodchuck range from 37.4° C. to 40° C., the lower being the human normal. During the lethargic state the rectal temperatures range from 8° to 17° C. (Hamilton 1934).

The Woodchuck's food consists mainly of fresh green plants, grasses,

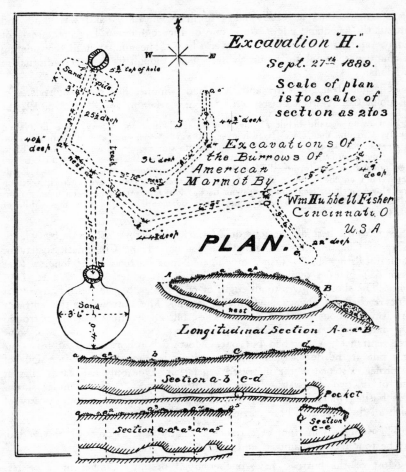

Fig. 62. Plan of a complicated burrow of Woodchuck, *Marmota monax*. After Wm. Hubbel Fisher, of Cincinnati, Ohio, Sept. 1889, Journal of the Cincinnati Society of Natural History, vol. 16.

clover, alfalfa, etc. Hahn (1907) reports one which he secured from a sassafras bush whose stomach was filled with sassafras leaves. It is not unusual for Woodchucks to climb small trees, but it is doubtful if they often do so for the sake of obtaining food. They also visit gardens for miscellaneous green vegetables and fruits. Probably they eat a bit of meat when opportunity presents.

All summer long the Woodchuck eats and eats, and by early autumn becomes very fat and before the weather is really cold, he retires to his den for the winter hibernation. Like most hibernating mammals, he rolls himself up into a large furry ball in his burrow and his physiological activities are all slowed down. He reappears in late winter while the weather is colder than when he went to bed. Popular folk-lore has it that he reappears on Candlemas Day, February 2. If the day is clear and the sun casts his shadow on the snow, he retires to his burrow for another six weeks' sleep. If the day is cloudy and no shadow is seen, it prognosticates an early spring and he remains abroad. Some have ascribed this weather forecasting legend of the Ground-hog to Negro folk-lore and others probably more correctly have connected it with a simliar German folk-lore legend in which the Badger is the actor. When the Germans first came to the eastern United States they found no Badgers, but in their place this Badger-like Ground-Squirrel and the transfer was easily made. That the prognosticative value of a clear or cloudy day on Ground-hog Day, as to a continuation of winter or an early spring, is without any scientific foundation is rather easily proved, in spite of the efforts of well meaning persons to make out a good case for the Ground-hog. The range of the Ground-hog is such that when it is storming in Indiana on February 1, the chances are it will be clear on February 2, the mystic day, and the storm or cloudy weather of the day before has moved eastward, as weather always does, and is about Philadelphia on February 2. Therefore, half the Ground-hogs in the range of the species will proclaim an early spring and the other half a continuance of six weeks more of winter. At any rate it is a good story and gives the newspapers something to write about on February 2, and certainly the Ground-hog, as a mere mammal, has appeared in more cartoons than any other except man himself and Elephant and Donkey.

The Ground-hog is a humble animal and without popularity except on one day of the year. His skin is tough and his fur of good quality, but not popular, at least that of the native species. Neither is the Ground-hog popular as an article of diet, though he is just a big fat squirrel that lives on the ground, and is meticulous in his choice of food and clean in all his habits. Only on one occasion have I heard of his being trapped for food and on that occasion a Badger was caught, at Claypool, Indiana.

Among the common names of the Woodchuck are the French Canadian, le Siffleur (the whistler), the German Murmeltier (which may come from murmeln to murmur, and Tier animal, or may be a corruption of the old Latin Mus montanus, the mountain rat) and Whistle-pig. Some of his western cousins are regularly called Whistlers. All these are based on his no mean vocal efforts, which consist of a trilling whistle as he sits at his den and a chuckling sort of warble of less intensity. My personal experience is that he is a rather quiet animal, at least in comparison with western relatives.

The Woodchuck seems to have more trouble with his front teeth than any other rodent. The incisors, as in all rodents, keep on growing from their persistent root pulps throughout his life. Any malocclusion of these teeth, or serious damage to one of them, causes them to develop into bizarre circles and spirals because they are not worn down by an opposing tooth. Many such freak skulls are picked up and considered great curiosities by the initiated so that even scientfic literature is filled with accounts of them.

Map 40. Published records, recent observations and specimens in collections of the Woodchuck or Ground-hog, *Marmota monax*, in Indiana.

Although the Woodchuck is one of the commonest of Indiana mammals and is probably found in suitable situations in every county, the published records are comparatively few. They are as follows: Carroll (Evermann and Butler 1894), Franklin (Haymond 1870, Quick and Langdon 1882, Evermann and Butler 1894), Jay (Montgomery 1864), Lagrange (Evermann and Butler 1894), Lake (Dinwiddie 1884, Blatchley 1898, Brennan 1923), Laporte (Brennan 1923), Lawrence (Hahn 1908), Marion (A. H. Howell 1915), Marshall (Evermann and Clark 1911, 1920, A. H. Howell 1915), Monroe (Evermann and Butler 1894, Banta 1907, McAtee 1907), Morgan (Major 1915), Newton (Hahn 1907, A. H. Howell 1915), Porter (Hahn 1907, Brennan 1923, Lyon 1923), Posey (Wied 1839-41, 1861-62, A. H. Howell 1910), Putnam (Anonymous 1881), Randolph (Cox 1894, Evermann and Butler 1894), St. Joseph (Anonymous 1880, Engels 1933), Vigo (Evermann and Butler 1894), Wabash (Evermann and Butler 1894), Wayne (Plummer 1844), Kankakee Valley (Reed 1920), throughout the state (Hahn 1909).

Ground-Squirrels
Genus **Citellus** Oken

The genus *Citellus* is found from Hungary eastward through Asia and North America to Indiana, Ohio, and southern Michigan.

The genus is strictly terrestrial, its members are of medium size, have a moderately bushy tail; internal cheek pouches are present; skull rather massive in comparison with that of the tree squirrels, the brain-case being much less convex above; molar teeth with the cross ridges high. Dental formula:

$$i \frac{1-1}{1-1}, \ c \frac{0-0}{0-0}, \ pm \frac{2-2}{1-1}, \ m \frac{3-3}{3-3}, = 22.$$

About thirty specific forms are recognized in North America and about eight in the Old World; two species occur in northwestern Indiana which before the clearing of the forests used to be the eastern limit of its range.

THIRTEEN-LINED GROUND-SQUIRREL, THIRTEEN-LINED GOPHER, STRIPED GROUND-SQUIRREL, STRIPED GOPHER
Citellus tridecemlineatus (Mitchill)

Sciurus tridecem-lineatus MITCHILL. Med. Repos., n.s. vol. 6, p. 248, 1821.
    Type locality: Central Minnesota.
Spermophilus tridecemlineatus Bailey 1893, Evermann and Butler 1894.
Citellus tridecemlineatus Hahn 1909.

    The Striped Ground-Squirrel ranges from southern Michigan and northern Ohio southwestardly into Texas, westwardly to Utah and northwest-

Fig. 63. Photograph, copyright by H. H. Pittman. Thirteen-lined Spermophile or Striped Gopher, *Citellus tridecemlineatus.*

wardly into Alberta, Canada. In this area eight subspecies have been described; the typical form occurs in the eastern part of its distribution.

The Thirteen-Striped Ground-Squirrel is easily distinguished from any other mammal, by the thirteen stripes which mark its back. General color above, dark brownish with seven long stripes of dull yellowish white between which are six rows of spots, irregularly shaped, and of essentially the same color as the seven solid light stripes. The stripes are much broken up on the top of the head and on the flanks. Underparts dull buffy, lighter on the chin. Tail light brownish with a fringe of coarse blackish hairs bearing yellowish white tips.

Total length 250 to 280 mm.. (10 to 11 in.); tail vertebrae, 90 to 100 mm. (3½ to 3⅞ in.); hind foot 33 to 40 mm. (1¼ to 1½ in.) greatest length of skull about 44 mm., greatest width about 24 mm. Weight from about 135 grams at the end of June to about 250 in September. (Wade 1930). Males larger than females.

Its natural habitat was the prairie and great plains region of central North America. With the clearing off of forests and the making of artificial fields and meadows, the Thirteen-lined Ground-Squirrel has extended its range to them. Undoubtedly in primitive times it was confined to the native prairie region of Indiana, but with the opening up of the country it has extended its distribution to take in the upper third of the state. It appears to like quiet fields, pastures and roadsides. Constant cultivation of the soil with the plow apparently interferes with its home life and normal activities. Every motorist in northern Indiana has seen it dart across the road to disappear in the grass of the opposite side. It is frequently found in golf courses. It is common on the campus of the University of Notre Dame.

The Striped Ground-Squirrel is strictly diurnal. When not feeding, it spends most of its time in subterranean burrows of its own digging. These are burrows about two inches in diameter and vary in length from two feet or less up to twenty feet, and in depth from four to 46 inches. Of a large number of burrows measured by Johnson (1917) two-thirds were four feet or less in length and thirteen inches or less in depth, only fourteen percent were longer than six feet or deeper than seventeen inches. Usually the burrows go straight down for two or three inches and then turn obliquely. They are never straight for any great distance. Usually a burrow has but one opening and usually all the excavated dirt is scattered from the opening which appears as a small inconspicuous hole in the sod, or partly obscured by a tuft of grass or weed. Many of the shorter and less deeply placed burrows are only for temporary use. In permanent hibernating and breeding burrows, at extremities or on side arms, the animal builds a nest of dry grass in excavated places ranging from four to eight inches in diameter. Nests seem to be placed in such a position that they are higher than the rest of the burrow so as to secure adequate drainage. The nests also serve as storehouses and frequently contain large quantities of stored grain or other seeds, carried in by means of the internal cheek pouches. When this food is eaten is unknown; certainly it is not used during the long winter sleep.

These Ground-Squirrels are rather omnivorous in diet. About half of the material in the stomachs examined by various observers consisted of animal matter, largely grasshoppers, cutworms, wireworms, etc., the other half or perhaps slightly more, consisted of grains and other seeds, roots, bark, and just plain herbage. They have even been known to kill young chickens and eat mice and birds. Examination of the cheek pouches has shown nothing but the presence of seeds of wild grasses and other plants, and oats and wheat, material which will keep and not rot when placed in storage nests.

The mating season is unusually brief and occurs shortly after the animals awake from their winter sleep and emerge from their winter nests in April. The young are usually born shortly before June in a very immature condition. The period of gestation is about one month. They have no hair until they are twenty days old and their eyes are closed until they are thirty days old. By July they come out of their birth burrows and shortly after begin shifting for themselves. By September they are fully grown and putting on fat, getting ready for their long winter sleep. But one brood is produced during a year. The number of young at a birth is from five to thirteen, averaging between eight and nine.

The hibernation of the Thirteen-lined Ground-Squirrel and that of its close relative, Franklin's Ground-Squirrel, is one of the most complete of any mammal and one of the best studied. When the animals become fat in late September and almost double their spring body weight, they become torpid and shortly after take to their deeper nests and curl themselves up into a ball, solidly plugging up the entrance to the burrows to keep out enemies and the unfriendly winter weather. The arched back is uppermost and the nose is placed under the body and touches the pelvic region. All the bodily functions are reduced to a minimum and the body temperature almost reaches that of the world about it. Rectal temperatures are reported as somewhat higher than cheek pouch temperatures (Wade 1930). The following summary of the hibernating state is quoted from Johnson (1928):

1. A torpid *Citellus tridecemlinatus* is rolled up, somewhat stiffly and is cold to the touch.

2. As contrasted with a rate of about 100 to more than 200 respirations a minute in active ground-squirrels the respiration rate in deeply torpid animals at external temperatures below 10° C may average from one-half to four a minute normally. Some records were made of no respiration for five minutes in animals long in hibernation.

3. Heart beats in animals awake and active usually ranged from 200 to 350 a minute. In forty-two torpid animals with body temperatures below 10° C the average was 17.4 beats a minute, and the lowest was five beats a minute.

4. Ground-Squirrels not in hibernation may have temperatures ranging from 30° to about 41° but a range of 35° to 39° is more common in a warm room, and a range of from 32° to 36° C is more prevalent in a cold room. High room temperatures produced a body temperature of 42.3° C. The minimum body temperature in hibernation appears to be between 0° and 2° C. The body temperature in deep hibernation is usually within 3° C of surrounding temperature.

5. Loss of weight in ground-squirrels may approach 40 percent in a winter of hibernation. The daily loss appears to be about 0.30 percent in nature and about 0.40 or 0.50 percent in the refrigerator.

Map 41. Published records, recent observations and specimens in collections of the Thirteen-lined Ground-Squirrel, *Citellus tridecemlineatus*, in Indiana.

The published records of the Thirteen-lined Ground-Squirrel are: Benton (Evermann and Butler 1894, Hahn 1909), Carroll (Evermann and Butler 1894, Evermann and Clark 1911, Hahn 1909), Kosciusko (Hahn 1909), Lagrange (Evermann and Butler 1894, Hahn 1909), Lake (Dinwiddie 1884, Blatchley 1898, Hahn 1909), Laporte (Hahn 1909), Marshall (Evermann and Clark 1911, 1920), Newton (Evermann and Butler 1894, Butler 1895, Hahn 1909), Porter (Blatchley 1898, Hahn 1907, 1909, Lyon 1923), St. Joseph (Anonymous 1880, Hahn 1909, Engels 1933), Tippecanoe (Evermann and Butler 1894, Butler 1895, Hahn 1909), Vigo (Evermann and Butler 1894, Hahn 1909, Evermann and Clark 1911), White (Evermann and Butler 1894, Hahn 1909), north and west of Wabash River (Bailey 1893), northern Indiana (Kennicott 1857).

FRANKLIN'S GROUND-SQUIRREL, FRANKLIN'S GOPHER, PRAIRIE SQUIRREL, GRAY GOPHER

Citellus franklinii (Sabine)

Arctomys franklinii SABINE. Trans. Linn. Soc., vol. 13, p. 587, 1822. Type locality: Vicinity of Carlton House, Saskatchewan, Canada.
Spermophilus franklini Bailey 1893, Evermann and Butler 1894.
Citellus franklinii Hahn 1909, Lyon 1932.

Franklin's Ground-Squirrel has a narrow distribution in central North America, from Alberta in the northwest, south to Kansas and Missouri and east to northwestern Indiana.

Fig. 64. Photographs courtesy U. S. Nat. Mus. Skulls of Indiana Ground-Squirrels, genus *Citellus*, natural size.

Upper group. Striped Ground-Squirrel or Gopher, *Citellus tridecemlineatus*, Cat. No. 250,129, U. S. Nat. Mus., White County, Sept. 7, 1931, M. W. Lyon, Jr.

Lower group. Franklin's Ground-Squirrel or Gopher or Gray Gopher, *Citellus franklinii*, Cat. No. 250,127, Tippecanoe County, Sept. 7, 1931, M. W. Lyon, Jr.

Fig 65. Photograph, copyright by H. H. Pittman. Franklin's Spermophile or Ground-Squirrel, or Gray Gopher, *Citellus franklinii*.

This Ground-Squirrel is a relatively large animal nearly equalling the Gray Squirrel in size and somewhat resembling it in color, its tail, however, is less bushy and shorter, upperparts a mixture of brownish gray and blackish with head and neck slightly darker, sides paler; the colors so arranged as to produce an obscurely coarse spotted effect; tail grayish and coarsely spotted like the body, the ends of the hairs tipped with whitish; feet grayish; underparts and inner side of legs dull yellowish white. Unless the animal is under

Fig. 66. Photograph courtesy Otis Wade and Journal of Mammalogy. Franklin's Spermophile or Ground-Squirrel or Gray Gopher, *Citellus franklinii*, beginning to waken from deep torpor.

some provocation, the hairs of the tail do not make it appear very bushy, but when excited they stand out and the tail seems as bushy as that of a Gray Squirrel.

Its total length is 355 to 375 mm. (14 to 15 inches), tail 115 to 125 mm. (4½ to 5 inches), hind foot, 50 to 55 mm. (about 2 inches); greatest length of skull about 50 mm. and greatest width nearly 30 mm. Weight, 370 to 700 grams, depending upon the time of year. They are heaviest before going into hibernation and lightest on emerging from winter sleep.

In food and habits Franklin's Ground-Squirrel is essentially like its near relative the Thirteen-lined Ground-Squirrel. Its food consists of grain, wild seeds, fruits, green vegetation, and a variety of insects such as grasshoppers, crickets, beetles and cutworms. It is rather omnivorous and eats eggs of ground-nesting birds, young birds and young mice, and has been known to kill and partially eat a young rabbit (Arthur M. Johnson, Journal of Mammalogy, vol. 3, p. 187, 1922). Bailey (1893) in a summary shows its food to consist of animal matter 30.3 percent; vegetable matter 68.5 percent, and and indeterminable matter 1.2 percent.

Franklin's Ground-Squirrel is active from about the first of April until the first of November. At the latter date, or before, it takes to its nest in its burrow and passes the winter in a state of hibernation similar to that of the Thirteen-lined Ground-Squirrel. Mating takes place soon after waking from the winter sleep and young numbering up to half a dozen are born before June. Only one litter is produced in a season. The animals are said to be easily tamed and to make interesting pets.

Their voice is much like that of the thirteen lined ground squirrel, but is as much heavier as they are larger. It is often heard in a long babbling trill from a weed patch and is almost bird-like in musical quality. (Bailey 1926).

Franklin's Ground-Squirrels are comparatively rare in Indiana. It is not so successful an animal in multiplying and spreading as is the Thirteen-lined Ground-Squirrel. In making inquiries about them in counties where they are known to occur, it is often difficult to find persons who are familar with them.

Map 42. Published records, recent observations and specimens in collections of Franklin's Ground-Squirrel, *Citellus franklinii*, in Indiana; 1, in Blatchley's collection.

The published records for Franklin's Ground-Squirrel are: Benton (Bailey 1893, Evermann and Butler 1894, Hahn 1907, Lyon 1932), Cass (Lyon 1932), Jasper (Evermann and Butler 1894, Hahn 1907, 1909, Lyon 1932), Lake (Dinwiddie 1884, Blatchley 1898, Lyon 1932), Laporte (Lyon 1932), Newton (Bailey 1893, Evermann and Butler 1894, Butler 1895, Hahn 1907, 1909, Lyon 1932), Porter (Blatchley 1898, Hahn 1907, 1909, Lyon 1932), Pulaski (Lyon 1932), St. Joseph (Anonymous 1880, Lyon 1932, Engels 1933), Tippecanoe (Lyon 1932), White (Evermann and Butler 1894, Hahn 1907, 1909, Lyon 1932).

Only on about three occasions have I seen it running across a road, and then rather leisurely, while the Thirteen-Striped Ground-Squirrel is seen running across roads everywhere, and usually so fast that one scarcely sees the stripes.

No one has complained of damage done by them though at corn planting time some farmers accuse them of eating the seed, but the same farmers have never been able to point out to me one of the animals or their burrows. They are easily caught in small steel traps set in the entrance to their burrows. These animals are good swimmers. I tried to drown one taken in a No. 1 steel trap, and the animal was not only able to keep itself afloat but to make progress through the water in spite of its handicap.

I have never found it elsewhere than in open fields and meadows. Originally it was certainly confined to prairie regions of the State, but with the clearing off of timber and rendering much of the State an artificial prairie, it has slowly spread a few miles to the eastward, but nowhere so extensively as its striped cousin. Its burrows are similar to those of the Thirteen-lined Squirrel but slightly larger. There is often more than one entrance to a burrow and usually the dirt is scattered away from the opening so that no mound about it exists.

CHIPMUNKS
Genus **Tamias** Illiger

The genus *Tamias* is confined to eastern North America, ranging from the southern Canadian provinces to Georgia and Louisiana, and from the Atlantic seaboard westward to eastern North Dakota and Oklahoma.

The Chipmunks are essentially small, striped squirrels living mainly on or in the ground, but readily climbing trees and bushes to a moderate height. The back is marked by five longitudinal blackish stripes and two whitish longitudinal stripes. Ears much longer than in the genus *Citellus*. The skull is relatively long and narrow and the brain case slightly flattened; interorbital construction narrow; postorbital processes broad at base and rather short; in general aspects resembling the two proceeding genera, rather than the tree squirrels.

Dental formula: $i\frac{1-1}{1-1}, c\frac{0-0}{0-0}, pm\frac{1-1}{1-1}, m\frac{3-3}{3-3}, = 20.$

Like the two ground-squirrels described above they possess large cheek pouches inside the mouth.

It contains but a single species which is divided into five subspecies or geographic races, one of which is widely distributed in Indiana and another found on the western border of the state.

FISHER'S CHIPMUNK
Tamias striatus fisheri Howell

[*Sciurus*] *striatus* LINNAEUS. Syst. Nat., ed. 10, vol. 1, p. 64, 1758. Type locality: Southeastern United States.
Tamias striatus Wied 1839-41, Evermann and Butler 1894, Hahn 1909.
Sciurus striatus Plummer 1844.

Fig. 67. Photograph courtesy N. Y. Zool. Soc. Chipmunk, *Tamias striatus*.

Tamias striatus fisheri A. H. HOWELL. Journ. Mamm. vol. 6, p. 51, 1925.
Type locality: Near Ossining, New York. A. H. Howell 1929, 1932.
Fisher's Chipmunk ranges from the seaboard of the Middle Atlantic States to the western edge of Indiana where it meets with the western subspecies *Tamias striatus griseus.*

Color: Head and rump russet or bay color, a narrow stripe from nose above eye nearly to ear, buff, a blackish patch behind the eye; sides of face and neck with a broad irregular stripe of russet bordered with cinnamon buff. Median dorsal stripe from between ears nearly to rump, black or blackish, and the two pairs of outer and shorter dorsal stripes also blackish; color on either side of mid-dorsal stripe grayish, and of the stripe between the pair of black dorsal stripes creamy white; rump and hinder back hazel; side of head cinnamon buff; underparts creamy white to pale pinkish buff; tail above, brownish black overlaid with grayish, beneath tawny or russet bordered with blackish and edged with grayish; front feet pinkish brown, hind feet brownish. In the winter coat seen in autumn and early spring the lower back is paler and the gray of the back more prominent.

Total length 230 to 280 mm., tail vertebrae 83 to 97 mm., hind foot 33 to 35 mm., ear about 15 mm. Weight 65 to 105 grams. Greatest length of skull about 40 mm., greatest width about 22 mm.

The eastern chipmunks spend a large part of their lives in burrows which they dig for themselves, often beneath a rock, a stone wall, the roots of a tree, or a building. The entrance holes are small and inconspicuous, and there is rarely any dirt thrown out about the used doorways. This is accomplished, apparently, by digging the burrow in some thicket or sheltered place, and after it is completed, closing up the original opening and making another entrance at the other end where it reaches the surface. Vernon Bailey excavated a chipmunk burrow at Elk River, Minn., July 4, 1930, which he found to be about 20 feet in length and from 1 to 3 feet below the surface. It had several branches and openings and four or five storage and nest cavities. A large old nest about 18 feet from the entrance, composed mainly of oak leaves rested on a foundation of stored food supplies, consisting of about 8 quarts of the previous year's acorns, a pint of old moldy corn, and a handful of the previous year's hazelnuts. This cavity would have held about a bushel. A smaller storage chamber at one side of the burrow contained a handful of freshly stored corn and about a pint of the previous year's acorns. At one side and about a foot below the nest cavity was a much used toilet; the nest and storage chambers were clean and sweet. (A. H. Howell, 1929).

The Chipmunk is most at home on the ground but it readily takes to bushes, and low trees. When pursued or in search of food, it can even climb far out on the branches of a large tree.

All through the summer and especially early in the fall the eastern chipmunks are busy gathering food materials, which they carry to their dens in their capacious cheek pouches. (A. H. Howell 1929).

The capacity of the cheek pouches is surprisingly large. They open between the lips and the molars and extend along the cheek and neck beneath the outer skin. They are simply folds of skin that have grown back from the lining of the lips and are not furred inside. (Hahn 1909).

Hahn has taken 145 grains of wheat from the cheek pouches. A. H. Howell (1929) reports that 25 kernels of corn have been found in one individual.. As many as 17 hazelnuts and 7 large acorns in each of two others. All kinds of nuts, seeds, and some fruits are eaten and stored. A few insects are credited to their diet as well as occasional eggs and young birds. Animal food is not stored.

Late in autumn the chipmunks disappear into their dens for the winter. Evermann and Clark (1920) give the latest date of their being seen as November 27 and their first date of appearance above ground in the spring as March 20, Marshall County. Frederick H. Test (Journal of Mammalogy, vol. 13 p. 278, 1932) reports Chipmunks in Parke County as running about in the open on February 1, 1932, during a rather mild winter. The profundity of their winter sleep is unknown with certainty, but it is probably deeper and much longer in higher latitudes. They do not put on nearly as much fat as the ground-squirrels of the genus *Citellus,* so it is not improbable that they eat some of their stored food, at least on the warmer days of winter. Col. Wirt Robinson (Journal of Mammalogy vol. 4, p. 256, 1923) reports finding a Chipmunk at West Point, N. Y. in as torpid a state of hibernation as that already described for the ground-squirrels. Before retiring for their winter's nap they perch as solitary individuals on some fence rail stump or log in the sunshine and issue a succession of hollow clucking sounds. They keep this up at intervals of two or three seconds for as long as an hour at a time. It seems to be a farewell hymn to the sun. In early spring this song is again repeated.

A second noise is the rapid chatter he makes in defiance as he dashes away from danger along a fence or wall. But the most startling sound that I have ever known to proceed from any rodent's throat, is the shrill whistle of this little animal. Its exact nature is indescribable, but it resembles the whistle of a bird more than any mammal note that I know of. I have been fooled by it myself, and once I knew of two very good ornithologists to search all over a hillside for some unknown bird, only to discover that the call that had lured them was not that of some feathered creature, but the ventriloquistic whistle of one of these little squirrels. (Hahn, 1909).

The mating period of the Chipmunk extends from the earliest spring to late in that season, with an additional breeding season from the latter half of July to early August. (Schooley 1934) Few records of young have been made. They have been found in dug out nests in the first third of May. A captured female (Henry, in Seton, 1929) gave birth to young on July 17. Half grown young have been seen with their mother as late as October. Schooley's observations (1934) show that more than one brood a season is raised and that females born the preceding year may breed in the late summer. There is some evidence that the young and parent or parents may hibernate in the same burrow. The young are born in a very immature state. At 11 days they measure 75 mm. (3 in.) total length, but are blind and the hair is just starting to grow. At 35 days of age the eyes are first opened. After about 40 days they appear half grown. By the end of August most of the young Chipmunks are fully grown and able to care for themselves. The number of young in a brood varies from four to six. The females have four pairs of mammae, one pair inguinal, two abdominal and one pectoral.

Chipmunks are bright attractive little animals and are not accused of any essentially bad habits. They are easily partially tamed about homes and summer resorts and readily learn to eat crumbs or other food passed to them. They are the most highly colored and attractive of our small mammals, with a delightful little chuckle. All too often they are used as targets for the small boy's air gun or rifle.

Map 43. Published records, recent observations and specimens in collections of Fisher's Chipmunk, *Tamias striatus fisheri*, in Indiana; 1, North Madison High School.

The published records for Fisher's chipmunk are: Boone (A. H. Howell 1929, 1932), Carroll (Evermann and Butler 1894), Dearborn (A. H. Howell 1932), Franklin (Haymond 1870, Quick and Langdon 1882, Butler 1886), Hamilton (A. H. Howell 1929), Jay (A. H. Howell 1932), Knox (A. H. Howell 1929), Lagrange (Evermann and Butler 1894), Lake (Dinwiddie 1884, Blatchley 1898), Lawrence (Hahn 1908), Laporte (Cory 1912, A. H. Howell 1929, 1932), Marshall (Evermann and Clark 1911, 1920, A. H. Howell 1929), Miami (A. H. Howell 1929, 1932), Monroe (Evermann and Butler 1894, Banta 1907, McAtee 1907), Newton (A. H. Howell 1929), Ohio (A. H. Howell, 1929), Porter (Blatchley 1898, Lyon 1923, A. H. Howell 1929), Posey (Wied 1839-41, 1861-62, A. H. Howell 1910), Randolph (Evermann and Butler 1894, Cox 1893), St. Joseph (A. H. Howell 1932, Engels 1933), Wabash (Evermann and Butler 1894), Wayne (Plummer 1844, Allen 1877, A. H. Howell 1929).

MEARNS' CHIPMUNK
Tamias striatus griseus Mearns

Tamias striatus griseus MEARNS. Bull. Amer. Mus. Nat. Hist., vol. 3, p. 231, 1891. Type locality: Fort Snelling, Minnesota. A. H. Howell, 1829, 1932.

Mearns' Chipmunk ranges from eastern North Dakota and Kansas east to the western border of Indiana and eastward north of the Great Lakes into the Province of Quebec.

Compared with the preceeding subspecies it is larger, sides of head and body paler, gray of upper parts paler and more extensive; underside of tail paler. The winter pelage is still grayer.

Total length, 250 to 300 mm., tail vertebrae, 95 to 110 mm., hind foot, 35 to 38 mm., ear 12 to 16 mm. No weights of this subspecies are recorded. Greatest length of skull about 41.5 mm., greatest width about 23 mm.

In order to differentiate this subspecies from the preceeding, it is practically necessary to have both subspecies at hand for actual comparison.

Mearns' Chipmunk has only been recorded with certainty from Parke County but it probably will be found to occupy the adjoining counties as indicated on the map, when proper material is collected.

In its life and habits it differs in no wise from Fisher's Chipmunk which is found elsewhere in the state.

Map 44. Specimens in collections and recent observations of Mearns' Chipmunk, *Tamias striatus griseus*, in Indiana. It is assumed that the recent observations, O on the map probably refer to this subspecies. They were sent in by observers as simply Chipmunks.

The published records of Mearns' Chipmunk are: Parke (Howell 1932) and perhaps Vigo (Evermann and Butler 1894).

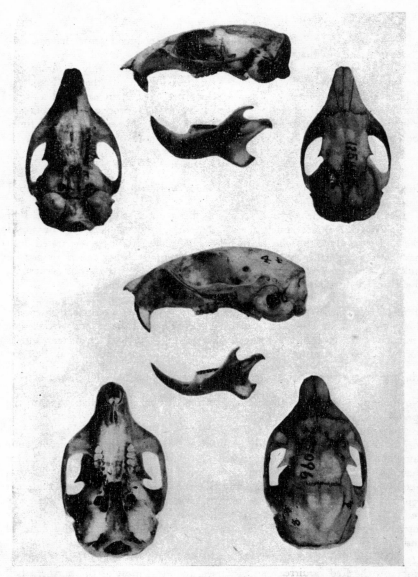

Fig. 68. Photographs courtesy U. S. Nat. Mus. Skulls of Chipmunk and Red Squirrel, natural size.

Upper group. Fisher's Chipmunk, *Tamias striatus fisheri*, Cat. No. 125,445, Bascom, Ohio County, W. L. Hahn.

Lower group. Red Squirrel, *Sciurus hudsonicus loquax*, Cat. No. 257,096, Notre Dame, St. Joseph County, W. L. Engels.

SQUIRRELS

Genus **Sciurus** Linnaeus

The true or tree Squirrels, genus *Sciurus* in its broad sense, have a distribution essentially that of family *Sciuridae*.

The Squirrels are strictly arboreal members of the family *Sciuridae* of medium size, with a bushy tail which is flattened and more than half as long as head and body. The skull has a strongly convex brain case and a weak rostrum, with slender posteriorly directed postorbital processes. Incisors are strongly compressed, anterior upper premolar usually present as a small functionless spike. It may be deciduous. Dental formula usually:

$$i\frac{1-1}{1-1}, \ c\frac{0-0}{0-0}, \ pm\frac{2-2}{1-1}, \ m\frac{3-3}{3-3}, = 22.$$

Crowns of the molars low, the upper ones with two moderately developed cross ridges.

Nearly 100 species or subspecies of the genus have been recognized in North America alone. They are as numerous in other parts of the world where the family *Sciuridae* is found. The genus has been separated into many well recognized subgenera which are gradually being raised to generic rank, so that at the present time it is impossible to define the genus accurately, give its exact distribution, or approximate numbers of species.

Three very distinct species of the genus are found in Indiana each one of them representative of a subgenus, defined by certain technical characters shown by the skull, teeth, penis bone or baculum, and the glands of the male genitalia. The Red Squirrel shows the most pronounced characters and is worthy of recognition as a full genus. The same is true of the Fox Squirrel which lacks the small upper premolars, which are thus pm $\frac{1-1}{1-1}$ instead of $\frac{2-2}{1-1}$.

No attempt is made to define these subgenera here, other than to state the species which are consigned to them.

Subgenus *Sciurus* Linnaeus, containing the Gray Squirrels, *Sciurus carolinensis* of North America and some other North American Squirrels quite unrelated to it, so much so that theree other subgenera have been proposed for them. The type of the subgenus *Sciurus* is the common squirrel of Europe, *Sciurus vulgaris* Linnaeus. The Gray Squirrels were separated from the other squirrels by Trouessart (Le Naturaliste, vol. 2, p. 292, 1880) as the subgenus *Neosciurus*. This subgenus with a single species *carolinensis* divisable into two geographic races is or was found throughout the entire state of Indiana.

Subgenus *Tamiasciurus* Trouessart (Le Naturaliste, vol. 2, p. 292, 1880), embraces the Red Squirrels or Chickarees, found in most of the northern half of North America from the limits of tree growth south to the higher mountains of North Carolina and in the west as far south as Arizona and New Mexico. It is common in the northern half or third of Indiana, very rare in the southern portions. *Tamiasciurus* is frequently regarded as a distinct genus, notably by Pocock, and by Mossman and his coworkers. The author concurs in this view and only follows customary usage in placing it in *Sciurus*.

Subgenus *Guerlinguetus* Gray (London Med. Repos. vol. 15, p. 304, 1821) embraces the Fox Squirrels of the southeastern United States, Mississippi Valley, western Texas and northeastern Mexico and some other species found mainly in Mexico and Central America. Among the four synonyms given for it there is only need to mention *Parasciurus* Trouessart (Le Naturaliste, vol. 2, p. 292, 1880), of which the type is *Sciurus niger* Linnaeus. Among other characters of the Fox Squirrels is the absence of the small upper premolar.

All these three distinct members of the *Sciuridae* have much in common as to their habits and manner of living. They are all arboreal, spending most of their lives in the trees, but they do not hesitate to come down to the ground, and the Red Squirrel has even been known to build its nest in subterranean passages. They are all diurnal. They nest in hollows of trees or stumps, or build outside nests in crotches or branches of trees. All have the habit of storing up some food for use on "rainy days." Often the nuts or other food are lightly and skillfully buried just beneath the ground. It is very doubtful if the squirrels can possibly remember all these caches of morsels. It seems more likely that when other food is lacking they either smell them out or dig around, hit or miss, till they are found by mere chance. They remain active all winter, and do not undergo any form of hibernation. On the stormiest days of winter they remain in their nests.

All the squirrels, sometimes either by accidently losing a foothold or under the stress of pursuit, have been known to fall to the ground from considerable heights, as much as 50 or 60 feet, and get up and run away immediately without apparent injury. The legs, feet and tail are all outspread in these falls, and the animal reaches the ground with a velocity much less than that of the usual compact falling body studied in physics.

EASTERN RED SQUIRREL, CHICKAREE, PINEY
Sciurus hudsonicus loquax Bangs

Sciurus vulgaris hudsonicus ERXLEBEN. Syst. Regni Anim., vol.. 1, p. 415, 1777. Type locality: Hudson Strait.

Sciurus hudsonicus loquax BANGS. Proc. Biol. Soc. Washington, vol. 10, p. 161, 1896. Type locality: New London County, Connecticut.

Sciurus hudsonicus Haymond 1870.

Sciurus hudsonicus Evermann and Butler 1894.

Sciurus hudsonicus loquax Allen 1898, Hahn 1909.

The Eastern Red Squirrel ranges from Massachusetts south to Maryland and Virginia, westward through northern Michigan, Indiana and Illinois into Wisconsin.

In winter the back is marked by a broad band of rufous extending from the top of the head nearly to the end of tail; sides of body and outside surface of legs olive gray; ear tufted with dusk colored hairs; underparts including lips, chin and throat grayish white; tail above with a broad central area of yellowish rufous bordered with a band of black, beneath, central area yellowish gray. In summer, it is distinctly brighter and redder; ears are not tufted and there is a conspicuous black lateral line separating the dorsal from the ventral region. Bangs (1896) refers to an albinistic series from Denver, Miami County.

This is the smallest of our tree squirrels. Total length of a pair from the dunes region of Porter County, 320 mm.; tail vertebrae 125 mm., hind feet 46 to 47 mm. Greatest length of skull about 45 mm., greatest width of skull about 21 mm. Weight (Hatt 1929) 170 to 265 grams. Weight (Evermann and Clark 1920) 6½ to 7 oz.

Fig. 69. Photograph courtesy A. B. Klugh and Journal of Mammalogy. Red Squirrel, *Sciurus hudsonicus.*

These squirrels though born in the trees spend many hours of their lives on and under the ground in search of food and water, in storage activities, and in travelling about. Squirrels do not seem so self-assured on the ground as in the trees, however, and travel more frequently from branch to branch or along such clear and comparatively safe highways as stone walls and rail fences.

The Red Squirrel voluntarily takes to water and can swim considerable distances. From the deck of a boat I once saw one swimming across the Wisconsin River at the Dells, Wisconsin. It was well down in the water and I could not make out what sort of animal it was until it hauled out on the bank. It looked very wet and much bedraggled. It weakly shook itself and walked leisurely away into some bushes. It made such good speed in the water that I was quite surprised to find that it was a squirrel.

The food of the Red Squirrel is very varied. It eats all kind of nuts and seeds of trees and shrubs. Seeds from the cones of evergreens are an important article of diet when it lives among such trees. On the campus at the University of Notre Dame are many pines and were it not for the policing of the grounds veritable middens of its cones would be found. In the spring it eats buds of various trees and shrubs. Klugh (1927) shows a beautiful picture of a Red Squirrel drinking sap as it hangs upside down on a limb. It eats a fair amount of animal food, most frequently, insect larva, then young birds and birds' eggs. Many observers report Red Squirrels living near birds' nests which they must obviously have seen, and yet never molested them. It is also fond of fruits and berries. Those that I trapped in Porter County were taken with apple as the bait. My wife once saw one making a meal of blackberries. The squirrel was hanging on to the blackberry bushes by its hind legs upside down. It picked off the berries by its hands in which it held them while it was eating. It frequently has regular feeding places to which it repairs with its food and leaves a heap of empty nutshells or empty cones on the ground at the base of some stump where it has fed. Many authors describe its fondness for mushrooms, and it seems to eat poisonous ones with impunity. Mushrooms are frequently stored in tree branches for future meals.

Its nests are mainly of two kinds, natural hollows in trees, or those dug out by woodpeckers, and outside nests built among the branches of trees. These are solid except for the nest cavity inside. It is also known to make elaborate underground tunnels with enlarged cavities for food storage as well as for a nest, very similar to those of the Chipmunk.

When the ground is covered with snow they make extensive tunnels in the snow in their search for food either that which might naturally be found there, or that which was buried by the squirrels themselves.

Red Squirrels are essentially diurnal in their activities from sunrise to twilight, though Merriam (1882-84) speaks of them as being out on moonlight nights. They are noisy inquisitive little creatures and do not quietly run away from the approach of an observer, but sit in the branches or run around the tree trunks either scolding, laughing or chattering at him.

Mating with the Red Squirrel varies with the latitude. In Indiana it probably occurs in late winter or early spring. During this season the testes become much swollen and descend from the abdomen to the scrotum. The period of gestation is about six weeks. The number of young at a birth varies from four to six. There are eight mammae four on each side extending from the inguinal region to the pectoral region. Like all squirrels the young are born in a very immature state, blind and naked. They are nursed by the mother for some time before coming forth from the nest, and are about one-third grown before venturing out. Most authors ascribe but one litter to a season. The few that I caught in Porter County (Lyon 1923) fell into three age groups, adult, young but nearly adult, and very young, fully haired, eyes open, but scarcely able to crawl about. A nursing female was trapped on September 27,1922, and about two days later a pathetic little Red Squirrel, not more than a third grown was found near our tent vainly trying to suck juice from some grapes which were resting on the ground. It was too immature to eat solid food. We fed it some warm canned milk and placed it in an improvised cotton nest, but it died during the night. These observations would indicate that perhaps in Indiana two broods per season are produced. Evermann and Clark (1920) report finding a young one just able to crawl about on September 24, 1900. They were successful in raising it.

Three elaborate accounts of the Red Squirrel have appeared in recent years, Klugh 1927, Hatt 1929, Seton 1929, giving their own personal observations

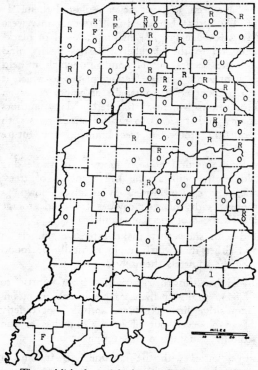

Map 45. Published records, recent observations, and specimens in collections of the Red Squirrel, *Sciurus hudsonicus*, in Indiana; 1, North Madison High School, and now deposited in the U. S. National Museum.

The published records for the Red Squirrel are: Blackford (Evermann and Butler 1894), Carroll (Evermann and Clark 1911), Clinton (Evermann and Clark 1911), Delaware (Hahn 1909), Franklin (Haymond 1870, Quick 1882, Langdon 1887, Evermann and Butler 1894, Hahn 1909), Fulton (Evermann and Butler 1894, Hahn 1909, Evermann and Clark 1911), Hamilton (Walker 1923), Huntington (Evermann and Butler 1894, Hahn 1909), Jefferson (Lyon 1934), Kosciusko (Hahn 1909), Lake (Butler 1895, Blatchley 1898, Hahn 1909, Brennan 1923), Lagrange (Evermann and Butler 1894, Hahn 1909), Laporte (Allen 1898, Elliot 1907, Hahn 1907, 1909, Cory 1912, Brennan 1923), Marion (Hahn 1909), Marshall (Evermann and Clark 1911, 1920), Miami (Evermann and Butler 1894, Bangs 1896), Newton (Butler 1895) Porter (Blatchley 1898, Hahn 1907, 1909, Brennan 1923, Lyon 1923), Randolph (Cox 1893, Evermann and Butler 1894, Hahn 1909), St. Joseph (Hahn 1909, Engels 1933), Steuben (Hahn 1909), Vanderburg (Lyon 1934), Wabash (Evermann and Butler 1894, Hahn 1909), Wells (Cory 1912).

and those of others recorded in complete bibliographies. The above account has been largely drawn from them.

The Red Squirrel is thought to have increased its range in Indiana in recent years. Rarely it is found in the southern counties. There is a specimen in the Field Museum from Evansville and one in U. S. National Museum donated by the North Madison High School, taken in Jefferson County, five miles west of North Madison in January 1934. As far back as 1870 it was reported as rare by Haymond in Franklin County, and it was reported by Cox in 1893 as far south as Randolph County. I think its alleged spread (Walker 1923) is not as real as appears at first glance and due largely to greater interest taken in natural history in the state. Also its natural enemies, predatory mammals and birds have decreased and it is not hunted as game as are the other two species of squirrels. It seems to stand civilization well as attested by its presence on the campus at Notre Dame and its occasional occupancy of man-built structures.

GRAY SQUIRREL
Sciurus carolinensis Gmelin

[*Sciurus*] *carolinensis* GMELIN. Syst. Nat., vol. 1, p. 148, 1788. Type locality: Carolina.
Sciurus cinereus Wied 1839-41
Sciurus carolinensis Plummer 1844.

The Gray Squirrel of which there are five varieties is found throughout southeastern North America from the southern Canadian provinces to Florida and Texas and from the Atlantic seaboard west to Minnesota and Texas. Two of the five recognized froms, *Sciurus carolinensis carolinensis* and *Sciurus carolinensis leucotis* were formerly found abundantly in Indiana, the former in the southern two-thirds of the state and the latter in the northern tier or two of its counties. In the middle of the state specimens are considered to be intermediate between the two forms.

As the older generation of naturalists did not distinguish between the two forms and as there are no differences in their habits, both forms are here treated together.

The general color above is a fine grizzled gray; the underfur plumbeous and each of the longer over- or guard-hairs plumbeous at base, then buffy, or tan, then blackish and at the tip whitish; on the head, back, feet and shoulders the gray is tinged with rusty yellow. The tail is large long and very bushy; its long hairs are colored from the base outward, tan, black, and finally white on the ends. In winter the pelage is longer, the buffy or tan color of the hairs less marked and the general gray color more pronounced. In the northern part of its range melanism is of frequent occurrence, the entire pelage being black or blackish, though close examination may reveal paler rings in some of the hairs. Sometimes the melanism is only partial. Half or more of the Gray Squirrels in a given locality may show this color phase; they are none the less Gray Squirrels. Both gray and black phases have been found in the same nest. Dr. Haymond writing in 1870 from Franklin County says:

The black squirrels were common—forming about one-third of the total number of squirrels in southeastern Indiana at the period of its first settlement. Now they have completely disappeared.

Hahn (1909) writes:

In southern Porter and northern Jasper counties in 1905 the black or partially black squirrels were nearly as numerous as the gray.

Black specimens were extremely rare at New Harmony in 1832-33 according to Wied (1861-62). In the museum of the University of Notre Dame

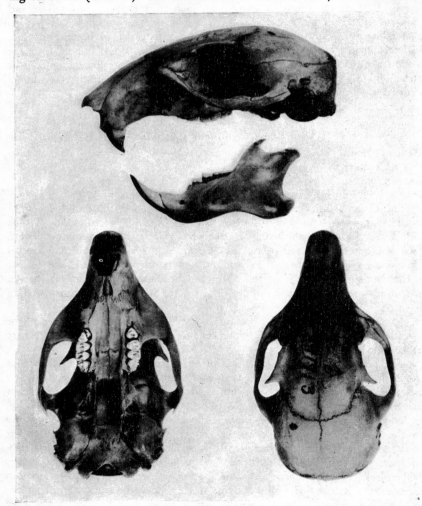

Fig. 70. Photographs courtesy U. S. Nat. Mus. Skull of Gray Squirrel, *Sciurus carolinensis leucotis*, natural size, Cat. No. 141,713, Hebron, Porter County, Aug. 25, 1905, W. L. Hahn.

are two mounted specimens of the Gray Squirrel in the black phase taken at Peru, Miami County.

In the popular mind these two color phases are almost universally regarded as distinct species. Even the early naturalists looked at them in the same light. The name *Sciurus niger* was frequently applied to the black form (Plummer 1844) while *Sciurus cinereus* was often used for the gray form. *Sciurus niger*, however, is the correct technical name to apply to the southern Fox Squirrel. (See below).

Total length, 475 to 500 mm. (19 to 20 in.); tail, 220 to 240 mm. (9 to

Fig. 71. Photograph courtesy N. Y. Zool. Soc. Gray Squirrel, *Sciurus Carolinensis*.

9¼ in.); hind foot 62.5 to 70 mm. (2½ to 2¾ in.). Weight from 1 to 1½ lbs. (450 to 680 grams). Greatest length of skull about 65 mm.; greatest width, about 36 mm.

The Gray Squirrel is the most arboreal of the three Indiana squirrels. It is an inhabitant of heavy woods where there is an abundance of nut-bearing trees. The few that I have seen in Indiana and those only in the southern part of the state, have been high in the branches of tall trees in bottom lands. It is surprising however to see how well this squirrel takes to civilization and adapts itself to city parks when it is supplied with adequate food and shelter.

Its food consists of all kinds of nuts including acorns, fruits, berries and grain, seeds, fleshy underground parts of plants, also fungi. It eats a small amount of animal food such as insects, young birds and eggs. As Seton (1929) aptly remarks if the practice of raiding birds' nests were at all regular, there would have been no tree-nesting birds left in the hardwood forests of the Mississippi Valley in the halcyon days of the Gray Squirrel. McAtee (1907) has "observed [them] foraging about garbage barrels on the edge of town [Bloomington.]" Hahn (1908) says:

The Gray Squirrel is very abundant on the University [Indiana] Farm [near Mitchell, Lawrence County], seeming to delight in using the large oaks and tulip-trees for homes. In the autumn of 1906 the crop of acorns was very large. I estimated that each of the large white oaks produced from two to eight thousand acorns during that season. Eighty acres are heavily wooded with white oaks and nearly a hundred acres more have a considerable growth of these trees. Before November 1, the immense crop of acorns had been so completely garnered by the squirrels that none were in sight on top of the leaves and only an occasional one could be found by the most careful search.

Merriam (1882-84) speaks of their food and storage thus:

Those who have observed the habits of this species in summer must have noticed their propensity for burying nuts just beneath the surface in various parts of the woods. They do not, so far as I am aware, make a great accumulation in any one place, but dig a thousand little holes, plant a nut or two in each, scrape a few leaves over the spot and hurry off, as if afraid some one would discover the treasure. In winter this habit is almost equally marked, and the first thing a squirrel thinks of after his hunger is satisfied is to secrete a portion of the food remaining at his disposal. In accomplishing this he tunnels into the snow in various directions, hiding some of the surplus provision in each excavation. Many persons who have observed this habit in summer regard it as an idle pastime, and question if the Squirrel ever finds the nuts again, knowing that he could never remember the exact positions of so many. . . . His sense of smell is very acute enabling him to detect the presence of a nut at some little distance; hence though he does not, of course, remember the exact spot where each one is buried under the leaves, he can, by moving carefully over the ground, discover a great many of them.

The nuts that the squirrel does not discover are planted and ready to germinate in the spring.

The Gray Squirrel uses two sorts of nest, probably in the colder weather hollow trees and holes in limbs; in summer outside nests built situated high in the larger tree branches or in crotches. These nests are a mass of twigs and leaves and are roofed over in a waterproof manner so that the interior remains dry. In extremely cold and in inclement weather they remain indoors. The bushy tail is thought to serve as a blanket as well as a balancing organ when they are leaping about the branches.

Mating takes place in winter and the young numbering from three to five are born early in the spring, the period of gestation being about 45 days. As usual in the family the young are born in a very immature state. Their eyes open in about five weeks. Shortly after, they venture forth from the nest and when about half grown and fully furred they begin eating solid food. A second litter is usually born sometime about the first of September. The mammae are eight, four on each side, from the inguinal to the pectoral region.

The following collected by Hahn (1909) show the former abundance of the Gray Squirrel in Indiana:

D. D. Banta (1888) writes: In 1821 four families living in White River township, did not succeed in saving a single bushel of corn from the squirrels and raccoons. In a four acre field of shocked corn, only a single ear was overlooked by the squirrels. Two hundred were killed by one man in one day.

In the History of Bartholomew County, Indiana, (Anonymous 1888, p. 378) is an account of a great squirrel hunt which took place in that county in 1834. There was strong rivalry between Sand Creek and Wayne townships as to which had the best squirrel hunters. Finally it was agreed that each township should select fifty men to compete in a three days' squirrel hunt, to be terminated by a great barbecue for which the losing side was to pay. The total number of squirrels killed is not recorded, but an idea of the destruction of the animals may be obtained from the statement that the individual championship was awarded for killing 900 squirrels in three days. The second largest number was 783. That was in the days before the heavy timber of nut-bearing trees had been cleared off.

One of the most interesting animal phenomena recorded by the early naturalists was the migration, or rather the emigration of the Gray-squirrel.

In the early natural histories this squirrel is called 'migratory' [also in scientific nomenclature *Sciurus migratorius* Audubon and Bachman] and amazing accounts are given of its armies appearing to devastate the farms of whole regions.

Dr. P. H. Hoy, knew of an 'Ohio hunter that killed 160 in one day. . . . In parts of Michigan, Illinois, Southern Wisconsin and Indiana, they were no less numerous. Dr. Bachman (Audubon and Bachman, 1846, vol. 1, p. 272) saw 130 miles of the Ohio strewed with them in 1819. [In attempting to cross wide rivers many of

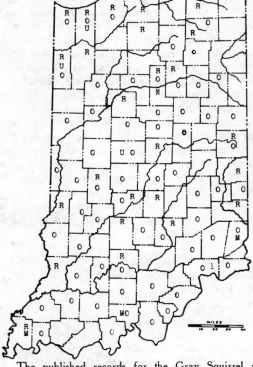

Map 46. Published records, recent observations, and specimens in collections of the Gray Squirrel, *Sciurus carolinensis*, in Indiana. In the two northern tiers of counties the Gray Squirrels are referable to the northern race, *Sciurus carolinensis leucotis*, while southward they are referable to the typical race, *Sciurus carolinensis carolinensis*. especially in the southern counties; 1, North Madison High School.

The published records for the Gray Squirrel are: Bartholomew (Hahn 1909), Carroll (Evermann and Butler 1894), Franklin (Haymond 1870, Quick and Langdon 1882, Butler 1885, Dury 1890, Evermann and Butler 1894, Hahn 1909), Hamilton (Anonymous 1906), Jasper (Hahn 1909), Johnson (Hahn 1909), Knox (Hahn 1909), Lagrange (Evermann and Butler 1894, Hahn 1909), Lake (Blatchley 1898, Brennan 1923), Laporte (Anonymous 1880, Brennan 1923), Lawrence (Hahn 1908, 1909), Marshall (Evermann and Clark 1911, 1920), Miami (Bangs 1896), Monroe (Evermann and Butler 1894, McAtee 1907, Hahn 1909), Morgan (Major 1915), Newton (Hahn 1907), Noble (Hahn 1909), Porter (Blatchley 1898, Hahn 1907, 1909, Brennan 1923), Posey (Wied 1839-41, 1861-62, Hahn 1909), Putnam (Anonymous 1881), Randolph (Cox 1893, Evermann and Butler 1894), St. Joseph (Anonymous 1880, Engels 1933), Vigo (Thomas 1819, Evermann and Butler 1894), Wabash (Evermann and Butler 1894, Hahn 1909), Wayne (Plummer 1844), southern Indiana (Audubon and Bachman 1849, Kennicott 1857).

the squirrels became exhausted and drowned though the Gray Squirrel is as good a swimmer as is the Red Squirrel described above]. . . . An old settler of Bay City, Michigan, records that in the migration of 1866, one of the last, he counted 1400 squirrels while driving 2 miles. (Seton, Journal of Mammalogy, vol 1, p. 53, 1920).

They appeared to be migrating to no place in particular, but were just leaving the home woods, though it was well supplied with food and shelter, a singular perversion of squirrel psychology.

There is a popular superstition that many male Gray Squirrels are emasculated or castrated by their supposed enemy the Red Squirrels or by rival males of their own species. The larvae of the bot fly, *Cuterebra emasculator* are accused of also emasculating squirrels.. Larvae of this fly are found in a great many mammals from the White-footed Mouse to the Deer. Occasionally and quite by accident these may be located in the scrotal region. Also occasionally and quite by accident the scrotum might be nipped off in the case of two squirrels fighting. Such stories are large apocryphal. As Seton (1929) aptly says the reason why male squirrels are so frequently found without evidence of testicles is that the vast majority of them are hunted and killed in autumn, not in the rutting season and when the testicles are reduced in size or withdrawn into the abdomen. Also many are young animals.

The Gray Squirrel in Indiana falls into two well marked subspecies described below. Owing to lack of specimens in collections the exact distribution of the two forms in the state is unknown either in the past or present. The frequency with which black squirrels were reported in the early days from comparatively southern portions of the state leads to the belief that the Northern Gray Squirrel extended farther south than recent writers (Bangs 1896) indicate. Melanism is rather characteristic of the northern race. The problem is further complicated by the enormous migrations that the Gray Squirrel used to undertake.

SOUTHERN GRAY SQUIRREL
Sciurus carolinensis carolinensis (Gmelin)

Sciurus carolinensis Evermann and Butler 1894, Hahn 1909.
Sciurus carolinensis carolinensis Bangs 1896.

Probably confined to the southern two-thirds of Indiana, where it is still fairly common.

Length of body about 9.50 inches [240 mm.], ranging from 8.50 to 10.25 [216 to 260 mm.]; tail vertebrae about 8.00 [200 mm.], ranging from 7.50 to 8.75 [180 to 215 mm.];. . . . Above brownish-yellow, varied with black, with generally the sides of the neck, shoulders, and thighs mixed with whitish; beneath white. Differs from var. *leucotis* in its smaller size, and in the general color of the dorsal surface being yellowish brown instead of whitish gray. (Allen 1877).

Melanism in this subspecies is rare. The back of the ear is never conspicuously whitish.

NORTHERN GRAY SQUIRREL
Sciurus carolinenis leucotis (Gapper)

Sciurus leucotis GAPPER. Zool. Journ., vol. 5, p. 206, 1830. Type locality: Between York and Lake Simcoe, Ontario.
Sciurus niger Plummer 1844.

Sciurus carolinensis leucotis Evermann and Butler 1894, Hahn 1909.

Probably confined to the northern tier or two of the counties where it is apparently rare. In numerous botanical excursions in the northern counties in recent years I have never encountered a Gray Squirrel.

Length of body about 10.50 inches [270 mm.], varying from 9 to 11.50 in. [230 to 290 mm.]; tail vertebrae, 8 in. [200 mm.]; varying from 7 to 9 in. [175 to 225 mm.]. . . . Above, whitish-gray, with a dorsal area and a lateral line brownish yellow, and with a more or less strong fulvous suffusion beneath the surface of the pelage, generally more or less apparent through the surface-tints; beneath, white. Varies through dusky and annulated phases to intense glossy black; rarely in the dusky phases with areas of yellowish brown below, more or less strongly annulated with black. Tail with the hairs yellowish-brown basally, with narrow black annulations and a broad conspicuous, subterminal black bar, with hairs all broadly tipped with white, giving a white surface tint, through which the yellowish brown and black bars are seen beneath. Ears are not tufted, with or without a conspicuous woolly tuft of white at the base posteriorly. (Allen 1877).

FOX SQUIRREL
Sciurus niger rufiventer (Geoffroy)

[*Sciurus*] *niger* LINNAEUS. Syst. Nat., ed. 10; vol. 1, p. 64, 1758. Type locality: Probably southern South Carolina.
Sciurus rufiventer GEOFFROY. Cat. Mamm., Mus. Nat. Hist. Nat., Paris, p. 176, 1803. Type locality: Mississippi Valley.
Sciurus ludovicianus CUSTIS. Barton's Med. and Phys. Journ., vol. 2, pt. 2, p. 47, 1806.
Sciurus rufiventris Wied 1839-41.
Sciurus vulpinus Haymond 1870.
Sciurus niger ludovicianus Evermann and Butler 1894.
Sciurus ludovicianus ludovicianus Bangs 1896.
Sciurus niger rufiventer Hahn 1909.

The Fox Squirrel has a geographic distribution almost coincident with that of the Gray Squirrel. It does not extend so far north, however. It occurs from southern New England to Florida and from the Atlantic seaboard westward to eastern South Dakota and Texas. Seven geographic races are recognized, one of which is found throughout the whole of Indiana. This subspecies is more widely distributed than the other six, occupying the greater part of the Mississippi Valley from northern Louisiana to southern Wisconsin.

The Fox Squirrel is the largest of the Indiana squirrels and readily distinguished from the others not only by its large size but by its characteristic "foxy" color. In general it is tawny brown grizzled with gray above, and yellowish brown or rufous on the underparts; tail mixed blackish and rufous. Sides of nose usually like the underparts.

Unlike the northern Gray Squirrel melanistic individuals are essentially unknown. The true southern Fox Squirrel of Florida and other southern states is blackish (whence the specific name *niger*) with whitish nose and ears. There is considerable individual variation in the amount and intensity of the rufous and blackish colors.

Total length, about 550 mm.; tail vertebrae, 245 mm.; hind foot, 67 mm.

Greatest length of skull, about 65 mm.; greatest width, about 37 mm.; essentially the same size as that of the Northern Gray Squirrel, from which it differs however in lacking the small upper premolars in the upper jaw. Weight, 750 to 900 grams.

The Fox Squirrel although in wilderness days occupying the same forests as the Gray Squirrel seems to be better adapted to civilization and partially cleared ground and wood lots. Apparently a century ago it was the rare squirrel in Indiana and never attained to the enormous numbers of its gray relative nor was it given to migrations. While it cannot be said to be common in the state today yet in northern Indiana it is much more abundant than the Gray Squirrel. The Fox Squirrel is often seen in open woods in the northern part of the state. In South Bend it is not infrequently seen in the streets bor-

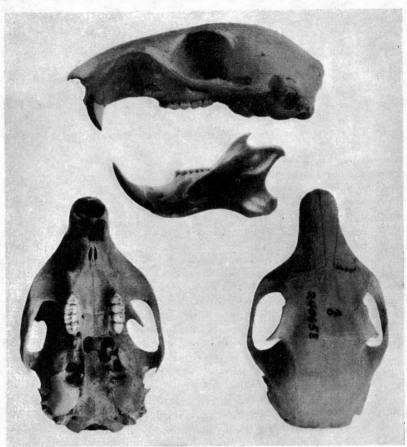

Fig. 72. Photographs courtesy U. S. Nat. Mus. Skull of Fox Squirrel, *Sciurus niger rufiventer*, natural size, Cat. No. 240,658, U. S. Nat. Mus., Chesterton, Porter County, Nov. 22, 1924, Elmer Johnson.

dered by large trees and in the city parks, sometimes within three blocks of the business district. It seems particularly sluggish in its movements especially when on the ground or in the middle of a street exposed to the dangers of motor cars, dogs and boys..

In its general habits the Fox Squirrel is essentially similar to the Gray Squirrel. It eats the same kinds of food and nests in similar situations. It is less active in its movements in the trees and on the ground, and it spends more time on the ground, but it is none the less a truly arboreal species. In autumn it gathers nuts and deposits them singly in the ground in the same manner and searches out these caches in winter when the trees and bushes are bare. When all else fails it feeds on buds and other tender parts of plants, as well as bulbs and tubers. It also eats corn and grain when these are left available. Evermann and Clark (1920) report them as feeding upon the seeds of the cocklebur in mid winter. "The squirrels would strip the burs from the plants and carry them to a nearby log on which they would sit on their haunches while they gnawed the burs and removed the seeds." It is the habit of all our squirrels to carry away the food from where it is found and eat it at some convenient place.

H. L. Stoddard (1920) writes of the nesting and breeding of the Fox Squirrel in northern Indiana as follows:

All accounts of the habits of the western fox squirrel (*Sciurus niger rufiventer*) that I have been able to find, speak of the young as being brought forth in hollow trees, no mention being made of the carefully constructed open nest used for this purpose in parts of the range of this squirrel.

In the sand dunes of northwestern Indiana particularly, where fox squirrels are still fairly abundant, the young born in early spring at least are usually brought forth in a very ingenious type of open nest, though hollow trees are common. These nests are round or oval in shape, tightly woven of freshly cut oak or other tough twigs. Inside of this twig shell comes a thick compact wall of large leaves, evidently pressed into shape while damp, making a smooth, tough lining capable of resisting wind, cold and rain. The nest proper is then made of soft inner bark, shredded leaves and other material.

The entrance hole is on one end and is just large enough to admit the owner, the surrounding fiber often nearly closing the opening. [An excellent illustration of such a nest is given in Stoddard's article.]

These nests are entirely different from the loosely constructed summer nests, and are so compactly built that they frequently remain in place many years, the squirrels using them a great deal even in coldest weather. From the ground they look something like hawks' nests, piles of sticks being all that are visible.

The three or four young, blind and nearly naked, are born in late February or March in this region, as the following records show. Nest containing three young near Miller, Indiana, March 8, 1914. Another nest located near-by the same day by my companion, Mr. L. L. Walters, contained four young about two weeks old. Miller, March 17, 1914, four young about two weeks old; Dune Park, Indiana, April 1, 1917, three young a week or ten days old. I have never found a second litter in the season.

Other nests, containing young, and dozens of empty nests examined by Mr. Walters and myself, have invariably been placed in pine trees, from twenty to forty or more feet above the ground. As a nest of this type must be built from the inside, a foundation of encircling limbs such as is offered by the northern scrub pine [*Pinus banksiana*] is necessary and may explain the absence of domiciles of this nature in the greater part of the range of this squirrel.

These winter nests are often placed in close proximity to some good old den tree,

Fig. 73. Fox Squirrel, *Sciurus niger rufiventer*, in city yard, South Bend,
photograph by M. W. Lyon, Jr.

to which the squirrel can retire if disturbed, and the surrounding trees are likely to contain one or more of the temporary nests used in summer, simply twigs and leaves cut green and piled into a convenient crotch.

When about 10 or 12 weeks old the young begin to come out of the nest. Mating occurs in December or January and the period of gestation is probably about the same as in the case of the Gray Squirrel, 45 days.

When it becomes necessary for squirrels to carry their young from one nest to another for safety or other reasons, the young are grasped by the mother by the belly and the young assists in grasping the mother's neck by means of the fore and hind feet. Dangling them from the mouth by the back

Map 47. Published records, recent observations, and specimens in collections of the Fox Squirrel, *Sciurus niger rufiventer*, in Indiana.

The published records for the Fox Squirrel are: Brown (Evermann and Butler 1894), Carroll (Evermann and Butler 1894), Franklin (Haymond 1870, Langdon 1881, Butler 1885, Butler 1886, Evermann and Butler 1894, Hahn 1909), Lake (Stoddard 1920, Brennan 1923), Laporte (Anonymous 1880, Brennan 1923), Lawrence (Hahn 1908), Marshall (Evermann and Clark 1911, 1920), Miami (Bangs 1896, Hahn 1909), Monroe (Evermann and Butler 1894, McAtee 1907), Morgan (Major 1915), Newton (Hahn 1907), Ohio (Hahn 1909), Porter (Hahn 1907, 1909, Stoddard 1920, Lyon 1923, 1925, Brennan 1923), Posey (Wied 1839-41, 1861-62, A. H. Howell 1910), Putnam (Anonymous 1881), Randolph (Cox 1893), St. Joseph (Anonymous 1880, Engels 1933), Vanderburg (Cory 1912), Vigo (Evermann and Butler 1894), Wabash (Evermann and Butler 1894), western Indiana (Kennicott 1857), throughout the state (Hahn 1909).

as is done in the case of cats which have longer legs would interfere with the squirrel's progress, either on the ground or in climbing about trees. (See Herbert Lang, Journal of Mammalogy, vol. 6, pp. 18-24, plate 3, 1925.)

FLYING SQUIRRELS

Genus **Glaucomys** Thomas

The Flying Squirrels constitute a separate subfamily of the *Sciuridae*, the *Pteromyinae*, all characterized by the presence of the flying membrane between the fore and hind limbs, and in some of the exotic genera by having the membrane extended from the hind limbs to the tail. The several members of the family *Sciuridae* described above all fall in the subfamily *Sciurinae*.

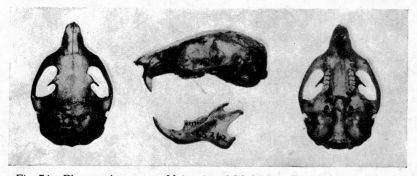

Fig. 74. Photographs courtesy University of Michigan. Dorsal, lateral and ventral views of skull of Flying Squirrel. *Glaucomys volans*, about natural size, Cat. No. 65,262, Univ. of Mich., Lake County, August 2, 1930, Paul Hickie and Thomas Harrison.

The genus *Glaucomys* is peculiarly North American. However, closely related genera are found in Europe, Asia and the Malay Region. The genus ranges in North America from Alaska to Quebec and southward in the eastern United States to the Gulf of Mexico. The species in it fall into two well marked groups: The large *Glaucomys sabrinus,* the northern animal and the small *Glaucomys volans* with a geographic distribution essentially the same as that of Fox Squirrel, from the Atlantic seaboard, Massachusetts to Florida, westward to Minnesota, Nebraska and Texas. Five subspecies of *Glaucomys volans* are recognized, one of them *Glaucomys volans volans* occupying the northern part of the range of the species from North Carolina and Arkansas northward. It is found throughout the whole of the state of Indiana.

The generic characters are mainly external ones. They are squirrels in which the fore and hind limbs are connected by a broad fold of skin extending from wrists to ankles supported anteriorly by a slender cartilaginous process growing from the wrist. The tail is broad, much flattened and its sides nearly parallel. In accordance with its nocturnal habits the eyes are larger than those of diurnal genus *Sciurus*. In addition to these there are certain technical differences in the skull. Dental formula:

$$i \frac{1-1}{1-1}, \ c \frac{0-0}{0-0}, \ pm \frac{2-2}{1-1}, \ m \frac{3-3}{3-3}, = 22.$$

The first upper premolar is very small.

FLYING SQUIRREL,
Glaucomys volans volans (Linnaeus)

[*Mus*] *volans* LINNAEUS. Syst. Nat., ed. 10, vol. 1, p. 63, 1758. Type locality: Virginia.

Fig. 75.   Flying Squirrel, *Glaucomys volans*, photograph by J. C. Allen, West Lafayette.

Sciurus volucella PALLAS. Nov. Spec. Glires, p. 351, 1778.
Pteromys volucella Wied 1839-41, Plummer 1844, Haymond 1870.
Sciuropterus volans Evermann and Butler 1894, Hahn 1909.
Glaucomys volans volans. A. H. Howell 1919.

The fur is very soft and dense. General color, above drab to pinkish cinnamon, washed with pinkish buff along the sides, hairs slate-colored at base; head grayish; ears small and rounded, light brown; tail above similar to the back but less pinkish, below light pinkish cinnamon; underparts white to creamy white to the roots of the hairs; forefeet whitish; hind feet brownish except for whitish toes. In summer the color is usually darker and redder than in winter.

The skull is distinguished from that of other Indiana *Sciuridae* by its small size and rounded form. The braincase is depressed at the back and the rostrum is short and sharply marked off from the broad interorbital region.

Total length, 220-240 mm.; tail vertebrae, 90-110 mm.; hind foot, 29-32 mm. Greatest length of skull 34-36 mm.; greatest width, 20-22 mm. Weight, 40-70 grams.

The Flying Squirrel is nocturnal and arboreal in its habits. It may be common in localities and yet seldom seen. Like the other arboreal squirrels it frequently comes on the ground. Although designated as a flying squirrel it does not possess true flight like the Bats. It is a glider and not a flier. Its mode of progression is not essentially different from that of other arboreal squirrels but its powers of leaping from place to place are highly specialized. By means of its development of skin between the fore and hind limbs and its broad flattened tail it can make unusually long leaps from branch to branch or tree to tree. It always starts from a higher position and lands at a lower one. The usual distance covered is not more than 25 or 30 feet but authentic instances of nearly 100 feet are recorded and even as much as 50 yards. It has the power of breaking its flight by an upward turn at the end of the glide. It is able to change the direction of its glide while in mid air.

Occasionally, in the evening twilight or on moonlight nights, a Flying Squirrel may be seen sailing in a gentle downward curve from one tree to another, the start being made from well toward the top of one tree and the place of alighting at a much lower point on the other. There is something ghost-like in this gliding flight; it is so unlike that of any other of our native creatures; there is not only an entire absence of fluttering wings, but perfect silence. (Evermann and Clark 1920).

These squirrels are inhabitants of woods and usually make their nests in holes in old dead or decaying trees. They may utilize a hollow limb, a decayed and hollowed out portion of the trunk or a deserted or usurped woodpecker's hole. Pounding the base of the tree will often induce them to come out and sail away to another tree even in broad daylight. They are resourceful animals and stand civilization well, frequently making their homes in lofts and attics. In the residential part of South Bend the occupants of a house were disturbed by the nightly running around of some animals thought to be rats in the attic. Some traps were set for them and the house owners were surprised to take Flying Squirrels out of them. One of these was mounted and is now in the posession of Mr. Henry Duncker of South Bend. Dr. R. B. Dugdale, of South Bend, says one got into his house in summer by way of the chimney and fireplace. Evermann and Clark (1920) speak of their taking up winter quarters in some suitable loft box or cupboard in the cottages about Lake Maxinkuckee.

In addition to nesting in holes in trees Flying Squirrels also make outside nests.

On August 19, 1906, while riding along a road west of the lake a squeaking sound attracted attention to the base of a small scrub oak at the roadside. On examining the place four young Flying Squirrels were discovered. They were quite small and wholly naked. A storm had probably blown them from their nest which was a large, globular affair, made of fibrous material, situated in the crotch of the tree. While we were only a few feet away, one of the parent squirrels, presumably the mother, came down the tree and, taking the young in her mouth, carried them, one at a time, back to the nest. (Evermann and Clark 1920).

These same authors tell of another instance in which two young were carried away from the ground, one at a time. After carrying the young up one tree the mother flew with each to another tree thirty feet away. The mother was so solicitous about the young that she permitted Evermann to take her in his hand.

On December 16, 1890, a family of six Flying Squirrels was found by Mr. J. M. Beck near Burlington. They were all full grown. On Thanksgiving Day, several years ago, Prof. U. O. Cox, then of Farmland, Indiana, found 15 Flying Squirrels in a small rotten stump a little higher than a man's head. (Evermann and Clark 1920).

Six may have been a pair and their young, of the last litter, but 15 in one hole indicates a gregarious habit on the part of the animal aside from any family relationship, a habit which is spoken of by various other authors.

They seem to breed chiefly in the spring, about sugar making time. A second or third litter may be produced later in the season. (Evermann and Clark 1920).

A. H. Howell (1918) says:

The number of young produced at birth varies from 3 to 6—usually 4 or 5. The period of gestation is said to be one month, but no definite evidence on this point is available.

There are eight mammae, two inguinal, four abdominal, and two pectoral.

Map 48. Published records and specimens in collections of the Flying Squirrel, *Glaucomys volans*, in Indiana.

The Flying Squirrel is probably found in every county in the state (Hahn 1909), but published reports are comparatively few. These are: Carroll (Evermann and Butler 1894), Franklin (Haymond 1870, Quick and Langdon 1882, Evermann and Butler 1894), Knox (A. H. Howell 1918), Lagrange (Evermann and Butler 1894), Laporte (Anonymous 1880, Elliot 1907, Cory 1912, A. H. Howell 1918), Lawrence (Hahn 1908), Marion (Brayton 1882), Marshall (Evermann and Clark 1911, 1920), Miami (Bangs 1896, A. H. Howell 1918), Monroe (Evermann and Butler 1894, McAtee 1907), Newton (A. H. Howell 1918), Posey (Wied 1839-41, 1861-62), Putnam (Anonymous 1881), Randolph (Cox 1893, Evermann and Butler 1894), St. Joseph (Anonymous 1880, Engels 1933), Vigo (Evermann and Butler 1894, Evermann and Clark 1911), Wabash (Evermann and Butler 1894), Wayne (Plummer 1844), Kankakee marshes (Hahn 1907, Cory 1912).

The food of flying squirrels consists in large part of nuts, including probably, most of the native species—chestnuts, acorns, beechnuts, hickorynuts, pecans and others. . . . they frequently gather and store seeds of the cultivated cherry. . . . Several stomachs taken at Red Fork, Okla., in June contained only remains of insect larvae. Buds of trees are said to be eaten in winter, and corn or other grain sometimes is taken. Beetles and perhaps other insects constitute part of the animals' fare. They have a decided taste for meat, and are so frequently caught by fur trappers in meat-baited traps set for larger game as to constitute a nuisance. . . . Stores of food laid up by flying squirrels for winter use have occasionally been found, indicating that the hoarding habit is probably general. (A. H. Howell 1918).

H. L. Stoddard (Journal of Mammalogy, vol. 1, p. 95, 1920) contributes the following as to its carnivorous propensities:

On April 6, 1914, an adult female flying squirrel (*Glaucomys volans*) was captured with her two young and placed in a roomy cage in the workshop with a section of tree trunk containing a flicker's hole as a nest. Two or three days later a fine male yellow-bellied sapsucker was captured unhurt, and placed in the same cage when he made himself at home on the stump. I was greatly surprised the next morning to find his bones on the bottom of the cage picked clean. This strong, hardy woodpecker in perfect health had been killed and eaten during a few hours of darkness, by the old mother flying squirrel, though she had other food in abundance. . . .

Flying Squirrels make interesting pets. Brayton (1882) contributes the following:

A pair, kept in confinement under the observation of the author, [probably in Indianapolis] made their nest in a crayon-box placed over a bay window. In the evening they would come to the floor and take up any kind of nuts, ends of ears of popcorn, and similar food, which was packed away in the box in excess of their daily meals. Their favorite amusement was to jump from the highest point of the transoms directly toward occupants of the sitting room, suddenly veering to the right or left when almost in one's face, and alighting on the floor or furniture at the opposite side of the room. The female joined with the male in these amusements until in April when, heavy with young, she became sluggish. The young, four in number, were brought forth in the drawer of the library table, at which some of the family sat every evening. The mother was very much annoyed, and even alarmed when the drawer was closed during her temporary absence. The male was not admitted to the drawer, but kept to the box. Finally, the whole family escaped from an open window and took to the woods. . . .

POCKET GOPHERS
Family Geomyidae

The family *Geomyidae* is confined to North America where it ranges from the plains of the Saskatchewan in Canada southward to Costa Rica. It attains its highest development in the western United States and Mexico. It extends eastward in the north to northwestern Indiana. In the Gulf States occurs a group separated from the other members reaching the Atlantic seaboard in Florida and Georgia, south of the Savannah River and westward to Alabama. It embraces nine genera one of which is found in extreme northwestern Indiana.

Miller and Gidley (1918) give the following technical definition of the living members of the family:

Skull fossorial; zygoma robust; infraorbital foramen always at end of a long canal, its orifice protected from muscle pressure by countersinking in an oblique sulcus; frontal without postorbital process; . . . Angular portion of mandible mostly above alveolar level; cheek teeth ever growing, the first and second adult molar consisting each of a single prism, with an enamel plate always present on the anterior surface in upper teeth and on posterior surface of lower teeth.

The skull is large, heavy and angular, with wide spreading zygometic arches and a heavily built rostrum.

They are readily distinguished from any other North American mammals by their generally compact rat-like form, comparatively short, essentially naked tail, large heavy incisors, heavy claws on front feet and especially by large external cheek pouches opening on either side of the mouth, and outside of it, extending as far back as the shoulder, and lined with fur. The mouth opening is very small and divided into two compartments by a sort of diaphragm between the incisors and the cheek teeth. All members are strictly fossorial in their habits and spend nearly all their lives in subterranean burrows which are dug by means of their large incisors and large strong forefeet. They have no noticeable external ears and very small eyes.

POCKET GOPHERS
Genus **Geomys** Rafinesque

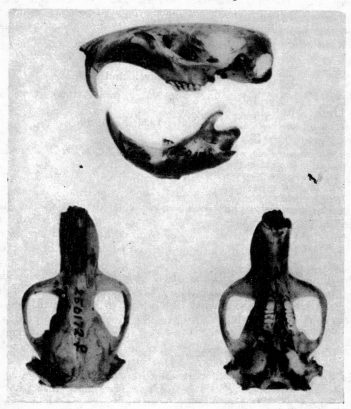

Fig. 76. Photographs courtesy U. S. Nat. Mus. Lateral, dorsal and palatal views of skull of Pocket Gopher, *Geomys illinoenşis*, natural size, Cat. No. 250,172, U. S. Nat. Mus., Rensselaer, Jasper County, July 4, 1931, M. W. Lyon, Jr. and W. L. Engels.

The genus *Geomys* ranges from North Dakota south to Louisiana, Texas and New Mexico, from northwestern Indiana west to Wyoming and Colorado; with an isolated group in southern Alabama, Georgia and northern Florida. About a dozen and a half species and subspecies are recognized one of which is found in the northwestern counties of Indiana.

The genus *Geomys* is distinguished from the other members of the family by having posterior enamel plates present on first and second upper molars, no enamel plate on posterior face of upper premolar. Each upper incisor has a rather large groove down its anterior face and also a smaller groove toward the inner side of the tooth. Dental formula:

$$i\frac{1-1}{1-1},\ c\frac{0-0}{0-0},\ pm\frac{1-1}{1-1},\ m\frac{3-3}{3-3},\ = 20.$$

The Pocket Gopher shows a peculiar sexual dimorphism of the pelvis. The males possess a normal rodent pelvis and normal symphysis pubis, also the female until the time of bearing her first litter. At that time under the influence of an ovarian hormone the pubic symphysis becomes absorbed, thus enlarging the birth canal. This absorption persists throughout the life of the animal (Hisaw 1925).

ILLINOIS POCKET GOPHER.
Geomys illinoensis Komarek and Spencer

Mus bursarius SHAW. Trans. Linn. Soc., vol. 5, p. 227, 1800. Type locality: Upper Mississippi Valley.
Geomys bursarius Evermann and Butler 1894, Hahn 1909.
Geomys pinctis (sic) Ball 1900.
Geomys bursarius illinoensis KOMAREK and SPENCER 1931. Type locality: Momence, Kankakee County, Illinois. Lyon 1932.

As the Illinois Pocket Gopher is not known to integrade with the more western dark brown *Geomys bursarius* it is here given the status of a full species. The existence of plumbeous or dusky colored animals was well known to Merriam (1895) and plumbeous colored ones are recorded by Baird (1857) from part of the present known range of *Geomys illinoensis*. Merriam referred to it as a color phase and Baird intimated that it might be of taxonomic significance.

The Illinois Pocket Gopher is slatey gray in color above, underneath similar, but the hairs tipped with light brownish or whitish, feet and tail whitish, the latter scantily covered with whitish hairs; a small whitish spot on the throat. The nasal bones are constricted in their middle portion. Total length, 250-325 mm.; tail, 70-100 mm.; hind foot, 32-36 mm. Weight, about 300 grams. Males larger than females. Greatest length of skull, about 48 mm., greatest width, about 28 mm.

The Pocket Gopher spends practically its entire life beneath the surface of the ground in burrows of its own making. The tunnels that I have examined are about a foot below the surface and of a size to admit comfortably one's hand. The main tunnel is often many yards in length. Coming off from it laterally at intervals of a few feet are short side passages used by the animal for carrying out the dirt from the main passages. The dirt is piled up into characteristic mounds of varying size. After the last load of dirt has been shoved out, the opening of the lateral on the outside is firmly plugged with dirt and obliterated. Indeed it is sometimes difficult to find the lateral burrow at all. Once found it leads to the main tunnel and by inserting one's arm one can move his hand in either direction into the main tunnel. The

Fig. 77. Pocket Gopher, *Geomys illinoensis*, Newton County, photograph by M. W. Lyon, Jr.

recent activity of the animals may be told by the freshness of the piles of excavated dirt.

The Pocket Gophers, in working their way through the earth in the construction of their tunnels, use the powerful upper incisors as a pick to loosen the ground. At the same time the fore feet are kept in active operation, both in digging and pressing the earth back under the body, and the hind feet are used also in moving it still further backward. When a sufficient quantity has accumulated behind the animal, he immediately turns in the burrow and by bringing the wrists together under the chin, with the palms of the hands held vertically, forces himself along by the hind feet, pushing the earth in front. When an opening in the tunnel is reached the earth is discharged through it, forming a little hillock. . . . (Merriam 1895).

The animal is able to run forward or backward with equal facility. The tail appears to serve as a tactile organ in running backward.

[The] cheek pouches are used exclusively in carrying food, and not in carting dirt as often erroneously supposed. The animals are great hoarders and carry away to their storehouses vastly more than they consume. The cheek pouches reach back as far as the shoulder and are so attached that they can not be completely everted without rupture of their connections. . . . As a rule one pouch was filled at a time, though not always, and the hand of the same side was used to push the food in. . . . A piece of potato, root, or other food is seized between the incisor teeth, and is immediately transferred to the fore paws, which are held in a horizontal position, the tips of the claws curving toward one another. . . . The piece is then passed rapidly across the side of the face with a sort of wiping motion which forces it into the open mouth of the pouch. Sometimes a single rapid stroke with one hand is sufficient; at other times both hands are used, particularly if the piece is large. . . . The most remarkable thing connected with the use of the pouches is the way they are emptied. The fore feet are brought back simultaneously along the sides of the head until they reach a point opposite the hinder end of the pouches; they are then pressed firmly against the head and carried rapidly forward. In this way the contents of the pouches are promptly dumped in front of the animal. (Merriam 1895).

Fig. 78. Workings of Pocket Gopher, *Geomys illinoensis*, Tippecanoe County, photograph by G. C. Oderkirk, Purdue University.

The food of Pocket Gophers consists of roots, including those of small trees, tubers and similar vegetation; some green stuff is eaten around the temporary openings of the burrows. Material is cut small enough to fit the pouches. It is necessarily cut by the incisors into small bits in order to pass the diaphragm-like structures between the incisors and cheek teeth. In cultivated regions they may become troublesome. Those that I have seen in Indiana were most frequently found in uncultivated land. Otis Wade reports a captive Pocket Gopher to which he fed small portions of fresh beef regularly and the animal seemed to enjoy it. (Journal of Mammalogy, vol. 8, p. 310, 1927.)

Pocket Gophers are solitary, surly animals; except at time of mating or breeding, but one individual occupies a tunnel. Little is known of their breeding habits. In their burrows they make a nest chamber, as well as food storage chambers. Bailey (1926) describes young in the nest as very immature, blind, hairless and pink in color. The number of young is probably about four. The mammae are six in number, two pairs inguinal and one pair pectoral. As soon as young are old enough to dig for themselves they leave the home burrows, and begin leading the usual solitary lives of their kind. The time of birth is probably in spring. Whether more than one litter a season is produced is unknown.

Pocket Gophers do not hibernate, but Bailey found them less active on cold days. In winter their tunnels are made beneath the frost line. They are helpless in water which may account for some peculiarities of distribution, such as the fact that the Illinois Pocket Gopher is only at present known between the Kankakee-Illinois river system and the Wabash.

Special traps have been devised for catching Pocket Gophers. No bait is used; the abhorrence of an unplugged doorway is sufficient to induce the animals to try to plug it and spring the trap. I have had better success with ordinary small steel traps placed level with the floor of the main tunnels so that the Gopher must cross the pan coming or going. After placing the trap the whole burrow is covered with stiff cardboard and dirt piled over it to exclude all light. If light enters, the animal is all too often likely to push dirt over the trap and bury it without springing it. When caught unkilled in traps, the animals appear sullen and give vent to a dull hissing sound. Those that I have taken were active in their tunnels during the day time.

Not many persons seem to be familiar with the Pocket Gopher in Indiana, although it is not uncommon in places in Newton and Jasper Counties; many express surprise when shown one. They can scarcely be called a menace to agriculture. Those I have found were inhabiting waste ground. Some agriculturists found their mounds a nuisance but the few that I have interviewed thought their damage to crops negligible.

Map 49. Published records and specimens in collections of the Pocket Gopher, *Geomys illinoensis*, in Indiana; 1, collection of Frederick H. Test; this specimen was taken north of the Wabash River which flows through Tippecanoe County.

The published records of the Pocket Gopher are: Jasper (Ball 1900, Lyon 1932), [Lake (Hahn 1909), probably erroneous record], Newton (Evermann and Butler 1894, Butler 1895, Hahn 1907, 1909, Komarek and Spencer 1931, Lyon 1932), [St. Joseph (Elliot 1907, Cory 1912), erroneous record,], Tippecanoe (Lyon 1932).

BEAVERS
Family Castoridae

Beavers formerly inhabited the forested portions of the Northern Hemisphere, extending south to the Mediterranean region and the southern United States. Today they are largely exterminated from much of this area.

Beavers are one of the three families of recent sciuroid or squirrel-like rodents occurring in Indiana, the other two being the *Sciuridae* and *Geomyidae*. They are large heavily built animals with a broad tail flattened from above downwards, its surface scaly. Hind feet, webbed, the second toe of the hind foot with a double claw, or split claw. Their habits are aquatic. The skull lacks postorbital processes. The cheek teeth are rootless, with reentrant enamel folds. Dental formula:

$$ i \frac{1-1}{1-1},\ c \frac{0-0}{0-0},\ pm \frac{1-1}{1-1},\ m \frac{3-3}{3-3}, = 20. $$

It contains but a single genus *Castor,* with four closely related species, one peculiar to the Old World and the other three to the northern portions of North America.

BEAVERS
Genus Castor Linnaeus

The geographic distribution and the distinguishing characters of the genus are the same as those of the family *Castoridae* given above. Three species are recognized in North America and ten additional subspecies, one or perhaps two of which were formerly found throughout the whole of Indiana in suitable localities.

BEAVER
Castor canadensis carolinensis Rhoads

Castor canadensis KUHL. Beitrage z. Zool., p. 64, 1820. Type locality: Hudson Bay.

Castor canadensis carolinensis RHOADS. Trans. Amer. Philos. Soc., n.s., vol. 19, p. 420, 1898. Type locality: Dan River, near Danbury, Stokes County, North Carolina.

Castor americanus Wied 1839-41.

Castor fiber Plummer 1844. Evermann and Butler 1894.

Castor canadensis carolinensis Hahn 1909.

There are no specimens of beaver from Indiana extant so far as I am aware except the imperfect skull which is figured. It is assumed on purely geographic grounds that the Beaver formerly occupying Indiana belonged to the subspecies *Castor canadensis carolinensis*. It might well be, however, that the north Michigan subspecies *Castor canadensis michiganensis* was the one that formerly inhabited the state, along with the Porcupine. It also may have

Fig. 79. Photograph courtesy N. Y. Zool. Soc. Beaver, *Castor canadensis*, once common in Indiana.

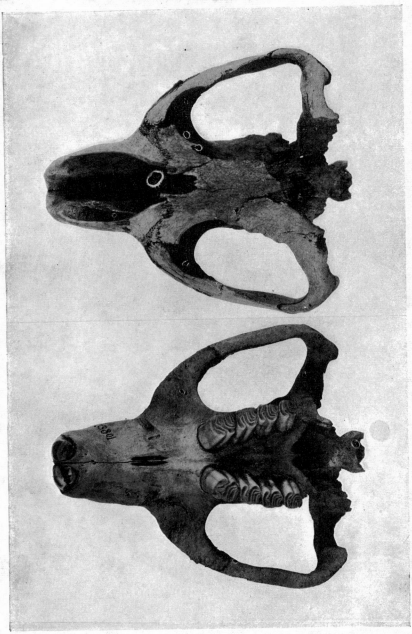

Fig. 80. Photograph courtesy Field Mus. Nat. Hist. Dorsal and palatal views of skull of Beaver, *Castor canadensis*, 8/11 natural size, Cat. No. 33,801, Field Mus. Nat. Hist., collected at Ogden Dunes, Porter County by D. A. Spencer. So far as known, this fragmentary skull is the only extant specimen of a Beaver from Indiana.

been the case that the northern *michiganensis*, was found in the northern third of the state in analogy with the Northern Gray Squirrel, and that the Carolina Beaver occupied the southern portion with an area of intergradation in between.

The general color of the Beaver is an almost uniform dark brown, the long or guard hairs chestnut brown, the soft, shorter under fur without any reddish tinge. The head is brighter in color than elsewhere, and the underparts are lighter and lack any reddish tinge. The Carolina Beaver is a duller, paler colored animal than the Beavers of the north, and is described as somewhat larger, and as having a broader tail, its fur is shorter and relatively harsher.

Total length about 45 in. (1100 mm.), scaly portion of tail 11 in. long by 6¼ in. wide (280 x 160 mm.), hind foot, 7.4 in. (184 mm.). Weight, 30 to 60 pounds (14-27 kgs.).

Beavers are very aquatic in their habits, but much of their feeding and other activities are done on land, but always near water. Their webbed hind feet constitute their chief mode of propulsion in the water, the tail being mostly a rudder. Seton (1929) estimates their best swimming speed at two miles per hour. Their progresssion on land is equally slow or worse. They are found in small lakes, ponds and small streams with suitable banks or in small ponds of their own construction. The undrained lake region of the Indiana of bygone days must have been ideal for them.

On account of their valuable fur they were among the first of the recent mammals to be exterminated from the region now occupied by Indiana. They seem to have disappeared even before the early days when naturalists and travellers were making casual mention of other large mammals. Dinwiddie (1884) speaking of Lake County region says that Beavers had dissappeared before the advent of the white man. Kennicott (1855) says remains of dams are found in northern Illinois. Plummer (1844) speaks of dams being found about Richmond, but knew of no one who had ever seen a beaver there. No Beaver skins are mentioned in the Hamilton County list of 1859 (Anonymous 1906).

Remains of dams are reported by various authors and the South Bend *Tribune* of Sunday, May 11, 1930 contains a photographic reproduction of a so-called beaver dam at Sousley Lake, St. Joseph County. I have seen this and some other so-called beaver dams. They were all made so long ago, over a century, that it is impossible from a superficial examination of them to say whether or not they are real beaver dams. The only way to determine this point is to dig down into them and see if they have as a base, branches showing the unmistakable cutting marks of the Beaver, or possibly to find a few Beaver bones. The Sousley Lake dam is wide and solid enough to drive a car across it and appears as a solid earth affair at the present time. I have been unable to investigate its interior.

Hahn (1909) writes that Mr. E. J. Chansler reports a beaver taken near Vincennes in 1840 by Mr. T. Dubois. Evermann (Evermann and Butler 1894) writes:

In September 1888, I saw a skull in Mr. Sampson's collection at New Harmony, that was taken near there not many years ago.

The Prince of Wied (1839-41) in 1832-33 reports beavers as formerly abundant along the lower Wabash. Evermann and Butler (1894) write:

This [the Beaver] was certainly rather common in Indiana in early days. 'Beaver Lake' [probably Newton County, not on modern maps] was, no doubt, so named because of the presence of beavers there. [In the same county on certain maps are found the places Beaver City, Beaver Timber.] Mr. C. L. Reynolds says he saw a beaver swimming in the Wabash river about twelve miles above LaFayette, in the summer of 1889. He says he is sure of it.

In 1932 newspapers reported Beavers working in Wells County, and reproduced photographs of undoubted cuttings. Father J. F. Luttmann has shown me similar cuttings in a tamarack swamp at Edwardsburg, Mich., just north of the Indiana line, made within the past two or three years. The source of these Beavers is a mystery.

Beavers are usually attributed with remarkable intelligence and foresight but it is doubtful if they possess these qualities to a higher degree than other rodents. Their valuable fur and large size has drawn attention to them. Observations are easier made on them than many of the smaller forms. Beavers do a few things that are worthy of brief mention. Those interested in more detailed accounts of their life and habits are referred to these authors: L. H. Morgan, The American Beaver and His Works, 1868; H. T. Martin, Castorologia or the History and Traditions of the Canadian Beaver, 1892; Enos A. Mills, In Beaver World, 1913; E. R. Warren, The Beaver, Its Work and Its Ways, 1927; C. E. Johnson, The Beaver in the Adirondacks, 1927; as well as Seton's account (1929).

Felling trees is its most important habit. The act is accomplished by gnawing around the base of the trunk until it is so thin that the tree falls by its own weight. As trees growing on the edges of ponds and streams naturally incline toward them, the trees fall toward the pond or stream according to natural laws and not according to any skill on the part of the Beaver. Once felled it is cut up. Its bark is eaten, branches are used for the framework of dams, sticks of suitable size for building houses, and pieces stored for winter use. The trees cut down are comparatively small, with trunk diameter of only a few inches though sometimes trunks a foot or over in diameter are cut through. It is believed that usually two, sometimes more Beavers work on the same tree. While connected with Long's Expedition to the Rocky Mountains 1819-1820 Thomas Say, one of Indiana's early naturalists writes thus:

Three Beavers were seen cutting down a large cottonwood tree, when they had made considerable progress, one of them retired to a short distance, and took his station in the water, looking steadfastly at the top of the tree. As soon as he perceived the top begin to move toward its fall, he gave notice of the danger to his companions, who were still at work gnawing at its base, by slapping his tail upon the surface of the water, and they immediately ran from the tree out of harm's way. [5]

---

5 In James's Account of S. H. Long's Expedition 1819-1820, p. 151, vol. 2, 1823, *Teste* Early Western Travels 1748-1846, by Reuben Gold Thwaites, vol. 15, p. 236, 1905—Cleveland, Ohio, Arthur H. Clark Company.

Probably the cracking of the wood as the tree is about to fall serves to alarm them. Mr. and Mrs. Wendell Chapman show a motion picture of a beaver struck by the branches of a new-felled tree. It was unhurt.

Beaver houses or lodges are of two kinds, like those of the Muskrat. First, a simple burrow into a stream or lake bank with an enlarged and lined nest cavity; and second, lodges built of a pile of sticks in the shallow water of a lake or pond, with a lined nest cavity or cavities in the center. The opening to both types of houses is from beneath the surface of the water.

Dams are made for the purpose of making a pond. Only small streams are dammed, those not over two feet in depth. Branches are placed with the butt end upstream and piled one on top of another and the whole weighted down and filled in with mud, sod and stones. As the water rises the dam has to be enlarged all along its front and continued on the side. Alleged remnants of these dams are all that remains of the Beaver in Indiana. Beavers are said to show much ability and engineering skill in the planning of these dams, but no doubt the facts are that they build dams more or less hit or miss and that only the successful ones that show engineering skill remain.

Canals are dug from the shore of lakes inland in order that they may reach more food supply. These may be of several hundred feet in length, and are wide and deep enough for the animal to navigate freely in and to carry branches from inland to their lodges.

The chief food of Beavers is bark of poplars, cottonwoods, aspens, willows, birchs and alders. They also feed on the roots of various aquatic plants.

They do not hibernate but remain active all winter and subsist on stored branches and on the vegetation at the bottom of their frozen lake. They can remain under water for periods of time up to six minutes, or more.

Mating is supposed to take place in the first few weeks of the year. Gestation lasts about three months. The young, termed kits, numbering from two to five, usually four, are born in a fair state of development, and need to be nursed by the mother only about a month before they begin to eat solid food. The young remain with parents for nearly a year.

The Beaver was one of the most sought for fur bearing animals of North America, and still is in many sections. The fur traders and trappers in its quest were among the foremost of the pioneers on the continent, so the Beaver has played his part in settling the wilderness, a costly part to him, for he has been exterminated over much of his former range. He cannot stand civilization, but given wild country and much of it and adequate protection he thrives well, and has been brought back in recent years to places from which he had been formerly exterminated. There are still probably some places left in Indiana where a few Beavers might thrive if introduced and given half a chance. I do not believe, however, there are areas in the state where Beavers could be raised for profit. Their introduction would only be done in the interest of nature lovers and conservationists who wished to preserve an interesting mammal that was found throughout Indiana in days before the White Man.

Map 50. Published records of the former occurrence and specimen in collection of the Beaver, *Castor canadensis carolinensis*, in Indiana.

The published records for the Beaver are: Allen (Dryer 1889), Bartholomew (Butler 1895), Dearborn (Anonymous 1885), Dekalb (Anonymous 1914), Franklin (Butler 1885, Evermann and Butler 1894), Grant (Phinney 1884), Jasper (Collett 1883), Knox (Butler 1895, Hahn 1909), Lagrange (Rerick 1882, Evermann and Butler 1894), Lake (Dinwiddie 1884, Ball 1894, Brennan 1923), Laporte (Brennan 1923), Marion (Anonymous 1906), Marshall (Evermann and Clark 1911, 1920), Morgan (Major 1915), Newton (Butler 1895, Ade 1911), Ohio (Anonymous 1885), Porter (Brennan 1923), Posey (Wied 1839-41, Evermann and Butler 1894), Putnam (Anonymous 1881), Randolph (Cox 1893, Evermann and Butler 1894), St. Joseph (Anonymous 1880, Engels 1933), Steuben (Anonymous 1888, Tippecanoe (Evermann and Butler 1894, Butler 1895, Cory 1912), Wayne (Plummer 1844), Kankakee Valley (Reed 1920), lower Wabash (Croghan 1834), formerly throughout the state (Hahn 1909).

GIANT BEAVERS
† Family **Castoroididae**

Zygomasseteric structure modified by the passage of the shaft of the incisor below the infraorbital foramen instead of above it, the ridge formed by the tooth dividing the area of masseteric origin or side of rostrum into two planes; posterior nares divided horizontally by the median fusing of palatine bones over roots of cheekteeth; teeth ever-growing, the enamel pattern a series of 5-7 parallel transverse ridges. Miller and Gidley (1918).

The family contains but a single genus of some uncertain species and one well known one, confined to the Pleistocene of North America.

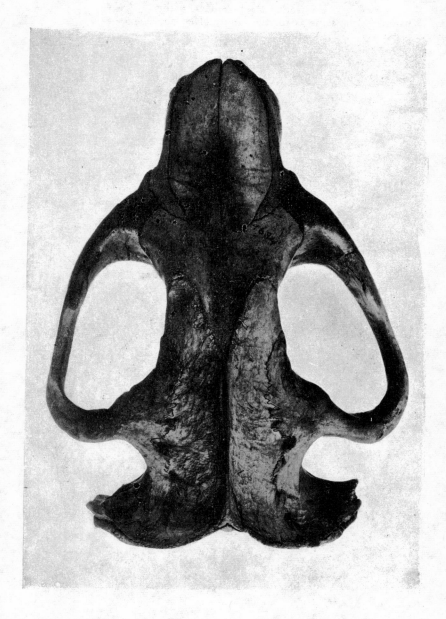

Fig. 81. Photograph courtesy U. S. Nat. Mus. Dorsal view of skull of Giant Beaver, *Castoroides ohioensis*, about 1/3 natural size, Cat. No. 1634, U. S. Nat. Mus., Logansport, Cass County, 1894, S. L. McFadin.

GIANT BEAVERS
Genus **Castoroides** Foster
Characters, the same as for the family given above.

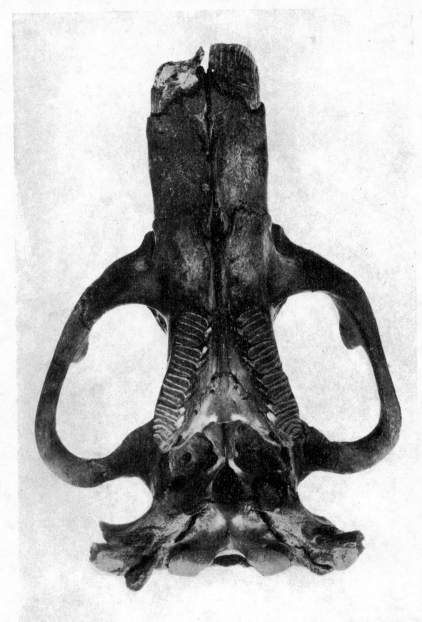

Fig. 82. Photograph courtesy U. S. Nat. Mus. Palatal view of skull of Giant Beaver, *Castoroides ohioensis*, about 1/3 natural size, Cat. No. 1634, U. S. Nat. Mus., Logansport, Cass County, 1894, S. L. McFadin.

Fig. 83. Photograph courtesy Amer. Mus. Nat. Hist. Restoration of the Giant Beaver, *Castoroides ohioensis*. The squirrel on the tree trunk in the foreground gives an idea of the great size of the Giant Beaver, more remains of which have been found in Indiana than in any other state.

GIANT BEAVER

† **Castoroides ohioensis** Foster

† *Castoroides ohioensis* FOSTER. 2nd Ann. Rep. Geol. Surv. Ohio, p. 81, 1838; Collet 1876, Hay 1902, 1912, 1923, 1930, Cahn 1932.

The Giant Beaver is one of the largest rodents known. Remains of it have been found in the North American Pleistocene from Central New York to the Great Plains and from Florida to Minnesota and even farther north.

It had the size of the Black Bear, greatest length of skull about 270 mm. (10½ in.), greatest width about 195 mm. (7½ in.). Its supposed external appearance is shown on Fig. 83. The latest author (Cahn 1932) dealing with *Castoroides* credits it with habits and activities similar to those of the modern beavers, genus *Castor*. More remains of it have been found in Indiana than

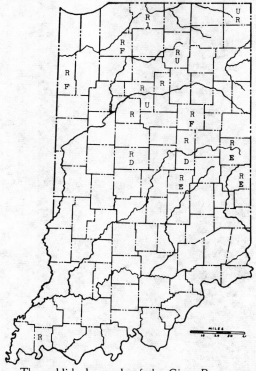

Map 51. Published records and specimens in collections of the Giant Beaver, *Castoroides ohioensis*, in Indiana; 1, Northern Indiana Historical Society.

The published records of the Giant Beaver are: Boone (Hay 1912, 1923, Cahn 1932), Carroll (Collett 1884, Hay 1912, 1923, Baker 1920, Cahn 1932), Cass (Hay 1912, 1923, Cahn 1932), DeKalb (Cahn 1932), Grant (Hay 1912, 1912B, 1923, Cahn 1932), Hancock (Moore 1893, 1900, Hay 1912, 1923, Baker 1920, Cahn 1932), Kosciusko (Collett 1884, Hay 1912, 1923, Baker 1920, Cahn 1932), Madison (Hay 1912, 1923, Cahn 1932), Miami (Hay 1923, Cahn 1932), Newton (Anonymous 1932, Cahn 1932), Randolph (Moore 1890 Aug., 1890 Oct., 1891, 1892, 1893, Hay 1912, 1914, 1923, Baker 1920, Cahn 1932), St. Joseph (Engels 1932), Starke (Hay 1923, Cahn 1932), Vanderburg (Collett 1876, 1884, Hay 1912, 1923, Baker 1920, Cahn 1932), Wayne (Moore 1890, 1893, Hay 1912, 1932, Cahn 1932).

in any other state. Not only are they more numerous but they are better preserved than any remains of its dwarf relative that was exterminated in the state
scarcely more than 100 years ago.

RAT OR MOUSE-LIKE RODENTS OR RODENTS OBVIOUSLY DERIVED FROM SUCH FORMS
Superfamily Muroidae Miller and Gidley (1918)

This superfamily contains six living families, only one of which the *Cricetidae* contains forms indigenous to Indiana, and another the *Muridae* represented by introduced species widely distributed throughout the state.

CRICETINE MUROIDS
Family Cricetidae

Infraorbital foramen usually enlarged and specialized, consisting of a rounded upper
portion for transmission of muscle and a narrow lower portion for transmission of nerve,
the zygomatic root developed into a broad oblique plate; skull varying excessively in
form, but always without postorbital process on the frontal; cheekteeth 3/3, the crown
structure showing all stages from brachydont to ever-growing, the fundamental structure quadritubercular, the enamel patterns varying from simple heptamerism to exces-
sive specialization, the tubercles in the maxillary teeth always presenting a longitudinally
biserial arrangement and never developing a functional third series on lingual side of
crown; external form murine or fossorial. (Miller and Gidley 1918).

WHITE-FOOTED MICE AND ALLIES AND CAVE RATS
Subfamily Cricetinae

Skull without special modification . . . the squamosal not developing a postorbital
ridge or process; molars rooted, their crowns varying gradually from tubercular and
brachydont to flat-crowned and strongly hypsodont. . . . (Miller and Gidley 1918).

AMERICAN HARVEST MICE
Genus Reithrodontomys Giglioli

The genus *Reithrodontomys* is peculiarly American, ranging from the southeastern
United States west to the Pacific, north to the Great Plains region and south into
Central America.

The members of this genus are small mice, with long tails, two rows of tubercles
on the upper teeth and most characteristic of all the upper incisors are longitudinally
grooved. There are many other technical characters and those interested are referred
to A. H. Howell's North American Fauna No. 36, 1914. It contains over 50 forms,
one of which will probably be found to occur in southeastern Indiana.

AMERICAN HARVEST MOUSE,
Reithrodontomys humulis merriami (Allen)

Mus humulis AUDUBON AND BACHMAN. Proc. Acad. Nat. Sci. Philadelphia, vol. 1,
    p. 97, 1841. Type locality; Charleston, South Carolina.

Ochetodon humilis Evermann and Butler 1894.

Reithrodontomys merriami ALLEN. Bull. Amer. Mus. Nat. Hist., vol. 7, p. 119,
    1895. Type locality: Near Alvin, Brazoria County, Texas.

Reithrodontomys lecontii Hahn 1909.

Reithrodontomys humulis merriami A. H. Howell. North Amer. Fauna, No. 36,
    p. 21, 1914.

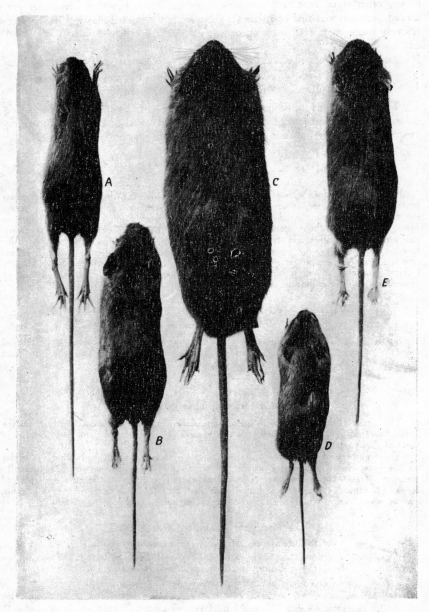

Fig. 84. Photographs courtesy U. S. Nat. Mus. Skins of Indiana long-tailed indigenous Mice, all in U. S. Nat. Mus., about 2/3 natural size.

A.—Jumping Mouse, *Zapus hudsonicus*, Cat. No. 239,797, Porter County, Oct. 27, 1923, M. W. Lyon, Jr.

Merriam's Harvest Mouse is one of three subspecies found in the southeastern United States, ranging from Louisiana northward to southern Ohio. I am assuming that specimens of *Reithrodontomys* from southwestern Ohio in the Cleveland Natural History Museum belong to this subspecies.

Externally Merriam's Harvest Mouse resembles a small House Mouse, brownish above, grayish white below, with a rather clear line of demarkation between upper and lower sides. . Its skull is at once distinguished by the tubercles of upper teeth being arranged in two parallel rows, and the upper incisors with longitudinal grooves.

Total length about 115 mm., tail vertebrae about 55 mm., hind foot about 16 mm.; greatest length of skull about 19 mm., greatest width about 9 mm.

In common with the other members of the genus it is an inhabitant of open grassy situations, particularly in neglected, overgrown fields and weedy borders of cultivated tracts.

There are no known specimens from Indiana but with the animal occurring so close to Indiana as southwestern Ohio, there is every likelihood of its occurring in the state when sufficient trapping is done in suitable habitats in the southeastern portion. Probably a few hundred White-footed Mice will have to be taken before a Harvest Mouse is caught. It was included by both Evermann and Butler (1894) and Hahn (1909) in their hypothetical lists.

WHITE-FOOTED MICE
Genus **Peromyscus** Gloger

Peromyscus is a peculiarly North American genus ranging throughout the continent from about the limits of tree growth in the north, south to Central America.

External form, mouse-like, with a long tail, at least more than a third of the total length, and often more than half; tail with scaly annulations more or less concealed by hair. The ears are large, delicate and thinly clothed with hair. The eyes are large. There are two pairs of inguinal and one pair of pectoral mammae and six tubercles on soles of hind feet in the great majority of species, including the two found in Indiana. More or less evident internal cheek pouches are present. The coloration in adults in general is some shade of brown above and white below, at once distinguishing the White-footed Mice from the ordinary House Mouse. Immature animals are slate colored or plumbeous above and whitish below.

The skull is delicate usually with a smoothly rounded thin-walled brain case. The upper incisor teeth are not longitudinally grooved. The molar teeth are low-crowned and rooted, and in general characterized by two rows of tubercles. Dental formula:

$$i \frac{1-1}{1-1}, \ c \frac{0-0}{0-0}, \ pm \frac{0-0}{0-0}, \ m \frac{3-3}{3-3}, = 16.$$

B.—Prairie White-footed Mouse, *Peromyscus maniculatus bairdii*, Cat. No. 239,024, Porter County, Oct. 4, 1922, M. W. Lyon, Jr.

C.—Rice Rat, *Oryzomys palustris*, Cat. No. 142,167, Suffolk, Va., Jan. 12, 1906, A. Royster. Not certainly known to occur in Indiana.

D.—Harvest Mouse, *Reithrodontomys humulis*, Cat. No. 254,166, Buckingham County, Va., Dec. 27, 1915, Wirt Robinson. Suspected to occur in southeastern Indiana.

E.—Woodland White-footed Mouse, *Peromyscus leucopus noveboracensis*, Cat. No. 239,071, Porter County, Oct. 13, 1922, M. W. Lyon, Jr.

There are many other technical characters and the more ambitious student is referred to the excellent monograph by Osgood (1909).

About 150 species and subspecies are recognized in the genus *Peromyscus*, only two of which are certainly known to be found in Indiana.

White-footed Mice are among our commonest mammals. They are attractive, dainty little creatures and although typically mouse-like in appearance and behavior, have nothing of the repulsiveness of the ordinary House Mouse. Their large delicate ears, large eyes, soft light brown or fawn-colored fur above and white underparts, and absence of musky odor, make them great favorites with those who know them. Considering how common these mice are they are seldom seen owing to their retiring and nocturnal habits.

They wander widely at night not over any beaten pathway, but at will through the fields and woods. However, they are frequently caught in the surface or subsurface runways of other animals which they do not hesitate to use. Their usual home range is about 100 yards, but their homing instinct is well developed. Marked specimens have been released far from their point of capture, as far as two to four miles, and been retaken shortly after in their home territory. (Murie and Murie 1931).

Their food consists mainly of weed seeds, and the smaller seeds and nuts of trees and shrubs, such as basswood or linden seeds, pits of wild cherries, beechnuts, hazelnuts and acorns. They are not given to feeding much on herbage. They store away considerable quantities of nuts and seeds in suitable holes about roots of trees or in trees, or in the ground, probably for use on the more inclement days of winter. These caches may amount to a pint in bulk. They are active the whole year and do not hibernate. Their tracks may be seen in abundance in the snow. Evermann and Clark (1920) report them as feeding on small snails and other small delicate mollusks. They probably eat a few insects. Their tastes are quite omnivorous so that they may be taken in traps baited with almost anything. It is not improbable that occasionally they eat birds' eggs and young birds.

Their nests are made of soft grasses and downy material and placed in cavities about roots of trees, in holes in trees, not too far from the ground or in underground burrows. About human habitations such as houses, summer cottages and cabins in primitive places, they nest in situations which in urban communities are utilized by the House Mouse.

Mating occurs apparently at any time during the year. The females are in heat immediately following the birth of a litter. The period of gestation varies from 22 to 37 days, being longest when the female is lactating. The male, female and newborn young seem to occupy the same nest until time for the birth of next litter, when father and young are driven from it. The number of young produced at a birth varies from one to six with an average of about four. At birth the young are wrinkled and bright flesh colored and "naked" although microscopic examination shows that the hairs have already passed through the outer layers of the skin. The whiskers or vibrissae at birth are three millimeters in length. Their eyes are closed and the ears folded. The ears unfold at three days and the eyes open at about 13 days

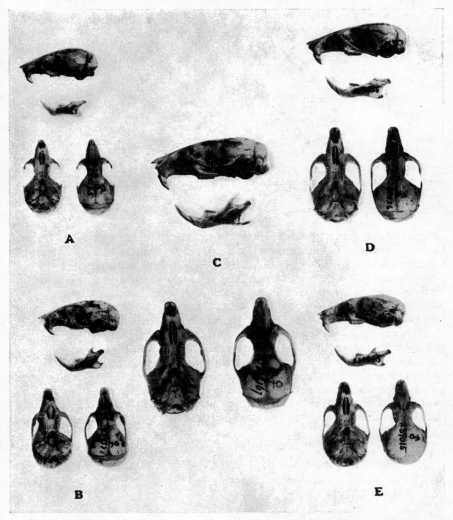

Fig. 85. Photographs courtesy U. S. Nat. Mus. Skulls of long-tailed Mice, all in U. S. Nat. Mus., all natural size.

A.—Harvest Mouse, *Reithrodontomys humulis*, Cat. No. 254,165, Nelson County, Va., July 6, 1903, Wirt Robinson. The Harvest Mouse has not yet been taken in Indiana.

B.—Jumping Mouse, *Zapus hudsonius*, Cat. No. 239,797, Porter County, Oct. 27, 1923, M. W. Lyon, Jr.

C.—Rice Rat, *Oryzomys palustris*, Cat. No. 142,167, Suffolk, Va., Jan. 12, 1906, A. Royster. No specimens of the Rice Rat have as yet been taken in Indiana.

D.—Woodland White-footed Mouse, *Peromyscus leucopus noveboracensis*, Cat. No. 239,036, Porter County, Sept. 28, 1922, M. W. Lyon, Jr.

E.—Prairie White-footed Mouse, *Peromyscus maniculatus bairdii*, Cat. No. 239,015, Porter County, Sept. 26, 1922, M. W. Lyon, Jr.

of age. Weight at birth of the Prairie White-footed Mouse averages about 1.67 grams and of the Woodland Mouse about 1.87 grams. Weaning takes place in from 22 to 37 days. In mice in captivity as many as 10 litters in a year have been observed with a total of 45 young, but much smaller figures apparently are the rule, such as five or six litters with total young from 16 to 25. (Svihla 1932).

Young are transported by the mother either collectively by dragging them attached to her elongated mammae or separately, carrying them one at a time in her mouth. In the first method, during the first few days after birth the young act as a dead weight to the mother but when older push with their hind feet against the ground. When carried by the second method, the mother picks the young mouse up in her paws and places it belly-side up in her mouth with her incisors around it, rather than pinching a piece of the skin between them. The young mouse if it is large enough, curls itself about the neck of the mother clinging with its tail and paws. (Svihla 1932).

Several observers have noticed a curious habit of the White-footed Mouse of drumming by moving their front paws rapidly up and down against some resonant object. They seem to do this when disturbed or in a state of excitement. Not all individuals drum. It is done by both sexes. (Svihla 1932).

White-footed Mice are as a rule comparatively harmless creatures and do little damage to crops and stores of grain. In rural and remote places to which the House Mouse has not penetrated, they may make the same nuisance of themselves that the House Mouse does in cities. The remedy is to build mouse proof structures and storage places for grain as well as not kill off their natural enemies, the predatory birds and mammals.

In northern Indiana I have found five to ten percent of these mice infested with a large fly larva, probably *Cuterebra emasculator*, only one larva to a mouse. The majority of the mice infested were nursing females. Only one was noticed in a male in which case the swelling caused by the subcutaneous larva superficially resembled a swollen testicle.

PRAIRIE WHITE-FOOTED MOUSE
Peromyscus maniculatus bairdii (Hoy and Kennicott)

Hesperomys maniculatus WAGNER. Arch. f. Naturg., vol. 11(1), p. 148, 1845. Type locality: Labrador.

Mus bairdii HOY and KENNICOTT in Kennicott. Agric. Rep. U.S. Pat. Off. 1856, p. 92, 1857. Type locality: Bloomington, Illinois.

Peromyscus michiganensis of authors, see Osgood 1909, p. 81.

Calomys michiganensis Evermann and Butler 1894.

Peromyscus maniculatus bairdii Osgood 1909, Hahn 1909.

Peromyscus maniculatus is the most widely distributed of any of the species of White-footed Mice, its range being practically coincident with that of the genus. Over 40 subspecies or closely allied forms are known. Usually the various subspecies intergrade with one another but occasionally two subspecies are found in the same locality, occupying different habitats and not intergrading. The Prairie White-footed Mouse, subspecies *bairdii* ranges from central Ohio westward across the northern three-fourths of Indiana to Kansas, northward to southern Wisconsin and southern Manitoba, and along the shores of Lake Michigan to the northern part of the lower peninsula of Michigan. It is found throughout nearly all of Indiana, though I know of no records from the extreme southern part.

The Prairie White-footed Mouse is the smaller of the two species found in Indiana; upperparts dark in color, especially the middle of the back which is very dark brown or even blackish, underparts creamy white; feet white; ears brownish black; tail rather heavily haired, especially at the tip, its dark uppersurface contrasting strongly with its white undersurface.

Total length of adults varies from 130 to 150 mm., usually about 140; tail vertebrae 52 to 62 mm., usually about 57; hind foot 17 to 18 mm., greatest length of skull about 24 mm., weight, 13 to 19 grams.

The Prairie White-footed Mouse is an inhabitant of cleared land, fields, natural meadows, prairies, and the sand beaches of Lake Michigan. It probably spends the daylight hours in underground passages. It certainly must do so in the dunes region of Lake Michigan, for in summer these are blistering

Fig. 86. Photograph, copyright by H. H. Pittman. Baird's or Prairie White-footed Mouse, *Peromyscus maniculatus bairdii.*

hot on the surface by day. It is active at night, as judged by foot prints in trails up and down the sand. Its usual mode of progression is by jumping on all four feet at once. Only rarely does one find tracks apparently made by walking, in which case what appears to be tail marks are sometimes present. In the jumping mode of progression the tail does not touch the ground.

In trapping in northern Indiana I have found this species to be rare in comparison with the next species: *Peromyscus leucopus noveboracensis*.

Map 52. Published records and specimens in collections of the Prairie White-footed Mouse, *Peromyscus maniculatus bairdii*, in Indiana; 1, collection of F. H. Test.

The published records for the Prairie White-footed Mouse are Knox (Osgood 1909), Laporte (Elliot 1907, Cory 1912), Marshall (Evermann and Clark 1911, 1920), Miami (Hahn 1909, Cory 1912), Monroe (McAtee 1907, Osgood 1909), Newton (Hahn 1907, 1909), Ohio (Hahn 1909), Porter (Evermann and Clark 1911. 1920, Lyon 1923, 1930), St. Joseph (Engels 1933).

WOODLAND WHITE-FOOTED MOUSE
Peromyscus leucopus noveboracensis Fischer

Musculus leucopus RAFINESQUE. Amer. Month. Mag., vol. 3, p. 446, 1818
        Type locality: Pine barrens of Kentucky.
[*Mus sylvaticus*] δ *noveboracensis* FISCHER. Synopsis Mamm., p. 318, 1829
        Type locality: New York.
Mus leucopus Wied. 1839-41.
Mus agrarias Gmel. Plummer 1844.

Hesperomys leucopus Haymond 1870, Coues 1877.
Calomys americanus Evermann and Butler 1894.
Peromyscus leucopus noveboracensis Osgood 1909, Hahn 1909.

The species *Peromyscus leucopus* ranges from the New England States southward to the Carolinas, westward to Wyoming, Arizona and southward into Mexico. About a dozen and a half subspecies or closely related species are known. The subspecies *noveboracensis* ranges from Virginia westward across northern Kentucky, Indiana to eastern Kansas, and South Dakota, northward to southern Ontario and Minnesota. It is found in every county in Indiana.

The Woodland White-footed Mouse is larger and lighter in color than the preceding species, and with a relatively longer tail. The upperparts are cinnamon-rufous in color lightly mixed with dusky lines on sides, more heavily on middle of back; underparts creamy white; hands and feet white; tail above similar to upperparts, beneath whitish, the line of demarkation between the upper and lower portion not so striking as in the preceding species and its tip less hairy.

The average total length of ten adult males from northern Indiana gave 172 mm., tail vertebrae 79 mm., hind foot 21 mm. Of ten adult females the corresponding figures are 176, 81 and 21. Weight, 17 to 24 grams. Greatest length of skull about 26 mm.

The Woodland White-footed Mouse is probably the most abundant mammal in Indiana and is found in suitable localities everywhere throughout the state. While primarily a woodland species, yet it is found in thickets and not infrequently taken in open fields. It makes its home in holes about the roots of trees, under logs, in holes in trees, etc. In flooded lowlands it is of necessity forced to an arboreal existence. It is not afraid of wet situations for I have trapped it in a very wet quaking bog where it had probably gone from nearby woods. They penetrate the caves in the southern part of the state far beyond the entrance of light but probably do not permanently live there. At one time Blatchley (1897) thought these cave forms were distinct from those found outside, but the differences noted by him come within the range of individual variation.

The last taxonomic student of the genus *Peromyscus*, Osgood (1909) regarded specimens from most of the state as unquestionably belonging to *Peromyscus leucopus noveboracensis*. Two specimens from New Harmony are identified as "position doubtful." It is not improbable that specimens from the extreme southern and southwestern portions of the state may incline toward *Peromyscus leucopus leucopus*, the type locality of which is not far away. In the absence of any opportunity to have all the Indiana material as well as material representing *Peromyscus leucopus leucopus* at hand at one time, and making a careful study of it, I am calling all the Indiana material *Peromyscus leucopus noveboracensis*, but it is not unlikely that material from Posey and adjoining counties may be referable to true *leucopus* or at least represent intermediate forms. *Peromyscus leucopus leucopus* averages darker in color, slightly smaller, and tail not so hairy as in its northern relative. It is only by actual comparison of a series of specimens that the determination can be made.

In the Murarium, Museum of Zoology, University of Michigan, many species of *Peromyscus* are kept alive and bred. All the subspecies of *Peromyscus maniculatus* there readily cross with one another. The same is true of the subspecies of *Peromyscus leucopus*. However, no subspecies of *maniculatus* will cross with any of those of *leucopus*, notwithstanding the close superficial resemblance of these two forms in Indiana.

Two other species of *Peromyscus* may possibly be found in southwestern Indiana, as they have been taken nearby in southern Illinois. Although considerable trapping has been done in Posey County, they have not come to light. Both species are con-

Map 53. Published records and specimens in collections of the Woodland White - footed Mouse, *Peromyscus leucopus noveboracensis*, in Indiana; 1, collection of F. H. Test.

The published records of the Woodland White-footed Mouse are: Carroll (Evermann and Butler 1894), Crawford (Blatchley 1897, 1899), Dubois (Osgood 1909), Franklin (Haymond 1870, Coues 1877, Quick 1881, Quick and Langdon 1882, Evermann and Butler 1894), Knox (Langdon 1881 Dec.), Lagrange (Evermann and Butler 1894), Laporte (Elliot 1907, Osgood 1909, Cory 1912), Lawrence (Hahn 1907, 1908, Elliot 1907, Osgood 1909, Cory 1912), Marshall (Evermann and Clark 1911, 1920), Miami (Osgood 1909), Monroe (Evermann and Butler 1894, Banta 1907, McAtee 1907), Newton (Hahn 1907, Osgood 1909), Porter (Hahn 1907, Osgood 1909, Lyon 1923), Posey (Wied 1839-41, 1861-62, Osgood 1909), Randolph (Cox 1893, Evermann and Butler 1894), St. Joseph (Engels 1933), Sullivan (Coues 1877), Vigo (Evermann and Butler 1894), Wayne (Plummer 1844).

spicuous enough to have attracted the attention of the Prince of Wied, as well as many naturalists since his time, but none has mentioned them.

Peromyscus gossypinus megacephalus Rhoads. It is similar to *Peromyscus leucopus* but larger, total length 185 mm., tail vertebrae 80 mm., hind foot 24 mm.; greatest length of skull 30 mm. A. H. Howell (1910) found it in swamps and wooded bluffs in southern Illinois.

Peromyscus nuttalli aureolus (Audubon and Bachman). The upper parts of this mouse are golden brown in color; total length about 170 mm., tail about 75 mm., hind foot 19 mm., greatest length of skull 25 mm. Kennicott (1858) first reported it from southern Illinois. He says it is locally known as Red Mouse. It is more strictly woodland in its habitat than *Peromyscus leucopus*, and is more arboreal. This species under the name *Calomys aureolus* was included in their hypothetical lists by Evermann and Butler (1894), and as *Peromyscus nuttalli* by Hahn (1909).

RICE RATS
Genus **Oryzomys** Baird

This genus as represented in the United States ranges southward from New Jersey along the Atlantic seaboard to southern Florida and from the Mississippi Valley in southern Illinois and Ohio and possibly southern Indiana, southward to the Gulf of Mexico.

For practical purposes the genus as represented by the above distribution may be defined as a very large coarse haired semi-aquatic *Peromyscus* with the supraorbital and temporal ridges forming a distinct bead on the side of the skull. Teeth in general resemble those of a large *Peromyscus*. The United States species superficially resemble a small House Rat.

The term Rice Rat has been given to them because they were at first best known from the rice fields of the Southern States, but they are found in many other equally damp or wet and other situations. The genus is a large one and attains its maximum development in South America. The genus has never been satisfactorily defined or delimited.

RICE RAT
Oryzomys palustris palustris Harlan

Mus palustris HARLAN. Amer. Journ. Sci., vol. 31, p. 385, 1837. Type locality: Near Salem, Salem County, New Jersey.
Calomys palustris Evermann and Butler 1894.
Oryzomys palustris Hahn 1909.
Oryzomys palustris palustris Goldman, North Amer. Fauna, No. 43, p. 22, 1918.

The fur is long and coarse. General color above grizzled grayish or buffy brown, darker along middle of back; below, whitish or cream colored. Tail long, sparsely haired, brownish above and whitish below.

Total length about 250 mm., tail vertebrae about 115 mm., hind foot about 30 mm.; greatest length of skull about 32 mm., greatest width about 17 mm.

Rice Rats are mainly nocturnal. They inhabit wet meadows, marshes and grassy lands. They are good swimmers. Rhoads (1903) speaks of them as using the same trails as Muskrats and living in holes in Muskrat houses, and frequently being caught in traps set for Muskrats. They are, however, known sometimes to leave their semi-aquatic habitat and inhabit woods. Mr. A. H. Howell tells me that those trapped by him in southern Illinois were taken along a railroad embankment.

The Rice Rat was included in their hypothetical lists by Evermann and Butler (1894) under the name *Calomys palustris*, and by Hahn (1909) under its current name. It is still in the hypothetical list. No one has been able to secure specimens in Indiana, although there is every likelihood of its occurrence in both the southeastern and southwestern portions of the state. Two skulls are reported from Ohio by Langdon (1891) near Cincinnati. It is also included in Brayton's list (1882) from Madisonville, Ohio. (See also Robert Kendall Enders, Some factors influencing the distribution of mammals in Ohio, Occ. Papers, Mus. Zool., Univ. Michigan, No. 212 April 23, 1930 p. 14.) It was reported by A. H. Howell (1910) in southern Illinois. Hahn (1909) produces the best evidence of its occurrence in Indiana. "Mr. E. J. Chansler, of Bicknell, Knox County, has written me as follows: 'There is a kind of a water rat found about ponds and streams. It is perhaps smaller than the house rat, has short front legs and long hind ones. The hind feet look to be somewhat webbed. Color light gray with dark reflections. Our boys caught some last winter while trapping for mink and muskrat along Flat Creek. They have usually been found among water lilies or about drift along Flat Creek.'

" . . . Mr. Chansler states that none of the rats have been seen for several years and he thinks they may have disappeared since the draining of Mintour's and other ponds."

The Rice Rat should be looked for in the southern counties. Persistent trapping will probably secure specimens from Posey County. Skulls should be sought for in owl pellets.

Map 54. Published but unconfirmed record of the Rice Rat, *Oryzomys palustris palustris*, in Indiana.

The published unconfirmed record for the Rice Rat is Knox, (Hahn 1909).

CAVE RATS OR WOOD RATS
Genus **Neotoma** Say and Ord

The genus *Neotoma* ranges from about 60° latitude in the Pacific Northwest southward along the coast and into Central America and southeastward to the Gulf of Mexico and Florida. In the eastern United States it ranges from southern New York southwestward, chiefly among the Alleghenies, into Ohio, southern Indiana and Illinois and Tennessee.

The Cave or Wood Rat is a large rat-like mammal bearing much superficial resemblance to the common House Rat, but its hair is longer, softer, and its tail much better haired, in fact in some species very hairy. Its ears are large and membranaceous. In many ways it is like a giant *Peromyscus*. The general form of the skull is somewhat like that of *Peromyscus* but much enlarged, more angular, with the brain case not thin walled and swollen. The teeth, however, are very different; the crowns of the teeth are flat with the enamel thrown into prismatic folds, closely resembling the enamel folds seen in the teeth of the subfamily *Microtinae*. Dental formula as in *Peromyscus* and the *Microtinae*. The genus contains about 75 species and subspecies, one of which is found in Indiana.

Allegheny Cave Rat
Neotoma pennsylvanica Stone

Neotoma pennsylvanica STONE. Proc. Acad. Nat. Philadelphia, 1893, p. 16, 1893. Type locality: South Mountain, Cumberland County, Pa.

Neotoma floridana Evermann and Butler 1894.

Neotoma pennsylvanica Hahn 1909, A. H. Howell 1910, Hickie and Harrison 1930.

The Allegheny Cave Rat occupies the Appalachian Mountain region from southern New York to northern Alabama, westward to Mammoth Cave, Kentucky, and western Tennessee, and northward again into southern Indiana and Ohio.

Color of the upper parts grayish or grayish buff, overlaid with blackish, especially along the back; under parts and feet white; upper half of tail similar to back and under half whitish, ears large and thin.

Measurements of four Indiana specimens, apparently not fully adult, at least not old adults: Total length 377 to 406 mm., tail vertebrae 175 to 184 mm., hind foot 40 to 44 mm., ear 27 to 32 mm., weight 238 to 342 grams. Greatest length of skull of the largest of these specimens 50 mm., greatest width 25 mm. These measurements are less than those given by Goldman (Revision of the Wood Rats of the genus *Neotoma*, North American Fauna, No. 31, p. 85, 1910) for the species, probably due to immaturity.

The Cave Rats are found in Indiana in small limestone caves or crevices in the cliffs along the Ohio River or its tributaries in Harrison County, and probably adjoining counties. They are mainly nocturnal and so escape observation. Into their caves or crevices they drag considerable quantities of sticks, other pieces of wood, corn cobs, stones and an occasional bone. Among the bones in one pile which I examined was a fragment of a lower jaw which proved to be a probable second specimen of the extinct deer *Odocoileus dolichopsis*. (See Engels 1932). The nest proper is placed inside this pile or it may be placed in a secure nitch with or without sticks, etc. piled in front of it. It is made of the bast fibers of trees loosely formed into a deep thick walled cup. This habit of piling up sticks inside a cave or in front of a crevice is very characteristic of Cave Rats, and has given origin to the term "pack rat" used in the West to designate these animals.

An interesting account of the habits of a Cave Rat from Mammoth Cave is given by Rhoads (1903):

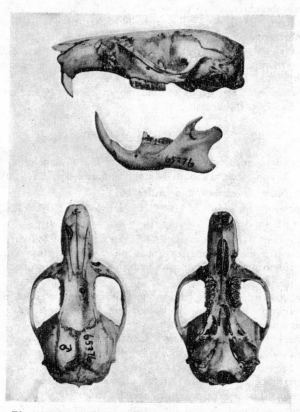

Fig. 87. Photographs courtesy University of Michigan. Lateral, dorsal, and palatal views of skull of Cave or Wood Rat, *Neotoma pennsylvanica*, about natural size, Cat. No. 65,276, Univ. of Mich., Tobacco Landing, Harrison County, 1930, Paul Hickie and Thomas Harrison.

Any suspicion of blindness or deficient eyesight, such as is exemplified in some of the lower orders of animal in the cave, cannot attach to this mammal. As in all the more strictly nocturnal rodents, the eyes of this species are greatly developed; nevertheless, they are able to make most intelligent use of them in broad daylight if need be. My pet cave rat was very sleepy by day, and if given the materials would quickly make a globular nest in which to hide. The favorite position of rest was on the side, coiled, with the nose resting on the abdomen and tail curled around the body. It frequently would 'sit on its head,' as it were, by leaning forward and placing its nose near the root of the tail, that member acting as a sort of prop to prevent the animal from turning a somersault in its sleep. Sometimes it would lie stretched out at full length

Fig. 88. Cave Rat or Wood Rat, *Neotoma pennsylvanica*, Tobacco Landing, Harrison County, 1930, photograph by Paul Hickie. From Amer. Midland Nat. vol. 12, p. 171, 1930.

on its side, the tail straight and the hind feet extended to their farthest limit. It invariably picked up objects with its teeth, though its fore feet were quite capable of the service, and the dexterity with which it would manipulate a nut with one or both paws was astonishing. In eating this kind of food it would quickly rasp a small hole, and, inserting the long lower incisors, clip off pieces of the kernel and extract them with great adroitness through an opening less than a quarter of an inch in diameter. All kinds of vegetable and animal foods were acceptable to it, but it seemed to prefer nuts and grain to anything else, though cabbage and apples were a favorite dessert, and it greatly enjoyed sharpening its teeth on candy toys. It was a great drinker, lapping water like a dog. In defending itself it would stand on its hind legs and strike with great force with the forefeet, at the same time laying hold on an object thrust toward it with great strength and forcing it toward a distant part of the cage. The odor of this animal, even under ordinary conditions of care, is almost suffocating, and far more mephitic than that of the Norway rat. When investigating an object, the coarse and prominent whiskers of this rat are vibrated with astonishing rapidity, forming a sort of halo about the face because of their incessant motion. The function of these organs must be highly specialized in this *Neotoma*, and undoubtedly has to do with its subterranean habits. On no occasion did any of my caged rats utter a cry, save a sort of grunting squeak when they yawned forcibly.

Little seems to be known of the Cave Rats' breeding habits. They prob-

Map 55. Published records and specimens in collections of the Allegheny Cave Rat, *Neotoma pennsylvanica*, in Indiana.

The published records for the Allegheny Cave Rat are: Crawford, unconfirmed records (Cope 1872, Packard 1888, Blatchley 1897), Harrison (Hickie and Harrison 1930), southern Indiana in cliffs along Ohio River, unconfirmed surmise (A. H. Howell 1910).

ably mate in mid-winter and two to four young are brought forth early in spring. The young are probably born in the same immature state as those of *Peromyscus* and develop more slowly in proportion to their larger size. The mammae are four in the inguinal region.

The first mention of *Neotoma* in Indiana was by Cope in 1873:

The rats also have brought into fissures and cavities communicating with the cave, seeds, nuts, and other vegetable matter.

No generic or specific names for "the rats" were used. The next mention was by Packard, 1888 who says:

A 'cave rat' was described to me by Mr. Rothrock as having been seen in the main Wyandotte Cave. It was said to be of the same color as the domestic rat, but with a body longer, somewhat like a weasel's; the whiskers are larger than those of a rat and the 'ears are nearly twice as large': It is probably a Neotoma.

Neither Hickie and Harrison nor I could find any trace of *Neotoma* in Wyandotte Cave in 1930, and the guides knew nothing of it. It may have become exterminated in the 42 years that have elapsed since Packard wrote. Evermann and Butler include *Neotoma* in their hypothetical list of 1894. Blatchley (1897) says that the rats mentioned by Cope and by Packard have been exterminated by cats. Hahn (1909) includes *Neotoma* in his hypothetical list and mentions there is much suitable habitat in southern Indiana for it. A. H. Howell (1910) says:

It [*Neotoma pennsylvanica*] probably occurs, also, in the cliffs on the Indiana side of the river [Ohio].

No further mention of its occurrence or probable occurrence in Indiana was made until 1930 when Hickie and Harrison reported the capture of four specimens at Tobacco Landing in August of that year.

Few persons know of their existence in the state. It is hoped that additional specimens will be secured and the range of this interesting species extended.

Neotoma floridana illinoensis A. H. Howell (1910) has been taken in southern Illinois. It might possibly occur in southwestern Indiana, but at the present time there is no evidence to lead to such a belief.

Voles, Lemmings, Meadow Mice, Muskrats, etc.
Subfamily **Microtinae**

Like the more hypsodont members of the subfamily Cricetinae but cheek teeth often growing from a persistent pulp, the enamel pattern always consisting of (at least partially) alternating triangles, the posterior termination of m1 and m2 never rounded; squamosal with distinct postorbital ridge or process. (Miller and Gidley 1918).

Dental formula: $i \frac{1-1}{1-1}$, $c \frac{0-0}{0-0}$, $pm \frac{0-0}{0-0}$, $m \frac{3-3}{3-3}$, $= 16$.

Most members of the subfamily possess a pair of scent glands located either on the sides of the body, the flanks or hips. While probably present in both sexes, these glands are much more conspicuous in the males than females and best developed during the rutting season. Also, anal glands are

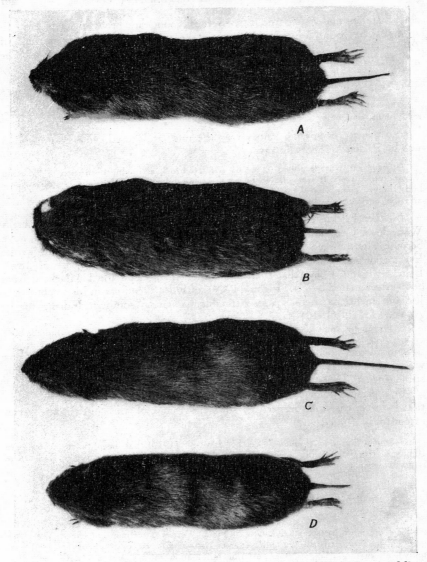

Fig. 89. Photographs courtesy U. S. Nat. Mus. Skins of Indiana Microtine Mice, all in U. S. Nat. Mus., about 2/3 natural size.

A.—Prairie Meadow Mouse, *Microtus ochrogaster*, Cat. No. 240,642, Porter County, Oct. 31, 1924, M. W. Lyon, Jr.

B.—Stone's Lemming Mouse, *Synaptomys cooperi stonei*, Cat. No. 143,703, Ohio County, Aug. 28, 1905, W. L. Hahn.

C.—Pennsylvania Meadow Mouse, *Microtus pennsylvanicus*, Cat. No. 239,814, Porter County, Nov. 2, 1923, M. W. Lyon, Jr.

D.—Pine Mouse, *Pitymys pinetorum scalopsoides*, Cat. No. 239,075, Porter County, Oct. 10, 1922, M. W. Lyon, Jr.

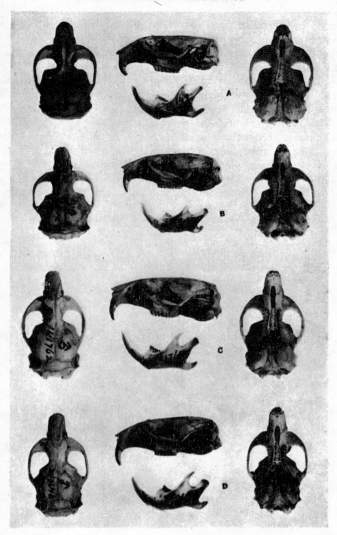

Fig. 90. Photographs courtesy U. S. Nat. Mus. Skulls of Microtine Mice, all in U. S. Nat. Mus., all natural size.

A.—Cat. No. 12,149/9,963, Lemming Mouse, *Synaptomys cooperi stonei*, Brookville, Franklin County, R. Haymond.

B.—Cat. No. 239,802, Pine Mouse, *Pitymys pinetorum*, Dunes State Park, Porter County, Nov. 1, 1923, M. W. Lyon, Jr.

C.—Cat. No. 141,762, Pennsylvania Meadow Mouse, *Microtus pennsylvanicus*, Hebron, Porter County, Aug. 23, 1905, W. L. Hahn.

D.—Cat. No. 240,646, Prairie Meadow Mouse, *Microtus ochrogaster*, Dunes State Park, Porter County, Nov. 7, 1924, M. W. Lyon, Jr.

present in many of these mice. Both types of glands have been recently studied histologically in European species by Dr. V. Vrtis 1930.

Their eyes are small and bead-like, tail usually short; hands and feet usually mouse-like.

The *Microtinae* contain about 30 generic or subgeneric groups confined to the northern portions of both hemispheres. They fall into three major divisions two of which, the LEMMI or Lemmings, and the MICROTI, the Voles or Meadow Mice, are represented in Indiana.

The Lemmings, represented in Indiana by the single genus *Synaptomys* are distinguished by their short thickset bodies and with tail usually shorter than hind foot, but in *Synaptomys* slightly longer. They have broad and massive skulls; the lower incisors are short with the roots ending on the inner side of the lower molars and not forming a conspicuous prominence on the outer side of the mandible.

The Voles or Meadow Mice represented in Indiana by three genera,

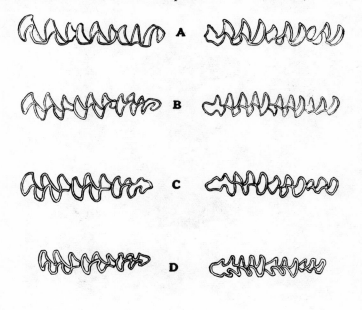

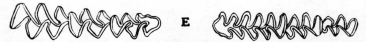

Fig. 91. Enamel patterns of Molar Teeth of Indiana Microtines, after Miller, North American Fauna, No. 12, 1896.

A.—*Synaptomys cooperi*, x5, fig. 8, p. 34.
B.—*Microtus (Microtus) pennsylvanicus*, x5, fig. 33, p. 63.
C.—*Microtus (Pedomys) ochrogaster*, x5, fig. 29, p. 56.
D.—*Pitymys pinetorum*, x5, fig. 31, p. 59.
E.—*Ondatra zibethica*, x2½, fig. 39, p. 72.

Microtus, Pitymys and *Fiber*, are distinguished by their more slender form; tail usually much longer than hind foot. They have more slender and lightly built skulls; lower incisors are long and with the roots ending on the outer side of and posterior to the lower molars.

The arrangement of the enamel pattern of the teeth is an important character in classifying the various groups of the subfamily.

LEMMING MICE
Genus **Synaptomys** Baird

The Lemming Mice are peculiar to North America, ranging from Labrador and New Brunswick in the east, south and westward through the Middle Atlantic States to eastern Kansas and northwestward from the Great Lakes region into the Canadian provinces and Alaska.

Synaptomys is at once distinguished from all other *Microtinae* by having the upper incisors grooved on their anterior face. Other generic characters are: Short well haired tail, scarcely longer than the hind foot; rather heavily built skull, with short rostrum; molars rootless, and ever-growing; reentrant angles on the tongue side of the upper molars, excessively deep; and on the cheek side of the lower molars equally deep; sole of hind foot with six tubercles; nail of first digit of forefoot, flat and strap-shaped. Skin glands on the hips are conspicuous in old males.

The genus is divided into two subgenera, *Synaptomys* and *Mictomys*, the latter occurrring in Canada and barely reaching the extreme northwest of the United States. The subgenus *Synaptomys* contains but a single species *cooperi* which splits up into three subspecies, one of which is found throughout Indiana except in the etrxeme southwestern portion.

STONE'S LEMMING MOUSE
Synaptomys cooperi stonei (Rhoads) 6

S[ynaptomys] cooperi BAIRD. Mamm. North Amer., p. 558, 1857. Type
    locality: Probably northern New Jersey.
Synaptomys stonei RHOADS. Amer. Nat., vol. 27, p. 53, 1893. Type locality:
    May's Landing, Atlantic County, New Jersey.
Synaptomys cooperi Quick and Langdon 1882, Evermann and Butler, 1894.
Synaptomys cooperi stonei Hahn 1909, A. B. Howell 1927.

Stone's Lemming Mouse ranges from Wisconsin eastward through most of Indiana to the Atlantic seaboard of New Jersey and Maryland and southward along the mountains to North Carolina.

Synaptomys has rather long and shaggy hair, mixed gray, yellowish brown and black giving a grizzled appearance with the general effect of a cinnamon-brown above; under parts dull whitish washing over the slate-colored underfur; tail brownish above and whitish below.

The Lemming Mouse is a comparatively small animal, total length, about

---

6 Specimens from St. Joseph County have never been critically compared with *S. cooperi cooperi*. They may possibly belong to that form or be intermediate.

115 mm.; tail vertebrae, about 18 mm.; hind foot, 17 mm.; ear, about 9 mm. Indiana specimens (Hahn 1909). Greatest length of skull about 26 mm.; greatest width, about 16 mm.; weight 20-27 grams.

Lemming Mice are comparatively rare animals. I have never been so fortunate as to take one in Indiana, probably looking for them in the wrong place. East of the Allegheny Mountains the favorite haunts of these mice seem to be cold bogs. Westward they are more like ordinary Meadow Mice and are found in old fields and hillsides. Hahn (1909) who collected many in the state, took just one specimen in a tamarack bog. All the others were taken in grass lands. Quick and Butler (1885) had more specimens of this rare mammal from around Brookville than had previously been captured in the entire range of the species. A skull of one of these old specimens is illustrated. These authors say it frequents hillsides and dry blue grass pastures where flat stones are scattered over the surface. Stegeman (1930) and Engels (1933) found them in essentially similar situations.

The Lemming Mice appear to be colonial and Stegeman estimates an average of about 14 per acre in the large colony studied by him. Although his specimens are identified as *Synaptomys cooperi cooperi* it is assumed that they do not differ in breeding and habits from those of *S. cooperi stonei* found in Indiana.

The runways are like those of *Microtus*, and at irregular intervals they have side chambers which seem to be used as feeding and resting places. Cut grass stems were found in these stations, and green colored feces, though scattered throughout the runways, were here accumulated.

The runways are heavily covered with dead grass and it is an easy matter to tell whether or not a runway is being used by the presence or absence in it of fresh feces and freshly cut sections of grass stems. When the runways are being used the grass is kept cut close to the ground, so there is no obstruction in the passage; they become obscured or obliterated very rapidly when they are no longer used. . . . The runways led to many burrows which seem to be used as retreats, since feces were found in them as well as occasional sections of grass stems.

The nests were usually found in a slight depression of the ground alongside the main runways. . . . The nests were made entirely of dry grass and resemble the nests of *Microtus pennsylvanicus*. (Stegeman 1930).

Quick and Butler (1885) state the nest is always under cover, generally in a hollow log or stump. Hahn (1909) reports:

A conical nest ten inches in diameter and five inches high placed on the ground with no covering except a very thin veil of dry grass blades. It was inconspicuous, however, for it was made of moss and grass and placed in a hummocky place among some sumach bushes. The lining was of fine grass.

Inside were four little mice about two and one-half inches long, with open eyes and body fully covered with hair. . . . An old mouse, apparently their mother, was caught at the site of the nest. She would have given birth to five more young in a week or ten days. The usual number of young at a birth seems to be four, but three and five are not infrequent.

Stegeman (1930) reports the number of young in a litter to be from two to four. Young born in his laboratory were blind and naked, weight of male 2.7 grams and of female 2.4, that is about one-tenth the body weight of the adults. Hair was present on the sixth day, and the eyes opened on the 12th day, at which time their weights were 11.6 and 10.9 grams.

There are two pairs of pectoral mammae and one pair of inguinal.

Of their food Hahn (1909) says:

These mice live on grass more exclusively than any other species that I know. However, they sometimes eat seeds and roots, and like some species of *Microtus*, sometimes store up supplies in winter.

Quick and Butler (1885) say:

Cooper's mice live in winter chiefly upon the stems of blue grass and the more tender portions of white clover, stores of which may be found near their winter quarters. They sometimes store large quantities of the tubers of the wild artichoke (*Helianthus*).

Stegeman (1930) reports them as eating principally grasses or other green material, rarely apple, and refusing carrots; very rarely eating insects (Coleoptera). He makes no mention of any storing habits.

Like the other *Microtinae*, it is active all winter.

Map 56. Published records and specimens in collections of Stone's Lemming Mouse, *Synaptomys cooperi stonei*, in Indiana. Specimens from Franklin County in collection of A. W. Butler.

The published records for Stone's Lemming Mouse are: Brown (Evermann and Butler 1894, Hahn 1909), Franklin (Coues 1877, Langdon 1881, Quick and Langdon 1882, Quick and Butler 1885, Merriam 1892, Butler 1892, Bangs 1894, Evermann and Butler 1894, Hahn 1909, A. B. Howell 1927), Jay (A. B. Howell 1927), Knox (A. B. Howell 1927), Lagrange (Hahn 1909), Lawrence (Hahn 1908, 1909, Cory 1912, A. B. Howell 1927), Monroe (Hahn 1909), Newton (Hahn 1907, 1909, A. B. Howell 1927), Ohio (Hahn 1909, Cory 1912, A. B. Howell 1927), Porter (Hahn 1907, 1909, Cory 1912, A. B. Howell 1927), St. Joseph (Engels 1933).

Synaptomys is one of Indiana's most interesting mammals, representing, as it does, the Lemmings, a truly boreal group. It is probably a left-over from the days when the last great glacier retreated and has adapted itself to the temperate climate of Indiana. It is probably much more common than specimens in collections would indicate, colonies being scattered here and there throughout most of the state.

MEADOW MICE
Genus **Microtus** Schrank,

The geographic distribution of the genus *Microtus* is essentially that of the subfamily given above.

In the genus *Microtus* the root of lower incisor extends to the outside of the lower molar roots, ascending posteriorly high above the level of the cutting surface of the molars and forms a noticeable protuberance on the outer surface of the ascending portion of the mandible at the base of the articular process. The molars, upper and lower are permanently rootless, growing continuously from a persistent pulp. The mammae are six to eight in number, the tubercles on soles of hind foot five to six. Claw of first toe of forefoot, pointed, not stump-shaped. Members of the genus are not modified in any way for aquatic or subterranean life.

Over 100 species are recognized in the genus, two of which occur extensively in Indiana, each representing a different subgenus.

Subgenus **Microtus** Schrank

The subgenus *Microtus* is characterized externally by normal fur, six tubercles on soles of hind feet, two pairs of inguinal and two pairs of pectoral mammae, eight mammae in all; ears moderately developed usually projecting beyond the fur; side glands well developed in the males at least. First lower molar with five closed triangles; second upper molar with four closed sections and often with a small additional posterior loop, third upper molar with three closed triangles.

This subgenus contains about 50 specific forms widely distributed in North America, one of which is found in Indiana.

PENNSYLVANIA MEADOW MOUSE
Microtus pennsylvanicus pennsylvanicus (Ord)

Mus pennsylvanica ORD. Guthrie's Geogr., 2nd Amer. ed., vol. 2, p. 292, 1815; Type locality: Meadows below Philadelphia, Pennsylvania.
Arvicola riparias Plummer 1844.
Arvicola riparius Haymond 1870.
Arvicola pennsylvanicus Evermann and Butler 1894.
Microtus pennsylvanicus Bailey 1900, Hahn 1909.

The Pennsylvania Meadow Mouse is found throughout the northeastern United States, southward in the Alleghenies to North Carolina and Tennessee and westward to Nebraska, and is found throughout the northern three-fourths of Indiana in moist meadows.

Upper parts are dark chestnutty brown with blackish hairs mixed in; under parts dull slaty, usually without any light brownish wash; side of body lighter than back; feet brownish; upper surface of tail similar to back, under surface paler; ears short but usually project beyond the fur of the head. Mammae, two pairs inguinal and two pairs pectoral.

Microtus pennsylvanicus is a large heavy-set animal. Total length, 160 mm.; tail vertebrae, 42 mm.; hind foot, 20 mm. (Average of ten Indiana specimens, Hahn, 1909) These measurements are slightly smaller than those given by Bailey (1900). Weight 35 to 45 grams. Greatest length of skull, about 28 mm.; greatest width, about 16 mm.

The Pennsylvania Meadow Mouse is an inhabitant of lowland fields and meadows. It is a capable swimmer and has been known to build its nests in tussocks of grass surrounded by water, so that it must of necessity have traveled by water to reach its feeding grounds. It is mainly nocturnal in its activities. It makes long intricate runways through the tall grass by cutting down and eating much of the grass along its pathway. It also makes underground tunnels. It is active throughout the year and in the winter makes pathways on the surface of the ground, tunnelling between the surface and the overlying snow.

Their large round nests are also constructed of the blades of this [blue] and kindred grasses. They are built much after the manner of musk rat houses, a miniature of which they closely resemble. The single opening is below, where it connects with the runways of the animal. These nests are found in almost every conceivable place; in thickets and briar patches, among the rank grass which grows there, in swampy places upon a tussock of grass, in a log or fence corner, under a pile of rubbish and very many on the open ground, especially in clover meadows where the mice may prey upon the nests of the humble bee. (Butler, 1886 Jan 9).

The lining is usually of soft downy material, or finely shredded grasses.

These mice subsist mostly on fresh grass or other green herbage, but they also eat grains and seeds as their occasional presence under corn and wheat shocks testifies. However, I have examined the stomachs of a number of individuals, principally in August when both seeds and grass are plentiful, and have found that about 80 per cent of the contents was grass. (Hahn 1909).

They probably eat a fair number of insects or their larvae and like most rodents eat flesh on occasion and when obtainable. Butler (1886 Jan. 9) gives this interesting note on its feeding:

This mouse has an ingenious and patient method of securing the head from a standing stalk of wheat. Selecting a stalk which gives promise of a large, well filled head, the mouse cuts it off as high up as it can reach; owing to the proximity of the surrounding grain the stem will not fall, the butt end falls to the ground and another cut is made about four inches up the stalk; the process of cutting off sections of this length is repeated until the grain is within reach. Here, after a square meal, the mouse leaves a collection of straws about four inches long, together with a shattered head of grain, to puzzle the farmer.

In winter they sometimes eat the inner bark of shrubs and small trees. They also eat wild tubers or tuberous roots. If they have a storage habit, it is not pronounced. Normally one of these mice will eat 55% of its weight in food per day.

Butler (1886 Jan. 9) speaks of them as breeding from February to January. Bailey (1900) reports finding young in nests at all seasons of the year. The number of young in a litter varies from two to eight; probably six is the most usual number. Like other mice they are born in a very immature state and develop rapidly. Weight at birth averages about 2.50 to 2.75 grams. The period of gestation is about 21 days. The period of nursing is probably another three weeks, and about a month later they are of adult size. The females begin to breed before attaining maturity and in captivity have been known to have young when only 45 days of age. Many litters may be raised in a year. (Bailey 1924, Hatt 1930.)

In well cared for fields and carefully handled corn and grain, these mice probably do little damage to agriculturalists. One of the best means of keeping down their numbers is Nature's own, protection of their natural enemies, hawks, owls and the carnivorous mammals.

Map 57. Published records and specimens in collections of the Pennsylvania Meadow Mouse, *Microtus pennsylvanicus,* in Indiana. Specimen from Franklin County in collection of A. W. Butler.

The published records for the Pennsylvania Meadow Mouse are: Carroll (Evermann and Butler 1894), Clinton (Evermann and Butler 1894), Franklin (Haymond 1870, Quick 1882, Quick and Langdon 1882, Quick and Butler 1885, Butler 1886, Evermann and Butler 1894), Lagrange (Hahn 1909), Laporte (Anonymous 1880, Cory 1912), Marshall (Evermann and Clark 1911, 1920), Monroe (McAtee 1907, Hahn 1909, Cory 1912), Newton (Hahn 1907, 1909), Ohio (Hahn 1909, Cory 1912), Porter (Hahn 1907, 1909, Lyon 1925, 1930), Randolph (Evermann and Butler 1894), St. Joseph (Hahn 1909, Engels 1933), Vigo (Evermann and Butler 1894), Wayne (Plummer 1844, Evermann and Butler 1894).

Subgenus **Pedomys** Baird

The subgenus *Pedomys* is characterized externally by rather long coarse fur, medium-sized ears, two pairs of inguinal and one pair of pectoral mammae, six mammae in all; tubercles on soles of hind feet five; side glands obscure or wanting. Skull high and narrow; molars with wide reentrant angles, first lower molar with three closed and two open triangles; second lower molar with anterior pair of triangles confluent; third lower molar with three transverse loops, the middle one sometimes constricted or divided into two more or less distinct triangles; second upper molar with four closed sections and without a small additional posterior loop.

PRAIRIE OR BUFF-BELLIED MEADOW MOUSE
Microtus ochrogaster (Wagner)

Hypudaeus ochrogaster WAGNER. Schreber's Säugethiere, Suppl., vol. 3, p. 592, 1842. Type locality: America.

Arvicola austerus LECONTE, Proc. Acad. Nat. Sci. Philadelphia, vol. 6, p. 405, 1853. Type locality: Racine, Wisconsin.

Arvicola xanthognata Plummer 1844, probably equals *ochrogaster*.

Arvicola austerus Evermann and Butler 1894.

Microtus austerus Bailey 1900.

Microtus ochrogaster Hahn 1909.

The Prairie Meadow Mouse is found in the north central part of the Mississippi Valley, from Indiana and southwestern Michigan west into eastern Nebraska and Kansas, north into southern Wisconsin. It is found throughout practically all of Indiana, though there are no records from the northeastern corner of the state.

The general color of *Microtus ochrogaster* above is a general brownish gray, with a salt and pepper appearance from the mixture of black and pale yellowish brown tips of the long hairs; sides are paler; under parts are washed with pale cinnamon or fulvous, whence the specific name of the animal was derived. The summer coat is darker than the winter. The pelage appears coarser than that of the preceding species, and the ears do not usually project beyond the hairs of the head. The tail is sharply bicolor; above similar in color to the back, and almost whitish below.

Ten Indiana specimens gave the following average measurements: Total length, 144 mm.; tail vertebrae, 36 mm.; hind foot, 20 mm. (Hahn 1909), slightly more than those given by Bailey (1900). Greatest length of skull, about 27 mm.; greatest width, about 15 mm. Weight, 35-50 grams.

The Prairie Meadow Mouse was probably originally confined to the natural prairie region of northwestern Indiana, but with the artificial making of fields everywhere in the state it is the common meadow mouse in upland fields, preferring drier locations than does the Pennsylvania Meadow Mouse. Otherwise its habits appear to be essentially the same. The following observations by Hahn (1909) are interesting:

The nest is of dry grass and is placed under ground or under a protecting log or rock. One that I found was in a little depression under a discarded railroad tie lying on the side of an embankment. At the time of discovery, about 4 p. m. on April 11, the mother was not at home, and I carefully replaced the tie over the nest containing three hairless and blind young. Early the next morning the old mouse was again absent but about ten o'clock I found her nursing her offspring. She began to run with the young still clinging to her teats, but the whole family was captured. They were confined in a roomy wire cage with plenty of dry grass and cotton for a nest and fresh grass, bread and water for food. Nevertheless, the next morning the cage contained only the mother; she had eaten her children. The old mouse lived only two days longer. She showed a surprising ability to climb, not only going up the sides of the cage, but creeping fly-like, across its wire top with her claws hooked in the meshes of the wire and her body hanging downward.

The breeding season evidently includes all the summer months, though I am positive that they do not, as a rule, breed between October and February. Sometimes they mate as soon as a litter is born. The period of gestation is short, probably not over three weeks. I have never found more than four young in any litter. Two and three at a birth are quite usual. (Hahn 1909).

The smaller number of young in a litter as compared with *Microtus*

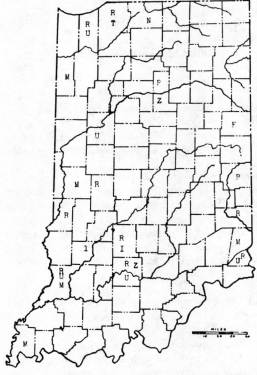

Map 58. Published records and specimens in collections of the Prairie Meadow Mouse, *Microtus ochrogaster*, in Indiana; 1, collection of Robert Goslin.

The published records for the Prairie or Buff-bellied Meadow Mouse are: Franklin (Quick and Langdon 1882, Quick and Butler 1885, Butler 1886 Jan., Butler 1892, Evermann and Butler 1894, Hahn 1909), Knox (Bailey 1900, Hahn 1909), Laporte (Hahn 1907, 1909, Cory 1912), Lawrence (Hahn 1908, 1909), Monroe (McAtee 1907, Hahn 1909), Ohio (Hahn 1909), Porter (Lyon 1923), Putnam (Hahn 1909), Vigo (Evermann and Butler 1894, Hahn 1909), Wayne (Plummer 1844, *Arvicola xanthognata* may be this species).

pennsylvanicus is probably correlated with the smaller number of mammae, six instead of eight.

Microtus ochrogaster has about the same economic status as that of *M. pennsylvanicus*.

PINE MICE
Genus **Pitymys** McMurtrie

In addition to being found in the eastern and southeastern United States, the genus *Pitymys* also is found in central and southern Europe, in Asia Minor and in southern Mexico.

The Pine Mice are rather small microtines, more or less adapted for a subterranean life. The fur is short, dense and mole-like, the claws on the front feet are the longest; tubercles on the hind feet, five; mammae four, two inguinal pairs; ears very small; tail short; lateral glands prominent on the hips of males. The skull is short and wide; first lower molar with three closed and two open triangles, second lower molar with the anterior pair of triangles confluent; third lower molar with three transverse loops.

PINE MOUSE
Pitymys pinetorum (LeConte)

Psammomys pinetorum LeConte. Ann. Lyc. Nat. Hist. New York, vol. 3, p. 133, 1830. Type locality: Pine forests of Georgia, probably near Riceboro, Liberty County.

Arvicola pinetorum Quick and Langdon 1832, Evermann and Butler 1894.

The Pine Mouse is distributed from southern New York to Georgia and westward to Nebraska, Kansas and Oklahoma. It does not extend farther north than southern Wisconsin, three subspecific forms and two closely allied species are embraced in this distribution. The species as a whole is found throughout the state of Indiana, one subspecies in the northern two-thirds and another in the southern third, differing slightly from one another in size and coloration. To appreciate the differences it is desirable to have typical specimens of each form for comparison, and as the two subspecies intergrade it will not always be possible to allocate specimens. There are no differences in the habits between the two forms.

Unlike the other three Microtines discussed above the Pine Mouse is a woodland animal, though it is frequently found in fields adjacent to woodlands. It is the most fossorial of our Microtines and spends nearly all of its life in underground passages. These underground runways resemble those of the mole in miniature. So mole-like are they in appearance that most persons mistake them to be the work of Moles. On digging down into them, one readily perceives they are much too small to accommodate a Mole, also they are closer to the surface and the line of partly broken, pushed up earth is much smaller. The Pine Mouse does not have the powerful digging forefeet of the Mole and its tunnels are, for that reason, made in looser, more easily worked soil. The mole-like nature of the fur, the relatively large forefeet, small ears, and short tail of the Pine Mouse all point to its subterranean life. They do, however, come out on to the surface of the ground and I remember on one occasion taking Pine Mice on three successive nights in a large rat trap baited with apple and placed in an open space with only short grass about it and at some distance from any woods. No signs of surface or underground runways were noticed in the vicinity. As a rule Pine Mice are easily caught by cutting into a runway and placing the trap so that its pan is level with its floor. Not infrequently White-footed Mice and Short-tailed Shrews are taken in these traps.

Pine Mice are more given to storage of food than the previously mentioned Microtines. Quick and Butler (1885) report them as storing young sprouts of white clover, fruits of the red haw, and tuberous roots of the violet. Such deposits sometimes contain as much as a gallon and extend 18 inches below the surface. Kennicott (1857) reports them as storing acorns.

The food of the Pine Mouse is not the green herbage of the Meadow Mice but for the most part wild roots and tubers as well as those in gardens, which it usually reaches by the underground route. It also eats seeds and fruits that have fallen from trees. It is the most destructive of our Microtines and frequently digs through the loose soil of gardens to eat planted seeds and bulbs. It also eats the inner bark of forest shrubs and trees, as well as those under cultivation either of the trunk at the ground or of the roots below the surface. The damage in the latter case is not seen until the tree is found to be in a poor or dying condition. Because of the likeness of its burrows to those of the Mole, the latter animal is often blamed for these depredations.

The nests of the Pine Mouse are always placed under the ground or under a log or stump, made of fine dry grass, root fibers or leaves. The number of young at a birth is from one to four. The latter number corresponds to the number of mammae, four placed in the inguinal region. The period of gestation has been unrecorded but it is probably about the same as in the genus *Microtus*. The young are probably born in the same undeveloped state and grow with about the same rapidity. The frequency of their breeding is unknown.

The success of their underground life is well illustrated by the fact that in an examination of owl pellets from the towers of the Smithsonian Institution, Dr. A. K. Fisher recovered 73 skulls of Pine Mice as against 3,730 skulls of the Pennsylvania Meadow Mouse. Probably they are not so immune from the carnivorous mammals. Methods for getting rid of these mice from gardens and orchards are described in detail in various circulars issued by the U. S. Department of Agriculture, which may be obtained on application.

Two subspecies of the Pine Mouse are recognized in Indiana. The descriptions of them below are taken almost verbatim from Bailey (1900). To make satisfactory identifications it is practically necessary to compare well made skins and adult skulls with those of typical examples of each form. It is probably safe to say that specimens from the lower fourth of the state represent the southern race or approach it, while those from the northern part represent the northern race.

Map 59. Published records and specimens in collections of the Pine Mouse, *Pitymys pinetorum*, in Indiana; 1, collection of Robert Goslin. Specimens from the southern third of the state are referable to *Pitymys pinetorum auricularis*, those from the northern two-thirds to *Pitymys pinetorum scalopsoides*. Specimens from Franklin County in collection of A. W. Butler.

The published records for the Pine Mouse are: Franklin (Coues 1877, Langdon 1881, Quick and Langdon 1882, Quick and Butler 1885, Butler 1886 Mar., Butler 1892, Evermann and Butler 1894, Bailey 1900, Hahn 1909), Knox (Hahn 1909), Lawrence (Hahn 1907, 1908, 1909), Marshall (Evermann and Clark 1920), Ohio (Hahn 1909), Porter (Lyon 1923), Randolph (Cox 1893, Evermann and Butler 1894), St. Joseph (Engels 1933), Vigo (Evermann and Butler 1894, Bailey 1900), Wabash (Evermann and Butler 1894, Cory 1912), Wayne (Kennicott 1857).

Northern Pine Mouse
Pitymys pinetorum scalopsoides (Audubon and Bachman)

Arvicola scalopsoides Audubon and Bachman. Proc. Acad. Nat. Sci. Philadelphia, vol. 1, p. 97, 1841. Type locality: Long Island, New York.
Microtus pinetorum scalopsoides Bailey 1900, Hahn 1909.

The geographic distribution of the Northern Pine Mouse is from southern New York westward to Illinois.

Its size is larger than that of the southern subspecies and its ears not so conspicuous. Upper parts dull brownish chestnut, slightly darkened by dusky-tipped hairs; sides paler; belly lightly washed with dull buff over plumbeous under fur; feet brownish gray; tail indistinctly bicolor, sooty above, grayish below. Total length, 122-125 mm., tail vertebrae, 20-22 mm.; hind foot, 16.5-17.5 mm. Greatest length of skull, about 27 mm.; greatest width, 16 mm.

Weight, probably slightly more than that of the southern subspecies which is about 15 grams.

SOUTHERN PINE MOUSE
Pitymys pinetorum auricularis (Bailey)

Microtus pinetorum auricularis BAILEY. Proc. Biol. Soc. Washington, vol. 12,
    p. 90, 1898. Type locality: Washington, Mississippi.
Microtus pinetorum auricularis Bailey 1900, Hahn 1909.

The geographic distribution of the Southern Pine Mouse is northern Mississippi, Tennessee, Kentucky and southern Indiana.

Its size is small, the ears large for the genus and conspicuous above the fur. Upper parts dark rich chestnut darkened by dusky tipped hairs; under parts washed with paler chestnut over dark under fur; projecting tip of ear with scattered dusky hairs; tail not bicolor, scarcely darker above, like the back or slightly darker. Total length, 120 mm.; tail vertebrae, 22 mm.; hind foot, 16 mm. Greatest length of skull, about 24 mm.; greatest width, 15.2 mm. Weight of an apparently adult male from Posey County, 15 grams.

Bailey (1900) says,

Specimens from Brookville, Ind. are dark and dull colored and might pass for either this [sub] species or *scalopsoides.*

MUSKRATS
Genus **Ondatra** Link [7]

The geographic distribution of the genus *Ondatra* is North America, north of the southern border of the United States. It is not found on the Atlantic seaboard south of North Carolina, nor on the Pacific seaboard south of Oregon. One species is found throughout Indiana wherever there is suitable aquatic habitat.

The Muskrat is essentially an overgrown *Microtus,* with a long laterally compressed, scaly, sparsely haired tail, adapted for an aquatic existence. The upper incisors have smooth anterior faces; the lower incisors have long roots extending backward located on the outside of the lower molars; molars rooted; enamel pattern of both upper and lower molars marked by an approximate equality of the reentrant angles on their inner and outer side. The hind feet are partially modified for swimming; large and so formed that they can be turned edgewise when carried forward, thus producing as little resistance to the water as possible when the animal is swimming; they are only inconspicuously webbed. The tail is large long and strongly compressed laterally so as to make an efficient rudder when swimming. The flattened form of the tail is scarcely noticeable in the young even when large enough to leave the nest, but develops rapidly as the Muskrat increases in size. One would infer from this that the peculiar tail is a character acquired late in the evolution of the genus. The fur of *Ondatra* is highly modified to produce a waterproof covering, the under fur being very dense and the long overhairs closely placed and glossy. There are certain other more technical characters in the skull and

---

7 In the older works the technical name of the genus is *Fiber* Cuvier.

those interested should consult the works of Miller (1896) and Hollister (1911).

The scent glands of the Muskrat are enormously developed compound sebaceous preputial glands, two in number right and left, between the skin and the abdominal muscular wall. Each gland is about two inches in length and about a third as thick in its widest portion. The glands open into the

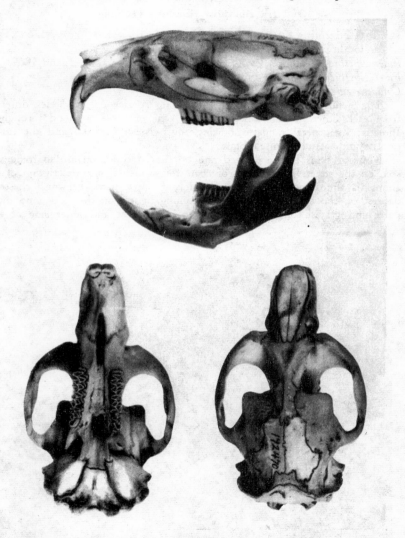

Fig. 92. Photograph courtesy U. S. Nat. Mus. Lateral, palatal and dorsal views of skull of Muskrat, *Ondatra zibethica*, natural size, Cat. No. 172,470, U. S. Nat. Mus., Newton County, 1910, Miss E. Settle.

preputial space. They increase in size during sexual activity. (Reisinger, 1916) Their function is to secrete the musky substance from which the animal derives its name. The expulsion of the musk takes place at the time of mating or just before. Actual copulation takes place while the animals are in the water or at least partially in the water. (Ulbrich, 1930; Svihla and Svihla, 1931).

MUSKRAT
Ondatra zibethica zibethica (Linnaeus)

[Castor] zibethicus LINNAEUS. Syst. Nat. ed. 12, vol. 1, p. 79, 1766. Type
    locality: Eastern Canada.
Fiber zibethicus Wied 1839-41, Evermann and Butler 1894, Hahn 1909.
Fiber zibethicus zibethicus Hollister 1911.
Ondatra zibethica Lyon 1923.

The genus Ondatra contains 14 existing species or subspecies differing from each other in minor details only. One of these is found throughout Indiana; its general range embracing southeastern Canada, and the north-eastern and central United States.

Muskrat skins in the undyed and unplucked condition are so frequently seen on the streets in the form of coats for women that a description of the animal is almost needless. General color of upper parts, brownish chestnut, darkest on top of head and back, becoming lighter on the sides, and much paler and grayish on under parts; chin and throat and inner side of legs

Fig. 93. Muskrat, Ondatra zibethica, photograph by J. C. Allen, West Lafayette.

whitish. In some localities melanistic individuals are fairly common. The feet
are brownish and the tail blackish.

Total length, about 560 mm.; tail vertebrae, 255 mm.; hind foot, 81 mm.
Weight, 1½-2 lbs. (680-900 grams). Greatest length of skull, about 65 mm.;
greatest width, about 38 mm.

Wherever aquatic conditions are suitable, marshes, ponds, lakes, brooks

Fig. 94. Partially drained marsh dotted with Muskrat houses. The fence post in
the foreground gives an idea of their size. St. Joseph County, photograph by M.
W. Lyon, Jr.

and rivers, Muskrats are usually found in Indiana. Although the animal is
common enough and large enough they are not frequently seen unless pains
are taken to find them, especially as they are largely nocturnal in activities.
Their houses, however, are conspicuous objects in almost any marsh in the
northern part of the state. Muskrats have rather readily adapted themselves
to civilization and are occasionally found within the corporate limits of some
of our larger towns. Their natural enemies have been decreased by man, and
in spite of much trapping the Muskrats have thrived accordingly. At Sousley's
Lake, a small body of water in St. Joseph County and within ten miles of
South Bend a farmer boy relates catching 300 Muskrats in the winter of
1931-32. (Engels 1933) They live in the small lakes which are part of the
campus of the University of Notre Dame.

They are so well adapted to cope with civilization that they have become
firmly established in central Europe, the only instance to my knowledge in
which an American mammal has invaded the Old World.

In 1906 Princess Colloredo-Mannsfeld imported four pairs of muskrats (*Fiber
zibethicus*) from America and turned them loose in Dobrisch, an estate southwest of
Prague, Bohemia. These animals subsequently increased in such numbers that at present

they have spread all over Bohemia, into Upper and Lower Austria and Moravia and also in Bavaria and Saxony, following the water courses.

The Muskrats have shown themselves to be very injurious, as they construct their burrows in the dams and embankments of the rivers and ponds, and thus by undermining the banks they endanger the whole system of waterways, subjecting the surrounding fields to the danger of floods. (Ahrens 1921).

A large German literature has sprung up regarding these animals and one of the best accounts of the Muskrat's ecology is that of Ulbrich (1930). Muskrats have two sorts of habitations. The most primitive is the simple hole in the bank, with its entrance under water and its interior with a nest cavity proper above the water level and back from the bank from a few to as many as thirty feet. In heavy soil the bank house may have an air shaft leading to the surface. In loose soil such an air shaft is usually absent. In some localities this is the only type of habitation used. The other type of habitation is the so-called house These houses vary much in size some being only a foot high above the water and not more than that in diameter at the base, others may be three or four feet high and eight or ten feet in diameter. They are made of whatever material any particular marsh or pond affords. The

Fig. 95. Muskrat house, amid cat-tails, Sousley's Lake, St. Joseph County, photograph by M. W. Lyon, Jr.

one illustrated was a medium sized house about four feet in diameter and about one and one-half feet above water line. It was made entirely of cat-tail stalks and leaves. Within the house is the nest or nests proper placed above the water level and lined with finer materials. The houses are entered and left by way of a plunge hole from below the water's surface. Larger houses contain several nests and one or more plunge holes. One Muskrat may make only a single small house, or at mating time a pair constructs a house. Probably the larger houses with several nests and plunge holes are family affairs, though the animals are fond of each other's company and are somewhat colonial. (Svihla and Svihla 1931) Some think that when conditions are suitable for both types of houses, the bank burrows are used in summer and the reed houses in winter. In extensive marsh land the reed houses are the only type available. According to Ulbrich (1930) the temperature of the interior of the house is usually always far above the outside temperature which may be much below the freezing point, while the inside at its lowest is a few degrees above freezing.

Evermann and Clark (1920) describe some curiously placed houses, such as on cross timbers under piers at Lake Maxinkuckee.

When living in an unflooded marsh the Muskrat makes runways and burrows similar to those of the other Microtines, only larger in proportion to the size of the maker.

While mainly aquatic the Muskrat often travels afar on dry ground. I once found one that had been run over on a highway; no evident water was in sight and there were cornfields on either side of the road. They are excellent swimmers and divers, but do not travel in the water rapidly, one to three miles per hour (Mizelle 1935). They can remain under water for considerable periods of time. Evermann and Clark (1920) attribute this to their ability to blow a small bubble of air just beyond the nostril and reinhale it again. Beneath the ice they are said to let small streams of bubbles pass upward to form a larger bubble and reinhale the latter. As the exhaled air passes through the water it loses its carbon dioxide and reabsorbs some of the oxygen dissolved in the water. C. E. Johnson (1925) is inclined to discredit these methods of purifying the breathed air. The method of propulsion in water is by means of the hind feet, which are only partly webbed, but are bordered by stiff hairs. Strokes are made by the hind feet alternately, the forefeet being held motionless beneath the chin, palms inward. The tail is a rudder in surface swimming. When swimming submerged the tail is used as an organ of propulsion in addition to the hind feet (Mizelle 1935).

On land the progress of the Muskrats is rather slow and awkward. In marshland the Muskrat makes runways in the manner of any other Microtine. It also makes small canals for purposes of travelling much as the Beaver does.

When cornered or in traps the animals are vicious and can inflict severe wounds with their powerful incisor teeth. They have been known to jump at an adversary.

The chief food of the Muskrat is the aquatic vegetation of its pond or marsh including the roots of pond lilies. It consumes about 1/3 of its weight in green vegetation daily. (Svihla and Svihla 1931). In cultivated lowlands they often come out at night and invade gardens and cornfields. Butler (1885) says they eat corn at all stages of its growth, but this damage to cultivated land is not material. Like most rodents they are not averse to eating flesh when obtainable. Occasionally they can catch a fish and eat it, and Evermann and Clark (1920) found them feeding on dead birds, as well as turtles. They write further:

The most important of the winter food of the Muskrat is the fresh water mussels or Unionidae. At various places along the shore [Lake Maxinkuckee], where an object projects out of the water, such as a log or pier, or fallen tree top, there will be found in autumn or early winter a pile of mussel shells where muskrats have been feeding. These piles are frequently of considerable size, containing sometimes a bushel or more of shells.

During the fall these operations are probably confined to mussels which they find in shallow water near shore. In winter, however, when ice-cracks form and extend well across the lake, the Muskrats go far out on the ice, dive through the cracks and bring up mussels which they eat sitting on the ice. . . .On January 4, a Muskrat was seen at the edge of this crack about 1,000 feet from shore eating mussels. It would dive through the crack and after a little while reappear with a mussel. . . . It would then sit on its haunches, holding the mussel in its paws and, by much clawing and chewing, finally succeed in opening the shell and removing the meat, which it usually licked out quite clean. In some case the muskrat failed to get the shell open. . . . It is our observation that the Muskrat, by inserting its claws or teeth between the valves succeeds in cutting or tearing loose the adductor muscles so as to permit the valves to spring open.

Butler (1885) refers to this same habit of eating mussels in winter and of eating dead birds. In addition to tearing the shells apart, Butler thinks the Muskrat may leave the larger molluscs out of water for the animal to become weakened or die, the shells naturally opening when the adductor muscles can no longer operate. C. E. Johnson (1925) ably discusses the methods of opening molluscs.

The first mating takes place in late winter or early spring depending much upon the condition of the weather. At this time the females utter hoarse squeals which attracts the males who utter grunts (Butler 1885). The Svihlas (1931) found them quite promiscuous in their sexual behavior. The exact period of gestation is unknown. Hollister (1911) quoting Lantz places it at about three weeks, Ulbrich (1930) places it at 27 days. The young are usually said to be born blind and naked, though the Svihlas (1931) found them thinly clothed with hair. The number of young in a litter varies from one to six, four being probably the most usual number. Hollister (1911) places it at six or eight. The weight of the new born is around 20 grams. Young of about 70 grams weight are able to feed upon grasses and grain. The Svihlas think six months ample time for the Muskrat to develop from birth to adult. The number of litters per year at Lake Maxinkuckee is at least two and probably three (Evermann and Clark 1920). Butler (1885) also speaks of a plurality of broods. The number of mammae is usually eight, two pairs inguinal and two pairs thoracic.

The Muskrat has an important economic status, not from its destructiveness to crops of agriculturists, which is practically negligible, but from the value of its fur. In certain cases, however, where artificial ponds or drainage ditches are maintained its presence may be objectionable owing to its construction of bank dwellings and unintentionally producing leaks.

In the last few years Muskrat fur has become one of the popular ones on the market. The 1932-33 prices of raw skins varied from 15 to 45 cents. Marshlands properly cared for and not trapped too closely ought to yield a considerable profit. Unfortunately at the present time there is a tendency to drain nearly all available land and turn it over to agricultural purposes. It is not unlikely that if these marshlands were allowed to remain as such the crop of Muskrats would prove quite as valuable as the farm products subsequently raised after the expensive operations of draining have been completed. The Muskrat requires no care. The chief enemy of the Muskrats appears to be Minks whose skins are worth even more than the Muskrats. In the old days of the Kankakee marshes Muskrats were very abundant, and the annual catch large; in Lake County alone it amounted to 20,000 to 40,000 skins. In those days skins were of little value. Following the World War the price of skins soared to well over a dollar and sometimes more for particularly choice skins. Hahn (1909) cites trappers who took from 300 to 700 skins in the Kankakee region per season, at a time when the skins were worth only 15 cents each. Engels (1933) cites a farmer boy who took over

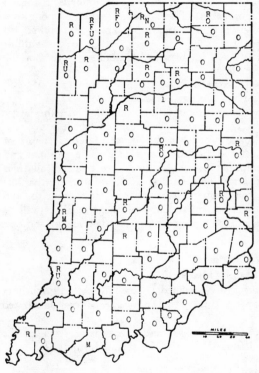

Map 60. Published records, recent observations and specimens in collections of the Muskrat, *Ondatra zibethica*, in Indiana; 1, Carnegie Museum, Pittsburgh, Pa.

The published records for the Muskrat are: Carroll (Evermann and Butler 1894), Fayette (Evermann and Butler 1894), Franklin (Haymond 1870, Quick and Langdon 1882, Butler 1886, Evermann and Butler 1894, Hahn 1909), Fulton (Evermann and Butler 1894), Hamilton (Shirts 1901), Jasper (Hahn 1909), Knox (Hollister 1911), Lagrange (Evermann and Butler 1894), Lake (Ball 1884, Dinwiddie 1884, Blatchley 1898, Hahn 1909, Brennan 1923), Laporte (Anonymous 1880, Elliot 1907, Hollister 1911, Cory 1912, Brennan 1923), Marshall (Evermann and Butler 1894, Evermann and Clark 1911, 1920), Monroe (Evermann and Butler 1894, McAtee 1907), Morgan (Major 1915), Newton (Hahn 1907, Hollister 1911, Ade 1911), Porter (Blatchley 1898, Hahn 1907, 1909, Hollister 1911, Brennan 1923, Lyon 1923, 1925), Posey (Wied 1839-41, 1861-62), Randolph (Cox 1893, Evermann and Butler 1894), St. Joseph (Anonymous 1880, Engels 1933), Vigo (Evermann and Butler 1894), Wabash (Evermann and Butler 1894), Kankakee Valley (Reed 1920).

300 skins in the 1931-32 season within ten miles of South Bend, averaging about 60 cents per skin. The fur of Muskrat is used very frequently in its undyed and unplucked condition. When the long guard hairs are removed and the soft under fur dyed it is usually sold under the name of "Hudson Seal." It is difficult to distinguish it at sight from the true fur-seal, but a garment made of it can instantly be told by its lighter weight and thinness of the leather of the skin. Plucked or unplucked the Muskrat fur is variously treated and sold under various trade names.. Today nearly all dealers in furs if asked point-blank will give the real name of the animal from which any "fancy" fur is made. The real knowledge of fur-bearing animals possessed by some saleswomen is truly remarkable. There is no attempt to hoodwink the buying public as in bygone days. Although Muskrats are worked up into handsome garments or fur pieces or trimmings, either in the natural state or under various guises it is not a fur of great durability like that of the seal, mink, otter and other carnivores.

According to figures received by the Department of Conservation 586,689 Muskrat skins were taken in Indiana during the season of 1931-32.

Another economic aspect of the Muskrat is its food value. In the larger cities of the Atlantic Seaboard, the carcasses of Muskrats which have been trapped for their fur are sold for almost a nominal price under the name of "marsh rabbits." I have never eaten it, but the flesh is said to be excellent and there is no reason why it should not be, as Muskrats are clean in all their habits and almost entirely vegetarian in their diet. It is unfortunate that the animal has been saddled with the opprobrious name of "rat." Had the old Indian name Ondatra remained the popular name of the animal as well as its scietnific name, Ondatras might have become a table delicacy in addition to a popular fur.

Old World Rats and Mice
Family **Muridae**

The family *Muridae* was originally confined to the Old World south of Arctic region, but members of two genera are now everywhere distributed through human agencies.

Their external form is rat- or mouse-like, and the general form of the skull is that of the Cricetidae discussed above. The dental formula is:

$$i\,\frac{1-1}{1-1}, \; c\,\frac{0-0}{0-0}, \; pm\,\frac{0-0}{0-0}, \; m\,\frac{3-3}{3-3}, = 16.$$

The molars are low-crowned and rooted. They are tuberculate, the tubercles of the upper molars being arranged in three principal longitudinal rows. The family contains about 50 genera, two of which are widely distributed, through introduction, in Indiana and the rest of North America.

Old World House Rats
Genus **Rattus** G. Fischer

The genus *Rattus* was originally confined to the temperate and tropical portions of the Old World, but is now essentially cosmopolitan through introduction by man, of two of its several hundred species.

The external form, skull, and teeth are all rat-like. The first upper molar is five-rooted; the upper incisors are compressed and set at such an angle that their outer sides are worn away smoothly by the action of the lower incisors.

HOUSE RAT
Rattus norvegicus (Erxleben)

[*Mus*] *norvegicus* ERXLEBEN. Syst. Regni Anim., vol. 1, p. 381, 1777. Type locality: Norway.
Mus decumanus PALLAS. Nov. Spec. Glires, p. 91, 1778. Plummer 1844, Haymond 1870, Evermann and Butler 1894.
Mus norvegicus Hahn 1909.
Rattus norvegicus Lyon 1923.

The House Rat is too well known to need any description, or account of its habits. For purposes of comparison the following measurements are given: Total length, 375-400 mm.; tail, 190-200 mm.; hind foot, 41-44 mm.; greatest length of skull, about 45 mm.; greatest width, about 21 mm. Besides being found about buildings, on farms, in villages and cities, it frequently wanders far afield, and is often taken in traps placed remote from any human habitation. Thus I have taken it on a wild island in the Potomac River, far above the City of Washington and so located that the animal had to reach it by swimming at least 100 yards. It was probably attracted by the presence of a week-end camp.

The House Rat is a most destructive pest, a great nuisance and a possible transmitter of disease, so that its depredations in the aggregate amount to an enormous sum. "Food and shelter are as essential to rats as to other animals, and removal of these offers a practical means of permanent rat control. The number of rats on premises and the extent of their destructiveness are usually in direct proportion to the available food supply and to the shelter afforded. Rat proofing in the broadest sense embraces not only the exclusion of rats from buildings of all types, but also the elimination of their hiding and nesting places and cutting off their food supply. Through open doors and in other ways, rats may frequently gain access to structures that are otherwise rat proof, but they can not persist there unless they find safe retreats and food. When rat proofing becomes the regular practice the rat problem will have been largely solved." (James Silver and W. E. Crouch, Rat proofing buildings and premises, U. S. Dept. Agric., Farmers' Bull. No. 1638. 1930). Those interested should apply for this bulletin, to the Superintendent of Documents, Washington, D. C., as well as for Leaflet No. 65, Red Squill powder in rat control, by James Silver and J. C. Munch, 1931. Both are sold at nominal cost.

The House Rat entered Indiana shortly after the advent of the white man and the settling of the state. The only exact dates we have are Brookville 1837 (Haymond 1870), Richmond 1835 (Plummer 1844) and Vincennes 1840 (Hahn 1909). It was preceded in these places by the Black Rat which it speedily drove out.

The House Rat is an excellent mammal to practice on in learning to pre-
pare study skins and skulls, as well as to dissect for learning mammalian
anatomy. The common White Rat is an albinistic form of the House Rat. It
is extensively raised in appropriate cages and used in the study of numerous
biological problems of great theoretical and practical importance.

Map 62. Published records
and specimens in collections of
the House Rat, *Rattus norvegicus,* in Indiana.

.The House Rat is found throughout the state. The few published records are:
Franklin (Haymond 1870, Langdon 1881, Quick and Langdon 1882), Monroe (Mc-
Atee 1907, Cockerell 1914), Newton (Hahn 1907), Porter (Hahn 1907, Lyon 1923),
St. Joseph (Engels 1933), Wayne (Plummer 1844).

BLACK RAT
Rattus rattus rattus (Linnaeus)

[*Mus*] *rattus* LINNAEUS. Syst. Nat., ed. 10, vol. 1, p. 61, 1758. Type
    locality: Upsala, Sweden.
Mus rattus Plummer 1844, Haymond 1870, Evermann and Butler 1894,
    Hahn 1909.

The Black Rat was formerly the common rat of Europe and the common
introduced rat of America. However, at an early date in America it was
rapidly supplanted by the common House Rat, so that it is rare indeed to
find examples of it today in the United States except in isolated localities
and except in the Southern States, where it exists as the true Black Rat or

more commonly as the subspecies known as Roof Rat or Alexandrine Rat. It is doubtful if any thoroughly established Black Rats are to be found in Indiana today. An occasional straggler may enter the state from the south. In the early settlements of the state it was probably common enough, playing the same role that the House Rat plays today. It was gone from the vicinity of Richmond by the time Plummer wrote, 1844. Haymond (1870) says it was common about Brookville up till 1827. It was last seen near Vincennes about 1845 (Hahn 1909). Hahn (1909) records a specimen in the State Museum, Indianapolis, taken at New Albany, December 6, 1904; and ventures the opinion that it reached there in a shipment of goods from some southern port. The specimen apparently was a true Black Rat.

The Black Rat is readily distinguished from the well known House Rat by its general slaty color, darker on the back which is sometimes almost black; by its more slender and lighter build, with a tail longer than the head and body. The skull is lighter in build, and the beading on the top of the skull caused by the attachment of the temporal muscles is gracefully bowed out-

Map 62. Published records and specimens in collections of the Black Rat, *Rattus rattus*, in Indiana.

The Black Rat became quickly exterminated in Indiana by its successor the Norway Rat. The only published records are: Floyd (Hahn 1909), Franklin (Haymond 1870, Langdon 1881, Quick and Langdon 1882, Evermann and Butler 1894), Knox (Hahn 1909), Wayne (Plummer 1844).

ward on each side instead of forming more or less parallel ridges as in the case of the House Rat.

Total length, about 390-400 mm.; tail, 200-225 mm.; hind foot, 36-38 mm.; greatest length of skull, about 43 mm.; greatest width, about 21 mm.

The southern variety of the Black Rat, *Rattus rattus alexandrinus* differs from *Rattus rattus rattus* in having the upperparts light brown in color; and the underparts strongly contrasted pale buff or light gray. There are no records of the occurrence of this subspecies in Indiana, but it might be found as a straggler or immigrant in the southern part of the state.

There is something pleasing and attractive about both varieties of the Black Rat in contrast to the repugnant appearance of the common House Rat.

OLD WORLD HOUSE MICE AND ALLIED FORMS
Genus **Mus** Linnaeus

The genus *Mus* was originally confined to the temperate and tropical portions of the Old World but is essentially cosmopolitan, through introduction by man of one of its two dozen species.

The external form, skull, and teeth are all mouse-like. The first upper molar is three-rooted; the upper incisors are compressed and set at such an angle that a sub-apical notch is cut in their outer sides by the action of the lower incisors.

HOUSE MOUSE
Mus musculus Linnaeus

[*Mus*] *musculus* LINNAEUS. Syst. Nat. ed. 10, vol. 1, p. 62, 1758. Type locality: Upsala, Sweden.

Mus musculus Plummer 1844, Haymond 1870, Evermann and Butler 1894, Hahn 1909.

H[esperomys] indianus WIED 1861-62.

The House Mouse is too well known to need any description or account of its habits. For purposes of comparison the following measurements are given: Total length, about 170 mm.; tail, about 90 mm.; hind foot, 17-18 mm.; greatest length of skull, about 21 mm.; greatest width, about 11 mm. Besides being found about buildings on farms, in villages and cities it frequently wanders far afield and is often taken in traps remote from any human habitation. Thus I have taken it while camped in an apparently wild place in the dunes of Lake Michigan, Porter County, in a situation as remote as a mile away from any permanent dwelling.

The House Mouse is as much of a pest and nuisance as is its larger relative the House Rat, but less so in proportion to its smaller size. It has never been accused of carrying any diseases that affect man.

The same remarks regarding the necessity of appropriate food and shelter for maintaining itself quoted under the account of the House Rat apply with equal force to the House Mouse. Buildings that are carefully and properly rat-proofed are for the most part mouse-proof, but mice can enter through much smaller openings and apparently are more quick to enter a dwelling by means of a door or window temporarily left open or unguarded by a screen.

The House Mouse entered America at an early date, and probably was in the settlements of Indiana almost as soon as they were formed. It was mentioned by Plummer in 1844 and while not specifically mentioned by Wied in 1839-41 or 1861-62, yet he collected a specimen at New Harmony which he mistook to be a new species of *Peromyscus* and described as *H[esper-omys]* *indianus*, "die *Wabasch-Waldmaus.*" J. A. Allen examined the speci-men in 1891 and R. T. Hatt in 1930 and both identified it as *Mus musculus*. I have seen the specimen myself and fully concur in their opinions. As so distinguished a naturalist as the Prince of Wied has made the mistake of confusing the House Mouse with the White-footed Mouse, it may be desir-able to point out its chief characters. First the skull and teeth should be carefully examined. The House Mouse has three longitudinal rows of tub-ercles on the upper molars, while the White-footed Mouse has but two such rows. The incisor teeth of *Mus* are without grooves, in *Reithrodontomys*, a genus not yet recorded from Indiana, but externally closely resembling *Mus* there are longitudinal grooves on the upper incisors. The House Mouse is

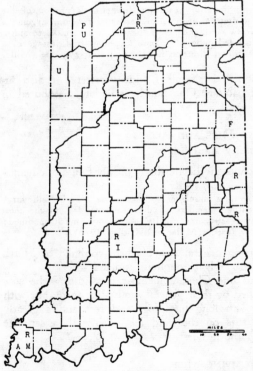

Map 63. Published records and specimens in collections of the House Mouse, *Mus musculus*, in Indiana.

The House Mouse is found in every county, however only these few published records have been found: Franklin (Haymond 1870, Quick and Langdon 1882), Mon-roe (McAtee 1907), Newton (Hahn 1907), Porter (Hahn 1907, Lyon 1923), Posey (Wied 1861-62, Allen 1891, Hatt 1930), Wayne (Plummer 1884), St. Joseph (Engels 1933).

uniformly gray throughout. Even though the under parts are a lighter gray than the upper parts, they are never white as in the White-footed Mouse. The adult White-footed Mouse is slightly larger than the adult House Mouse. The Harvest Mouse, *Reithrodontomys*, has the closest resemblance of any of our native mice to the House Mouse, especially immature specimens. Externally they are more slender in build and have relatively longer tails, and lighter under parts. The only certain criterion is the structure of the teeth; incisors grooved in the Harvest Mouse, and the upper molars with but two longitudinal rows of tubercles instead of three such rows.

The common White Mouse of animal dealers is an albino House Mouse. It is used occasionally as a pet by children, but is very extensively employed as an experimental laboratory animal, in the fields of applied medicine, genetics, physiology, bacteriology, etc.

JUMPING MICE, JEROBAS, ETC.
Superfamily Dipodoidae

Masseter lateralis superficialis with anterior head not distinct, this portion of the muscle attaching along a considerable area on an anterior border of zygoma; zygomatic plate nearly horizontal, always narrow and completely beneath infraorbital foramen. Angular portion of mandible not distorted outward at base to permit free passage of a branch of the masseter lateralis, its general direction not parallel with zygoma. (Miller and Gidley 1918).

This superfamily contains eight living families, widely scattered in distribution, and variable in form and habitat. One family is widely distributed in North America.

JUMPING MICE AND ALLIES
Family Zapodidae

The family *Zapodidae* is found in the northern portions of both hemispheres.

Infraorbital foramen large, transmitting muscle as well as nerve; cheek teeth varying in number from 5/4 in the earlier members of the group to 3/3 in the most advanced; the quadritubercular crown structure usually not always much modified; metatarsals not reduced in number or fused. (Miller and Gidley 1918).

The family contains four living genera, two of them confined to North America, one of which occurs sparingly throughout Indiana.

The American members and one Chinese member constituting the subfamily *Zapodinae* are distinguished by their general mouse-like form, but with body enlarged posteriorly and with long hind legs and feet and a greatly elongated tail. There are five toes on the hind feet each with a separate metatarsal, the middle one being the heaviest.

JUMPING MICE
Genus Zapus Coues

The genus *Zapus* ranges throughout most of northern North America, extending as far south as North Carolina and New Mexico.

The skull is essentially mouse-like, with a rather high and rounded brain case; large oval antorbital foramina; zygomata broadly expanded anteriorly where the malar extends upward to the lachrymal bone. Dental formula:

$$i \frac{1-1}{1-1}, \ c \frac{0-0}{0-0}, \ pm \frac{1-1}{0-0}, \ m \frac{3-3}{3-3}, = 18.$$

Enamel of the molars much folded; upper incisors compressed, curved and deeply grooved. See Fig. 85, p. 235.

The genus contains 20 species or subspecies, one of which is found sparingly throughout Indiana.

JUMPING MOUSE
Zapus hudsonius hudsonius Zimmermann

Dipus hudsonius ZIMMERMANN, Geogr. Gesch., vol. 2, p. 358, 1780. Type locality: Hudson Bay.
Dipus canadensis DAVIES, Trans. Linn. Soc. London, vol. 4, p. 157, 1798.
Gerbillus canadensis Wied 1839-41, Plummer 1844.
Zapus hudsonius Evermann and Butler 1894, Preble 1899, Hahn 1909.

The Hudson Bay Jumping Mouse ranges from the southern shores of Hudson Bay, south to New Jersey and in the mountains to North Carolina, west to Iowa and Missouri and northwest to Alaska. It is apparently found throughout Indiana, though none have as yet been reported from or taken in the southeastern counties. The animal is nowhere common in the state. Hahn (1909) who did much trapping failed to take one specimen. In the dunes region of Porter County, I took one *Zapus* in a total of some 200 mammals. Others have been more fortunate as Engels (1933) and Paul Hickie took two out of a total of seven mammals trapped near Mongo, Lagrange County.

The Jumping Mouse in general is yellowish brown above, darkest and band-like along the middle, due to black tipped hairs; the bases of the hairs are slaty colored; underparts white or whitish, and feet whitish; sides yellowish orange, unmixed with black tipped hairs, and with bases of hairs white; tail brownish above and whitish below, scantily haired but somewhat tufted at tip. The colors are brightest in spring and early summer. The pelage is rather coarse.

Total length, 200 to 215 mm., tail vertebrae, 120 to 130 mm., hind foot, 28 to 31 mm. Greatest length of skull, about 23 mm., greatest width, about 12 mm. Summer weight, 11.5 to 13.5 grams. Before hibernating their weight is about a third heavier (Hamilton 1935, Sheldon 1934). New born young, 0.7 to 0.9 gram.

Jumping Mice are found in meadows, shrubby fields, and thickets along the edges of woods, usually in moist situations. They are most often seen in meadows and fields during the mowing season when they are driven from their hiding places and jump away in a series of frog-like leaps, the long tail being used as a balance and rudder. They are credited with leaps of 6 to 8 feet, truly remarkable distances for so small an animal. They can clamber about the lower branches of shrubs with ease. They have no beaten paths through the grass but wander about at will. Their food consists of green vegetation seeds and grains. In late summer they make globular nests of

Fig. 96. Photograph, copyright by H. H. Pittman. Jumping Mouse, *Zapus hudsonius*, nearly natural size.

grass, about four inches in diameter with a small entrance on the side. These nests are placed on the ground, in thick grass or in small bushes.

Breeding nests are ordinarily placed underground or under some convenient object. Four to six young are born at a birth, in late spring or early summer. One collected by Paul Hickie in Posey County on July 5, contained four embryos. Preble (1899) reports young born in September, so probably they breed throughout the summer season. New born young are pink, hairless, not even the vibrissae being visible, in contrast to the known young of other North American rodents (Svihla and Svihla, 1933). The period of gestation and rate of development appears to be unknown. The mammae are eight in number, four on each side from the inguinal to the pectoral region.

Late in summer Jumping Mice begin putting on fat preparatory to hibernation shortly after the frosts of autumn. The one that I trapped in Porter County on October 26 was apparently still active although the thermometer a few nights previous registered five degrees of frost. They often lay up stores of food in nests or burrows during summer, but it is unknown if they use these in winter. The hibernating animal, they are usually found singly, occupies a nest in holes at a depth of from a few inches to two or three feet below the surface. Rarely hibernation takes place in a nest above ground.

A most interesting account of a Jumping Mouse exhumed at Vincennes was published by Prof. Sanborn Tenney in 1872, and is quoted in full.

On the 18th of January of the present year (1872), I went with Dr. A. Patton of Vincennes, Indiana, to visit a mound situated about a mile and a half in an easterly direction from Vincennes. While digging in the mound in search of relics that might throw light upon its origin and history, we came to a nest about two feet below the surface of the ground, carefully made of bits of grass, and in this nest was a Jumping Mouse (Jaculus Hudsonius Baird) apparently dead. It was coiled up as tightly as it could be, the nose being placed upon the belly, and the long tail coiled around the ball-like form which the animal had assumed. I took the little mouse into my hand. It exhibited no motion or sign of life. Its eyes and mouth were shut tight, and its little fore feet or hands were shut and placed close together. Everything indicated that the mouse was perfectly dead, excepting the fact that it was not as rigid as perhaps a dead mouse would be in the winter. I tied the mouse and nest in my handkerchief and carried them to Vincennes. Arriving at Dr. Patton's office I untied my treasures, and took out the mouse and held it for some time in my hand; it still exhibited no sign of life, but at length I thought I saw a very slight movement in one of the hind legs. Presently there was a very slight movement of the head, yet so feeble that one could hardly be sure it was real. Then there came to be some evidence of breathing, and a slight pressure of my fingers upon the tail near the body was followed by an immediate but feeble movement of one of the hind legs. At length there was unmistakable evidence that the animal was breathing, but the breathing was a labored action, and seemingly performed with great difficulty. As the mouse became warmer the signs of life became more and more marked; and in the course of the same afternoon on which I brought it into the warm room it became perfectly active, and was as ready to jump about as any other member of its species.

I put this mouse into a little tin box with holes in the cover, and took him with me in my journeyings, taking care to put in the box a portion of an ear of corn and pieces of paper. It ate the corn by gnawing from the outside of the kernel, and it gnawed the paper into bits with which it made a nest. On the fourth day after its capture I gave it water which it seemed to relish. On the 23rd of January I took it with me to Elgin, Illinois, nearly three hundred miles farther north than the region where I found the specimen. The weather was extremely cold. Taking the mouse from the box, I placed it on a newspaper on a table, and covered it with a large glass bell, lifting the edge of the glass so as to admit a supply of air. Under this glass was placed a good supply of waste cotton. Soon after it was fairly established in its new and more commodious quarters, it began to clean every part of its body in the most thorough manner, washing itself very much in the same manner as a cat washes. On coming to the tail it passed that long member, for its whole length, through the mouth from side to side, beginning near the body and ending at the tip. At night as soon as the lights were put out the mouse began gnawing the paper, and during the night it gnawed all the newspaper it could reach, and made the fragments and the cotton into a large nest perhaps five or six inches in diameter, and established itself in the centre. Here it spent the succeeding day. The next night it was supplied with more paper, and it gnawed all it could reach, and thus spent a large part of the night in work. I could hear the work going on when I was awake. In the morning it appeared to be reposing on the top of its nest; but after watching it for some time, and seeing no motion, I lifted up the glass and took the mouse in my hand. It showed no signs of life. I now felt that

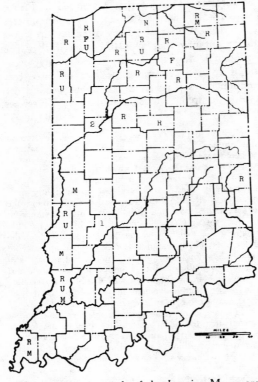

Map 64. Published records and specimens in collections of the Jumping-Mouse, *Zapus hudsonius*, in Indiana; 1, collection of Robert Goslin; 2, collection of Frederick H. Test.

The published records of the Jumping Mouse are: Carroll (Butler 1892, Evermann and Butler 1894, Hahn 1909), Fulton (Evermann and Clark 1920), Howard (Evermann and Butler 1894), Knox (Tenney 1872, Butler 1892, Evermann and Butler 1894, Hahn 1909, Cory 1912), Kosciusko (Hahn 1909), Lagrange (Butler 1892, Evermann and Butler 1894, Hahn 1909), Lake (Hahn 1909), Marshall (Evermann and Clark 1911, 1920), Newton (Butler 1895, Hahn 1909), Noble (Hahn 1909), Porter (Lyon 1924), Posey (Wied 1839-41, 1861-62, Hahn 1909), St. Joseph (Engels 1933), Stark (Butler 1892, Evermann and Butler 1894, Hahn 1909), Vigo (Evermann and Butler 1894, Preble 1899), Wabash (Butler 1892, Evermann and Butler 1894, Hahn 1909), Wayne (Plummer 1844, Hahn 1909), Kankakee Valley (Hahn 1907).

perhaps my pet was indeed really dead; but on remembering what I had previously seen, I resolved to try to restore it again to activity. By holding it in my hand and thus warming it, the mouse soon began to show signs of life, and although it was nearly the whole day in coming to activity, at last it was as lively as ever, and afterward, on being set free in the room, it moved about so swiftly by means of its long leaps, that it required two of us a long time to capture it uninjured.

On the evening of February 6th I reached my home in Williamstown, and on my arrival the mouse was in good condition. But the next morning it was again apparently dead; in the course of the day, however, being placed where it was warm, it gradually came back again to activity as before.

This mouse, then, when dug from the mound was in a state of the most profound lethargy,—if torpidity be too strong a term—and it is safe to infer that it would have so remained until spring, had it not been removed into a warmer temperature; and this lethargy or torpidity was as intense, so far as least as regards external appearances, as that seen in other animals, not excepting reptiles and batrachians.

I may add that the observations above detailed show that this mouse is capable of passing into the deepest lethargic state in a single night, and of returning, when warmed, to activity again on the succeeding day.

The Jumping Mouse is very quiet in the daytime, but very active at night. When disturbed in its nest it vigorously repels the attack by striking with its fore feet with the greatest rapidity. It apparently does not seek to bite me.

Since the above was written the mouse has repeated the exhibitions detailed above, and at least once since the bginning of April. A colder night than usual seems to furnish the occasion for it to go into a state of the most profound lethargy.

HYSTRICOMORPH RODENTS
Superfamily **Hystricoidea**

Zygomasseteric structure as in the Dipodoidae except: Angular portion of mandible distorted outward to allow passage of a specialized enlarged distal end of anterior limb of the masseter lateralis superficialis muscle. Masseter medialis arising from side of rostrum and passing through large infraorbital foramen. (Miller and Gidley 1918).

This is a large superfamily widely distributed throughout the warmer portions of the world. It attains its highest development in South America, and the single North American representative of the superfamily probably had its origin there but it has long since become adapted to the rigors of northern winters and is now chiefly confined to the northern United States and Canada.

AMERICAN PORCUPINES
Family **Erethizontidae**

Mandibular rami with conspicuous postsymphyseal buttresses which prevent movement at the symphysis; lower border of angular process folded inward; cheekteeth subhypsodont, [rooted], flat crowned, with reduced-heptamerous enamel pattern characterized by narrow ridges and wide reentrant spaces, the spaces on the paramere tending to become transformed into pits. Upper zygomatic root over anterior part of toothrow, feet noticeably modified for arboreal life. (Miller and Gidley 1918).

This family confined to America contains the porcupines of North America and two other genera found in South or Central America.

NORTH AMERICAN PORCUPINES
Genus **Erethizon** F. Cuvier

The North American Porcupines are, or were formerly, distributed throughout the colder portions of North America from southern Indiana, Nebraska, Arizona and California, northward into Alaska and Labrador. They contain two well marked species which in turn fall into several geographic races, one of which formerly occupied nearly the whole of Indiana.

The genus *Erethizon* is chiefly distinguished by its external form, a thick-set clumsy animal about a meter or a little less in length, and pelage of three very different sorts of hairs, long soft woolly hairs, long coarse hair, and highly

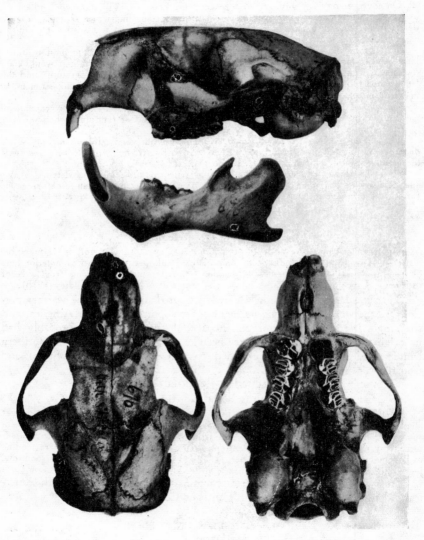

Fig. 97. Photograph courtesy U. S. Nat. Mus. Lateral, dorsal and palatal views of skull of Porcupine, *Erethizon dorsatum*, about 7/9 natural size, Cat. No. 676, U. S. Nat. Mus., Lycoming County, Penn., S. F. Baird. Though the Porcupine was once common in Indiana, no skulls of Indiana specimens are known to be extant.

developed spines or quills. The latter are narrow and pointed, barbed at the free end; the loosely attached end is also narrow, the intervening or main shaft of the quills is thick, stiff, hollow and air filled. There are four toes on the front feet and five on the hind, all armed with strong curved claws. The tail is short and thick and heavily armed with quills.

The skull is about the same in size as that of the Woodchuck and seen from above, bears a striking resemblance to it except that it lacks the conspicuous postorbital processes, but anatomically it is vastly different. The teeth are built along an entirely different pattern with the enamel intricately folded. Dental formula:

$$i \frac{1-1}{1-1}, \ c \frac{0-0}{0-0}, \ pm \frac{1-1}{1-1}, \ m \frac{3-3}{3-3}, = 20.$$

PORCUPINE, sometimes HEDGEHOG [1]

Erethizon dorsatum dorsatum Linnaeus

Hystrix dorsata LINNAEUS. Syst. Nat., ed. 10, vol. 1, p. 57, 1758. Type locality: Eastern Canada.
Hystrix dorsata Wied 1839-41. Plummer 1844.
Hystrix Hudsonius Haymond 1870.
Erethizon dorsatus Evermann and Butler 1894.
Erethizon dorsatum Hahn 1909.

The color of the Porcupine is everywhere slaty to brownish black with considerable sprinkling of yellowish white hairs on the upperparts and sides. The quills are lacking about the face, the entire underparts and inner side of legs; they are present on the under side of the tail; the quills are yellowish white in color with black tips; they are most conspicuous on rump and tail. They vary in length from less than an inch to four inches or slightly over.

Total length 36 to 40 in. (900 to 1000 mm.), tail vertebrae 6 in. (150 mm.), hind foot 3.5 to 4 in. (87 to 100 mm). Weight 15 to 25 lbs. (7 to 10 kgms.) or even considerably more when very fat. Greatest length of skull about 90 mm., greatest width about 63 mm.

Of their habits Rhoads (1903) writes:

They are nowhere in their element. In water they can just manage to paddle and skull along, being too fat to sink [and being buoyed up by the air-containing quills]. On land they crawl like a huge tortoise both in pace and gait. When pursued on land they seek preferably the nearest hole that will at least cover the head, wedging themselves tightly therein, leaving the huge bristling back and the ponderous tail for the enemy to fool with. Sometimes they take to a tree, ascending to the summit, but they are slow climbers. The tail is used as a flail to parry attack. The quills are not detached except by contact, anchoring themselves by the finely barbed points, and thus become detached from their loose hold on the porcupine's skin. They work their way into the skin and muscles automatically, and are found in all parts of wild animals which sometimes eat porcupines when driven by hunger. Porcupines are said to be arboreal. They do ascend and descend trees to get bark and twigs for food. In doing so they again display their innate awkwardness, the huge tail lurching from side to side as they shin slowly up, threatening at every step to throw the animal to the ground, but their strength is enormous, and sheer might of hugging and clawing, tooth and nail,

---

1 A name properly applied to a spiny Insectivore of the Old World.

Fig. 98.   Photograph courtesy N. Y. Zool. Soc.   Porcupine, *Erethizon dorsatum*,
once common in Indiana.

gets him his breakfast. Unless they can reach the top of a large or tall tree before being seen, they will hastily descend a smaller tree when discovered and bolt for their rocky dens in the most ludicrous and stupid fashion. They are more at home among rock piles and caverns than anywhere else and once jammed head foremost in such retreats neither man nor beast can dislodge them. In these places they bring forth their young. They spend a part of the winter here in semi-hibernation. [Merriam (1882-84) and Struthers (1928) say they do not hibernate and that fresh tracks may be found during winter in snow.]

At the same time they can remain indefinitely during the same season in the lofty forks of a hemlock or pine or other tree. They are to some extent destructive to timber by girdling the bark. Owing to their love of salt they visit camp and cabins [and privies] and eat away the woodwork and utensils which have become saturated with saline matter, causing great annoyance by the nightly noise and destruction. . . . They eat the flesh, bones and horns of dead animals in the woods with great avidity. . . . It appears that they eat a large variety of vegetable food, but that the staple article is from pine and hemlock [and other] timber, the inner bark being especially relished.

Porcupines mate in late autumn. Young, generally one (rarely two in number) are born about the first of May, the period of gestation being 16 weeks. The young are monstrous for the size of the species. They are actually larger, and relatively more than 30 times larger, than the young of the black bear at birth. Weight at birth 510 to 567 grams (about one to one and one quarter pounds). Total length, at birth 270 to 285 mm. (about 11 inches), the head and body, 195 mm. (about seven and three-fourths inch). They are born with their eyes open and fully clothed with black hair and sometimes short quills. Within a few hours the young are able to walk, reminding one of the guinea pig, which is also a hystricomorph rodent. (From Merriam 1882-84 and Struthers 1928). The mammae are four in number in the pectoral region.

Because of the Porcupine's sluggish habits it easily fell a victim to man; the clearing off of the forests was also an aid in its extermination. It is disliked by man because of its propensities of gnawing any salt-containing wood found about farm buildings, as well as because most dogs have too much curiosity and too often come home with a nose full of quills which have to be extracted one by one. I recall one dog in the Adirondacks that never learned his lesson and almost daily had to have quills extracted.

Its former distribution in Indiana is shown on the map together with dates of observations. The Prince of Wied reports it as very rare in Posey County 100 years ago. Plummer (1844) says several were killed in Wayne County in the past few years. Haymond (1870) speaking of Franklin County says: "Now very rare." The latest published record is that of Brennan (1923) who reports one killed in Porter County 1918. Hahn (1909), in addition to many other records all included on the accompanying map, reports two specimens in the State Museum "said to have been taken in Laporte County not many years ago." Dr. B. W. Rhamy of Fort Wayne tells me that as a small boy, about 1881, he distinctly remembers seeing porcupines that had been taken in a large swamp lying east of Fort Wayne and extending into Ohio. Mr. George Burgner, now 85 years of age says porcupines were plentiful in Wells County in early days.

Map 65. Published records with dates of observation and specimens in collection of the Porcupine, *Erethizon dorsatum*, in Indiana; 1, see text.

The published records for the Porcupine are: Daviess (Butler 1895), Dearborn (Anonymous 1885), Dekalb (Anonymous 1914), Elkhart (Weaver 1916), Franklin (Haymond 1870, Langdon 1881, Quick and Langdon 1882, Butler 1885, Evermann and Butler 1894), Grant (Evermann and Butler 1894, Cory 1912), Hancock (Binford 1882), Huntington (Evermann and Butler 1894), Jay (Montgomery 1864), Knox (Butler 1895, Cory 1912), Lagrange (Evermann and Butler 1894), Laporte (Blatchley 1898, Hahn 1907, 1909, Cory 1912), Lake (Dinwiddie 1884, Hahn 1909), Marion (Anonymous 1906), Marshall (Evermann and Clark 1911, 1920), Miami (Hahn 1909), Noble (Hahn 1909), Ohio (Anonymous 1885), Porter (Brennan 1923), Posey (Wied 1839-41, Hahn 1909), Putnam (Anonymous 1881), Randolph (Cox 1893, Evermann and Butler 1894), St. Joseph (Engels 1933), Steuben (Anonymous 1888), Tippecanoe (Evermann and Butler 1894), Vigo (Thomas 1819), Wayne (Plummer 1844, Young 1872, Hahn 1909, Cory 1912), Kankakee marsh (Hahn 1909), northern Indiana (Kennicott 1857), south of Great Lakes and north of Ohio River (Allen 1877).

HARES, RABBITS AND ALLIES, ORDER LAGOMORPHA

The Lagomorphs are widely distributed throughout most of the world, but were never indigenous in Madagascar, Australia and New Zealand. Through introduction by man of certain members of it, the order as a whole has become practically cosmopolitan.

The order *Lagomorpha* has long been associated, as the suborder *Duplicidentata*, with the order *Rodentia* with which it has much in common. More recent students of mammals, however, regard the two groups as ordinally distinct, and account for the resemblances between them as the result of parallel convergence rather than phylogenetic relationships. (See J. W. Gidley, Science n.s. vol. 36, pp. 285-286 August 30, 1912). The upper incisors are 2 - 2, their enamel covering extending to the posterior surface. The first of these upper incisors are large and very suggestive of the simple pair of incisors in the Rodentia. The second pair of incisors is small, without a cutting edge and nearly circular in cross section. The distance between the tooth rows of the lower jaws is less than between the tooth rows of the upper jaws; so that only one pair of rows is capable of opposition at the same time and the motion of the jaws in mastication is from side to side instead of fore and aft. The premolars are $\frac{3\text{-}3}{2\text{-}2}$ instead of being reduced to $\frac{2\text{-}2}{1\text{-}1}$ or less in the Rodentia. The fibula always is fused for a half or more of its extent with the tibia and articulates with the calcaneum. In the Rodentia the two bones remain separate and the fibula does not articulate with the calcaneum. The testes are extra-abdominal and in a more or less well defined scrotum. No baculum or penis bone is present as occurs in the Rodentia.

The well-defined order Lagomorpha contains two families, the *Leporidae* and the *Ochotonidae*. Only the former is represented in Indiana.

HARES AND RABBITS
Family **Leporidae**

The geographic distribution is co-extensive with that of the order.

The *Leporidae* are large-sized Lagomorphs, with large, long ears, often as long or longer than the head; elongated hind legs and feet, the soles of which are well furred, very short tail. The pelage is soft and furry and under the throat is a patch of hair of coarser texture and different in color from the surrounding fur. In accordance with their mainly crepuscular and nocturnal habits their eyes are large. The postorbital processes of the skull are well developed and either conspicuously outstanding or so closely applied to the rest of the skull as to be almost unnoticeable. Dental formula:

$$i \frac{2\text{-}2}{1\text{-}1}, \; c \frac{0\text{-}0}{0\text{-}0}, \; pm \frac{3\text{-}3}{2\text{-}2}, \; m \frac{3\text{-}3}{3\text{-}3}, = 28.$$

(Lyon, Classification of the Hares and their Allies, Smiths. Misc. Coll. vol. 45, pp. 321-447, June 15, 1905). The family is divided into about ten generic or subgeneric groups, two of which are known to inhabit Indiana and a third may possibly have occurred in the state within recent years.

HARES
Genus **Lepus** Linnaeus

The genus *Lepus* has nearly the same geographic distribution as the order *Lagomorpha*, but is unknown in the Malay region and in South America. It contains about 80 species, one of which probably occurred in Indiana in not very remote historical or geological times.

The genus is chiefly distinguished by the broad triangular postorbital processes, which have free anterior and posterior portions unattached to the sides of the cranium; the radius and ulna are relatively long and slender, and the ulna itself much reduced in size along the middle of its shaft. The young are active at birth, the eyes being open and the body completely furred.

VARYING HARE
Lepus americanus phaeonotus Allen

Lepus americanus ERXLEBEN. Syst. Regni Anim., vol. 1, p. 330, 1777. Type locality Hudson Bay.
Lepus americanus phaeonotus ALLEN. Bull. Amer. Mus. Nat. Hist., vol. 12, p. 11, 1899. Type locality: Hallock, Kitson County, Minnesota.
Lepus americanus Kennicott 1855, 1857 for Cook County, Illinois.
Lepus campestris Evermann and Butler 1894.
Lepus americanus phaeonotus Hahn 1909.

Lepus americanus of which there are eight subspecies ranges from the northeastern United States and eastern Canada, northwestwardly to Alaska. It may have been a common inhabitant of northern Indiana in comparatively recent times.

The Varying Hare is a medium-sized rabbit with large hind feet. Its general color, in summer, above is a grayish or buffy brown rather liberally sprinkled with blackish along the back; underparts whitish; tail blackish above, white below. In winter the

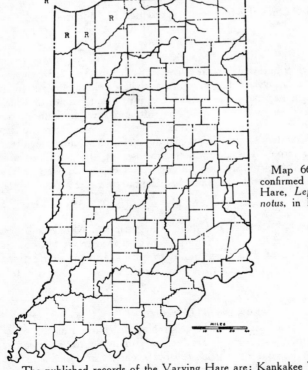

Map 66. Published but unconfirmed records of the Varying Hare, *Lepus americanus phaeonotus*, in Indiana.

The published records of the Varying Hare are: Kankakee Valley, doubtful (Hahn 1909), Cook County, Illinois is the nearest for which there is a positive statement (Kennicott 1855, 1857).

color is everywhere white except for dark tipped ears, although in the southern part of its range, its winter coat is not much different from its summer one.

Total length about 470 mm., tail vertebrae 45 mm., hind foot 135 mm., ear 65 mm. Weight 1400 to 1700 grams, (3 to 3¾ lbs.). Greatest length of skull about 75 mm., greatest width about 37 mm.

There are no actual specimens to establish the existence of *Lepus americanus* in Indiana. Kennicott (1855, 1857) records it as having been formerly found in Cook County, Illinois, just across the Indiana line. Hahn (1909) was led to include the Varying Hare in his hypothetical list on the statement of Mr. I. N. Lamb who was familiar with the Kankakee Valley from 1870 to 1875. He speaks of large rabbits saying: "[they] resemble the western jack rabbit, but is not so large; really they look more like the Wisconsin rabbit." One day in early spring Mr. E. A. Preble accompanying me in walking through a tamarack swamp in the dunes region of Porter County, pointed out signs which he said were very suggestive of this rabbit, and advised me to return when snow was on the ground and settle the matter. Occasion has never presented itself to visit that swamp in winter. Mr. Preble remarked that the Varying Hare, unlike the Cottontail, did not flush when disturbed but slowly and quietly sneaked away without being seen as a rule. In company with Mr. William Engels and Dr. Theodor Just, I visited a tamarack swamp with a decided northern cast to its flora when ground and snow conditions were suitable, but we only found tracks of cottontails. If the Varying Hare should still be represented in Indiana by a colony or two in some unexplored tamarack swamp, it is unlikely that it turns white in winter, otherwise attention would be directed to it. It will be recalled that only a small portion of the weasels in Indiana turn white in winter.

I have followed Hahn in assuming that the Indiana Varying Hare, if such exists or has existed, is the Minnesota race *Lepus americanus phaeonotus* Allen.

Cottontails and Swamp Rabbits
Genus **Sylvilagus** Gray

The genus *Sylvilagus* is peculiarly American, ranging from the northern border of the United States southward into South America; it just reaches into the adjoining Canadian provinces, especially Ontario.

The postorbital process is long and narrow and closely applied to the side of cranium with which it may completely fuse or the posterior limb form the outer limits of a clavate or slit-like foramen. The radius and ulna are moderately elongated, the two bones being subequal in size. The young are born blind and naked.

The genus *Sylvilagus* is separated into two or three well marked subgenera. Two of these are found in Indiana and their characters so marked that they might with propriety be considered as distinct genera.

Cottontails
Subgenus **Sylvilagus** Gray

So far as known the subgenus *Sylvilagus* does not reach farther south than Central America. It contains about 45 species and subspecies, one of which occurs throughout the whole of Indiana.

The Cottontails are chiefly characterized by the long, narrow postorbital process being so applied to the side of the cranium as to leave a clavate or slit-like foramen between it and the cranium. They are woodland or dry land animals, with soft furry hair.

COTTONTAIL

Sylvilagus floridanus mearnsii (Allen)

Lepus sylvaticus BACHMAN. Journ. Acad. Nat. Sci. Philadelphia, vol. 7, p. 403, 1837.

Lepus sylvaticus mearnsii ALLEN. Bull. Amer. Mus. Nat. Hist., vol. 6, p. 171, 1894. Type locality: Fort Snelling, Hennepin County, Minnesota.

Lepus americanus DESMAREST. Mammalogie, vol. 2, p. 351, 1822, Wied 1839-41, Plummer 1844.

Lepus sylvaticus Evermann and Butler, 1894.

Sylvilagus floridanus mearnsi Hahn 1909, Nelson 1909.

The Cottontail Rabbits of the species *Sylvilagus floridanus* extend from the Atlantic seaboard, New York south to Florida, westward to Colorado and parts of Mexico, northward to North Dakota and Ontario. The subspecies *Sylvilagus floridanus mearnsii* ranges from west of the Allegheny Mountains through Ohio, Indiana and most of Illinois to northeastern Kansas.

The Cottontail is such a common and well known animal that any detailed description is superfluous. The upper parts are dark buffy brown with a grayish wash finely sprinkled with black; back of neck rufous; under parts white except for dark buffy throat patch; tail above, brownish, below conspicuously white; ears buffy gray bordered with blackish.

Total length about 425 mm., tail vertebrae 45 mm.; hind foot 100 mm., ear 60 mm., weight (Indiana summer specimens) 1200 to 1600 grams., (2¾ to 3½ lbs.) Greatest length of skull about 67 mm., greatest width about 33 mm.

The Cottontail is Indiana's largest and commonest game animal. It is found everywhere throughout the state except in the centers of large cities. I have seen them in the alleys of South Bend within ten blocks of the business district. I have flushed them in all sorts of situations from open fields to dense woods and swamp land. They are probably more frequently found in thickets, brushy places and open woods. They are mainly crepuscular and nocturnal in their habits, and early in the evening are frequently seen along roadsides, as well as in the road itself. They are one of the commonest of animals run over by motor cars and their flattened bodies are frequent objects on any highway. They seem to be dazzled and held spellbound by the bright lights of the car. By day they live in nest-like forms on the surface of the ground in sheltered spots in grass and weed patches or in thickets, or in natural hollows of the ground, in stone piles, or hollow logs. They do not dig burrows of their own but at times may use abandoned ones made by other animals. Mainly a dry land animal, the Cottontail at times voluntarily takes to water where it is a fair swimmer.

The food of the Cottontail is practically any sort of soft green vegetable matter. They do not care for hard, dry food such as seeds and grains and they do not dig up bulbs and tubers. They seem to be readily taken in box traps baited with apple, whether they are attracted by the fruit or think the trap just another hole and safe retreat, cannot be said. The domestic rabbits of the closely allied genus *Oryctolagus* however, readily eat fleshy and tuberous parts of plants as well as dry hay. In winter when the Cottontail is hard

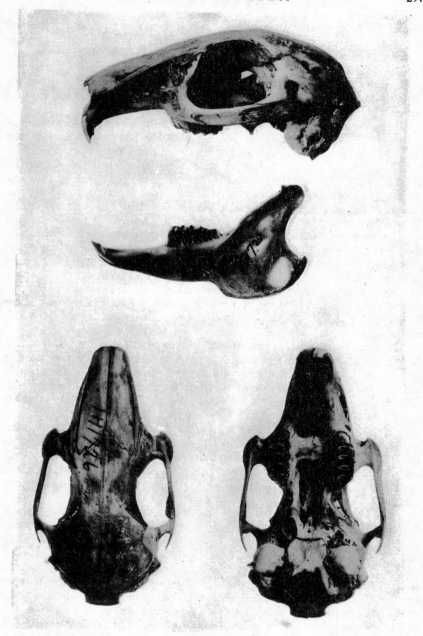

Fig. 99. Photographs courtesy U. S. Nat. Mus. Lateral, dorsal and palatal views of Mearns' Cottontail Rabbit, *Sylvilagus floridanus mearnsii* natural size, Cat. No. 141,726, U. S. Nat. Mus., Hebron, Porter County, 1905, W. L. Hahn.

pressed for food, it eats young twigs within its reach and gnaws the bark of young trees. The damage done by the Cottontail is rather high up on the young tree trunk and the tooth marks large, that done by the Pine Mouse, *Pitymys*, is low down, under the snow line, or even under ground and the tooth marks are much smaller. The Cottontail is about as strictly vegetarian as any animal can be, very much more so than the rodents, but a few isolated instances of their eating flesh are recorded.

Considering the abundance of the Cottontail, little exact information concerning its breeding is recorded. Mating probably takes place early in the year. In southern Indiana young have been found as early as January 8, and in northern Indiana pregnant females not at term have been taken August 21 (Hahn 1909). The breeding period is long so that several litters, as many as three and possibly four, may be produced in a season. The young are brought forth in a surface form or in one protected by some natural object. These nests, in addition to the usual dried grasses composing them, are lined with fur from the mother; whether this is actually plucked out or fur naturally shed is not known. Unlike the members of the genus *Lepus*, the young in the genus *Sylvilagus* are born blind, helpless and naked or essentially so; weight at birth 24 grams (¾ oz.), length 4¼ in. (105 mm.) (Seton, 1929). They develop rapidly and long before attaining adult size are able to take care of themselves. The number brought forth at a birth is said to vary from three to seven; four seems to be the most frequent number reported in a nest. Mammae, four pairs.

Cottontails and other rabbits have no means of defense, their only safety is in flight or concealment. With the continual destruction of their natural enemies, the carnivorous mammals and birds, they hold their own remarkably well in spite of the annual slaughter by hunters and trappers. In some localities they are important sources of food supply. Their skins have a slight value 5 to 10 cents per pound; the fur while thick and soft does not wear well nor last long. Through artifice, it is plucked, sheared and dyed so as to resemble almost any sort of fur. It is largely used for trimming and garments for children; it masquerades as seal skin under the name of "electric seal" and similar mysterious names. It is not to be confused with plucked and dyed muskrat sold as "Hudson seal." The latter is a worthwhile and fairly serviceable fur.

In recent years Cottontails have been found to be transmitters of an important human disease, tularemia or Francis' disease. Obviously sick rabbits that are shot should not be used as food. The danger comes in skinning and cleaning the animals. If proper precautions are taken, no infection need take place in handling diseased rabbits. The flesh when once cooked is harmless. Rabbits are popularly supposed to be unfit for food in the summer because of infestation with various subcutaneous parasites, but these may be carefully cut out and on camping trips I have eaten many rabbits in summer, and have found them just as palatable as in winter. The external parasites of rabbits are for them alone and while frequently getting on to human beings who are carrying freshly killed animals, yet they do not find man a suitable host and quickly disappear.

When the mammalian fauna of Indiana is better known it would not be surprising if the cottontails of southwestern Indiana were found to incline toward *Sylvilagus floridanus alacer* (Bangs) instead of being true *S. f. mearnsii* (Allen) in analogy with the distribution of the next species, *Sylvilagus aquaticus* (Bachman).

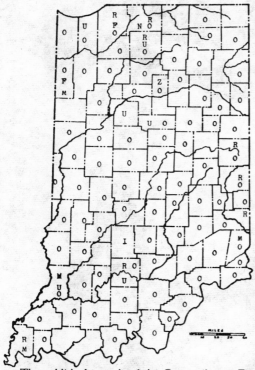

Map 67. Published records, recent observations, and specimens in collections of the Cottontail, *Sylvilagus floridanus mearnsii*, in Indiana.

The published records of the Cottontail are: Franklin (Quick and Langdon 1882), Laporte (Anonymous 1880, Cory 1912), Lawrence (Hahn 1907, 1908, Nelson 1909), Marshall (Nelson 1909, Evermann and Clark 1911, 1920), Monroe (McAtee 1907), Porter (Nelson 1909, Lyon 1922, 1925), Posey (Wied 1839-41), Randolph (Cox 1893), St. Joseph (Anonymous 1880, Engels 1933), Wayne (Plummer 1844), Kankakee marsh (Hahn 1907), Every county in the state (Evermann and Butler 1894, Hahn 1909).

SWAMP RABBITS AND ALLIES
Subgenus **Tapeti** Gray

The Swamp Rabbits are chiefly distinguished by the complete fusion of the postorbital processes with the sides of the cranium. Their hair is shorter and harsher than that of the Cottontails. They are inhabitants of marsh and swampy areas of the South Atlantic and Gulf States, reaching as far north as southern Indiana; they are also found in the heavy tropical forests of

Mexico, Central and South America. Ten North American species and sub-species are known, one of which is found in extreme southwestern Indiana.

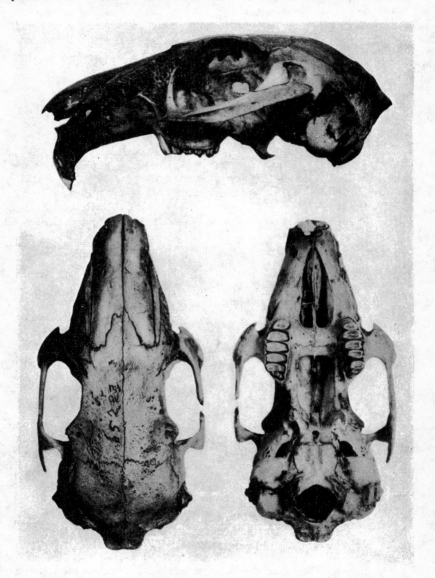

Fig. 100.   Photographs courtesy University of Michigan.   Lateral, dorsal and palatal views of skull of Swamp Rabbit, *Sylvilagus aquaticus*, Cat. No. 65,283, Univ. of Mich., Posey County, 1930, Paul Hickie and Thomas Harrison.   Natural size.

Swamp Rabbit
Sylvilagus aquaticus aquaticus (Bachman)

Lepus aquaticus BACHMAN. Journ. Acad. Nat. Sci. Philadelphia, vol. 7, p. 319, 1837. Type locality: western Alabama.

Lepus aquaticus Evermann and Butler 1894, Hahn 1909.

Sylvilagus aquaticus aquaticus Harrison and Hickie 1931.

The Swamp Rabbits range from the gulf coast of Alabama and Texas, northward to southern Illinois and Indiana; they are separable into two sub-species, *Sylvilagus aquaticus littoralis* Nelson, occupying a narrow coastal strip from Mississippi to Texas and *Sylvilagus aquaticus aquaticus* Bachman occupying the rest of the range of the Swamp Rabbits.

The Swamp Rabbit has the same color pattern as the Cottontail described above; in general it is dark brown above, coarsely and much peppered with black. In comparison its fur is coarse, harsh and short and hind feet much less supplied with hair.

Measurements and weights of four Indiana specimens: Total length 402 to 523 mm., tail 40 to 55 mm., hind foot 98 to 113 mm., ear 66 to 72 mm., weight 1409 grams to 2474 grams (3 to 5½ lbs.) (Harrison and Hickie, 1931). Greatest length of skull about 90 mm., greatest width about 42 mm. (Indiana specimen).

The Swamp Rabbit usually lives in moist woodland river bottoms and cane brakes, though it is occasionally found in drier situations. The only Indiana specimens were obtained in wooded swamps in which there was cane, in southern Posey County. It is described by various authors as an excellent swimmer and good diver. Like the other members of the genus *Sylvilagus*, it is mainly crepuscular and nocturnal, and probably spends the day in suitable forms. The four Indiana specimens were shot after being flushed by dogs.

The mating and breeding habits of the Swamp Rabbit, based upon a few observations are apparently essentially similar to those of the Cottontail. Mammae probably three pairs. Ruth Dowell Svihla (Journal of Mammalogy, vol. 10, pp. 315 to 319), writing of the related subspecies *littoralis*, however, has seen new-born young which were clothed with hair, and has seen well developed fetuses that were distinctly covered with hair. Weight at birth of this subspecies 55.7 grams. The daily green food consumed by one of these rabbits was 42.2% of the body weight, average weight being three pounds, five and a half ounces (1615 grams).

Although the Swamp Rabbit was long suspected of being an inhabitant of Indiana, no specimens were taken until the summer of 1930 when four were secured in Posey County. A youth near Yankeetown, Warrick County, described rather accurately very large, dark colored rabbits which he had shot in a cane brake in the vicinity.

In Indiana, at least, the Swamp Rabbit prefers the wilderness or what little is left of it, to association with man, being unlike the Cottontail in this respect. We made a meal off one of the specimens shot and as was to be expected, found it as good eating as the ordinary rabbit.

Map 68. Published records and specimens in collections of the Swamp Rabbit, *Sylvilagus aquaticus*, in Indiana.

The published records for the Swamp Rabbit are: Knox (Butler 1895, Hahn 1909), Posey (Allen 1877, Harrison and Hickie 1931), Warrick (Harrison and Hickie 1931).

PIGS, OXEN, SHEEP, ANTELOPES, DEER AND ALLIES
ORDER ARTIODACTYLA

The order *Artiodactyla* is so called because its members, for the most part, possess an even number of toes on each foot. The first or inner digit is suppressed so that the functional toes are four, or by reduction or even complete suppression, only two in number. Among other characters are the following. The premolar and molar teeth not alike, the former being single and the latter two-lobed. The last lower molar of both first and second dentition almost invariably three-lobed, and the first tooth of the upper cheek series always without a milk predecessor. Third and fourth digits of both feet almost equally developed, and their terminal phalanges flattened on their inner or contiguous surfaces, so that each is not symmetrical in itself, but when the two are placed together they form a figure symmetrically disposed to a line drawn between them. The calcaneum has an articular facet for the lower end of the fibula. There is no penis bone and the testicles are permanently carried in a scrotum. These last three characters are found in the *Lagomorpha*.

The *Artiodactyla* are traceable from the Eocene period and reach their culmination today in the hollow-horned ruminants. The order has representatives on all the larger land masses, except Australia. It contains such diverse forms as the pigs, hippopotamus, camels, antelopes, sheep, oxen and deer. Two families were represented in Indiana by recntly living forms, and another family is known only from the Pleistocene.

KEY TO THE FAMILIES AND GENERA OF LIVING ARTIODACTYLA

Bony outgrowths, antlers, from the frontal bones in the males periodicaly developed and shed, _____CERVIDAE 302

   Size very large, brow tine of antler directed forward, upper canines usually present, elks, _____*Cervus* 303

   Size medium, brow tine of antler directed upward, upper canines absent, deer, _____*Odocoileus* 307

Bony outgrowths from the frontal bone, permanently covered with true horn, present in both sexes, throughout life, _____BOVIDAE, *Bison*, 315

PECCARIES
† Family **Tayassuidae**

The Peccaries have a close external resemblance to the pigs but differ in several important respects. In the living forms the dental formula is:

$$i \frac{2-2}{3-3}, c \frac{1-1}{1-1}, pm \frac{3-3}{3-3}, m \frac{3-3}{3-3}, = 38.$$

(The pigs, family *Suidae* have an extra incisor above and an extra premolar above and below.) The upper canines are directed downward, with sharp cutting hinder edges. In the living forms there are four toes on the front feet, three on the hind. The stomach is complex. The group is confined to the New World, at the present time to the warmer portions from Texas, southward into South America. In late geologic times it extended much farther northward, probably due to a milder climate than that of today. Three genera have been recorded from Indiana.

LIVING AND EXTINCT PECCARIES
† Genus **Tayassu** Fischer

Dental formula:

$$i \frac{2-2}{3-3}, c \frac{1-1}{1-1}, pm \frac{3-3}{3-3}, m \frac{3-3}{3-3}, = 38.$$

Molars with four low crowns and weak accessory conules. Four digits on front feet, three on hind feet; the third and fourth metatarsals coosified in proximal half.

This genus includes the living peccaries and a few extinct species, one of which is represented in Indiana by very fragmentary remains.

GENTLE PECCARY
† **Tayassu lenis** (Leidy)

Dicotyles lenis LEIDY 1869.
Tayassu tajacu Hay 1902.
Tayassu lenis Hay 1912, 1914, 1923, 1930.

Hay (1912) provisionally referred to this species part of a ramus of the lower jaw with roots of three premolars and the first molar and part of another left ramus with a good first true molar and impressions of the succeeding molars. They were found in the stalagmitic deposit of an old cave near Williams, Lawrence County. In the same cave were some other bones, probably of a peccary and the fragmentary remains of *Platygonus vetus* mentioned below. The fragments are said to be in Indiana University.

Map 69. Published records and specimens in collections of the extinct Gentle Peccary, † *Tayassu lenis*, in Indiana.

The published records of the Gentle Peccary, † *Tayassu lenis*, are: Lawrence (Hay 1912, 1923).

LONG-SNOUTED PECCARIES
† Genus **Mylohyus** Cope

Dental formula:

$$i\frac{2\text{-}2}{2\text{-}2},\ c\frac{1\text{-}1}{1\text{-}1},\ pm\frac{3\text{-}3}{3\text{-}3},\ m\frac{3\text{-}3}{3\text{-}3},\ = 36.$$

Forefeet with four digits, the second and fifth being present with all their elements; the hind feet apparently with but two digits, the second and fifth entirely lacking.

This genus comprises a half dozen species, extinct, and is represented in Indiana by a single species and specimen.

LONG-SNOUTED PECCARY
† Mylohyus nasutus (Leidy)

"Peccary" Leidy 1860.
Dicotyles nasutus LEIDY 1868, 1869, Cope and Wortman 1885, Kindle 1898.
    Type locality: Gibson County, Indiana.

Mylohyus nasutus Cope 1889, Hay 1912, 1914, 1923, 1930, Gidley 1920.
Tayassu nasutus Hay 1902.

The type specimen of *Mylohyus nasutus* was discovered in Gibson County many years ago in the digging of a well at a depth of between 30 and 40 feet below the surface. The exact location of this find in Gibson County

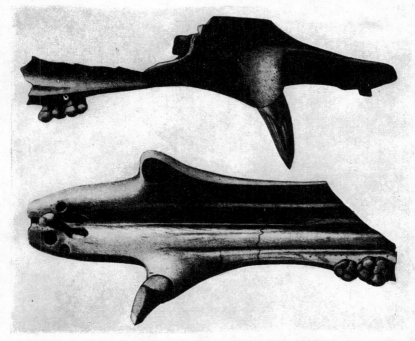

Fig. 101. Long-snouted Peccary, *Mylohyus nasutus* Leidy. Right lateral and palatal views of the type specimen from Gibson County, about 2/3 natural size. After the original illustration in the Journal of the Academy of Natural Sciences of Philadelphia, vol. 7, pl. 28, fig. 1 and 2. The specimen itself appears to be lost.

is not known, nor is its exact geologic age. Hay assigns it to the early part of the Pleistocene. The specimen was sent to Joseph Leidy by David Dale Owen. Its location was unknown to Hay in 1912. I was unable to find it in the Philadelphia collections in 1931. Fortunately it was well illustrated by Leidy whose figures are here reproduced. The original description is accompanied by a detailed set of measurements republished by Hay and the interested reader is referred to these two authors for them. The animal was larger than any of the living peccaries and had a much longer and narrower snout. The type specimen is the only known Indiana remains of this species.

Map 70. Published records of the extinct Snouted Peccary, † *Mylohyus nasutus*, in Indiana.

The published records of the Snouted Peccary, † *Mylohyus nasutus*, are: Gibson (Leidy 1860, 1868, 1869, Cope and Wortman 1885, Hay 1912, 1914, 1923, Gidley 1920).

Two-toed Peccaries
† Genus **Platygonus** LeConte

The peccaries of the genus *Platygonus* have moderately elongated snouts; no premolars have more than one pair of cusps; molars with the four primary cusps very strongly developed; dental formula:

$$i \frac{2-2}{3-3}, c \frac{1-1}{1-1}, pm \frac{3-3}{3-3}, m \frac{3-3}{3-3}, = 38;$$

fore and hind feet with only two digits each. In this last respect it is much more highly specialized than the two preceding genera. It is known from North America by eight species, two of which are represented by very fragmentary remains in Indiana.

ANCIENT PECCARY
† **Platygonus vetus** Leidy

Platygonus vetus LEIDY Proc. Acad. Nat. Sci. Philadelphia, 1882, p. 301, 1882. Hay 1902, 1912, 1923, 1930. Type locality: Mifflin County, Pennsylvania.

This species is represented by "the hinder upper molar of the right side and a part of the next tooth in front of it" (Hay 1912). The specimens are said to be in the collection of Indiana University. These fragments were found in Rock Cliff quarry, northwest of Williams, Lawrence County. With them were the scanty remains of *Tayassu lenis* already referred to above.

Map 71. Published records and specimens in collections of the extinct Ancient Peccary, † *Platygonus vetus*, in Indiana.

Published records of the Ancient Peccary, † *Platygonus vetus*, are: Lawrence (Hay 1912, 1923).

NARROW-SNOUTED PECCARY
† **Platygonus compressus** LeConte

Platigonus compressus LECONTE Amer. Journ. Sci., ser. 2, vol. 5, p. 103, 1848. Type locality: Pleistocene of lead region of Illinois.

Platygonus compressus Cope and Wortman 1885, Hay 1902, 1912, 1914, 1923, 1930.

Platygonus compressus is a widely ranging species of extinct peccary, remains of it having been found in New York, at many places in the

Mississippi Valley and probably in Mexico. It is known by excellent material from outside of Indiana. One of Leidy's illustrations of it is reproduced by Hay (1912), who also gives complete measurements of the skull and teeth. The species is represented in Indiana by a single find from Laketon, Wabash County. Cope and Wortman state that in the collection of the Geological Survey of Indiana there was the symphysial portion of the lower jaw and a large part of the left ramus supporting all the premolar teeth, except the last. Hay (1912) failed to find the specimen. He reported what appeared to be photographs of this specimen and of part of an upper jaw in the collection of Earlham University. The photographs were labeled as having been identified by Cope and the specimens as having been found in Wabash County.

Map 72. Published records of the Narrow-snouted Peccary, † *Platygonus compressus*, in Indiana.

The published records of the Narrow-snouted Peccary, † *Platygonus compressus*, are: Wabash (Cope and Wortman 1885, Hay 1912, 1923).

DEER AND ALLIES
Family **Cervidae**

The most striking character of the family *Cervidae* is the presence in the males (only rarely in the females) of antlers. These are true bony outgrowths from the frontal bone, covered during their growth with skin richly supplied with blood vessels and covered with short hair or velvet. When the growth of the antler is complete, the supply of blood to it ceases, the skin dies and peels off, leaving the bone bare and insensible, and after a time, by a process of absorption near the base it becomes detatched from the skull and is shed. A more or less elongated portion or pedicle always remains on the skull, from the summit of which a new antler is developed. The process of antler formation is repeated with great regularity at the same period of time each year. The antlers reach their height at the rutting season. The antlers in most deer are much branched, but the antlers of young are much simpler than in fully adult animals. In addition to this may be mentioned the following other characters which are also found in the next family, the *Bovidae*. There are no upper incisors, or canine-like premolars; upper canines generally absent. Lower incisors three on each side with an incisor-like canine in contact with them. The other teeth are six molar-like ones on each side of each jaw, making the dental formula:

$$i\ \frac{0-0}{3-3},\ c\ \frac{0\text{-}0\ or\ 1\text{-}1}{1-1},\ pm\ \frac{3-3}{3-3},\ m\ \frac{3-3}{3-3}, = 32\ or\ 34.$$

The third and fourth metacarpals and metatarsals are confluent; the outer toes are small and rudimentary. The stomach has four complete compartments and the animals ruminate or chew their cud.

The deer are distributed over all the larger land masses except Australia and Africa south of the Desert of Sahara, are also found in the Malay and Philippine Archipelagos. About 16 genera are recognized in the family.

Two genera until within recent historic times were found throughout Indiana, and the same two genera are found in Pleistocene deposits.

TYPICAL DEER
Genus **Cervus** Linnaeus

The genus *Cervus* is found in north temperate regions of both hemispheres; but it has been exterminated over much of its former range. One species once was found throughout the whole of Indiana.

The genus is distinguished by having what may be termed normal antlers, that is generally round in cross-section, with many and pointed branches, one tine of which projects characteristically forward more or less over the forehead and is termed the brow tine. Upper canines present in both sexes so that the dental formula is:

$$i\ \frac{0-0}{3-3},\ c\ \frac{1-1}{1-1},\ pm\ \frac{3-3}{3-3},\ m\ \frac{3-3}{3-3}, = 34.$$

The vomer is low posteriorly and does not divide the posterior nares into two distinct portions. The proximal extremities of the lateral (second and fifth) metacarpals persist.

AMERICAN ELK OR WAPITI
Cervus canadensis (Erxleben)

[*Cervus elaphus*] *canadensis* ERXLEBEN. Syst. Regni Anim., vol. 1, p. 305, 1777. Type locality: Eastern Canada.

Cervus canadensis Wied 1839-41, Plummer 1844, Evermann and Butler 1894, Hahn 1909.

The Elk formerly had a range covering most of the United States (the extreme southern states excepted) and the adjoining Canadian provinces. It is now confined in the wild state to a narrow strip of the Rocky Mountain region, to Manitoba and Saskatchewan and the Pacific coast. The subspecies *Cervus canadensis canadensis* formerly was found throughout Indiana.

The Elk is such a well known animal from living specimens seen in public and private parks and zoological gardens that no description of it is necessary. Males have a total length of about 9 feet (2745 mm.); tail, about 6 inches (150 mm); hind foot, about 25 inches (625 mm); height at shoulder, about 5 feet (1525 mm.); weight, about 700 pounds (315 kgms.). Each antler of the adult carries from 5 to 7 points. Females are decidedly smaller; total length, about 7½ feet (2287 mm.); tail, about 5 inches (125 mm.); height at shoulder, about 56 inches (1425 mm.); weight, about 500 pounds (225 kgms.).

The food of the Elk consists of grasses, twigs, leaves and herbage.

Mating occurs in autumn at which time the antlers are fully developed and used as weapons of offense and defense in the struggle of the males for mates. The animals are very polygamous. Cows do not breed until three or four years old, and the males are probably older before they can succeed in mastering rivals for mates. The period of gestation is about eight and one-half months, and the young are born in early summer. As a rule only one calf is produced at birth. They are well developed when born, and within a few hours are able to stand up and walk. Like most of the family *Cervidae* the young are spotted with white, but on the assumption of the first winter coat the spots are lost. The mammae are four in the inguinal region.

A glance at the map shows how few published records there are for Indiana and at what early dates the Elk became exterminated in the state. It was doomed from the start not only because of its large size, but because of its gregarious habits. There are no places in Indiana today where the Elk could exist in an untrammeled wild condition. It is regrettable that in the days of its abundance no Indiana specimens were saved for posterity. The same remark applies to all the other eastern states where Elk once dwelt. The only certain specimen of recent Indiana Elk that I know of is a fine set of antlers owned by Mr. H. F. Goppert of Walkerton. Between 30 and 35 years ago Mr. Goppert and several companions were seining for fish in the Kankakee River, in St. Joseph County, close to the Laporte County line. During one of the hauls a handsome pair of Elk Antlers was pulled out, illustrated as Fig. 102, p. 306. The following description of these was published by me in 1931:

The greater part of the cranial bones of the skull are present, the foramen magnum and occipital condyles being essentially intact. None of the facial portion of the skull is present. The antlers, themselves, are essentialy perfect. They do not appear to be of any great antiquity and must certainly be regarded as Recent rather than Pleistocene in age. The fact that they were not buried in the river bed would bespeak their Recent origin although the Kankakee flows through a region from which many Pleistocene mammal remains have been taken. There is not a break in the antlers and scarcely a scratch or worn spot on them.

The antlers and cranium together, weight 23½ pounds. They are strikingly asymmetrical, the right appearing heavier and shorter and with eight points instead of the usual six seen on the left antler. In addition to the normal royal tine, the right antler bears a large accessory royal tine, about 12 inches in length and diverted backward. The points of these two royal tines can be seen in the picture, though rather indistinctly. The following measurements were made with Mrs. Goppert's tape measure: Distance between terminal points 37 inches (940 mm.); greatest width of antlers, 45½ inches (1155 mm.). Circumference of right antler above burr, 10½ inches (266 mm.). Circumference of left antler above burr, 11¼ inches (285 mm.). Length of right antler along convexity, 52 inches (1320 mm.). Length of left antler along convexity, 54½ inches (1383 mm.). Length of right brow tine, from burr, 14 inches (355 mm.). Length of left brow tine, from burr, 15½ inches (394 mm.). Distance between tips of brow tines, 15 inches (381 mm.). (Lyon 1931).

The "Stags" of the early voyageurs were probably Elks. Father Marest

Map 73. Published records and approximate dates when last seen of the Elk, *Cervus canadensis*, in Indiana; 1, fine pair of antlers in possession of Mr. H. F. Goppert of Walkerton; 2, antler fragments owned by Amos W. Butler, † Pleistocene specimens.

The published records for the Elk are: Allen (Butler 1934), Daviess (Hahn 1909), Dearborn (Anonymous 1885, Hahn 1909), Franklin (Butler 1885, Evermann and Butler 1894, Hahn 1909), Marshall (Evermann and Clark 1911), Morgan (Major 1915), Ohio (Anonymous 1885, Hahn 1909), Posey (Wied 1839-41), Ripley (Butler 1885, Evermann and Butler 1894, Hahn 1909, Butler 1934), St. Joseph (Anonymous 1880, Howard 1907, Lyon 1931, Engels 1933), Vigo (Thomas 1819), Wayne (Plummer 1844), Kankakee valley (Reed 1920).

Fig. 102. Antlers of Indiana Cervidae. Photographs by M. W. Lyon, Jr.
Upper figure. Virginia Deer, *Odocoileus virginianus*, North Liberty, St. Joseph County, killed about 60 years ago, owned by Robert Hawblitzel.
Lower figure. American Elk, Walkerton, St. Joseph County, owned by H. F. Goppert.

(1846) in his journey of 1712 mentions stags along the Kankakee River.

The pieces of Elk antlers from Jasper and Newton Counties, mentioned by Hahn (1909) as being in the State Museum are probably of Pleistocene age.

PLEISTOCENE AMERICAN ELK OR WAPITI
† Cervus canadensis (Erxleben)

Cervus canadensis Elrod and Benedict 1892, Hay 1902, 1912, 1923, 1930.

Elk of Pleistocene Age have been recorded from eight counties in Indiana, as indicated on the map and listed below. The remains are mostly antler fragments, but a skull from Randolph County is now in Earlham University. No perfect specimens have been found. The remains so far have all come from the more recent Pleistocene deposits indicating that the Elk was a late comer into the state.

The published records of the Elk in Pleistocene deposits are: Bartholomew (Edwards 1902), Jay (M'Caslin 1883, Hay 1912, 1923), Jasper (Hahn 1909, Hay 1912, 1923), Lake (Blatchley 1898, Hay 1912, 1923), Laporte (Lyon 1931), Newton (Hahn 1909, Hay 1912, 1923), Randolph (Phinney 1883, Hay 1912, 1923), Wabash (Elrod and Benedict 1892, Hay 1912, 1923), Wayne (Hay 1912, 1923).

NORTH AMERICAN DEER
Genus Odocoileus Rafinesque

The genus *Odocoileus* is or was generally distributed throughout most of North America, but is not found in the extreme north; it ranges through Mexico, Central America and into South America.

The genus has smaller antlers than those of the genus *Cervus;* the brow tine is short, directed upwards and arises from the inner side of the main antler beam, instead of from the front. Upper canines are absent in both sexes so that the dental formula is:

$$i\ \frac{0-0}{3-3},\ c\ \frac{0-0}{1-1},\ pm\ \frac{3-3}{3-3},\ m\ \frac{3-3}{3-3},\ =32.$$

The vomer is high posteriorly and divides the posterior nares into two distinct portions. The distal extremities of the lateral (second and fifth) metacarpals persist. About 30 species and subspecies are recognized in North America, one species of which was formerly found throughout the whole of Indiana.

VIRGINIA OR WHITE-TAILED DEER
Odocoileus virginianus (Boddaert)

[*Cervus*] *virginianus* BODDAERT. Elenchus Anim., vol. 1, p. 136, 1784. Type
    locality: Virginia.
Cervus virginianus Wied 1839-41, Plummer 1844.
Cariacus virginianus Evermann and Butler 1894.
Odocoileus virginianus Hahn 1909.

The Virginia or White-tailed Deer formerly occupied most of the United States and adjoining Canadian provinces from the entire Atlantic seaboard westward to the Great Plains; about half a dozen geographic races are known, one or perhaps two of which were found in Indiana until about 50 or 60 years ago.

The Virginia Deer is such a well known animal in private and public parks and zoological gardens that any description of it seems unnecessary. In comparison with the Elk it is a small deer. Total length of adult males, about 6 feet (1825 mm.); tail, 6-10 in. (150-250 mm.); hind foot, about 20 in. (500 mm.); weight, about 150-200 lbs. (68-90 kgms.); females smaller and lighter. In summer the general color is reddish tan or yellowish brown, in winter a grizzled gray, with the hairs much longer. The under parts, inner side of legs white or whitish, particularly and conspicuously the under side of the tail. The young are reddish brown with white spots until the first winter coat is assumed. The beam of the antlers is first directed backward and then

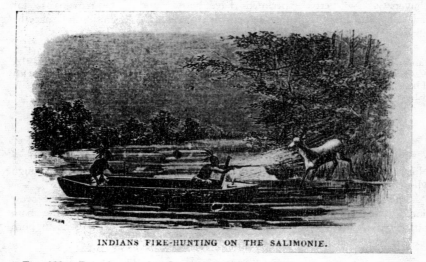

INDIANS FIRE-HUNTING ON THE SALIMONIE.

Fig. 103. Deer hunting by the aborigines on the Salimonia River, Jay County, about a century ago. After M. W. Montgomery, History of Jay County, Indiana, 1864, p. 108.

the axis curves forward with a variable number of tines, usually about five.

The food of the Deer is rough vegetation, twigs and leaves, and beechnuts and acorns; they are not particularly fond of grass. Curious and probably very exceptional instances of deer eating fish are reported by Thornton W. Burgess (Journal of Mammalogy, vol. 5. pp. 64-65, 1924). They eat all parts of the plant of the common yellow water lily.

The mating occurs in autumn when the antlers are fully matured. As in the case of the Elk they are used as offensive and defensive weapons in the buck's fights for does. They are polygamous but probably not to the same extent as the Elk. Like the Elk their antlers at times become interlocked in their combats, and the two combatants either starve to death or become ready prey to various carnivores. The young are born the following spring or early summer, and are usually two in number.

In pioneer days Deer were among the commonest of Indiana mammals. Brown (1817) counted three Deer in traveling seven miles in Dearborn County, and says the woods on the Wabash near Ft. Harrison (Vigo County) abound with Deer, Bears and Wolves. They were present in Posey County at the time of the Prince of Wied's visit. In the same county Bolton (1929) reports them as abundant in the cane brakes in 1850, but none have been seen since 1870. As many as 1130 were purchased by a fur dealer in Hamilton County in 1859 (Anonoymous 1906). Werich (1920) speaks of Deer as being plentiful in the Kankakee region and relates of 65 being killed in a single day in 1878. An anonymous author in Ball's Lake County, 1884, writes as follows:

When putting on the roof of the Rockwell house in Crown Point, V. Holton and others saw coming out from Brown's Point and passing out across the prairie to School Grove a drove of deer, one bounding after the other, according to their best count, in number one hundred and eleven.

Goodspeed (1883) in writing of Warren, Benton, Jasper and Newton Counties, refers to herds of Deer and a day's hunt yielding 160. Vogel (1914) mentions [date not given] 13 Deer killed in one morning in Brown County and refers to a Deer knocked in the head with an ax as it attempted to run past a man making fences. Mrs. George Burgner now 85 years of age says her husband and brother killed six Deer in one day in Wells County. In 1844 they were rare around Richmond (Plummer 1844). They were apparently gone from Franklin County by 1870 (Haymond 1870). Hahn (1909) quoting D. D. Banta in the History of Johnson County tells of a settler killing 370 Deer in the autumn of 1822.

The last stand of the Deer in the state was in the northwest in the Kankakee region and in Knox County. Butler (1895) records one killed in Jasper County, 1890; and one seen in Newton County in 1891. Mr. Chansler says that the last wild Deer were seen near Red Cloud in Knox County in 1893. The history of St. Joseph County (Anonymous 1880) speaks of them as being rare at time of writing. The anonymous historian of Putnam County (1881) speaks of Deer as numerous in the county in pioneer days, but the last were killed about 1876. The anonymous historian of Dekalb County 1914 says the last Deer was shot 20 years ago. Dinwiddie (1884) says:

Deer, once numerous, are still occasionally seen and more rarely shot on the islands of the Kankakee marsh.

Dryer (1889) writes of Allen County: "Deer, bear and wolf are nearly extinct." Gilbert (1910) says of Vanderburg County, Deer were killed as late as 1878. Mr. Henry Duncker of South Bend, tells me that the last Deer killed in St. Joseph County was at "Long Island" in the old Kankakee marsh, in 1881. It was a buck and its mounted head adorned a local saloon for many years in preprohibition days. He does not know what became of it. Mr. Charles Coonley, another old resident of South Bend, once drove me to a point in the western part of St. Joseph County, in the now drained Kankakee marsh, where he had seen Deer in his boyhood. Deer were fairly numerous in the Indiana dunes of Lake Michigan about 1875, but were shortly after all killed off (Lyon 1923).

The only extant specimens of Indiana deer that I know of at the present

time are a few antler fragments and a lower jaw that I picked up in the dunes
of Porter County in 1922, now in the U. S. National Museum; a mounted

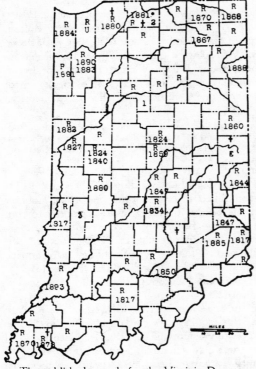

Map 74. Published records
with approximate dates of observation, and specimens of the
Virginia Deer, *Odocoileus virginianus,* in Indiana; U, fragments of antlers and a lower jaw
in United States National Museum; 1, stuffed skin of doe in
pool room, Royal Center, killed
50-60 years ago; 2, mounted
head in Robert Hawblitzel's bar-
bershop, North Liberty, killed
50-60 years ago; 3, several antlers owned by several persons in
Clay County; 1881*, see text;
† Pleistocene specimens.

The published records for the Virginia Deer are: Allen (Dryer 1889, Hahn 1909),
Brown (Vogel 1914), Cass (Lyon 1932), Dearborn (Anonymous 1885, Brown 1817),
Dekalb (Anonymous 1914), Elkhart (Weaver 1916), Fountain (Cox 1860), Franklin
(Haymond 1870, Quick 1882, Butler 1885, Evermann and Butler 1894), Hamilton
(Cox 1860, Shirts 1901, Anonymous 1906), Hancock (Binford 1882), Jackson
(Lazenby 1914), Jasper (Battle 1883, Butler 1895, Hahn 1909, Evermann and
Clark 1911), Jay (Montgomery 1864), Johnson (Banta 1888, Hahn 1909), Knox
(Butler 1895, Hahn 1909, Cory 1912), Lagrange (Rerick 1882, Evermann and But-
ler 1894), Lake (Anonymous 1884, Dinwiddie 1884, Blatchley 1898, Brennan 1923),
Laporte (Anonymous 1880, Brennan 1923), Lawrence (Hahn 1907), Marion (Anony-
mous 1906), Marshall (Evermann and Clark 1911), [Miami] (Eel River bottoms,
Hahn 1909), Montgomery (Cox 1860, Parsons 1920), Morgan (Major 1915), Newton
(Butler 1895, Hahn 1909, Ade 1911, Evermann and Clark 1911, Cory 1912), Noble
(Hahn 1909), Ohio (Anonymous 1885), Orange (Brown 1817), Porter (Blatchley
1898, Brennan 1923, Lyon 1923), Posey (Wied 1839-41, 1861-62, Bolton 1929),
Putnam (Anonymous 1881), Ripley (Butler 1885, Evermann and Butler 1894, Hahn
1909), St. Joseph (Anonymous 1875, 1880, Howard 1907, Engels 1933), Steuben
(Anonymous 1888, Hahn 1909), Tippecanoe (at Ouiatanon, near Lafayette, Hutchins
1778), Tipton (Cox 1860), Vanderburg (Gilbert 1910), Vigo (Brown 1817), Wabash
(Hahn 1909), Warren (Goodspeed 1883), Warrick (Hahn 1909), Wayne (Plummer
1844, Young 1872), Kankakee valley (Hahn 1907, 1909, Reed 1920, Werich 1920),
northern counties, prairie region (Owen 1862), lower Wabash (Croghan 1834, Cox
1860).

head in Mr. Robert Hawblitzel's barber shop in North Liberty, St. Joseph County, killed locally about 50 to 60 years ago; and a badly mounted and much bleached doe, in a pool room at Royal Center, Cass County. The last mentioned was killed locally some 50 or 60 years ago. It possesses a pair of spike antlers and is said to have contained a single mature fetus, which is also mounted and in the same case with the doe, along with several other animals. The North Liberty head is an eight-point buck. Length of left antler along convexity, 16¾ in. (420 mm.); right antler, 17 in. (425 mm.); length of left brow tine, 3 in. (75 mm.); right brow tine 2½ in. (63 mm.); distance between tips of antlers 8½ in. (213 mm.); distance between brow tines 4 in. (100 mm.); greatest spread of antlers, 14 in. (350 mm.); circumference of each antler at base, above burr, 3¾ in. (94 mm.).

In a recent letter, T. N. James of Brazil, says he knows of a few Deer antlers owned by various persons in Clay County.

There were three chief methods of hunting Deer in the early days: stalking, which was considered the most sportsmanlike; baiting with salt, for Deer, like all ruminants, are fond of salt, and came with great regularity to where it was placed; and firehunting, which was picturesque, and is here illustrated from an old cut in the History of Jay County. This last was nothing more than modern jacking; a fire was placed in the canoe's bow in place of the modern lantern.

It is unfortunate that deer were exterminated at so early a date before modern conservation came into vogue. I have seen considerable territory in Indiana that seems suitable for Deer. Had the old Kankakee area not been drained but preserved in a wild state, it would have continued to be a veritable haven for Deer. There is no reason why with properly enforced game laws and a few natural refuges, Indiana might not have its Deer-hunting season as well as such thickly populated states as Massachusetts and New Jersey. But the Deer are gone now and no specimens are left to tell to which race of Virginia Deer the Indiana Deer belonged. It was probably the typical race *Odocoileus virginianus virginianus*. The Deer of the Lower Wabash Valley may perhaps have been *Odocoileus virginianus louisianae* (G. M. Allen).

PLEISTOCENE VIRGINIA DEER
† Odocoileus virginianus (Boddaert)

Cervus virginianus Leidy 1854, Elrod and Benedict 1892, Kindle 1898.
Dama virginiana Hay 1902.
Odocoileus virginianus Hay 1912, 1923, 1930; Lyon 1931.

The Virginia Deer is found in scattered Pleistocene deposits in Indiana. The best example is one from Laporte County owned by Mr. Henry Duncker, of South Bend, and described and figured by me in 1931. The same specimen is illustrated here again.

The published records of the Virginia Deer, in Pleistocene deposits are: Bartholomew (Edwards 1902), Laporte (Lyon 1931), Randolph (Hay 1923), Vanderburg (Leidy 1854-55, 1860, Hay 1912, 1923), Wabash (Elrod and Benedict 1892, Hay 1912, 1923).

Fig. 104. Photograph of skull of Pleistocene Virginia Deer, *Odocoileus virginianus*, Laporte County, owned by Henry Duncker, South Bend. View with antlers about 1/6 natural size, palatal view about about 1/4 natural size. From Amer. Midland Nat., vol. 12, p. 407, 1931.

Cope's Deer
† Odocoileus dolichopsis (Cope)

† *Cariacus dolichopsis* Cope 1878 March, 1878, Cope and Wortman 1885, Kindle 1898. Type locality: Harrison or Vanderburg County, Indiana.

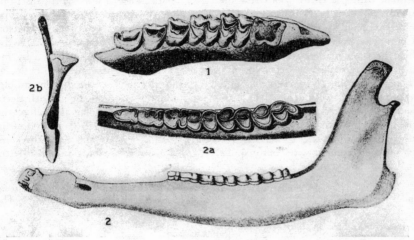

Fig. 105. *Odocoileus.* After O. P. Hay, Pleistocene Period and its Vertebrata, 36th Ann. Rep. Dept. Geol. Nat. Res. Indiana for 1911, p. 614, 1912; taken from E. D. Cope and Jacob L. Wortman, Post-pliocene Vertebrates of Indiana, Indiana Dept. Geol. Nat. Hist. 14th Ann. Rep., 1884, pl. 2, 1885.

1.—Crown view of left maxillary teeth of *Odocoileus "virginianus."*
2.—Lateral view of mandible of Cope's Deer, *Odocoileus dolichopsis.*
2a.—Crown view of teeth in same jaw.
2b.—View of same jaw seen from behind. The specimen is apparently lost.

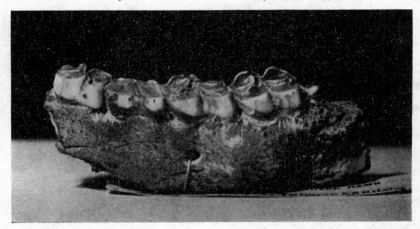

Fig. 106. Fragment of lower jaw of Cope's Deer, *Odocoileus dolichopsis*, from a Wood Rat's cave, Harrison County, 1930, M. W. Lyon, Jr. In collection University of Notre Dame, photograph by Th. Just. About natural size.

† *Dama dolichopsis* Hay 1902.
† *Odocoileus dolichopsis* Hay 1912, 1914, 1923, 1930; Engels 1932.

The type material of Cope's Deer was the left mandible of an old individual, with the entire tooth row intact. The specimen is apparently lost, but fortunately was well illustrated by Cope and Wortman (1885). The type locality is not at all certain. It was first thought to have come from Harrison County, later it was said to have come from Vanderburg County, which is the final decision made by Hay (1923). A second specimen was collected by me in 1930, among some debris of a Cave Rat's nest in the limestone cliffs, at Tobacco Landing, Harrison County. It is a portion of the left mandible, approximately two and one-half inches long and three-fourths of an inch deep, with the lower edge broken away, but bearing the last premolar and all of the molar teeth. This specimen was described by Engels (1932) and is now in the collection of the University of Notre Dame. Engels subsequently compared the fragment with many skulls of *Odocoileus virginianus* and in a letter makes these further remarks:

Examination of the skulls of *Odocoileus virginianus* in the U. S. National Museum indicates that the length of the mandibular molar series is not especially constant. The

Map 75.   Published records and specimens in collections of Cope's Deer, † *Odocoileus dolichopsis*, in Indiana.

The published records of Cope's Deer are: Vanderburg (Cope 1878 March, 1878, Cope and Wortman 1885, Hay 1912, 1923), Harrison (Engels 1932).

skulls of four old adults were found to have molar series of approximately the same length as the Tobacco Landing specimen. In each of these, however, the molars were proportionately narrow in comparison with examples of *virginianus* with a longer tooth row. No specimen of *virginianus* in the National Museum has molars as wide as in the specimen under discussion, whose molars are as wide as the much longer molars of *macrourus*. . . . It is in the great width of the molars then that the distinction of this specimen lies.

Oxen, Sheep, Goats and Antelopes
Family **Bovidae**

The most striking character of the family *Bovidae* is the presence of true horns, present in both sexes, but larger in males. Each horn consists of a permanent, conical, usually curved bony process of the frontal bone into which air cells continued from the frontal sinuses often extend, called horn-cores; ensheathed in a covering of true horn, an epidermic development of fibrous structure, which grows continuously though slowly, from the base, and wears away at the apex. There are no upper incisors, or canine-like pre-molars, upper canines absent. Lower incisors, three on each side with an incisor-like canine in contact with them. The other teeth are six molar-like ones on each side of each jaw, making the dental formula:

$$i \frac{0-0}{3-3}, c \frac{0-0}{1-1}, pm \frac{3-3}{3-3}, m \frac{3-3}{3-3}, = 32.$$

As in the Cervidae, the third and fourth metacarpals and metatarsals are confluent, the outer toes small and rudimentary; the stomach has four complete compartments and the animals ruminate or chew their cud. There are many other finer technical differences between the Cervidae and the Bovidae and the interested student is referred to the works of Fowler and Lydekker (1891) and others.

The family reaches its greatest development in Africa, and is found on all the larger land masses except Australia and South America. It contains about 50 living genera, one of which occurred in Indiana in recent historic times as well as in Pleistocene times, and another extant genus found only in Pleistocene deposits; while a third genus has been found only in such deposits.

Bisons
Genus **Bison** Hamilton Smith

The Bisons are *Bovidae* with rounded, slightly curved, pointed horns, directed upward and outward. The horns are about equally developed in the two sexes. The spinous processes of the dorsal vertebrae are unusually long so that the animals stand very high at the shoulders in comparison with the hind quarters. The genus is very closely related to *Bos*, to which the domestic cattle belong.

In historic times the genus *Bison* had an extensive range over a large part of North America from the Rocky Mountains almost to the Atlantic seaboard; it was also found rather extensively in Europe. In the Pleistocene period it had a much more extensive range in both continents, and several Pleistocene species existed in North America. Two recent species are recognized, the European and the American. Three geographic races of the latter are known; one, or perhaps two, of these, used to be found abundantly in Indiana.

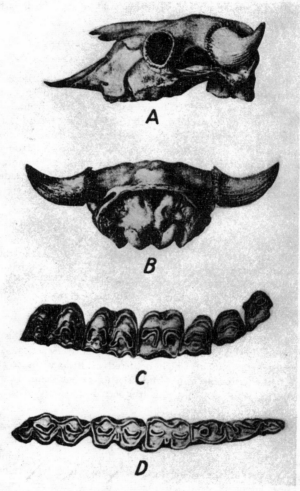

Fig. 107. Plains Bison or Buffalo, *Bison bison bison*. After J. A. Allen 1876 in O. P. Hay, 1912.

A.—Lateral view of skull, pl. 6, fig. 1.

B.—View of skull from rear, pl. 5, fig. 1.

C.—Left upper molars and premolars, pl. 10, fig. 11.

D.—Right lower molars and premolars, pl. 10, fig. 9.

The plate and figure numbers refer to Allen's publications.

PLAINS BISON OR BUFFALO
Bison bison bison (Linnaeus)

[*Bos*] *bison* LINNAEUS. Syst. Nat., ed. 10, vol. 1, p. 72, 1758. Type locality: Mexico.

Bos bison Wied 1839-41.

Bos americanus Plummer.

Bison bison Evermann and Butler 1894, Hahn 1909.

The Plains Bison had a former range from northern Mexico north into Alberta and Saskatchewan where it met the range of the Wood Bison, *Bison bison athabascae* Rhoads, and from the plains of the Columbia River eastward across the Great Plains to the forested region of the United States.

The Bison or Buffalo is so frequently seen in public parks and zoological gardens as to need no description. A representation of it is on the great seal of the State of Indiana. It was the largest Indiana mammal known in historic times. Total length of males, about 11 ft. (3355 mm.); tail vertebrae, 2 ft. (600 mm.); hind foot, 2 ft. (600 mm.); height at shoulder about 70 inches (1750 mm.); weight, about 1800 lbs. (818 kgms.). Females are much smaller, the corresponding figures being: 7 ft. (2135 mm.); 18 in. (460 mm.); 20 in. (500 mm.); 60 in. (1500 mm.); 1000 lbs. (455 kgms.)

The Buffalo was a gregarious, polygamous animal. Only a century ago it existed on the Great Plains in millions. Beginning with the middle of the last century a ruthless slaughter for meat and hides began, continuing until a few years ago when it was almost exterminated. Since then, due to the activities of a small group of interested persons, the last remnant was preserved and in parks and reservations it has been increasing in numbers in recent years.

The cows brought forth but one young (rarely twins) annually.

In summer the Buffalo lost much of its shaggy coat of woolly hair, particularly on the posterior half of the body, which became almost naked subjecting the animals to the annoyance of insect pests. It is thought that the familiar mud wallowing of the Buffalo was an attempt to cover this part of its body with as much mud as possible to proctect it against insects. Remains of some of these wallows were said to be still present in southern Indiana. (Wilson 1910).

The Buffalo was somewhat migratory in its habits or at least travelled over well beaten paths from one feeding ground to another. The animals made several paths through the state; one of the best known is described in detail by George R. Wilson (1910). It was variously termed "Buffalo Trace," "Mud Holes" (referring to the frequent wallows), "Governor's Trace," "Kentucky Road," "Louisville Trace," and "Vincennes Trace." The animals entered the state from the prairies of Illinois. Crossing the Wabash River near Vincennes and travelling southeastwardly to the Falls of the Ohio River (near Louisville, Kentucky) there they crossed that river to seek the salt of Big Bone Lick, Kentucky, and the blue grass regions of that state. The "Trace" was surveyed in 1805. Wilson says no Buffaloes were seen in the state after 1808.

Fig. 108. Photograph courtesy South Bend Park Board and South Bend Tribune, Bison or Buffalo, *Bison bison bison*, in Pottawattomie Park, South Bend.

Buffaloes were probably formerly found in every county of Indiana but seem to have been most numerous in the southwest where great herds crossed the state as cited above. Croghan (1831, 1834, 1846, 1875,) has the following entry in his journal under date of June 13, 1765: "Buffaloes, deer and bears are here [lower Wabash], in great plenty." Hutchins (1778) leaves the impression that there were plenty of Buffaloes along the Ohio. Craig (1893) quotes from an old document regarding Ouiatanon [near Lafayette]:

From the summit of this elevation nothing is visible to the eye but prairies full of buffaloes.

Charlevoix (1763) writing for 1721 says:

All the country that is watered by the Ouabache [Wabash] and by the Ohio that runs into it, is very fruitful . . . where the wild Buffaloes feed by Thousands.

The same author refers to herds of two or three hundred in the meadows of the Theakiki [Kankakee]. This may possibly have been in Illinois instead of adjacent Indiana. Marest (1846) writing of his travels in 1712 says:

We ascended the River Saint Joseph to where it is necessary to make a portage [at present, city of South Bend] about thirty leagues from its mouth. . . We were but two days in making this portage which is a league and a half in length. . . . At last we perceived our own agreeable country, the savage buffaloes and heards of stags [elks] wandering on the borders of the river [Kankakee].

At an earlier date Father Hennepin found Buffaloes numerous at the same portage, so numerous that the Miami Indians sometimes killed from 100 to 200 daily. Howard (1907) describes the parklike banks of the St. Joseph River as once a great Buffalo range, frequented especially by cows with calves. The early French hunters and traders called that part of this strip lying above and below the sites of South Bend and Mishawaka parc aux vaches, (park of the cows), which was corrupted to parkovash by the later settlers. The name is commemorated in the present Parkovash Street of South Bend. There is almost no mention of Buffaloes in the interior wooded portions of Indiana. McDonald (1908) refers to the last Buffalo being killed about 1818 along the Wabash between where are now the sites of Wabash and Huntington. Lahontan (1735) writing for 1687 says:

We find wild Beeves [Buffaloes] upon the banks of two pleasant Rivers [Maumee, Sandusky] that disembogue into it [Lake Erie].

While not in Indiana this is not far away. While it is only a guess I strongly suspect that the Buffalo once found throughout the forested area of Indiana and Ohio was the subspecies *Bison bison pennsylvanicus* (Shoemaker). If such was the case, Indiana was evidently the place where the Plains and Eastern Bisons met and intergraded.

I know of no specimens of the Bison from Indiana in any public collection, or owned by any person, not even a fragment of a skull. The largest recent mammal of the state has been completely wiped from the map. According to Chansler (Hahn 1909), the Buffaloes disappeared from around Vincennes about 1808 to 1810. Hornaday (1889) gives essentially the same date of extermination in the state, 1810.

Map 76. Published records
with approximate dates of observation of the Buffalo, *Bison
bison*, in Indiana. Before the
close of the 18th Century it was
probably found throughout the
area now embraced by the state.
† Pleistocene records.

The published records for the Buffalo are: Crawford (Wilson 1910, 1919),
Daviess (Butler 1895), Dearborn (Anonymous 1885, Wilson 1919), Dubois (Wilson
1910, 1919), Floyd (Wilson 1910), Franklin (Butler 1885), Everamnn and Butler
1894), Harrison (Wilson 1910), Jasper (Collett 1883), Knox (Butler 1895, Hahn
1909, Cory 1912, Wilson 1910, 1919), Lake (Dinwiddie 1884, Blatchley 1898),
Laporte (Anonymous 1880), Orange (Wilson 1910, 1919), Pike (Wilson 1910, 1919),
Porter (Blatchley 1898), Posey (Wied 1839-41), St. Joseph (Anonymous 1880,
Bartlett 1904, Howard 1907, Engels 1933), Tippecanoe (Craig 1893), Vanderburg
(Gilbert 1910), Vigo (Thomas 1819), Wayne (Plummer 1844), northern Indiana
(Allen 1876, 1877), Kankakee valley (Charlevoix 1763, Marest 1846, Beckwith 1881,
Reed 1920), prairie region (Audubon and Bachman 1851, Owen 1862), upper
Wabash valley between Wabash and Huntington (McDonald 1908), lower Wabash
valley (Charlevoix 1763, Croghan 1834), southern Indiana, along Ohio River
(Hutchins 1778, Allen 1876, 1877).

PLEISTOCENE AMERICAN BISON
† **Bison bison** (Linnaeus)

Bison americanus Leidy 1854. Identification doubtful.
Bison bison Hay 1902, 1912, 1923, 1930.

The American Bison has been reported in Pleistocene deposits in two
counties.

The published records of the American Bison in Pleistocene deposits are: Jasper
(Collett 1883, Hay 1912, 1923), Vanderburg (Leidy 1854, 1860, Hay 1912, 1923).

ANCIENT BISON
† **Bison antiquus** Leidy

† *Bison antiquus* LEIDY Proc. Acad. Nat. Sci. Philadelphia, vol. 6, p. 117,
  1852. Type locality: Big Bone Lick, Kentucky. Middleton and Moore
  1899, Hay 1902, 1912, 1930.

Bison antiquus is known by but few specimens, ranging from Kentucky
to California. The type specimen came from Big Bone Lick, Kentucky, and
was part of a collection presented to the American Philosophical Society by
President Thomas Jefferson. It consisted of the right horn-core and the
attached part of the cranium. The species is distinguished from all other
American Bisons in that the horn-cores stand at right angles to the skull.
The horn-cores are roundly subtriangular in section; they are long and slightly
curved; length along lower convexity 355 mm.; along upper concavity, 290 mm.

A fine example of this species is at Earlham University, illustrated as Fig.
109, a line drawing after Hay (1912) from photographs. It was first described
and figured by Middleton and Moore (1899). It was found in 1896 by a
Mr. Brower, a few miles from Vincennes, Indiana, in a ditch at a depth of
six feet. It is a much finer specimen than the original type.

Fig. 109. Frontal and occipital views of Ancient Bison, *Bison antiquus*, Vincennes,
Ind., in the collection of Earlham University. After O. P. Hay, Pleistocene Period
and its Vertebrata, 36th Ann. Rep. Dept. Geol. Nat. Res. Indiana for 1911, figs. 50
and 51, p. 650, 1912. Actual distance between tips of horn-cores about 880 mm.

Map 77. Published records and specimens in collections of the Ancient Bison, † *Bison antiquus*, in Indiana.

The pubilshed records of the Ancient Bison are: Knox (Middleton and Moore 1899, Hay 1902, 1912, 1913, 1914, 1923).

Wide-browed Bison
† **Bison latifrons** (Harlan)

† *Bos latifrons* Harlan. Fauna Amer., p. 273, 1825. Type locality: near Big Bone Lick, Kentucky.

† *Bison latifrons* Collett, J. in Cope and Wortman Dept. Geol. Nat. Hist. 14th Ann. Rep. 1884, p. 24. 1885; Hay 1902, 1912, 1913, 1923, 1930.

Bison latifrons is the largest species of American bison and inhabited the Mississippi Valley and the southeastern states in Pleistocene times. The type is in the Academy of Natural Sciences, Philadelphia. One of the best specimens is in the collection of the Cincinnati Society of Natural History, here illustrated as Fig. 110. The species is characterized by the great size and length of the horn-cores. The evidence of its occurrence in Indiana is not satisfactory, but the southern part of the state being so close to the type locality, there can be little question of its former actual range in the state. Remains of it are merely said to have been found in Vanderburg County without details or description of a specimen.

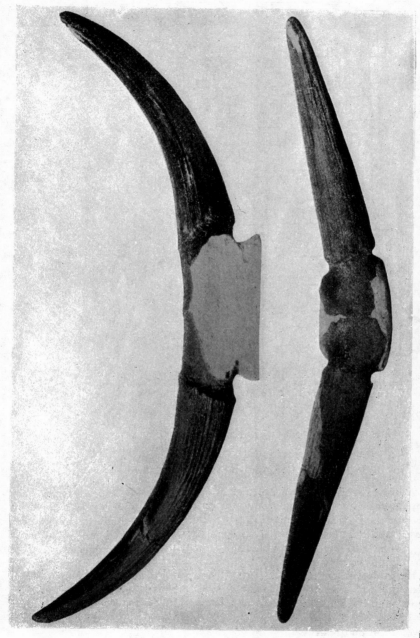

Fig. 110. Horn-cores of the extinct Wide-browed Bison, *Bison latifrons* Harlan. After Lucas in Proc. U. S. Nat. Mus., vol. 21, pl. 82, 1899. Specimen from Adams County, Ohio, i n collection of Cincinnati Society of Natural History.

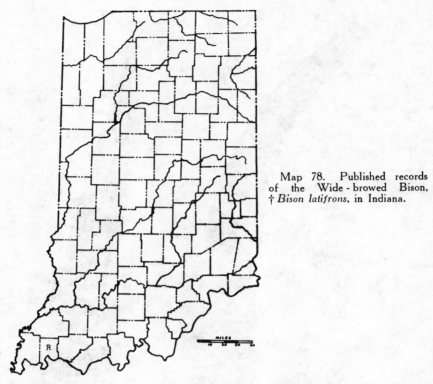

Map 78. Published records of the Wide-browed Bison, † *Bison latifrons*, in Indiana.

Published records of the Wide-browed Bison are: Vanderburg (Collett in Cope and Wortman 1885; Hay 1912, 1923).

MUSK-OXEN

† Genus **Ovibos** DeBlainville

Musk-oxen received their generic designation *Ovis* + *Bos* because they actually are intermediate in many respects between the ovine and bovine sections of the *Bovidae*. The horns of the adult males are rounded, smooth and closely approximated at their bases, where they are depressed and rugose; curving downwards, and then upwards and forwards. They are animals the size of small cattle with coarse shaggy hair. They are confined at the present time to the most northern parts of North America. In Pleistocene times they ranged over northen Siberia, the plains of Germany and France, and they also occurred in Ohio, Indiana and Iowa. They probably fed at the foot of the great ice sheets that covered North America and as the glaciers retreated, they followed them northward.

Fig. 111. Fragment of skull (base of horn-cores) of Musk-ox, *Ovibos moschatus*, Richmond, Ind., in collection of Earlham University. After O. P. Hay, Pleistocene Period and its Vertebrata, 36th Ann. Rep. Dept. Geol. Nat. Res. Indiana for 1911, pl. 9, fig. 2, p. 640, 1912.

MUSK-OX

† **Ovibos moschatus** (Zimmermann)

† *Bos moschatus* ZIMMERMANN Geogr. Geschichte, vol. 2, p. 86, 1780.
    Type locality: Between Seal and Churchill Rivers, Keewatin, Canada.

† *Ovibos moschatus* Desmarest. Mammalogie, vol. 2, p. 492, 1822; Hay 1902,
    1912, 1923, 1930.

Only one specimen of the true Musk-ox is known from Indiana. It is a fragmentary portion of the skull, mainly the bases of the horn-cores, unearthed near Richmond, Indiana. It is in the collection of Earlham University and is illustrated as Fig. 111 after Hay (1912).

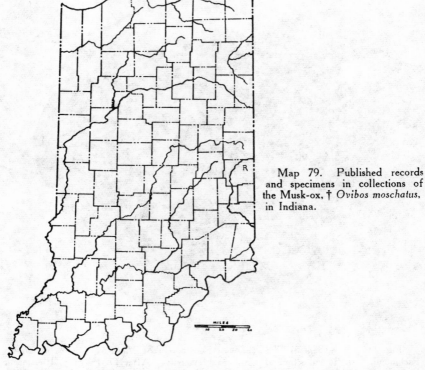

Map 79. Published records and specimens in collections of the Musk-ox, † *Ovibos moschatus*, in Indiana.

Published records of the Musk-ox are: Wayne (Hay 1912, 1923).

UNITED-HORN MUSK-OXEN

† Genus **Symbos** Osgood

The genus *Symbos* is similar in most respects to *Ovibos* except that the horn-cores are united at the base and that there is no "part" between them. The horns were evidently solidly united across the top of the head. Two species have been described but I strongly suspect that more material will show them to be identical. It ranged from Mississippi to Alaska and Pennsylvania to Oklahoma.

Fig. 112. Photograph courtesy Amer. Mus. Nat. Hist. Palatal view of skull of United-Horn Musk-ox, *Symbos cavifrons*, Amer. Mus. Nat. Hist. Hebron, Porter County.

Fig. 113. Photograph courtesy Amer. Mus. Nat. Hist. Dorsal view of skull of United-Horn Musk-ox, *Symbos cavifrons*, Amer. Mus. Nat. Hist., Hebron, Porter County.

United-horn Musk-ox
† Symbos cavifrons (Leidy)

† *Bootherium cavifrons* LEIDY. Proc. Acad. Nat. Sci. Philadelphia, vol. 6, p. 59, 1852, Bradley 1870. Type locality: Fort Gibson, Indian Territory near junction of Neosho and Arkansas rivers.

† *Ovibos cavifrons* Hay 1902.

† *Scaphoceros cavifrons* Osgood. Smiths. Misc. Coll., vol. 48, pls. 40-42, 1905.

† *Symbos cavifrons* Hay 1912, 1914, 1923, 1930; Allen 1913.

The United-horn Musk-ox appears to be the common Pleistocene Musk-ox of America. There are six published records of it for Indiana and probably there are a few specimens in local collections unrecognized and unpublished. In the United States National Museum exhibition series is a beautiful skull from Union township, Miami county. So far as I know it has never been previously reported.

Map 80. Published records and specimens in collections of the United-horn Musk-ox, † *Symbos cavifrons*, in Indiana; 1, Northern Indiana Historical Society; 2, Henry Duncker, South Bend.

The published records of the United-horn Musk-ox are: Bartholomew (Hay 1912, 1923, Allen 1913), Laporte (Lyon 1931), Newton (Bradley 1870, Hay 1912, 1923), Porter (Hay 1912, 1914, 1923, Allen 1913), Randolph (Hay 1912, 1923), St. Joseph (Lyon 1926).

TAPIRS, RHINOCEROSES, AND HORSES, ORDER PERISSODACTYLA

The order *Perissodactyla* is so called because its members for the most part possess an odd number of toes on each foot. The middle or third digit of both fore and hind feet is larger than any of the others and symmetrical in itself. This may be the only functional toe as in the horse; or the second and fourth toes may be subequally developed on either side of it; or the fifth toe may be present on the forefoot as in the tapirs and many extinct forms. The premolar and molar teeth form a continuous series, with massive, quadrate, transversely ridged or complex crowns; the posterior premolars often resemble the true molars in size and structure. The stomach is simple. The mammae are inguinal. The order is an old one and the few living forms are but a remnant of the hosts that existed in past geologic times. It is represented in Indiana by two fossil forms, tapir and horse.

TAPIRS
† Family **Tapiridae**

Tapirs are medium sized *Perissodactyls*, with four digits on the front feet, and three on the hind. The cheek-teeth are simply two-lobed; the hinder premolars resemble the molars in complexity. Tapirs had a wide geographic distribution in past ages, but are now confined in the living state to Central and South America and the Malay region. In the Pleistocene period they were found over the greater part of the southern United States from South Carolina to California. Two or three genera are currently recognized.

TAPIRS
† Genus **Tapirus** Cuvier

Characters as for the family given above. Dental formula:

$$i \frac{3-3}{3-3}, \ c \frac{1-1}{1-1}, \ pm \frac{4-4}{3-3}, \ m \frac{3-3}{3-3}, = 42.$$

Several living and several extinct species are recognized, one of the latter has been found in southern Indiana represented by a single tooth.

HAYS' TAPIR
† **Tapirus haysii** Leidy

† *Tapirus haysii* Leidy Proc. Acad. Nat. Sci. Philadelphia, vol. 6, p. 106, 1852 (nomen nudum), 1860; Type locality; Probably Big Bone Lick, Kentucky. Hay 1902, 1912, 1914, 1923, 1930.

† *Tapirus* [no specific name given] Leidy 1854.

† *Tapirus terrestris* Cope and Wortman 1885, Kindle 1898.

This species is represented in Indiana by but a single tooth, a lower molar that had been found on the banks of the Ohio River, near the mouth of Pigeon Creek, below Evansville, by Mr. Francis A. Lincke. With it were

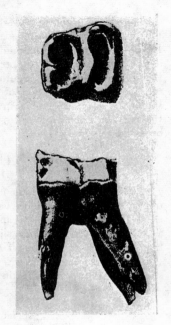

Fig. 114. Lower Molar Tooth, probably second, of Hays' Tapir, *Tapirus haysii*, natural size, near mouth of Pigeon Creek, Evansville, Indiana, Francis A. Lincke. After Joseph Leidy in Holmes' Post-Pliocene Fossils of South Carolina, pl. 17, figs. 9 and 10, 1860. This figure is reproduced by O. P. Hay in Pleistocene Period and its Vertebrata, 36th Ann. Rept. Geol. Nat. Res. Indiana for 1911, figs. 38 and 39, p. 591, 1912. The illustration herewith is taken from Hay. The specimen appears to be lost.

Map 81. Published records of Hays' Tapir, † *Tapirus haysii*, in Indiana.

The published records of Hays' Tapir are: Vanderburg (Leidy 1854, 1860, 1869, Cope and Wortman 1885, Hay 1912, 1923).

associated fragments of *Megalonyx jeffersonii, Bison americanus?, Cervus* [*Odocoileus*] *virginianus, Equus americanus* and *Canis primaevus* [*dirus*]. Joseph Leidy made a preliminary report of this material in 1854-55, but gave it no specific name. The specimen was afterwards figured by him in Holmes' Post-pliocene Fossils of South Carolina, 1860. A copy of this figure is here reproduced. The location of the tooth at the present time is unknown. It should be in Philadelphia in the Academy of Natural Sciences along with the type of *Aenocyon dirus*. Hay (1912) failed to find it and I had no better success in 1931.

HORSES AND ALLIES
† Family Equidae

Perissodactyla with long crowned molars, with the outer columns of the upper ones flattened, the valleys completely filled with cement, and the enamel thrown into folds and plications; upper premolars are as complex as the molars, which they slightly exceed in size. Digits of both fore and hind feet three to one, but if more than one, only the middle digit functional. The family *Equidae* comprises the genus *Equus* with both living and extinct species as well as many extinct genera.

HORSES
† Genus Equus[1] Linnaeus

Each foot with a single complete digit, the third, the terminal phalanx of which is covered with the well known hoof. Remnants of the proximal portions of the second and fourth metapodials persist. The teeth are high-crowned and prismatic the premolars closely resembling the molars, see Fig. 115. Dental formula: $i\frac{3-3}{3-3}$, $c\frac{1-1}{1-1}$, or wanting, $pm\frac{4-4}{3-3}$, the first upper premolar very small and often wanting, $m\frac{3-3}{3-3}$. About a dozen species of the genus *Equus* are known from the Pleistocene of North America ranging from the Atlantic to the Pacific and from the Great Lakes down into Mexico. The genus was extinct in the New World at the time of its discovery, and the wild horses of the plains of both North and South America are the descendants of those brought over by the Europeans.

Only two finds of Pleistocene horses are known from Indiana and they are so fragmentary as to be indeterminable.

HORSE
† Equus sp. indet.

† *Equus americanus* Leidy 1854.
† *Equus complicatus* Leidy 1858, Hay 1912, 1923.
† *Equus fraternus* and *major* Cope and Wortman 1885.

The first known specimen of *Equus* from Indiana is only the last dorsal

---

1 Originally spelled by Linnaeus *Eqvus*.

vertebra, found along the banks of the Ohio, below Evansville, by Mr. Francis Linke associated with fragmentary remains of *Megalonyx, Bison, Odocoileus, Tapirus* and *Aenocyon*. The other find is in collection of Mr. Henry Duncker of South Bend and consists of two teeth found in digging the drainage ditch of the Kankakee region, in association with remains of *Mammut, Symbos, Cervus,* and *Odocoileus*. One of these two teeth was examined by the late

Fig. 115. Crown nd lateral views of two upper cheekteeth of Horse, *Equus* sp., x1, associated with P eistocene remains of Mastodon, Musk-ox, Elk and Deer, La-porte County. Owne by Henry Duncker, South Bend, Ind.

J. W. Gidley and identified by him as the second right upper molar of a small horse about the size of a pony. The other tooth is probably the first right upper molar.

Map 82. Published records and specimens in collection of Pleistocene Horse, † *Equus sp.* in Indiana; 1, Henry Duncker, South Bend.

The published records of Pleistocene horse are: Laporte (L y o n 1931), Vanderburg (Leidy 1854, 1858, 1860, Hay 1912, 1923).

ELEPHANTS, MASTODONS AND DEINOTHERES, ORDER † PROBOSCIDEA

The order *Proboscidea* contains some of the largest land mammals known. It comprises two well marked groups, the *Elephantidae* and the *Deinotheriidae*, the latter an Old World group, lacking upper tusks but possessing conspicuous lower ones. These two groups are here treated as families for the sake of convenience. For a recent view of this subject the serious student should consult Osborn's article, Evolution and Geographic Distribution of the Proboscidea in the Journal of Mammalogy, vol. 15, pp. 177 to 184, figures 1 to 3. August, 1934.

ELEPHANTS, MAMMOTHS AND MASTODONS
† Family Elephantidae

The family *Elephantidae* is typified by the existing Elephants which are so well known that it is only necessary to point out some of its chief characters. The nose is extended into the well-known long muscular proboscis commonly called the trunk. The toes are five on each foot enclosed in a common integument and the terminal phalanges usually covered with distinct broad short hoofs. Mammae two, placed pectorally. Testes permanently abdominal. An excellent detailed and illustrated account of the osteology of the group as known in Indiana is given by Hay (1912) to which the interested reader is referred.

The incisor teeth are of great size, ever-growing usually limited to a single pair in the upper jaw, the well known tusks of the Elephant. Occasionally a small pair may be present in the lower jaw. The canines are absent. The cheek teeth are six on each side of each jaw. None of them have milk predecessors and the first three teeth on each side of each jaw are interpreted as milk molars which have no successors. The dental formula is:

$$i \frac{1\text{-}1}{0\text{-}0} \text{ or } \frac{1\text{-}1}{1\text{-}1}, \ c \frac{0\text{-}0}{0\text{-}0}, \ pm \frac{3\text{-}3}{3\text{-}3}, \ m \frac{3\text{-}3}{3\text{-}3}.$$

In primitive forms as the Mastodon the cheek teeth have a comparatively simple structure, being composed of a series of elevated transversely placed tubercles, and in the most highly specialized forms, Elephants and Mammoths, of a series of compressed transverse enamel ridges embedded in cement. This structure is illustrated in longitudinal section in Fig. 119, which shows the gradual evolution of the primitive Mastodon tooth into that of the Mammoth. The number of transverse rows of tubercles or of enamel plates increases with the age of the teeth and also varies with the different species. In the Mastodon of the United States the cross ridges of the six cheek teeth above and below are represented by the formula: 2, 2, 3, 3, 3, 4 or 5; in the African Elephant 3, 6, 7, 7, 8, 10; in the Indian Elephant 4, 8, 12, 12, 16, 24; in the Hairy Mammoth 4, 6-9, 9-12, 9-15, 14-16, 18-27, and probably the same in the Columbian Mammoth. The teeth are large and heavy and not all are functional at the same time. Each tooth as it is worn out is succeeded by another coming in from behind, until the last molar is in place. In the Elephants and Mammoths there may be in each side of each jaw at the same time only one tooth or parts of two teeth. In the Mastodon, however, as many as three teeth may be in place in each half of each jaw.

The family *Elephantidae* has a wide geographic distribution, their remains being found in suitable deposits in all large land masses except Australia. It comprises numerous fossil genera and species as well as the two living genera *Elephas* of the Indo-Malay region and *Loxodonta* of Africa. Numerous remains of Elephants and Mastodons have been found throughout the whole of Indiana.

MASTODONS
† Genus Mammut Blumenbach

Elephantidae characterized by the cheek teeth having from two to five

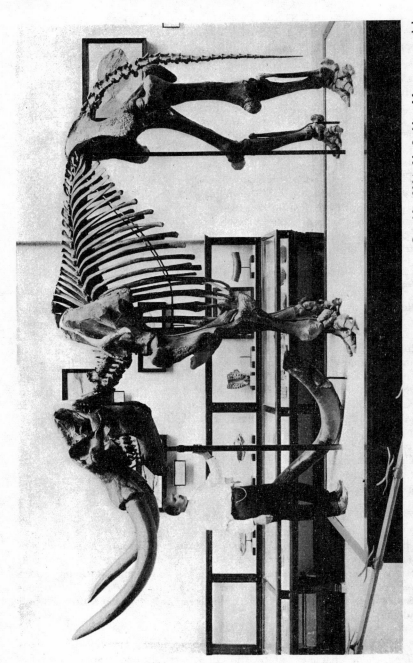

Fig. 116. Photograph courtesy U. S. Nat. Mus. Mastodon, *Mammut americanum*, Cat. No. 8204, U. S. Nat. Mus., presented by Major H. H. Patison and W. D. Patison, Winnemac, Pulaski County. Collected and assembled in 1914 by the late J. W. Gidley, who is standing beneath the head.

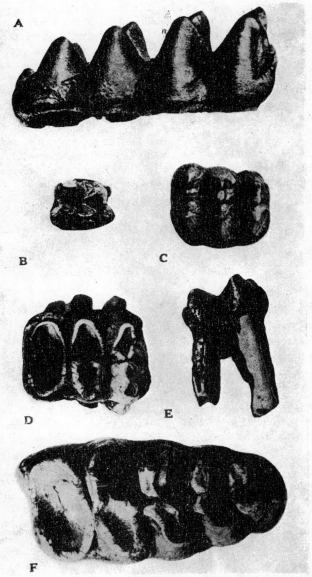

Fig. 117. Teeth of Mastodon, *Mammut americanum*. After O. P. Hay, Pleisto-cene Period and its Vertebrata, 36th Ann. Rep. Dept. Geol. Nat. Res. Indiana for 1911, pl. 15, p. 673, 1912.

A.—Third right lower molar, lateral view, outer face, only crown of tooth is pres-ent, roots are lacking. B.—Second right upper milk molar, crown view. C.—Third right upper milk molar, crown view. D.—First right upper molar, crown view. E.—Second right upper milk molar, lateral view. F.—Last left lower molar, crown view. All about 1/3 natural size, except E which is reproduced slightly larger.

cross ridges or cross rows of conspicuous nipple-like tubercles; crowns of teeth low; upper jaw with a pair of well developed tusks; the lower jaw rarely with one or two short tusks. Mastodons do not stand as high as the Elephants, but are more heavily built and wider and thickset. Most authors consider the Mastodon to have been covered with coarse dun-colored hair, but Hay (1914) thinks this assumption is not based on sufficient evidence. No Mastodons have been found frozen in ice as in the case of the Hairy Mammoth. Nor did Cave Men have the opportunity of recording it in their sketches as they did with the Mammoth and many other mammals.

The range of the genus *Mammut* in time is from the middle of the Miocene to the end of the Pliocene in the Old World when it became extinct. In the New World it persisted much longer, into the late Pleistocene. Several species are recognized, remains of the most common are *Mammut americanum*, being abundantly found in Indiana.

MASTODON

† **Mammut americanum** (Kerr)

† *Elephas americanus* KERR. Anim. Kingd. p. 116, 1792.

† *Mammut ohioticum* BLUMENBACH Handb. Naturgesch., ed. 6, p. 698, 1799.

† *Mastodon giganteum* G. CUVIER. Regne Anim. vol. 1, p. 232, 1817.

† *Mastodon giganteus* Warren 1855.

† *Mastodon americanus* Cope and Wortman 1884.

† *Mammut americanum* Hay 1902, 1912, 1923, 1930.

The American Mastodon probably has as many if not more published records than any other Indiana mammal. These are all indicated on the accompanying map and the list of published records. Many of the records are based on finds of single teeth, but several excellent nearly complete mounted skeletons are in various museums viz: Miami County, Milwaukee Public Museum; DeKalb County, Carnegie Museum, Pittsburgh; DeKalb County, Colorado Museum of Natural History; Pulaski County, United States National Museum; Grant County, Taylor University, Upland Indiana (not yet mounted); Randolph County, Earlham University. Remains are found in the most recent Pleistocene deposits of Indiana, so that the Mastodon evidently persisted until comparatively recent times, at least geologically speaking. No satisfactory evidence has been brought forward that the Mastodon and Man were contemporaneous in Indiana. Some idea as to the recentness of its extinction is shown by the statement of Collett (1881) in regard to Mastodon remains found in Fountain County:

When the larger bones were split open the marrow, still preserved, was utilized by the bog cutters to 'grease' their boats, and that chunks of sperm-like substance 2½ to 3 inches in diameter (adipocere) occupied the place of the kidney fat of the monster.

Fig. 118. Photograph courtesy Amer. Mus. Nat. Hist. Restoration of the American Mastodon, *Mammut americanum.*

Map 83. Published records and specimens or parts of specimens (often a single tooth) in collections of the Mastodon, † *Mammut americanum*, in Indiana; 1, Public Museum of Milwaukee, mounted skeleton; 2, Henry Duncker, South Bend; 3, Public Library, Walkerton; 4, W. W. Place, near Walkerton; 5, Buffalo Museum of Science, unmounted skeleton; 6, Taylor University, Upland, unmounted skeleton; 7, Carnegie Museum, Pittsburgh, mounted skeleton; 8, Yale University; 9, Wabash College; 10, Mr. William G. Thompson, Argos, Marshall Co. The specimen in the U. S. National Museum, Pulaski Co., is a complete mounted skeleton, shown as figure 116. Remains of Mastodon, reported by R. A. Gantz (Proc. Indiana Acad. Sci. vol. 34, p. 393, 1925) for Delaware County are in the collection of the Indiana State Normal School, Muncie. There are Mastodon remains in the Field Museum of Natural History from Newton County not shown on this map.

The published records for the Mastodon are: Allen (Lydekker 1886, Dryer 1889, Hay 1912, 1923), Bartholomew (Edwards 1902), Cass (Hay 1923), Clark (Borden 1874, Hay 1912, 1923), Dearborn (Warder 1873, Bigney 1832, Hay 1912, 1923), Decatur (Hay 1923), Dekalb (Holland 1905, Hay 1912, 1923, Simpson 1934), Delaware (Helm 1881, Phinney 1882, Hay 1912, 1923, Gantz 1925), Dubois (Mitchell 1818, Collett 1872, Hay 1912, 1923), Floyd (Borden 1874, Hay 1923), Fountain (Collett 1881, Mason 1882, Hay 1912, 1923), Franklin (Haymond 1870, Langdon 1881, Hay 1912, 1923), Fulton (Hay 1923), Gibson (Blainville 1839-64, Warren 1855, Hay 1912, 1923), Grant (Phinney 1884, Hay 1912, 1923), Hendricks (Hay 1912, 1923), Henry (Hay 1912, 1923), Jackson (Cox 1875, Hay 1912, 1923), Jasper (Collett 1883, Hay 1912, 1923), Jay (M'Caslin 1883, Hay 1912, 1923), Knox (Hay 1923), Lagrange (Rerick 1882, Hay 1912, 1923), Lake (Ball 1894, Blatchley 1898, Hay 1923), Laporte (Lyon 1931), Madison (Forkner 1897, Anonymous 1911, Hay 1912, 1923), Marion (Hay 1912, 1923), Marshall (Thompson 1890), Martin (Cox 1871, Hay 1912, 1923), Miami (Hay 1912, 1914, 1923, Kintner 1930), Montgomery (Hay 1912, 1923), Newton (Bradley 1870, Hay 1912, 1923), Noble (Meyers 1868, Hay 1923), Orange (Hay 1912, 1923), Parke (Collett 1881, Hay 1912, 1923), Porter (Blatchley 1898, Hay 1912, 1923, Posey (Blainville 1839-64, Warren 1855, Owen 1862, Hay 1912, 1923), Pulaski (Hay 1923), Putnam (Hay 1912, 1923), Randolph (Phinney 1883, Pleas 1891, Moore 1897, Hay 1912, 1923), St. Joseph (Hay 1912, 1923, Engels 1933), Steuben (Hay 1912, 1923), Vigo (Bradsby 1891), Wabash

(Elrod and Benedict 1892, Hay 1912, 1923), Wayne (Plummer 1841, 1843, Hay 1912, 1923).

The so-called Garrett Mastodon, recorded by Simpson (1934), is said to have been mounted and to be in the Colorado Museum of Natural History.

In a letter dated October 26, 1935, Dr. C. E. Cummings of the Buffalo Museum of Science states that the Mastodon remains from Noble County in that museum, are still in storage. Dr. John T. Sanford, who excavated the remains, has written the full description of the work that was done on it in vol. 7, no. 5 of the Proceedings of the Rochester Academy of Science, Rochester, N. Y.

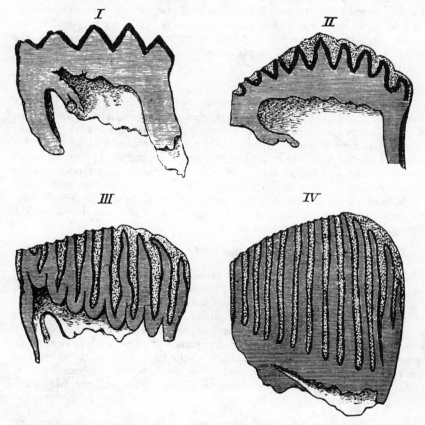

Fig. 119. Longitudinal sections of the crown of a molar tooth of various Proboscideans, showing stages in the gradual modification from the simple to the complex form.

I.—Mastodon, *Mammut americanum*.
II.—A primitive extinct Elephant, *Stegodon insignis*.
III.—African Elephant, *Loxodonta africana*.
IV.—Mammoth, *Elephas primigenius*.
The dentine is indicated by transverse lines, the cement by a dotted surface, and the enamel by solid black. After Flower and Lydekker, An Introduction to the Study of Mammals Living and Extinct, p. 420, 1891.

ELEPHANTS AND MAMMOTHS

† Genus **Elephas** Linnaeus

Living members of the genus *Elephas* are usually termed Elephants, while the extinct members are usually referred to as Mammoths, though there are no essential anatomical differences or striking differences in size. As already mentioned the teeth of *Elephas* are composed of relatively broad and deep plates of dentine covered by a layer of enamel; the various plates thus formed are held together by intervening plates of cement. These teeth constitute one of the most highly developd grinding or triturating devices known in the animal world. The number of plates varies with different teeth, and varies with the different species.

Two groups of fossil Elephants are known from Indiana. As not all authorities identify the same specimen as the same species and as in many instances it is impossible to tell from the published descriptions of teeth which of the two groups is meant, the accompanying map and list of published records have been prepared to include the fossil Elephants as a whole, and a review of the scientific names applied to them is appended. It is to be hoped that a scientific revision of the group will be prepared and its nomenclature straightened out. Finds of Elephants are nowhere as numerous as those of the Mastodons and so far as I am aware only one essentially perfect skeleton has been secured from Indiana, that from Grant County and now in the American Museum of Natural History.

The two groups of fossil Elephants found in Indiana are:

1. Hairy Mammoth, *primigenius* group, ridge formula of teeth 4, 6-9, 9-12, 9-15, 14-16, 18-27. During the Pleistocene this group of Elephants had a greater range than that of almost any other mammal. Several entire specimens have been found in the frozen soils of Siberia. The remains have been so well preserved that meat from them has been used to feed dogs. Not only from these remains have the external appearance of these animals been made known to us but also from the drawings of the Cave Men in the caverns of Europe. The Hairy Mammoth and Man were contemporaneous there at least. There is not sufficient evidence to say that Man and the Mammoth were contemporary in North America.

2. The Columbian Mammoth, ridge formula of teeth essentially the same as that of the Hairy Mammoth, although the ridges may be fewer. The ridge plates are described as thicker and more liable to be channeled and crimped. The sheaths for the bases of the tusks are shorter than in case of the Hairy Mammoth. It had a more southern range than the Mammoths of the preceding group.

The three groups of names that have been used for the Hairy Mammoths of Indiana are given below; there has been more uniformity in the names applied to the Columbian Mammoth.

American Hairy Mammoth
† Elephas boreus Hay

† *Elephas primigenius* BLUMENBACH. Handb. Naturgesch., 1st French ed., vol. 2, p. 407, 1803.

† *Elephas primigenius* Cope and Wortman 1885, Hay 1902, 1912, 1923.

† *Elephas boreus* HAY. Observations on Some Extinct Elephants, 1-19 pages, pls. 1-4, text figs. 1-10. Washington. Privately printed, 1922.

The Hairy Mammoths of the Old and New Worlds were long considered identical. Hay (1922) seems to have been the first to recognize their distinctness, and applied the specific name *boreus* to what had previously been called *primigenius*.

Theodore Roosevelt's Hairy Mammoth
† Elephas roosevelti Hay

† *Elephas roosevelti* HAY. Proc. Biol. Soc. Washington, vol. 35, p. 101, 1922, Hay 1925, 1930.

† *Elephas primigenius* Osborn 1922, Hay 1923.

† *Mammonteus primigenius compressus* OSBORN. Amer. Mus. Novit., no. 152, 1924.

The type of Osborn's *Mammonteus primigenius compressus* was found near Rochester, Fulton County. It is the skull of an adult female now in the American Museum of Natural History, New York. Illustrations of it are given as Fig. 120. The skull is remarkably compressed from before backwards. The molar teeth have the maximum number of enamel ridges which are closely packed into the tooth. Hay (1925) regards *Mammonteus primigenius compressus* as a synonym of *Elephas roosevelti* Hay.

Thomas Jefferson's Hairy Mammoth
† Elephas jeffersonii Osborn

† *Elephas columbi* Osborn 1907.

† *Elephas primigenius* Hay 1912, 1923.

† *Elephas jeffersonii* OSBORN. Amer. Mus. Novit., no. 41, pp. 1-16, 1922.

† *Parelephas jeffersonii* Osborn 1924.

The type of Osborn's *Elephas jeffersonii* is the practically complete skeleton of an adult male found in Grant County and now in the exhibition halls of the American Museum of Natural History. It was originally identified by Osborn as *Elephas columbi*, and identified by Hay in 1912, as *Elephas primigenius*. Through the courtesy of American Museum of Natural History a photograph of this skeleton is reproduced as Fig. 122, and a reproduction of Knight's restoration of it as Fig. 121.

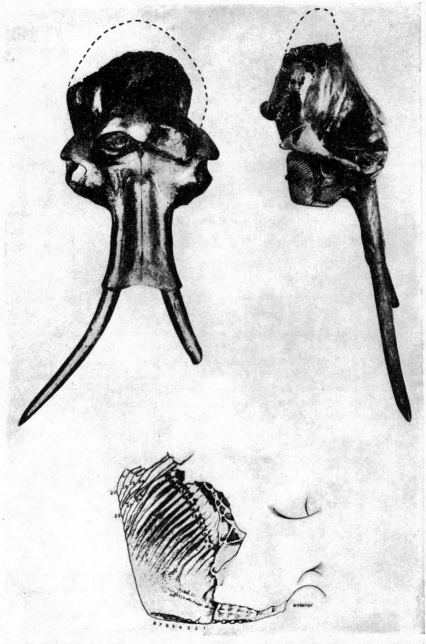

Fig. 120. Photographs courtesy Amer. Mus. Nat. Hist. Left upper figure: Frontal view of skull. Right upper figure: Lateral view of skull. Lower figure: Superior molar showing 27 enamel plates. Compressed Hairy Mammoth, *Mammonteus primigenius compressus* Osborn. Type, adult female, Cat. No. 14,559, Amer. Mus. Nat. Hist., Rochester, Fulton County.

Fig. 121. Photograph courtesy Amer. Mus. Nat. Hist. Restoration of the Jeffersonian Mammoth, *Parelephas jeffersonii* Osborn.

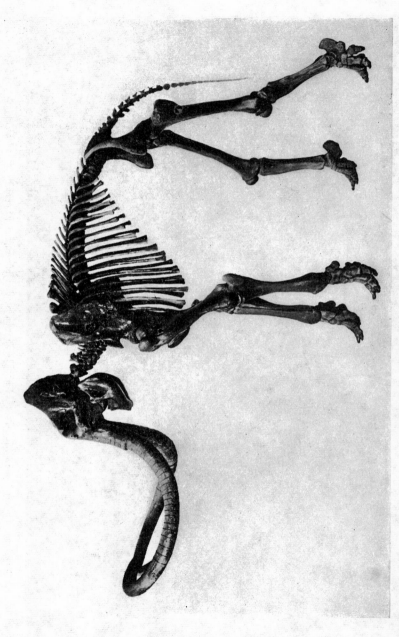

Fig. 122. Photograph courtesy Amer. Mus. Nat. Hist. Jeffersonian Mammoth, *Parelephas jeffersonii* Osborn, Type, Cat. No. 9950, Amer. Mus. Nat. Hist., Jonesboro, Grant County.

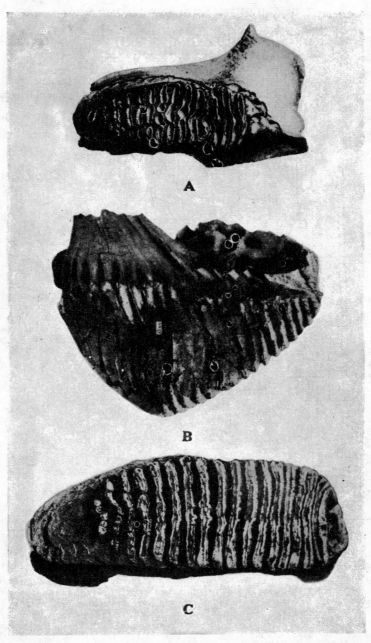

Fig. 123. Teeth of Mammoth, *Elephas primigenius*. After O. P. Hay, Pleisto-cene Period and its Vertebrata, 36th Ann. Rep. Dept. Geol. Nat. Res. Indiana for 1911, pl. 20, p. 724, 1912. A.—Fragment of right upper jaw, with part of much worn second milk molar and the entire third milk molar. B.—Lateral aspect of last right upper molar. C.—Crown or grinding surface of the same tooth. About 1/3 natural size.

Columbian Mammoth
† **Elephas columbi** Falconer

† Elephas columbi Falconer. Quart. Journ. Geol. Soc. London, vol. 13,
	p. 319, 1857. Hay 1902, 1912, 1923, 1930. For essential characters
	see p. 342.

Map 84. Published records
and specimens or fragments of
specimens in collections of the
Mammoth, *† Elephas* in Indiana;
1, Public Library, Walkerton;
2, W. W. Place, near Walkerton; 3, University of Nebraska;
4, Bert Morris, North Liberty;
5, Amos W. Butler.

The published records for the Mammoth are: Allen (Dryer 1889, Hay 1912,
1923), Bartholomew (Edwards 1902, Hay 1923), Carroll (Hay 1923), Dearborn
(Warder 1873, Bigney 1892), Delaware (Hay 1923), Fayette (Hay 1923), Franklin
(Plummer 1843, Haymond 1844, 1870, Hay 1912, 1923), Fulton (Hay 1912, 1923,
Osborn 1922, 1924, 1930), Grant (Osborn 1907, 1922, 1924, 1930, Hay 1912, 1914,
1923, Matthew 1915), Hamilton (Collett 1881, Hay 1923), Jasper (Collett 1883, Hay
1912, 1923), Jefferson (Leidy 1869, Cope and Wortman 1885, Hay 1912, 1923),
Lake (Blatchley 1898, Hay 1912, 1923), Martin (Cox 1871, Hay 1912, 1923), Mon-
roe (Wylie 1859, Hay 1912, 1923), Morgan (Hay 1912, 1923), Montgomery
(Thompson 1887, Hay 1912, 1923), Owen (Wylie 1859, Hay 1923), Parke (Collett
1881, Hay 1912, 1923), Putnam (Collett 1881, Hay 1912, 1923), Randolph (Hay
1923), St. Joseph (Hay 1912, 1923, Engels 1933), Switzerland (Hay 1923), Tipton
(Hay 1912, 1923), Vanderburg (Collett 1876, 1881, Hay 1912, 1923), Vermillion
(Collett 1881, Hay 1912, 1923), Vigo (Collett 1881, Hay 1912, 1923), Wabash
(Elrod and Benedict 1892, Hay 1912, 1923), Wayne (Collett 1881, Hay 1912, 1923).

AMERICAN EDENTATES, ORDER † XENARTHRA

The order *Xenarthra* is peculiarly American. During Tertiary times there existed in South America a very large number of genera of the Xenarthra. During the Pliocene and Pleistocene epochs some of these migrated into North America and spread over the larger part of the United States. A single representative of the order has been found in Indiana. The order is divided into two groups, series Loricata, represented by the existing armadillos and the allied extinct glyptodonts, none of this series ever extended as far north as Indiana; and series Pilosa represented by the existing tree-sloths and ant eaters and the extinct ground-sloths of the suborder Gravigrada, which had a much more northern range than the other members.

Teeth, when present, are column-like in form and ever-growing. They are devoid of enamel and composed principally of dentine, usually with a layer of cement. The dentine of the interior is softer and wears away more rapidly than the harder outer surface, giving each tooth a more or less distinct cutting edge.

GROUND-SLOTHS
† Suborder **Gravigrada**

The *Gravigrada* in Pleistocene times ranged from Pennsylvania and California southward to Patagonia. They were for the most part large or medium sized clumsy animals, some reaching the bulk of the elephant but very differently proportioned. The skull was small in comparison to the rest of the body, the tail heavy, the legs short, and the forefeet furnished with very large stout claws. The body was covered with coarse shaggy hair. Their food consisted of the leaves of bushes and trees which their great bulk enabled them to pull down or uproot. A rather detailed and illustrated account of their osteology is given by Hay (1912) and the more interested reader is referred to it. The *Gravigrada* is composed of three families, one of which is represented by very fragmentary remains from southern Indiana.

LARGE-CLAWED GROUND-SLOTHS
† Family **Megalonychidae**

The family *Megalonychidae* possessed five teeth in each half of the upper jaw and four in the lower; the two foremost teeth in each jaw were separated from the others by a considerable space and were more or less tusk-like in form. Forelegs shorter and more slender than the hind; feet with five digits, three of which carried claws of large size. Of the several genera comprising the family, mere fragments of one have been found in Indiana.

THOMAS JEFFERSON'S GROUND-SLOTHS
† Genus **Megalonyx** Jefferson

This genus was first described and named by President Jefferson in 1805, being based on an ungual phalanx found in a cave in Virginia. Jefferson imagined that it belonged to a lion of gigantic size that was probably still

living in the mountains of western Virginia. Its true nature was shortly recognized and the name *Megatherium jeffersonii* given to it by Desmarest in 1822.
Shortly after that the distinctness of *Megalonyx* from *Megatherium* was
recognized, so that the current name of the species is *Megalonyx jeffersonii*.

JEFFERSON'S GROUND-SLOTH
† **Megalonyx jeffersonii** (Desmarest)

† *Megatherium jeffersonii* DESMAREST. Mammalogie, p. 366. 1822.
† *Megalonyx jeffersonii* Leidy 1854, Cope and Wortman 1885, Hay 1902,
    1912, 1923, 1930.

Two finds of Jefferson's Ground-sloth have been reported from Indiana,
the first by Leidy in 1854, from the banks of the Ohio River, near Pigeon
Creek, below Evansville, Vanderburg County. This material was collected by

Map 85.   Published records of
Jefferson's Ground-sloth, † *Megalonyx jeffersonii*, in Indiana.

The published records of Jefferson's Ground-sloth are: Switzerland (Warder 1873),
Vanderburg (Leidy 1854, Collett 1876, Hay 1912, 1923, Moodie 1929).

Mr. Francis A. Lincke and consisted of the shafts of two tibiae of a young individual, an axis, a piece of calcaneum, one metacarpal, one metatarsal, and one ungual phalanx. Associated with it were remains of *Bison, Odocoileus, Equus, Tapirus* and *Aenocyon*. The other find is less definite; Warder (1873) reports finding bones of a sloth at Bryant's Creek, Switzerland County.

Fig. 124. External appearance of Jefferson's Ground Sloth, *Megalonyx jeffersonii*. After William B. Scott, History of the Land Mammals in the Western Hemisphere, New York, Macmillan Company, 1913. By permission of Macmillan Company.

ADDENDUM

The following notes, records and photographs were received or discovered too late to be included in the main body of the text.

BLACK BEAR
Euarctos americanus

In the Archives of the University of Notre Dame are some notes of the period of 1841 to 1854 written by Brother Augustus, C.S.C. He says forests are all around. Of the many kinds of animals in them one Bear was killed.

Dr. Amos W. Butler of Indianapolis succeeded in borrowing for examination what is probably the only extant skull of a Black Bear from Indiana. The skull is part of a skeleton that was found in a hollow tree near Brookville, Franklin County, in 1882. The specimen was originally owned by Dr. Rufus Haymond, who gave it to Dr. Butler, who in turn gave it to Edgar R. Quick, all of whom have written of Indiana mammals. The skeleton is now owned by, and in the possession of Mr. Quick's son, Mr. J. W. Quick of Brookville. As the last Black Bear was seen in Franklin County about 1840, the skeleton had remained in the tree about 40 or more years. Probably the Bear had gone into hibernation and died. It is a young adult individual; many of the skull sutures are plainly visible and the teeth show no sign of wear. The skull gives these measurements: Length between perpendicular planes, 255; width between similar planes, 148; upper toothrow from front of canine to end of last molar (alveoli), 95; lower toothrow, 110; width between frontal processes, 78; postorbital constriction, 60; greatest cranial width, 87; greatest width of rostrum, 56 mm. This skull is illustrated as plate 125.

Muskrat
Ondatra zibethica

In addition to being found in central Europe the Muskrat has been introduced in various parts of the British Isles, according to recent accounts being found in 26 English, 3 Welsh, 9 Scottish counties, in Ireland and in the Isle of Man.

Elk
Cervus canadensis

Prof. J. E. Potzger in a note dated November 9, 1935 reports the finding of Elk antlers at Summit, Henry County. These are probably of Pleistocene Age. They are not indicated on the map, page 305.

Mr. Samuel E. Perkins III. has kindly sent me on November 15, 1935 a photograph of a large six-tined single antler which was taken from the Tippecanoe River near Delong, Fulton County, about 1882 by Nicholas J. Busart of Culver, Indiana. This record is not shown on map, page 305.

Virginia Deer
Odocoileus virginianus

Prof. J. E. Potzger in a note dated November 9, 1935 reports the finding of Deer antler fragments near Summit, Henry County. These are probably of Pleistocene Age. They are not indicated on the map, page 310.

Mastodon
Mammut americanum

Prof. J. E. Potzger, under date of November 9, 1935 writes that there is a set of Mastodon tusks and jaw with an almost perfect set of teeth from Henry County in the Museum at New Castle.

Miss Louise Husband, in a letter dated November 9, 1935 reports the finding of a rather complete Mastodon skeleton found four miles east of New Harmony on Cox Creek.

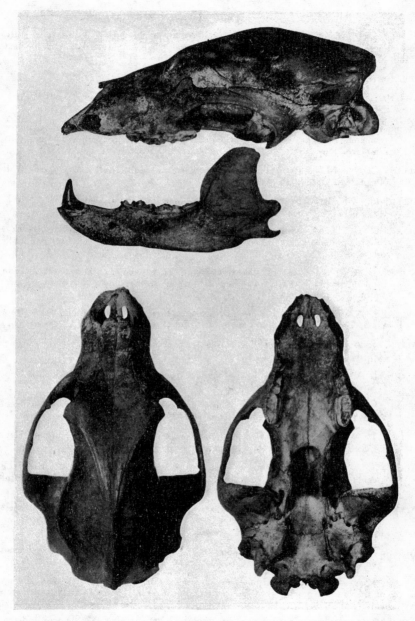

Fig. 125. Lateral, dorsal and palatal views of skull of Black Bear, *Euarctos americanus*, taken with remainder of skeleton from a hollow tree near Brookville, Franklin County, 1882. Owned by Mr. J. W. Quick and kindly made available by him for this illustration; about 1/3 natural size. The large upper canines have been lost.

BIBLIOGRAPHY OF INDIANA MAMMALS

* Denotes general works or papers referred to in the text, but not specifically mentioning Indiana specimens. Many other general papers are referred to in the text in full.

ADE, JOHN.—Newton County. The Bobbs-Merrill Company. 1911.

AHRENS, THEODOR G.—Muskrats in Central Europe, Journ. Mamm., vol. 2, pp. 236-7, 1921.

*ALDRICH, THOMAS B.—A chemical study of the anal glands of the *Mephitis mephitica* (common skunk) with remarks on the physiological properties of this sub-substance. Jour. Exp. Med., vol. 1, pp. 323-340, 1896.

ALLEN, GLOVER M.—Bats of the genus Corynorhinus. Bull. Mus. Comp. Zool., vol. 60, pt. 9, p. 336, 1916 April.

ALLEN, H.—Monograph of the bats of North America. Smiths. Misc. Coll., vol. 7, (No. 165) p. 53, 1864.

ALLEN, J. A.—The American Bisons, living and extinct. Mem. Geol. Surv. Kentucky, vol. 1, pp. 1-246, 12 pl. 1876. Also in Mem. Mus. Comp. Zool. Harvard Coll. vol. 4, 1876.

ALLEN, J. A.—Descriptions of some remains of an extinct species of wolf and an extinct species of deer, from the lead region of the upper Mississippi. Amer. Journ. Sci. ser. 3, vol. 11, pp. 47-51, 1876.

ALLEN, J. A.—History of the American bisons *(Bison Americanus)*. 9th Ann. Rep. U. S. Georgr. Geol. Surv. Terr. part 3, Zool., pp. 441-587, 1877.

ALLEN, J. A.—Monographs of the North American Rodentia. No. II. Leporidae. Rep. U. S. Geol. Surv. Terr. vol 11, pp. 265-377, 1877.

ALLEN, J. A.—Monographs of North American Rodentia. No. III. Hystricidae. Rep. U. S. Geol. Surv. Terr., vol. 11, pp. 385-398, 1877.

ALLEN, J. A.—Monographs of North American Rodentia. No. V. Castoroididae. Rep. U. S. Geol. Surv. Terr., vol. 11, pp. 419-426, 1877.

ALLEN, J. A.—Monographs of North American Rodentia, No. XI. Sciuridae. Rep. U. S. Geol. Surv. Terr., vol. 11, pp. 631-939, 1877.

ALLEN, J. A.—Notes on new or little known North American mammals, based on recent additions to the collection of mammals in the American Museum of Natural History. Bull. Amer. Mus. Nat. Hist., vol. 3, p. 290, 1891.

ALLEN, J. A.—On the mammals of Aransas County, Texas, with descriptions of new forms of Lepus and Oryzomys. Bull. Amer. Mus. Nat. Hist., vol. 6, p. 193, 1894.

ALLEN, J. A.—Revision of the chickarees or North American red squirrels, (subgenus Tamiasciurus.) Bull. Amer. Mus. Nat. Hist., vol. 10, p. 258, 1898.

ALLEN, J. A.—Ontogenetic and other variations in muskoxen, with a systematic review of the muskox group, recent and extinct. Mem. Amer. Mus. Nat. Hist. new ser. vol. 1, pt. 4, 1913.

ANONYMOUS.—Indiana Gazeteer or Topographical Dictionary of the State of Indiana. 1850, p. 14. Remarks on occurrence of various mammals.

ANONYMOUS.—An Illustrated Atlas of St. Joseph Co., Indiana. Higging Belden & Co., Chicago, 1875. P. 13, picture of apparently freshly killed deer.

ANONYMOUS.—History of St. Joseph County, Indiana. Chas. C. Chapman & Co., Chicago, 1880, p. 340. Partial list of living and exterminated mammals.

ANONYMOUS.—Fauna of LaPorte County. In History of LaPorte County, Indiana. Charles C. Chapman & Co., Chicago, 1880. Partial list of mammals.

ANONYMOUS.—Biographical and Historical Record of Putnam County, Indiana. The Lewis Publishing Company, Chicago, 1881, p. 195. Remarks on various mammals, living and exterminated.

ANONYMOUS.—American Field, vol. 18, p. 435, 1882 Dec. 23. Refers to abundance of foxes interfering with poultry raising, Bedford.

ANONYMOUS.—In Ball, T. H., Lake County, Indiana 1884. Refers to recent occurrence of deer.

ANONYMOUS.—History of Dearborn and Ohio Counties, Indiana. F. E. Weakley & Co., Chicago, 1885. Remarks on various conspicuous mammals.

ANONYMOUS.—History of Bartholomew County, Indiana. Brant & Fuller, Chicago, 1888, p. 378.

ANONYMOUS.—History of Steuben County, Indiana. Interstate Publishing Co., Chicago, 1888, p. 264. Remarks on various more conspicuous mammals.

ANONYMOUS.—Chicago and the West. Forest and Stream, vol. 39, p. 161, 1892 Aug. 25. Refers to fox shot while squirrel hunting, Landersdale [Morgan County].

ANONYMOUS.—Gray Squirrel migration. Forest and Stream, vol. 60, p. 205, 1903 March 14. Refers to squirrels swimming Ohio River.

ANONYMOUS.—American Field, vol. 61, p. 203, 1904 Feb. 27. Refers to lynx killed in Patoka bottoms, Gibson County.

ANONYMOUS.—Wild animals of Indiana. Indiana Mag. Hist. vol. 2, pp. 13-16, March 1906. Publishes records of 1859 by A. B. Cole of Noblesville, an agent who purchased of local trappers: 3,230 raccoon skins, 120 fox skins, 48 wild cat skins, 3 wolf skins, 1,130 deer skins, 1,126 mink skins, 1 cub bear skin, 1 fisher skin, 13 otter skins. Also additional notes.

ANONYMOUS.—Mastodon's bones in Indiana ditch. Forest and Stream, vol. 77, p. 141, 1911 July 22. Refers to Mastodon remains found eight miles northwest of Anderson, Madison County.

ANONYMOUS.—Driving for foxes. Forest and Stream, vol. 78, p. 468, 1912 Apr. 13. Describes drives for foxes north of Lafayette both in Tippecanoe and White Counties. Foxes numerous, 1200 men in a single drive.

ANONYMOUS.—History of Dekalb County, Indiana. B. F. Bowen & Company, Indianapolis, 1914. p. 45, remarks on various more conspicuous mammals.

ANONYMOUS.—Field Mus. Nat. Hist. Publ. 306. Report Series. vol 9, p. 131, 1932. Records jaw of Castoroides from Mount Ayr, Newton County.

*ANTHONY, H. E.—Field Book of North American Mammals. G. P. Putnam's Sons, New York-London 1928, pp. iii-xxv; 1- -625, plates I-XLVIII, figs. 1-150. Dr. Anthony has graciously given permission to quote portions of this book.

AUDUBON, JOHN JAMES AND JOHN BACHMAN.—The Viviparous Quadrupeds of North America. vol. 1, 1846, vol. 2, 1851, vol. 3, 1854. Also another edition with small bound in plates, entitled: The Quadrupeds of North America, vol 1, 1852, vol. 2, 1851, vol. 3, 1854.

AUDUBON, JOHN JAMES.—Delineations of American Scenery and Character. G. A

Baker & Company, New York, 1926. P. 102 mentions bear in cane brake in what is now Vanderburg County.

BAILEY, VERNON.—The Prairie Ground Squirrels or Spermophiles of the Mississippi Valley. U. S. Dept. Agric. Div. Onrithol. Mamm., Bull. No. 4, 1893.

BAILEY, VERNON.—Revision of American voles of the genus Microtus. North Amer. Fauna, No. 17, 1900 June 6.

*BAILEY, VERNON.—Mammals of the District of Columbia. Proc. Biol. Soc. Washington, vol. 36, pp. 103-138. 1923 May 1.

*BAILEY, VERNON.—Breeding, Feeding and Other Life Habits of Meadow Mice (Microtus). Journ. Agric. Research, vol. 27, no. 8, pp. 523-536, 1924.

*BAILEY, VERNON.—A Biological Survey of North Dakota. North American Fauna. No. 49, 1926.

BAILEY, VERNON.—Cave Life of Kentucky. Amer. Midland Nat., vol. 14, pp. 439-440, 1933 Sept.

*BAIRD, SPENCER F.—Mammals [of North America]. Rep. Explor. Surv. Railroad Mississippi Riv. to Pacific Ocean. vol. 8, pt. 1, pp. i-xxxii, 1-737, 43 pls., 1857.

BAKER, FRANK C.—The life of the Pleistocene, or Glacial Period. Univ. Illinois, Bull. 17, 1920 June 7. Numerous references to Indiana mammals, based on reports published elsewhere.

BALL, T.H.—Lake County, Indiana 1884, pp. 181-183, 1884. Remarks on abundance of fur bearing animals, muskrats and minks.

BALL, T. H.—Extinct fauna of Lake County. Proc. Indiana Acad. Sci., for 1894, pp. 54-57, 1895 Oct.

BALL, T. H.—Northwestern Indiana from 1800 to 1900, p. 448, 1900. Records Geomys pinctis (sic) as occurring in Newton and Jasper Counties.

BANGS, OUTRAM.—Synoptomys cooperi Baird in eastern Massachusetts; with notes on Synaptomys stonei Rhoads, especially as to the validity of this species. Proc. Biol. Soc. Wash., vol. 9, p. 101, 1894 Apr. 14.

BANGS, OUTRAM.—A review of the weasels of eastern North America. Proc. Biol. Soc. Washington, vol. 10, p. 13, 1896 Feb.

BANGS, OUTRAM.—A review of the squirrels of eastern North America. Proc. Biol. Soc. Washington, vol. 10, pp. 149-166, 1896 Dec. 28.

BANGS, OUTRAM.—A new race of Chickaree. Proc. New England Zool. Club. vol. 1, p. 28, 1899.

BANTA, ARTHUR M.—The Fauna of Mayfield's Cave, Carnegie Institution of Washington, Pub. No. 67, pp. 17-21, 1907 Sept.

BANTA, D. D.—History of Johnson County, Brant & Fuller, Chicago, 1888, pp. 326-360.

BARTLETT, CHARLES H.—Tales of Kankakee Land. Charles Scribner's Sons, New York, 1904.

BATTLE, J. H.—Counties of Warren, Benton, Jasper and Newton, Indiana. F. A. Battey & Co., Chicago, 1883.

BECKWITH, H. W.—History of Montgomery County. Chicago. H. H. Hill and N. Iddings, 1881.

BENTON, ROBERT.—Legends of Lost River [Kankakee] Valley as Related by Joseph Pontus. Champlin & Carlisle, Chicago, 1903.

BIGNEY, A. J.—Preliminary notes on the geology of Dearborn County. Proc. Indiana Acad. Sci., for 1891, pp. 66-67, 1892.

BINFORD, J. H.—History of Hancock County, Indiana, from its earliest settlement by the "pale face" in 1818 down to 1882. King and Binford. Greenfield, Indiana, 1882.

BIRKBECK, MORRIS.—Notes on a Journey in America from the Coast of Virginia to the Territory of Illinois. Ed. 2, p. 147. James Ridgway, London, 1818.

BLAINVILLE, H. M. DUCROTAY DE.—Ostéographie de Mammifères. vol. 3, p. 340, 1839-1864.

BLATCHLEY, W. S.—Indiana caves and their fauna. 21st Ann. Rep. Dep. Geol. Nat. Res. Indiana, 1896, pp. 121-212, 1897.

BLATCHLEY, W. S.—Notes on the fauna of Lake and Porter Counties. Indiana Dep. Geol. Nat. Res. 22nd Ann. Rep., 1897, pp. 89-91, 1898.

BLATCHLEY, W. S.—Gleanings from Nature. The Nature Publishing Company, Indianapolis, 1898.

BLATCHLEY, W. S.—The life zones of Indiana as illustrated by the distribution of Orthoptera and Coleoptera within the state. Proc. Indiana Acad. Sci., for 1908, pp. 185-191, 1909.

*BLOSSOM, PHILIP M.—A pair of long-tailed shrews (Sorex cinereus cinereus) in captivity. Journ. Mamm., vol. 13, pp. 136-143, 1932 May.

BOLTON, FRANCIS D. IN CHARLES C. DEAM.—Grasses of Indiana. State of Indiana Department of Conservation. Pub. 82, pp. 33-34, 1929.

BORDEN, WM. W.—Report of a geological survey of Clarke and Floyd Counties, Indiana. 5th Ann. Rep. Geol. Surv. Indiana, 1873, p. 176, 1874.

BRADLEY, FRANK H.—Geology of Kankakee and Iroquois Counties. Geol. Surv Illinois, vol. 4, p. 229, 1870.

BRADSBY, H. C.—History of Vigo County, Indiana. S. B. Nelson & Co., Chicago, 1891, p. 46.

BRAYTON, A. W.—Report on the mammals of Ohio. Rep. Geol. Surv. Ohio, vol. 4, pt. 1, pp. 3-185, 1882. Of this book, Dr. Stanley Coulter, in letter, 1929, writes, "Some 30 or 40 years ago, the late Dr. A. W. Brayton prepared a monograph on the mammals of Indiana. The Department of Geology thought it too extended to print. Dr. Brayton then substituted Ohio for Indiana on the title page and it was printed by the Ohio Department of Geology." This is a very complete work, with full lists of synomyms, descriptions, habits, etc. Dr. Brayton, however, did much more than change the title page, as he frequently mentions Ohio specimens by museum catalogue numbers and otherwise gives Ohio records. It contains several Indiana records.

BRENNAN, GEORGE A.—The Wonders of the Dunes. The Bobbs-Merrill Company. Indianapolis, pp. 242-262, 1923. Chapter 19, pp. 242-262 is devoted to the present and former mammals of the dunes region of northern Indiana.

BROWN, SAMUEL R.—The Western Gazeteer or Emigrant's Directory. H. C. Southwick, Auburn, N. Y. 1817, pp. 48, 78.

BUTLER, A. W.—Local weather lore. Amer. Meteorl. Journ., vol. 1, pp. 313-317, 1884 Dec.

BUTLER, AMOS W.—Observations on the muskrat. Amer. Nat., vol. 19, pp. 1044-1055, 1885 Nov.

BUTLER, AMOS W.—The Muskrat. Amer. Field, vol. 24, p. 513, 1885 Nov. 28., cont'd. p. 537, 1885 Dec. 5.

BUTLER, AMOS W.—Observations on faunal changes. Bull. Brookville Soc. Nat. Hist. No. 1, pp. 5-10, 1885.

BUTLER, AMOS W.—Mammals. Journ. Soc. Nat. Hist. Cincinnati, vol. 9, p. 261, 1886 Jan.

BUTLER, AMOS W.—The common meadow-mouse. Indiana Farmer, 1886 Jan. 9, p. 9.

BUTLER, AMOS W.—Some more mice. Indiana Farmer, 1886 March 6, p. 3.

BUTLER, AMOS W.—Meadow mice in southeastern Indiana. The Hoosier Naturalist, vol. 1, pp. 144-145, 1886 April and May.

BUTLER, AMOS W.—The periodical Cicada in southeastern Indiana. U. S. Dep. Agric. Div. Entomol. Bull. 12, pp. 24-31, 1886.

BUTLER, AMOS W.—Observations on the Muskrat. Proc. Amer. Ass. Adv. Sci., vol. 34, pp. 324-328, 1886.

BUTLER, AMOS W.—Zoological miscellany. Journ. Soc. Nat. Hist., Cincinnati, vol. 10, pt. 4, p. 214, 1888 Jan.

BUTLER, A. W.—Our smaller mammals and their relation to horticulture. Trans. Indiana Hort. Soc., for 1891, Rep. of 31st ann. meet., pp. 117-123, 1892.

BUTLER, A. W.—On Indiana shrews. Proc. Indiana Acad. Sci., for 1891, pp. 161-

BUTLER, AMOS.—[Blarina parva in Indiana]. Amer. Nat., vol. 27, p. 573, 1893 June.

BUTLER, A. W.—The mammals of Indiana. Proc. Indiana Acad. Sci., for 1894, pp. 81-86, 1895 Oct.

BUTLER, AMOS W.—Wild and domesticated Elk in the early days of Franklin County, Indiana. Journ. Mamm., vol. 15, pp. 246-248, 1934 August.

CAHN, ALVIN R.—Records and distribution of the fossil Beaver, Castoroides ohioensis. Journ. Mamm., vol. 13, pp. 225-241, 1932 Aug.

*CABRERA, ANGEL.—Manual de Mastozoologia. "Calpe," Madrid, 1922, 440 pages, 176 text figures, 10 plates. Excellent small handbook of Mammalogy.

CHARLEVOIX, FATHER [Pierre Francois Xavier de].—Letters to the Duchess of Lesdiguieres; giving an account of a voyage [1721] to Canada and travels through that vast country and Louisiana to the Gulf of Mexico. Printed for R. Goadby, London, 1763. English Translation. Page 281, a description of the Theakiki [Kankakee].

CLINE AND MCHAFFIE.—The Peoples Guide. etc., also a Historical Sketch of Hendricks County. Indianapolis, 1874, p. 134.

CLINE AND MCHAFFIE.—The Peoples Guide . . . also a Historical Sketch of Johnson County, Indianapolis, 1874, p. 137.

COCKERELL, T. D. A., LEWIS I. MILLER AND MORRIS PRENTZ.—Bull. Amer. Mus. Nat. Hist., vol. 33, p. 355, p. 361, 1914.

COLLETT, JOHN.—Geology of Dubois County, Indiana. Third and Fourth Ann. Reps. Geol. Surv. Indiana, 1871-1872, p. 214, 1872.
163, 1892.

COLLETT, JOHN.—Geological report on Vanderburg, Owen and Montgomery Counties, Indiana. 7th Ann. Rep. Geol. Surv. Indiana, 1875, p. 245, 1876.

[COLLETT, JOHN].—The Mammoth and Mastodon. Remains in Indiana and Illinois. State of Indiana, Second Ann. Rep. Dept. Statistics Geol., 1880, pp. 384-386, [1881].

[COLLETT, JOHN].—List of fossils found at Porter's Quarry, one and one-fourth miles west of Rensselaer on the south side of the Iroquois River. Indiana Dept. Geol. Nat. Hist. 12th Ann. Rep., 1882, p. 73, 1883.

COLLETT, J. in E. D. Cope and J. Wortman.—Post-Pliocene Vertebrates of Indiana. Indiana Dept. Geol. Nat. Hist. 14th Ann. Rep., 1884, p. 24, footnote, 1885.

COLLETT, JOHN,—Bats in Wyandotte Cave, Indiana. Amer. Nat., vol. 24, p. 189, 1890.

COPE, E. D.—Observations on Wyandotte Cave and its fauna. Amer. Nat., vol. 6, pp. 406-422, 1872 July.

COPE, E. D.—Report on the Wyandotte Cave and its fauna. Third and Fourth Ann. Repts. Geol. Surv. Indiana 1871 and 1872, [1873].

COPE, E. D.—A new Deer from Indiana. Amer. Nat., vol. 12, p. 189, 1878 March.

COPE, E. D.—Descriptions of new extinct Vertebrata from the Upper Tertiary and Dakota formations. Bull. U. S. Geol. Geogr. Surv. Terr., vol. 4, p. 379, 1878.

COPE, E. D.—The Artiodactyla. Amer. Nat., vol. 22, p. 1089, 1888.

COPE, E. D.—The Artiodactyla. Amer. Nat. vol. 23, p. 134, 1889 Feb.

COPE, E. D. AND JACOB L. WORTMAN.—Post-pliocene vertebrates of Indiana. Indiana Dept. Geol. Nat. Hist. 14th Ann. Rep. 1884, pt. 2, pp. 4-62, 6 pls. [1885].

CORY, CHARLES B.—The Mammals of Illinois and Wisconsin. Field Mus. Nat. Hist., pub. 153, Zool. Ser. vol. 11, pp. 1-505, Maps 71. Numerous unnumbered plates and text figures, 1912. The maps show the distribution of the various species of mammals occurring in Illinois and Wisconsin, and neighboring states. In many instances Indiana specimens are included under the heading "Specimens examined." Nearly every Indiana-occurring species is mentioned in lists of synonyms; many comments are made about Indiana records, and several quotations of letters from E. J. Chansler regarding old time mammals are given.

COUES, ELLIOTT.—Fur-bearing animals: A monograph of North American Mustelidae. U. S. Geol. Surv. Terr. Misc. Pub. No. 8, pp. 1-348, pls. 1-20, 1877.

COUES, ELLIOTT.—Monographs of North American Rodentia. No. I. Muridae. Rep. U. S. Geol. Surv. Terr., vol. 11, pp. 1-264, 5 pls. 1877.

COX, E. T.—Martin County. Second Rep. Geol. Surv. Indiana, 1870, p. 103, 1871.

COX, E. T.—Jackson County. Sixth Ann. Rep. Geol. Surv. Indiana, 1874, p. 59, 1875.

COX, SANFORD C.—Recollections of the early settlement of the Wabash Valley. Lafayette, 1860.

COX, ULYSSES O.—A list of the birds of Randolph County, Ind. with some notes on the mammals of the same county. Ornithol. and Ool., vol. 18, pp. 2-3, 1893 Jan.

CRAIG, OSCAR J.—Ouiatanon. A study in Indiana history. Indiana Hist. Soc. Pubs., vol. 2, p. 329, 1893.

CROGHAN, COL. GEORGE.—The Journal [1765] of Col. Croghan.—Mo. Amer. Journ.

Geol. Nat. Sci., vol. 1, p. 264, 1831 Dec. Also in A History of the Common-wealth of Kentucky by Mann Butler, A. M. Wilcox, Dickerman and Co., Louisville, Ky. 1834. Also in Olden Time, vol. 1, 1846. Also separately printed as Journal of George Croghan [Burlington, N. J. Enterprise Book and Job Printing Establishment, 1875.]

*DEARBORN, NED—Foods of some predatory fur-bearing animals in Michigan. Univ. Michigan School of Forestry and Conservation. Bull. No. 1, pp. 1-52, 1932. Foods of following mammals given: Opossum, raccoon, red fox, coyote, wild cat, mink, weasel, skunk, and badger.

DICE, LEE RAYMOND.—The mammals of Warren Woods, Berrien Co., Michigan. Occ. Papers Mus. Zool. Univ. Michigan, No. 86, pp. 1-20, 2 pls. 1920 June 24. An ecological study of the mammals of a locality three miles north of the Indiana-Michigan line.

DICE, L. R.—The Least Weasel in Indiana. Journ. Mamm., vol. 9, p. 63, 1928 Feb. 9.

DINWIDDIE, EDWIN W.—The fauna of Lake County. In Ball, T. H. Lake County, Indiana 1884, pp. 151-152, 1884.

*DOWNING, ELLIOTT ROWLAND.—A naturalist in the Great Lakes region. The University of Chicago Press, Chicago, 1922.

DRYER, CHARLES R.—Report upon the geology of Allen County, Indiana Dept. Geol. Nat. Res. 16th Ann. Rep. 1888, p. 129, 1889.

DURY, CHAS.—North American Sciuridae or squirrels. Journ. Cincinnati Soc. Nat. Hist. vol. 12, p. 67, 1889-1890.

DUVERNOY.—Notices pour servir a la monographie du genre Musaraigne (Sorex, Cuv.) 1re partie, comprenant l'histoire naturelle systematique ou classique du genre et des quinze espèces figurés dans ces notices. Comptes Rendus, vol. 15, p. 10, 1842.

DUVERNOY, M.—Notices pour servir à la monographie du genre Musaraigne. Sorex. Cuv. Mag. de Zool., ser. 2, vol. 4, pp. 1-48, 1842.

EDWARDS, J. JEP.—Paleontology of Bartholomew County, Indiana, Mammalian Fossils. Proc. Indiana Acad. Sci., for 1901, pp. 247-248, 1902.

ELLIOT, DANIEL GIRAUD.—A catalogue of the mammals in the Field Columbian Museum. Field Columbian Mus. Publ. 115, zool. ser., vol. 8, 1907.

ELROD, MOSES N. AND A. C. BENEDICT.—Geology of Wabash County: Fossil bones of the drift. 17th Ann. Rep. Indiana Dept. Geol. Nat. Res., pp. 240-241, 1892.

*ENDERS, ROBERT KENDALL.—Some factors influencing the distribution of mammals in Ohio. Occ. Papers Mus. Zool. Univ. Michigan, No. 212, p. 7, April 23, 1930.

ENGELS, WILLIAM L.—Long-tailed Shrews in northern Indiana. Journ. Mamm., vol. 12, p. 312 1931 Aug.

ENGELS, WILLIAM L.—Two new records of the Pleistocene beaver, Castoroides ohioensis. Amer. Midland Nat., vol. 12, pp. 529-531, 1 pl., 1931 Nov.

ENGELS, WILLIAM L.—A probable second record of the extinct deer, Odocoileus dolichopsis (Cope). Amer. Midland Nat., vol. 13, pp. 12-15, 1 pl., 1932 Jan.

ENGELS, WILLIAM L.—Notes on the mammals of St. Joseph County, Indiana. Amer. Midland Nat., vol. 14, pp. 1-16, 1933 Jan.

EVERMANN, B. W.—The occurrence in Indiana of the Star-nosed Mole (Condylura cristata L.). Amer. Nat., vol. 22, p. 359, 1888 April.

EVERMANN, BARTON WARREN.—A century of zoology in Indiana, 1816-1916. Proc. Indiana Acad. Sci., for 1916, pp. 189-207, 1917.

EVERMANN, B. W. AND A. W. BUTLER.—Bibliography of Indiana Mammals. Proc. Indiana Acad. Sci., for 1893, pp. 120-124, 1894 Aug.

[EVERMANN, B. W. AND A. W. BUTLER].—Preliminary list of Indiana mammals. Proc. Indiana Acad. Sci., for 1893, pp. 124-139, 1894 Aug.

EVERMANN, BARTON WARREN AND HOWARD WALTON CLARK.—Notes on the mammals of the Lake Maxinkuckee region. Proc. Washington Acad. Sci., vol. 13, pp. 1-34, 1911 Feb. 15.

EVERMANN, BARTON WARREN AND HOWARD WALTON CLARK.—Lake Maxinkuckee. A Physical and Biological Survey. Indiana Department of Conservation. Pub. No. 7., vol. 1, pp. 452-480, 1920.

*FISHER, A. K.—The economic value of predaceous birds and mammals. Yearbook U. S. Dept. Agric. 1908, pp. 187-194.

FORKNER, JOHN L. AND BYRON H. DYSON.—Historical Sketches and Reminiscences of Madison County, Indiana. Anderson, Indiana, 1897, pp. 8-9.

GANTZ, R. A.—Finds of the American Mastodon (Mammut americanum) in Delaware County, Indiana. Proc. Acad. Sci. Indiana, vol. 34, p. 393, 1925.

GIDLEY, JAMES WILLIAMS.—Pleistocene peccaries from the Cumberland Cave deposit. Proc. U. S. Nat. Mus., vol. 57, p. 674, 1920.

GILBERT, FRANK M.—History of the City of Evansville and Vanderburg County, Indiana. The Pioneer Publishing Company, Chicago, 1910, vol. 1, pp. 13-15.

GOODSPEED, WESTON A.—History of Brown County in Counties of Morgan, Monroe and Brown, Indiana. F. A. Battey & Co., Chicago, Charles Blanchard, Editor, 1884, p. 723.

GOODSPEED, WESTON A.—History of Monroe County in loc. cit. supra, p. 501.

GOODSPEED, WESTON A.—Counties of Warren, Benton, Jasper and Newton, Indiana. F. A. Battey & Co., Chicago, 1883, p. 46.

*GUTHRIE, MARY J.—The reproductive cycles of some cave bats. Journ. Mamm., vol. 14, pp. 199-216, 1933 August.

HAHN, WALTER L.—The mammalian remains of the Donaldson Cave [3 miles southeast of Mitchell]. Proc. Indiana Acad. Sci., for 1906, pp. 142-144, 1907.

HAHN, WALTER L.—Notes on the mammals of the Kankakee Valley. Proc. U. S. Nat. Mus., vol. 32, pp. 455-464, 1907 June 15.

HAHN, WALTER LOUIS.—Some habits and sensory adaptations of cave-inhabiting bats. Biol. Bull., vol. 15, pp. 135-193, 1908.

HAHN, WALTER L.—Notes on the mammals and cold-blooded vertebrates of the Indiana University Farm, Mitchell, Indiana. Proc U. S. Nat. Mus., vol. 35, pp. 545-581, 1908 Dec. 7.

HAHN, WALTER LOUIS.—The mammals of Indiana. 33rd Ann. Rep. Dep. Geol. Nat. Res. Indiana, pp. 419- 654, 1909. An annotated and descriptive list of the living and exterminated mammals of Indiana.

HAHN, WALTER L.—An analytic study of Faunal changes in Indiana. Amer. Midland Nat., vol. 1, pp. 145-156 and 171-186, 1910.

*HAHN, W. L.—Hibernation of certain animals. Pop. Sci. Mo., vol. 84, pp. 147-157, 1914 Feb.

*HAMILTON, WILLIAM JOHN, JR.—Habits of the Star-nosed Mole, Condylura cristata. Journ. Mamm., vol. 12, pp. 345-355, 1921 Nov.

*HAMILTON, WILLIAM J., JR.—Breeding Habits of the Short-tailed Shrew. Journ. Mamm., vol. 10, pp. 125-134, plates 10-12, 1929 May.

*HAMILTON, W. J., JR.—The food of the Soricidae. Journ. Mamm., vol. 11, pp. 26-39, 1930 Feb.

*HAMILTON, W. J., JR.—The insect food of the Big Brown Bat. Journ. Mamm., vol. 14, pp. 155-156, 1933 May.

HAMILTON, W. J., JR.—The Weasels of New York. Their natural history and economic status. Amer. Midland Nat., vol. 14, pp. 289-344, figs. 1-3, pls. 6-9, 1933 July.

*HAMILTON, W. J., JR.—The life history of the rufescent woodchuck, Marmota monax rufescens Howell. Ann. Carnegie Mus., vol. 23, pp. 85-178, pls. 15-19, figs. 1-8, 1934 July.

*HAMILTON, W. J., JR.—Habits of Jumping Mice. Amer. Midland Nat., vol 16, no. 2, pp. 187-200, 1935 March [Feb. 21].

HAMPTON, O. H.—The ways of gray squirrels. Forest and Stream, vol. 67, p. 860, 1906 Dec. 1.

HARDEN, FRANKLIN.—Through Johnson County fifty-five years ago[i. e. 1826]. In Banta, D. D. A Historical Sketch of Johnson County. J. H. Beers & Co., Chicago, 1881, Chap. 8.

HARRISON, THOMAS AND P. F. HICKIE.—Indiana's Swamp Rabbit. Journ. Mamm., vol. 12, pp. 319-320, 1931 Aug.

*HARTMAN, CARL G.—Studies in the development of the opossum (Didelphys virginiana). Anat. Record, vol. 19, pp. 251-261, 1920 Oct.

*HARTMAN, CARL G.—A brown mutation of the opossum (Didelphis virginiana) with remarks upon the gray and the black phases in this species. Journ. Mamm., vol. 3, pp. 146-149, 1922 August.

*HARTMAN, CARL G.—Breeding habits, development and birth of the opossum. Ann. Rep. Smiths. Inst. for 1921. 1923.

*HARTMAN, CARL G.—The breeding season of the opossum (Didelphis virginiana) and the rate of intrauterine and postnatal development. Journ. Morph. and Physiol., vol. 46, pp. 143-211, pls. 1-3, figs. A-H. 1928.

*HARTMAN, CARL G.—On the survival of spermatozoa in the female genital tract of the bat. Quart. Rev. Biol. vol. 8, no. 2, pp. 185-193, 1933 June.

*HATT, ROBERT T.—The Red Squirrel. Bull. New York State Coll. Forestry, Roosevelt Wild Life Annals, vol. 2, no. 1, pp. 11-146, March 1929.

*HATT, ROBERT T.—The Voles of New York. Bull. New York State Coll. Forestry, Roosevelt Wild Life Bull., vol. 5, no. 4, 1930.

HATT, ROBERT T.—Identity of Hesperomys indianus Wied. Journ. Mamm., vol. 11, pp. 317-318, 1930 Aug.

HAY, OLIVER PERRY.—Bibliography and Catalogue of the Fossil Vertebrata of North America. Bull. U. S. Geol. Surv., No. 179, 1902.

HAY, OLIVER P.—The recognition of Pleistocene faunas. Smiths. Misc. Coll., vol. 59, No. 20, pp. 1-16, 1912.

HAY, OLIVER P.—The Pleistocene Period and its Vertebrata. 36th Ann. Rep. Dept. Geol. Nat. Res. Indiana, 1911, pp. 541-784, 1912.

HAY, OLIVER P.—The extinct Bisons of North America; with description of one new species, Bison regius. Proc. U. S. Nat. Mus., vol. 46, pp. 161-200, 19 pls. 1913 Dec. 6.

HAY, OLIVER P.—The Pleistocene mammals of Iowa. Iowa Geol. Surv., vol. 23, pp. 1-662, 75 pls., 1914. Contains many references to Indiana mammals.

HAY, OLIVER P.—The Pleistocene of North America and its vertebrated animals from the states east of the Mississippi River and from the Canadian provinces east of longitude 95°. Carnegie Institution of Washington, Pub. No. 322, pp. i-viii, 1-499, 1923 Feb. 24.

HAY, OLIVER P.—A further and detailed description of Elephas roosevelti Hay and description of three referred specimens. Proc. U. S. Nat. Mus., vol. 66, No. 34, pp. 1-5, 4 pls., 1925.

*HAY, OLIVER PERRY.—Second bibliography and Catalogue of the fossil Vertebrata of North America. Carnegie Inst. Washington, Pub. No. 390, vols. 1-2, 1930.

HAYMOND, RUFUS.—Notice of remains of Megatherium, Mastodon and Silurian fossils. Amer. Journ. Sci., vol. 46, p. 294, 1843-1844.

HAYMOND, RUFUS.—Geology of Franklin County. First Ann. Rep. Geol. Surv. Indiana, 1869, pp. 199-200 [1870].

HAYMOND, RUFUS.—Mammals found at the present time in Franklin County, Indiana. First Ann. Rep. Geol. Surv. Indiana, 1869, pp. 203-208 [1870].

[HELM, THOMAS B.].—History of Delaware County, Indiana. Kingman Brothers, Chicago, 1881.

*HENDERSON. JUNIUS AND ELBERTA L. CRAIG.—Economic Mammalogy. Charles C. Thomas, Springfield and Baltimore, 1932, pp. i-x and 1-397.

HENNEPIN, FATHER LOUIS, 1683.—A Description of Louisiana. Translated by John Gilmay Shea, 1880. Pp. 129-150. Includes an account of the voyage up the St. Joseph River and the portage [at South Bend] to the Kankakee.

HENNINGER, W. F.—Two mammals new for Ohio. Journ. Mamm., vol. 2, p. 239, 1921 November.

HENNINGER, W. F.—On the status of Mustela allegheniensis. Journ. Mamm., vol. 4, p. 121, 1923 May 9.

HICKIE, P. F. AND THOMAS HARRISON.—The Alleghany wood rat in Indiana. Amer. Midland Nat., vol. 12, pp. 169-174, 1 pl., 1930 Nov. [3].

*HISAW, FREDERICK L.—Feeding Habits of Moles. Journ. Mamm., vol. 4, pp. 9-20, 1923 Feb.

*HISAW, FREDERICK L.—Observations on the burrowing habits of moles (Scalopus aquaticus machrinoides.) Journ. Mamm., vol. 4, pp. 79-88, 1923 May.

*HISAW, FREDERICK L.—The influence of the ovary on the resorption of the pubic bones of the pocket gopher, Geomys bursarius (Shaw). Journ. Exp. Zool., vol. 42, 411-441, pls. 1-4, 1925 Oct.

*HISAW, FREDERICK L. AND MARION L. ZILLEY.—A study of the pelvic girdle of

20-mm. embryos of the mole, Scalopus aquaticus machrinus (Raf.) Journ. Mamm., vol. 8, pp. 115-118, figs 1-3, 1927 May.

HOLLAND, J. W.—The hyoid bone in Mastodon americanus. Ann. Carnegie Mus., vol. 3, pp. 464-467, figs. 1-5, 1905. Very complete mounted skeleton in Carnegie Museum from Waterloo, Dekalb Co.

HOLLISTER, N.—Remarks on the long-tailed shrews of the easte.n United States with description of a new species. Proc. U. S. Nat. Mus., vol. 40, pp. 377-380, 1911 Apr. 17.

HOLLISTER, N.—A systematic synopsis of the Muskrats. North Amer. Fauna, No. 32, 1911 Apr. 29.

HORNADAY, WILLIAM T.—The extermination of the American Bison. Rep. U. S. Nat. Mus., 1886-1887, pp. 369-548, 22 pls., map. 1889.

HOWARD, TIMOTHY EDWARD.—A History of St. Joseph County, Indiana. Lewis Publishing Company, Chicago, 1907, vol. 1, p. 44.

HOWELL, A. BRAZIER.—Revision of the American Lemming Mice. North Amer. Fauna, No. 50, 1927 June 30.

HOWELL, ARTHUR H.—Revision of the skunks of the genus Chincha. North Amer. Fauna, No. 20, 1901 Aug. 31.

HOWELL, ARTHUR H.—Description of a new bat from Nickajack Cave, Tennessee. Proc. Biol. Soc. Washington, vol. 22, p. 46, 1909 Mar. 10.

HOWELL, ARTHUR H.—Notes on the distribution of certain mammals in the southeastern United States. Proc. Biol. Soc. Washington, vol. 22, p. 66, 1909 Apr. 17.

HOWELL, ARTHUR H.—Notes on the mammals of the middle Mississippi Valley, with description of a new Woodrat. Proc. Biol. Soc. Washington, vol. 22, pp. 23-34, 1910 March 23.

HOWELL, ARTHUR H.—Notes on the Skunks of Indiana, with a correction. Proc. Biol. Soc. Washington, vol. 27, p. 100, 1914 May 11.

HOWELL, ARTHUR H.—Revision of the American Marmots. North Amer. Fauna, No. 37, 1915 April 7.

HOWELL, ARTHUR H.—Revision of the American Flying Squirrels. North Amer. Fauna, No. 44, 1918 June 13.

HOWELL, ARTHUR H.—Revision of the American Chipmunks. North Amer. Fauna, No. 52, 1929 Nov.

HOWELL, ARTHUR H.—Notes on range of the Eastern Chipmunk in Ohio, Indiana, and Quebec. Journ. Mamm., vol. 13, pp. 166-167, 1932 May.

HUTCHINS, THOMAS.—A Topographical Description of Virginia, Pennsylvania, and North Carolina, comprehending the Rivers Ohio, Kanawha, Scioto, Cherokee, Wabash, Illinois, Mississippi, etc. London, 1778.

JACKSON, HARTLEY H. T.—A review of the American Moles. North Amer. Fauna, No. 38, 1915 Sept. 30.

JACKSON, HARTLEY H. T.—The Georgian bat, Pipistrellus subflavus, in Wisconsin. Journ. Mamm., vol. 1, p. 38, 1919 Nov. 28. Records a specimen from Sauk County, Wisconsin. The occurrence of this species as far north as Wisconsin would indicate that it is found throughout the entire state of Indiana.

JACKSON, HARTLEY H. T.—A taxonomic review of the American Long-tailed Shrews. North Amer. Fauna, No. 51, 1928 July.

*JOHNSON, CHARLES EUGENE.—The Beaver in the Adirondacks: Its economics and natural history. Roosevelt Wild Life Bull., vol. 4, no. 4, pp. 501-641, figs. 87-127, 1927 July.

*JOHNSON, CHARLES E.—The Muskrat in New York: Its natural history and economics. Roosevelt Wild Life Bull., vol. 3, no. 2, pp. 205-320, pls. 5, figs. 48-87, 1925 March.

*JOHNSON, GEORGE E.—The Habits of the Thirteen-lined Ground Squirrel. Quart. Journ. Univ. North Dakota, vol. 7, no. 3, 1917 April.

*JOHNSON, GEORGE EDWIN.—Hibernation of the thirteen-lined ground-squirrel, Citellus tridecemlineatus (Mitchell). Journ. Exp. Zool., vol. 50, pp. 15-30, 1928 Jan. 5.

KENNICOTT, ROBERT.—Catalogue of animals observed in Cook County, Illinois. Trans. Illinois State Agric. Soc., vol. 1, 1853-54, pp. 577-580, 1855.

KENNICOTT, ROBERT.—The quardupeds of Illinois injurious and beneficial to the farmer. U. S. Pat. Off. Rep. Agric., 1856, pp. 52-110, 1857.

KENNICOTT, ROBERT.—The quadrupeds of Illinois injurious and beneficial to the farmer. U. S. Pat. Off. Rep. Agric., 1857, pp. 72-107, 1858.

KENNICOTT, ROBERT.—The quadrupeds of Illinois injurious and beneficial to the farmer. U. S. Pat. Off. Rep. Agric., 1858, pp 241-256, 1859.

KINDLE, EDWARD M.—A catalogue of the fossils of Indiana, accompanied by a bibliography of the literature relating to them. Indiana Dept. Geol. Nat. Res. 22nd. Ann. Rep., 1897, p. 485, 1898.

KINTNER, EDWARD.—Notes on unearthing parts of a mastodon skeleton. Proc. Indiana Acad. Sci., vol. 39, pp. 237-239. 1930 [Oct.].

*KLUGH, A. BROOKER.—Notes on Eptesicus fuscus. Journ. Mamm., vol. 5, pp. 42-43. 1924 Feb.

*KLUGH, A. BROOKER.—Ecology of the Red Squirrel. Journ. Mamm., vol. 8, pp. 1-32, pls. 1-5, 1927.

KOMAREK, E. V. AND DON A. SPENCER.—A new pocket gopher from Illinois and Indiana. Journ. Mamm., vol. 12, pp. 404-408, 1 fig., 1 pl., 1931 Nov.

LAHONTAN, BARON.—New Voyages to North America [1687]. English ed. vol. 1, p. 217, 1735.

LANGDON, FRANK W.—The Mammalia of the vicinity of Cincinnati. Journ. Cincinnati Soc. Nat. Hist., vol. 3, pp. 297-313, 1881 Jan.

LANGDON, F. W.—Zoological miscellany. Mammalogy. Journ. Cincinnati Soc. Nat. Hist., vol. 4, pp. 336-337, 1881 Dec.

LANGDON, F. W.—Department of zoological miscellany. Journ. Cincinnati Soc. Nat. Hist., vol. 9, pp. 261-262, 1886 [1887].

LAZENBY, JOHN C.—Jackson County prior to 1850. Indiana Mag. Hist., vol. 10, No. 3, p. 257, 1914 Sept.

LECONTE, JOHN L.—Notice of five new species of fossil Mammalia from Illinois. Amer. Journ. Sci., ser. 2, vol. 5, pp. 102-106, 1848.

LEIDY, JOSEPH.—Notice of some fossil bones discovered by Mr. Francis A. Lincke, in the banks of the Ohio River, Indiana. Proc. Acad. Nat. Sci. Philadelphia, vol. 7, pp. 199-201, 1854-1855.

LEIDY, JOSEPH.—Description of some remains of extinct Mammalia. Journ. Acad. Nat. Sci. Philadelphia, new ser., vol. 3, pp. 167-168, pl. 17, 1856.

LEIDY, JOSEPH.—Notice of remains of extinct Vertebrata from the Valley of the Niobrara River, collected during the Exploring Expedition in 1857 in Nebraska under the command of Lieut. G. K. Warren, U. S. Top. Eng., by F. V. Hayden, geologist to the expedition. Proc. Acad. Nat. Sci. Philadelphia, 1858, p. 21, 1858.

LEIDY, JOSEPH.—Description of vertebrate fossils. In Holmes' Post-pliocene Fossils of South Carolina, pp. 99-122, 1860.

LEIDY, [JOSEPH].—No title. Proc. Acad. Nat. Sci. Philadelphia, 1860, p. 416. Dr. Leidy "exhibited fore part of the skull of another extinct Peccary."

LEIDY, JOSEPH.—Notice of some remains of extinct pachyderms. Proc. Acad. Nat. Sci. Philadelphia, 1868, No. 4, pp. 230-231, 1868 Sept. and Oct.

LEIDY, JOSEPH.—The extinct mammalian fauna of Dakota and Nebraska, including an account of some allied forms from other localities, together with a synopsis of the mammalian remains of North America. Journ. Acad. Nat. Sci. Philadelphia, vol. 7, pp. 28-472, 30 pls. 1869.

LEIDY, JOSEPH.—Fossil Vertebrates. Rep. U. S. Geol. Surv. Terr., vol. 1, pp. 230, 315, 1873.

LYDEKKER, RICHARD.—Cat. Foss. Mamm., Brit. Mus., vol. 4, p. 17, 1886.

LYON. M. W., JR.—A stray coati in Indiana. Journ. Mamm., vol. 4, pp. 184-185, 1923 Aug. 10.

LYON, MARCUS WARD, JR.—Notes on the mammals of the dune region of Porter County Indiana. Proc. Indiana Acad. Sci., for 1922, pp. 209-221, 1923.

LYON, MARCUS WARD, JR.—New records of Indiana mammals. Proc. Indiana Acad. Sci., vol. 33, pp. 284-285, 1924.

LYON, MARCUS WARD, JR.—New record of the Small Short-tailed Shrew in Indiana. Proc. Indiana Acad. Sci., vol. 34, p. 391, 1925.

LYON, MARCUS WARD, JR.—A specimen of the extinct musk-ox, Symbos cavifrons (Leidy) from North Liberty, Indiana. Proc. Indiana Acad. Sci., vol. 35, pp. 321-324, 1 fig., 1926.

LYON, MARCUS WARD, JR.—A pile of Microtus. Journ. Mamm., vol. 11, p. 320, 1930 Aug.

LYON, MARCUS WARD, JR.—A pair of Elk antlers from St. Joseph County, Indiana. Amer. Midland Nat., vol. 12, pp. 213-216, 1 fig., 1931 Jan.

LYON, MARCUS WARD, JR.—A small collection of Pleistocene mammals from Laporte County, Indiana. Amer. Midland Nat., vol. 12, pp. 406-410, 1 pl., 1931 July.

LYON, MARCUS WARD, JR.—Bat oil for rheumatism. Journ. Mamm., vol. 12, p. 313, 1931 Aug.

LYON, MARCUS WARD, JR.—Franklin's Ground Squirrel and its distribution in Indiana. Amer. Midland Nat., vol. 13, pp. 16-20, 1 map, 1 pl., 1932 Jan.

Lyon, Marcus Ward, Jr.—Remarks on *Geomys bursarius illinoensis* Komarek and Spencer. Journ. Mamm., vol. 13, pp. 77-78, 1932 Feb.

Lyon, Marcus Ward, Jr.—The badger, Taxidea taxus (Schreber), in Indiana. Amer. Midland Nat., vol. 13, pp. 124-129, 1 pl., 1 map, 1932 May.

Lyon, Marcus Ward, Jr.—Two new records of the Least Weasel in Indiana. Amer. Midland Nat., vol. 14, pp. 345-349, figs. 1-2, 1933 July.

Lyon, Marcus Ward, Jr.—Origins of Indiana's Mammals. Proc. Indiana Acad. Sci., vol. 43, pp. 27-43, 1934 [June].

Lyon, Marcus Ward, Jr.—Distribution of the Red Squirrel in Indiana. Amer. Midland Nat., vol. 15, pp. 375-376, 1934 [Aug. 1].

Major, Noah J.—The pioneers of Morgan County. Indiana Hist. Soc. Pubs., vol. 5, no. 5, pp. 313-316, 1915.

Marest, Father Gabriel.—Journeys through Illinois and Michigan, 1712. In Kip. William Ingraham. The early Jesuit Missions in North America. Wiley and Putnam, New York, Part 1, pp. 223-224, 1846.

[Mason, O. T.]—Recent extinction of the mastodon. Amer. Nat., vol. 16, p. 75, 1882.

Matthew, W. D.—Mammoths and Mastodons. A guide to the collections of fossil proboscideans in the American Museum of Natural History, 1915 Nov.

M'Caslin, David. Geology of Jay County, Indiana. Dept. Geol. Nat. Hist. 12th Ann. Rep. 1882, p. 169, 1883.

McAtee, W. L.—A list of the mammals, reptiles and batrachians of Monroe County, Indiana. Proc. Biol. Soc. Washington, vol. 20, pp. 1-16, 1907 Feb. 25.

McDonald.—A Twentieth Century History of Marshall County, Indiana. The Lewis Publishing Co., Chicago, 1908, vol. 1, pp. 2-3.

*Merriam, Clinton Hart.—The Vertebrates of the Adirondack Region, Northeastern New York. Mammalia. Trans. Linn. Soc. New York, vol. 1, pp. 27-106, 1882, vol. 2, pp. 9-214, 1884.

Merriam, C. Hart.—The occurrence of Cooper's Lemming Mouse *(Synaptomys cooperi)* in the Atlantic States. Proc. Biol. Soc. Washington, vol. 7, pp. 175-177, 1892 Dec. 22.

*Merriam, C. Hart.—Monographic Revision of the Pocket Gophers. North American Fauna, No. 8, 1895.

Merriam, C. Hart.—Revision of the Shrews of the American genera Blarina and Notiosorex. North Amer. Fauna, No. 10, 1895 Dec. 31.

Merriam, C. Hart.—Synopsis of the American Shrews of the genus Sorex. North Amer. Fauna, No. 10, 1895 Dec. 31.

Merriam, C. Hart.—Revision of the Lemmings of the genus *Synaptomys*, with descriptions of new species. Proc. Biol. Soc. Washington, vol. 10, pp. 55-64, 1896.

*Merriam, C. Hart.—Synopsis of the Weasels of North America. North Amer. Fauna, No. 11, pp. 1-35, pls. 1-5, 1896.

Merriam, John C.—The fauna of Rancho La Brea. Mem. Univ. California, vol. 1, pp. 218--246, 1912.

MERRIAM, JOHN C.—Note on the systematic position of the Wolves of the Canis dirus group. Bull. Dept. Geol. Univ. California, vol. 10, pp. 531-533, 1918.

MEYERS.—[Mastedons]. Amer. Nat., vol. 2, p. 56, 1868 Jan.

MIDDLETON, W. G. AND JOSEPH MOORE.—Skull of fossil bison. Proc. Indiana Acad. Sci. for 1899, pp. 178-181, 1 pl., 1900.

MILLER, GERRIT S., JR.—Revision of the North American Bats of the family Vespertilionidae North Amer. Fauna, No. 13, 1897 Oct. 16.

MILLER, GERRIT S., JR. AND GLOVER M. ALLEN.—The American Bats of the genera Myotis and Pizonyx. Bull. U. S. Nat. Mus., No. 144, 1928.

*MILLER, GERRIT S., JR. AND JAMES W. GIDLEY.—Synopsis of the supergeneric groups of Rodents. Journ. Washington Acad. Sci., vol. 8, pp. 431-448, July 19, 1918.

MITCHELL, SAMUEL L.—Cuvier. Essay on the Theory of the Earth to which are now added Observations on the Geology of North America. Kirk & Mercein, New York, 1818, p. 363.

*MIZELLE, JOHN D.—Swimming of the Muskrat. Journ. Mamm., vol. 16, no. 1, pp. 22-25, 1935 Feb.

*MOHR, CHARLES E.—Observations on the young of cave-dwelling bats. Journ. Mamm., vol. 14, pp. 49-53, 1933 Feb.

MONTGOMERY, M. W.—History of Jay County, Indiana. Church, Goodman and Cushing, 1864.

MOODIE, ROY L.—The Geological History of the Vertebrates of Indiana. Department of Conservation, Pub. No. 90, pp. 1-115, 1929.

MOORE, JOSEPH.—A recent find of Castoroides. Amer. Nat., vol. 24, pp. 767-768, 1890 Aug.

MOORE, JOSEPH.—Concerning a skeleton of the great fossil beaver, Castoroides ohioensis. Journ. Cincinnati Soc. Nat. Hist., vol. 13, pp. 138-169, 1890 Oct.

MOORE, JOSEPH.—Concerning some portions of Castoroides Ohioensis not heretofore known. Proc. Amer. Ass. Adv. Sci. for 39th meeting held at Indianapolis, August 1890, pp. 265-267, 1891 July.

MOORE, JOSEPH.—[Castoroides]. Proc. Indiana. Acad. Sci., for 1891, p. 26, 1892.

MOORE, JOSEPH.—The recently found Castoroides in Randolph County, Indiana. Amer. Geol., vol. 12, pp. 67-74, 1 pl., 1893 Aug.

MOORE, JOS.—The Randolph mastodon. Proc. Indiana Acad. Sci., for 1896, pp. 277-278, 1 pl., 1897.

MOORE, JOSEPH.—A cranium of Castoroides found at Greenfield, Ind. Proc. Indiana Acad. Sci., for 1899, pp. 171-173, 2 pls., 1900.

MOSELEY, E. L.—The number of young red bats in one litter. Journ. Mamm., vol. 9, p. 249, 1928 Aug.

*MOSSMAN, H. W., JOHN W. LAWLAH, AND J. A. BRADLEY.—The male reproductive tract of the Sciuridae. Amer. Journ. Anat., vol. 51, pp. 89-155, figs. 1-16, pls. 1-7, 1932 Sept.

*MURIE, O. J. AND ADOLPH MURIE.—Travels of Peromyscus. Journ. Mamm., vol. 12, pp. 200-209, 1931 August.

NELSON, E. W.—The Rabbits of North America. North Amer. Fauna, No. 29, 1909 Aug. 31.

*NELSON, EDWARD W.—Wild Animals of North America. National Geographic Society, Washington, D. C., 1918. A handsomely illustrated account of the more important mammals of North America.

NEWTON, L. H.—History of Allen County, Indiana. Kingman Brothers, Chicago, 1880, p. 154.

OSGOOD, WILFRED H.—Revision of the Mice of the American genus *Peromyscus.* North Amer. Fauna, No. 28, 1909 April 17.

OSBORN, HENRY FAIRFIELD.—A mounted skeleton of the Columbian mammoth (Elephas columbi). Bull. Amer. Mus. Nat. Hist., vol. 23, pp. 255-257, 1 fig., 1907 March 30.

OSBORN, HENRY FAIRFIELD.—Species of American Pleistocene Mammoths. *Elephas jeffersonii* new species. Amer. Mus. Novit., No. 41, pp. 1-16, 12 figs., 1922 July 6.

OSBORN, HENRY FAIRFIELD.—Parelephas in relation to phyla and genera of the family Elephantidae. Amer. Mus. Novit., No. 152, pp. 1-7, 1924 Dec. 20.

OSBORN, HENRY FAIRFIELD.—Final conclusions on the evolution, phylogeny and classification of the Proboscidea. Proc. Amer. Phil. Soc., vol. 64, pp. 17-35, 1925.

OSBORN, HENRY FAIRFIELD.—The romance of the woolly mammoth. Nat. Hist., vol. 30, pp. 227-241, 1930 May-June.

OSBORN, HENRY FAIRFIELD.—Parelephas floridanus from the Upper Pleistocene of Florida compared with P. jeffersonii. Amer. Mus. Novit., No. 443, pp. 1-17, 1930 Dec. 18.

OWEN, RICHARD.—Report of a Geological Reconnaissance of Indiana made during the years 1859 and 1860 under the direction of the late David Dale Owen, State Geologist, 1862.

PACKARD, A. S.—The cave fauna of North America, with remarks on the anatomy of the brain and origin of the blind species. Mem. Nat. Acad. Sci., vol. 4, p. 16, 1888.

PARSONS, JOHN, edited by Kate Milner Rabb.—A Tour through Indiana in 1840. Robert M. McBride & Co., New York, 1920.

PHINNEY, A. J.—Geology of Delaware County. Indiana Dept. Geol. Nat. Hist., 11th Ann. Rep. 1881, p. 131, 1882.

PHINNEY, A. J.—Geology of Randolph County. Indiana Dept. Geol. Nat. Hist., 12th Ann. Rep., 1882, p. 181, 1883.

PHINNEY, A. J.—Geology of Grant County. Indiana Dept. Geol. Nat. Hist., 13th Ann. Rep., 1883, p. 143, 1884.

PLEAS, ELWOOD.—[Communication without title]. Nautilus, vol. 4, p. 131, 1891 March.

PLUMMER, JOHN T.—Miscellaneous observations on insects, &c. Tooth and Grinder of a Mastodon. Amer. Journ. Sci. Arts, vol. 40, p. 149, 1841.

PLUMMER, JOHN T.—Suburban geology, or rock soils and water about Richmond, Wayne County, Indiana. Amer. Journ. Sci. Arts, vol. 44, p. 302, 1843.

PLUMMER, JOHN T.—Scraps in natural history (Quadrupeds). Amer. Journ. Sci. Arts, vol. 46, pp. 236-249, 1844.

*POCOCK, R. I.—The Classification of the Sciuridae. Proc. Zool. Soc. London, 1923, vol. 1, pp. 209-246, 1923.

PREBLE, EDWARD A.—Revision of the Jumping Mice of the genus Zapus. North Amer. Fauna, No. 15, 1899 Aug. 8.

QUICK, EDGAR R.—Mammalogy. Journ. Cincinnati Soc. Nat. Hist., vol. 4, p. 337, 1881 Dec.

QUICK, EDGAR R.—Mammalogy. Journ. Cincinnati Soc. Nat. Hist., vol. 5, p. 52, 1882 Apr.

QUICK, EDGAR R. AND A. W. BUTLER.—The habits of some Arvicolinae. Amer. Nat., vol. 19, pp. 113-118, 1885 Feb.

QUICK, EDGAR R. [AND] F. W. LANGDON.—Mammals found in Franklin County, Indiana. Atlas of Franklin County, Indiana. J. H. Beers & Co., Chicago, 1882, pp. 9-10.

REED, EARL H.—Tales of a Vanishing River [Kankakee]. John Lane Company, New York, 1920.

*REISINGER, LUDWIG.—Die spezifischen Drüsen der Bisamratte. Anat. Anz., vol. 49, pp. 321-328, figs. 1-5, 1916 Sept. 23.

RERICK, J. H.—History of LaGrange County. In Counties of LaGrange and Noble, Indiana. F. A. Battey & Co., Chicago, 1882.

*RHOADS, SAMUEL N.—The Mammals of Pennsylvania and New Jersey. Philadelphia, privately published, 1903.

SANBORN, COLIN C.—Mammals of the Chicago Area. Field Museum of Natural History, Zool. Leaflet, No. 8, pp. 1-23, 1925.

SANBORN, COLIN CAMPBELL.—Notes from northern and central Illinois. Journ. Mamm., vol. 11, p. 222, 1930 May.

*SCHEFFER, THEO. H.—American moles as agricultural pests and as fur producers. U. S. Dept. Agric. Farm. Bull., No. 1247, pp. 1-22, 16 figs., 1922 March.

SCHOOLEY, J. P.—A summer breeding season in the Eastern Chipmunk, Tamias striatus. Journ. Mamm., vol. 15, pp. 194-196, 1934 August.

SETON, ERNEST THOMPSON.—The mane on the tail of the Gray Fox. Journ. Mamm., vol. 4, pp. 180-182, figs. 1-2, 1923 Aug.

*SETON, ERNEST THOMPSON.—Lives of Game Animals. Doubleday. Doran & Company, Inc., Garden City, New York, 1929. Four volumes of detailed information, numerous bibliographic citations, drawings and photographs by the author. Mr. Seton has graciously given permission to quote portions of his valuable lives in the text.

*SHELDON, CAROLYN.—Studies on the life histories of Zapus and Napaeozapus in Nova Scotia. Journ. Mamm., vol. 15, no. 4, pp. 290-300, 1934 Nov.

SHIRTS, AUGUSTUS FINCH.—A History of the Formation, Settlement and Development of Hamilton County, Indiana, from the year 1818 to the Close of the Civil War, 1901. Privately printed.

SIMPSON, PAUL F.—The Garrett Mastodon. Proc. Indiana Acad. Sci., vol. 34, pp. 154-155, fig. 1, 1934 June.

SLONAKER, JAMES ROLLIN.—A preliminary report on the eye of the mole (Scalops aquaticus machrinus). Proc. Indiana Acad. Sci., for 1899, pp. 146-149, 1900.

*STEGEMAN, LEROY C.—Notes on *Synaptomys cooperi cooperi* in Washtenaw County, Michigan. Journ. Mamm., vol. 11, pp. 460-466, 1930 November.

STODDARD, H. L.—Nests of the Western Fox Squirrel. Journ. Mamm., vol. 1, pp. 122-123, 1 pl., 1920 June 19.

*STONE, WITMER, AND WILLIAM EVERETT CRAM.—American Animals. Doubleday Page & Company, New York, 1905.

*STRUTHERS, PARKE H.—Breeding habits of the Canadian Porcupine. Journ. Mamm., vol. 9, pp. 300-308, pls. 22-23, 1928 November.

STUART, BENJ. F.—History of the Wabash and Valley. Longwell-Cummings Co., 1924, pp. 245-247. An old timer describes red fox hunt.

*SVIHLA, ARTHUR.—Habits of the Louisiana Mink (Mustela vison vulgivagus). Journ. Mamm., vol. 12, pp. 366-368, 1931 Nov.

*SVIHLA, ARTHUR.—A comparative life history study of the genus Peromyscus. Univ. of Michigan Mus. Zool. Miscell. Pub., No. 24, pp. 1-39, 1932 July 8.

*SVIHLA, ARTHUR AND RUTH DOWELL SVIHLA.—The Louisiana Muskrat. Journ. Mamm., vol. 12, pp. 12-28, 1931 Feb.

*SVIHLA, ARTHUR AND RUTH DOWELL SVIHLA.—Notes on the Jumping Mouse, Zapus trinotatus Rhoads. Journ. Mamm., vol. 14, pp. 131-134, 1933 May.

TENNEY, SANBORN.—Hibernation of the Jumping Mouse. Amer. Nat., vol. 6, pp. 330-332, 1872.

THOMAS, DAVIS.—Travels through the western country in the summer of 1816 [1819] in Lindley, Harlow. Indiana Historical Commission. Indianapolis, 1916.

THOMPSON, ALEXANDER C.—History of Marshall County, Indiana, 1890, p. 66.

THOMPSON, W. H.—A geological survey of Clinton County, Indiana. Dept. Geol. Nat. Hist., 15th Ann. Rep., 1886, p. 159 [1887].

TROUESSART, E. - L.—Catalogus Mammalium tam Viventium quam Fossilium. 1897-1899.

TRUE, FREDERICK W.—The puma or American lion: Felis concolor of Linnaeus. Rep. U. S. Nat. Mus., 1889, p. 596, 1891.

TRUE, FREDERICK W.—A revision of the American moles. Proc. U. S. Nat. Mus., vol. 19, pp. 1-112, 1896 Dec. 21.

TYNDALL, JOHN W. AND O. E. LESH.—Standard History of Adams and Wells Counties, Indiana. Lewis Publishing Company, Chicago and New York, 1918.

*ULBRICH, JOHANNES.—Die Bisamratte, Lebensweise, Gang ihrer Ausbreitung in Europa, wirtschaftliche Bedeutung und Bekämpfung. C. Heinnich, Dresden, 1930, 137 pp., 46 pls., 2 maps.

VOGEL, WILLIAM FREDERICK.—Wild game and hunting. Indiana Mag. Hist., vol. 10, p. 17, 1914 June.

*VRTIS, V.—Ueber die s. g. Seitendrüsen der Wasserrate "Arvicola" und des Hamsters "Cricetus." Arch Zool. Italiano, vol. 16, pp. 790-795, pl. 25, 1931.

*VRTIS, V.—The anal glands and the anus of the field-vole (Microtus arvalis [Pall.]) Biol. Spisy, Vysoké Skoly Zverol., vol. 8, fasc. 11, pp. 1-43, figs. 1-4, 1929.

*VRTIS, V.—The development of the sebaceous anal glands of the field-vole (Microtus arvalis [Pall.]) and their changes during breeding season and aging. Biol. Spisy, Vysoké Skoly Zverol., vol. 8, fasc. 12, pp. 1-43, figs. 1-7, 1929.

*VRTIS, V.—Glandular organs on the flanks of the water rat, their development and changes during breeding season. Biol. Spisy, Vysoké Skoly Zverol., vol. 9, fasc. 4, pp. 1-51, figs. 1-13, 1930.

*WADE, OTIS.—The behavior of certain Spermophiles with special reference to aestivation and hibernation. Journ. Mamm., vol. 11, pp. 160-188, 1 pl., 1930 May.

WALKER, ERNEST P.—The Red Squirrel extending its range in Indiana. Journ. Mamm., vol. 4, pp. 127-128, 1933 May 9.

WARDER, ROBERT B.—Geology of Dearborn, Ohio, and Switzerland Counties. 3d and 4th Ann. Repts., Geol. Surv. Indiana, 1871 and 1872, p. 402, [1873].

WARREN, JOHN C.—The Mastodon giganteus of North America. Ed. 2, p. 170, 1855. Records mastodon found at White River, between Vincennes and Harmony (Knox-Gibson County line). Bones and drawings, and other bones nearer entrance of Wabash to Ohio, skin and hair said to have been present.

WEAVER, ABRAHAM E.—Standard History of Elkhart County, Indiana. 1916, vol. 1, pp. 38-39.

*WEBER, MAX.—Die Säugetiere, ed. 2, vol. 1, anatomischer Teil. i-xv, 1-444, 1927, vol. 2, systematischer Teil. i-xxiv, 1-898, 1928. Gustav Fischer, Jena. This is the most complete modern work dealing with mammals in a technical manner.

WERICH, J. LORENZO.—Pioneer Hunters of the Kankakee. 1920. Privately printed.

*WHITNEY, LEON F.—The Raccoon and its hunting. Journ. Mamm., vol. 12, pp. 29-38, 1931 Feb.

WIED, MAXIMILIAN, PRINZ ZU.—Reise in das Innere Nord-Amerika in den Jahren 1832 bis 1834, vols. 1 and 2, 1839-41. List and notes of the mammals about New Harmony, observed during the winter of 1832 to 1833. This is the earliest list of Indiana mammals.

WIED, MAXIMILIAN, PRINCE OF.—Travels in the Interior of North America, translated from the German by H. Evans Lloyd. Ackerman and Co., London, 1843. Reprinted in Reuben Gold Thwaites. Early Western Travels, 1748-1846. The Arthur H. Clark Company, Cleveland, Ohio, vols. 22 and 23, 1906. The translation is rather free.

WIED, MAXIMILIAN, PRINZ ZU.—Verzeichniss der auf seiner Reise in Nord-Amerika beobachteten Säugethiere. Berlin, pp. 1-240, 4 pls. Reprinted from Arch. f. Naturg., vol. 27, pt. 1, pp. 181-288, [equals pp. 5-112 of reprint], 1861; and Arch. f. Naturg., vol. 28, pt. 1, pp. 66-190 [equals pp. 113-237 of reprint]. 1862. Plates 1-3 in vol. 27, and 4 in vol. 28.

*WIGHT, H. M.—Reproduction in the Eastern Skunk (Mephitis mephitis nigra). Journ. Mamm., vol. 12, pp. 42-47, 1931 Feb.

WILSON, GEORGE R.—History of Dubois County from its Primitive Days to 1910. Published by author, 1910.

WILSON, GEORGE R.—Early Indiana Trails and Surveys. Indiana Hist. Soc. Publ., vol. 6, pt. 3, pp. 364-380, 1919.

WOOD, NORMAN A.—Notes on the mammals of Berrien County, Michigan. Occ Papers Mus. Zool. Univ. Michigan, No. 124, pp. 1-4, 1922 July 10. Lists 19 species of mammals from across the northern border of Indiana.

WRIGHT, N. W., in C. HART MERRIAM.—The Mink (Lutreola vison). Ann. Rep. Dept. Agric., 1888, p. 490, 1889.

WYLIE, T. A.—Teeth and bones of Elephas primogenius, lately found near the western fork of White River, in Monroe County, Indiana. Amer. Journ. Sci. Arts, ser. 2, vol. 28, pp. 283-284, 1859.

YOUNG, ANDREW W.—History of Wayne County, Indiana. Cincinnati, 1872.

YOUNG, CALVIN M.—Notes from Calvin M. Young. Indiana Mag. Hist., vol. 8, pp. 33-34, 1912. Records Canada lynx from Starke County "over 60 years ago".

INDEX

Figures in bold face indicate principal references; others, synonyms and secondary references. For the sake of simplicity all names have been treated as binomials.

Adelonycteris fuscus 74
Aenocyon **155**
     dirus 10, **156**
afer, Homo **168**
africana, Loxodonta 341
agrarias, Mus 238
allegheniensis, Mustela **103**
     Putorius 103
Allegheny Cave Rat **243**
American Indian 168
American Porcupines 281
americana, Martes **99**
     Mephitis 128
     Mustela 99
     Taxidea 131
americanum, Mammut **338**, 341
americanus, Bison 320
     Bos 317
     Calomys 239
     Castor 220
     Elephas 338
     Equus 332
     Euarctos 89, **93**
     Homo 168
     Lepus 288, 290
     Mastodon 338
     Scapanus 27
     Ursus 89, **93**
Amphisorex leseurii...............9, 39
     lesueurii 39
Ancient Bison **321**
     Peccary **301**
antiquus, Bison **321**
Apes **167**
aquaticus, Lepus 295
     Scalops 28
     Scalopus **28**
     Sorex 28
     Sylvilagus 295
Arctomys franklinii 182
     monax 172
     pruinosus 172
Armadillo 5
Artiodactyla **296**
arundivaga, Felis **158**
Arvicola austerus 257
     pennsylvanicus 254
     pinetorum 259
     riparias 254
     riparius 254
     scalopsoides 261

     xanthognata 257
Atalapha cinerea **80**
     noveboracensis **78**
ater, Canis 150
athabascae, Bison **317**
aureolus, Peromyscus **241**
auricularis, Pitymys **262**
austerus, Arvicola 257
Austral Region 12
austroriparius, Vespertilio **62**
avia, Chincha 129
     Mephitis **129**

Bachman's Shrew 14, **43**
Badger **131**
bairdii, Mus **236**
     Peromyscus **236**
Bat, Big Eared **14**
     Common **56**
     Georgian **71**
     Hairy-Tailed **78**
     Hoary **80**
     Howell's **63**
     Indiana **66**
     Leib's **67**
     Large Brown **74**
     Little Brown **60**
     Mouse-Eared **57**
     Rafinesque's **83**, **84**
     Red **78**
     Serotine **74**
     Silver-Haired **68**
     Trouessart's **65**
Bats 12, **53**
Bay Lynx **164**
Bear, Black 89, **351**
Beaver **220**
     Giant **226**, **228**, **230**
Big Eared Bat 14, **85**, **86**
Bison **315**
     americanus 320
     Ancient **321**
     antiquus **321**
     athabascae 317
     bison 317, **320**
     latifrons **322**
     pennsylvanicus **319**
     Plains **317**
     Wide-browed **322**
bison, Bison 317, **320**
     Bos 317

Black Bear 89
Black Rat 272
Blarina 47
    brevicauda 47, 53
    carolinensis 53
    cinerea 45
    exilipes 45
    parva 45
    platyrhinus 39
Bob-cat 161, 164
Bonaparte's Weasel 109
Bootherium cavifrons 329
Boreal Region 12
borealis, Lasiurus 78
    Nycteris 78
    Vespertilio 78
boreus, Elephas 342, 343
Bos americanus 317
    bison 317
    latifrons 322
    moschatus 325
Bovidae 315
Brachysorex harlani 45
brevicauda, Blarina 47, 53
breweri, Parascalops 27
    Scalops 27
Brewer's Mole 27
Buff-bellied Meadow Mouse 257
Buffalo 317
bursarius, Geomys 216
    Mus 216

Calomys americanus 239
    michiganensis 236
    palustris 241
campestris, Lepus 288
Canada Lynx 162
canadensis, Castor 220
    Cervus 303, 307
    Dipus 277
    Gerbillus 277
    Lutra 117
    Lynx 162
    Mustela 100
    Scalops 28
Canidae 134
Canis 143
    ater 150
    cinereoargentatus 141
    cinereoargenteus 141
    dirus 156
    fulvus 136
    indianensis 156
    lacyon 150
    latrans 143, 150
    lupus 150
    nubilis 150
    nubilus 150
    occidentalis 150

primaevus 156
Cariacus dolichopsis 313
    virginianus 307
Carnivora 88
Carolina Short-Tailed Shrew 53
carolinensis, Blarina 53
    Castor 220
    Sciurus 199, 204
    Sorex 53
Castor 220
    americanus 220
    canadensis 220
    carolinensis 220
    fiber 220
    michiganensis 220
    zibethicus 264
Castoridae 220
Castoroides 228
    ohioensis 230
Castoroididae 226
Cat 157
Catamount 164
Cave Rat 231, 242
    Allegheny 243
cavifrons, Bootherium 329
    Ovibos 329
    Scaphoceros 329
    Symbos 329
Cervidae 302
Cervus 303
    canadensis 303, 307, 352
    virgianus 307, 311
Chickaree 195
Chincha avia 129
    putida 128
Chipmunk 187
    Fisher's 187
    Mearns' 12, 191
Chiroptera 53
cicognanii, Mustela 109
cinerea, Atalapha 80
    Blarina 45
cinereoargentatus, Canis 141
    Urocyon 141
cinereoargenteus, Canis 141
    Urocyon 141
Cinereous Shrew 14, 39
cinereus, Lasiurus 80
    Sciurus 199
    Sorex 39
    Vespertilio 80
Citellus 178
    franklinii 182
    tridecemlineatus 179
Colored Man 168
columbi, Elephas 343, 348
Columbian Mammoth 342 348
Common Moles 28
Common Short-Tailed Shrew............................47

complicatus, Equus 332
compressus, Mammonteus 343
         Platigonus 301
         Platygonus 301
concolor, Felis 158
Condylura 34
       cristata 35
cooperi, Synaptomys 251
Cope's Deer 313
Corynorhinus 14, 85
       macrotis 86
       megalotis 86
       rafinesquii 86
Cottontail 289, 290
Cougar 158
cougar, Felis 158
Couguar, Felis 158
Coyote 134 143
       Pleistocene 150
Cricetinae 231
Cricetine Muroids 231
cristata, Condylura 35
cristatus, Sorex 35
Cryptotis 45
       parva 45

Dama dolichopsis 314
       virginiana 311
decumanus, Mus 271
Deer 296, 302, 303
       Cope's 313
       North American 307
       Virginia 307, 352
       White-tailed 307
Deinotheriidae 334
Dental formula 17
Dicotyles lenis 297
       nasutus 299
Didelphiidae 19
Didelphis 19
       pigra 19
       virginiana 19
Dipodoidae 276
Dipus canadensis 277
       hudsonius 277
Dire Wolf 12, 155, 156
dirus, Aenocyon 156
       Canis 156
Dogs 143
dolichopsis, Cariacus 313
       Dama 314
       Odocoileus 313
dorsata, Hystrix 283
dorsatum, Erethizon 283
dorsatus, Erethizon 283

Eastern Red Squirrel 195
Eastern Skunk 127
Ecologic areas 10

Edentates 349
Elephantidae 335
Elephants 334, 335, 341
Elephas 341
       americanus 338
       boreus 342, 343
       columbi 343, 348
       jeffersonii 343
       primigenius 341, 342, 343
       roosevelti 343
Elk 303, 352
Eptesicus 74
       fuscus 74
Equidae 332
Equus 332
       americanus 332
       complicatus 332
       fraternus 332
       major 332
Erethizon 281
       dorsatum 283
       dorsatus 283
Erethizontidae 281
erminea, Mustela 104
       Putorius 104
Euarctos 89
       americanus 89, 93, 351
       luteolus 89
exilipes, Blarina 45

Felidae 157
Felis 157
       arundivaga 158
       concolor 158
       cougar 158
       couguar 158
       rufa 164
Fiber 262
fiber, Castor 220
Fiber, zibethicus 264
Fisher 99, 100
fisheri, Tamias 187
Fisher's Chipmunk 187
Flesh-Eaters 88
floridana, Neotoma 243, 247
floridanus, Sylvilagus 290
Flying Squirrel 210, 211
Fox 134
       Gray 140, 141
       Red 136
Fox Squirrel 205
franklinii, Arctomys 182
       Citellus 182
       Spermophilus 182
Franklin's Gopher 182
       Ground-Squirrel 12, 182
fraternus, Equus 332
fulva, Vulpes 136
fulvus, Canis 136

fumeus, Sorex 44
fuscus, Adelonycteris 74
          Eptesicus 74
          Vespertililio 74

Gentle Peccary **297**
Geology, Glacial 13
Geomyidae **214**
Geomys **215**
          bursarius **216**
          illinoensis **216**
          pinctis **216**
Georgian Bat 71
Gerbillus canadensis **277**
Giant Beaver **226, 230**
giganteum, Mastodon **338**
giganteus, Mastodon **338**
Glacial Geology 13
Glaucomys **210**
          volans **211**
Gnawing Mammals **169**
Gopher, Franklin's **182**
          Gray **182**
          Pocket **214, 215**
          Thirteen-lined **179**
gossypinus, Peromyscus **241**
Gravigrada **349**
Gray Fox **140, 141**
Gray Gopher **182**
Gray Squirrel **14, 199**
          Northern **204**
          Southern **204**
Gray Wolf **150**
grisescens, Myotis 63
griseus, Tamias **191**
Ground-hog **172**
          Southern **172**
Ground-Sloth **12, 349**
Ground-Squirrel **178**
          Franklin's **12, 182**
          Striped **179**
          Thirteen-lined **12, 179**
gryphus, Vespertilio **60, 66**
Guerlinguetus **195**
Gulo **113**
          luscus **113**
Guloninae 99

Hairy Mammoth **342**
Hairy-Tailed Bats 78
Hairy-tailed Mole **26, 27**
Hare **286, 287**
          Varying **288**
harlani, Brachysorex 45
Harvest Mice **231**
Hays' Tapir **330**
haysii, Tapirus **330**
Hedgehog **283**

Hesperomys indianus **10, 274**
          leucopus **239**
          maniculatus **236**
Hoary Bat 80
Holarctic Region 12
Hominidae **167**
Homo **168**
          afer **168**
          americanus **168**
          sapiens **168**
Horse **332**
House Mouse **274**
House Rat **270, 271**
Howell's Bat 63
hoyi, Microsorex 45
          Sorex 45
Hoy's Pigmy Shrew 45
hudsonica, Lutra **117**
hudsonicus, Sciurus **195**
hudsonius, Dipus **277**
          Hystrix **283**
          Zapus **277**
humeralis, Nycticeius 84
          Vespertilio 84
humulis, Mus **231**
          Ochetodon **231**
Hypudaeus ochrogaster **257**
Hystricoidea **281**
Hystricomorph Rodents **281**
Hystrix dorsata **283**
          hudsonius **283**

illinoensis, Geomys **216**
          Neotoma **247**
Illinois Pocket Gopher **216**
Illinois Skunk **129**
Indian, American **168**
Indiana Bat 66
indianensis, Canis **156**
indianus, Hesperomys **274**
Insectivora 25
insignis, Stegodon **341**

jeffersonii, Elephas **343**
          Megalonyx **350**
          Megatherium **350**
          Paralephas **343**
Jefferson's ground-sloth **349, 350**
Jefferson's Mammoth **343**
Jerboas **276**
Jumping Mouse **276, 277**

lacyon, Canis **150**
Lagomorpha **286**
Large Brown Bat 74
Lasionycteris 68
          noctivagans 68

Lasiurus 78
      borealis 78
      cinereus 80
lataxina, Lutra 117
latifrons, Bison 322
      Bos 322
latrans, Canis 143, 150
Least Weasel 103
lecontii, Reithrodontomys 231
leibii, Myotis 67
Leib's Bat 67
Lemming Mouse 14, 251
            Stone's 251
Lemmings 247
Lemurs 167
lenis, Dicotyles 297
      Tayassu 297
Leporidae 287
Lepus 287
      americanus 288, 290
      aquaticus 295
      campestris 288
      phaeonotus 288
      sylvaticus 290
leseurii, Amphisorex 39
lesueurii, Amphisorex 39
leucopus, Hesperomys 239
      Mus 238
      Musculus 238
      Peromyscus 239
leucotis, Sciurus 204
Life Zones 12
Little Brown Bat 60
littoralis, Sylvilagus 295
Long-snouted Peccary 298, 299
longirostris, Sorex 43
loquax, Sciurus 195
lotor, Procyon 95
      Ursus 95
louisianae, Odocoileus 311
Lower Austral Zone 12
Loxodonta 335
        africana 341
lucifugus, Myotis 60, 66
        Vespertilio 60
ludovicianus, Sciurus 205
lupus, Canis 150
luscus, Gulo 113
      Ursus 113
luteolus, Euarctos 89
Lutra 115
      canadensis 117
      hudsonica 117
      lataxina 117
lutreocephalus, Lutreola 109
Lutreola lutreocephalus 109
      vison 109
Lutrinae 99
Lyncus rufus 164

Lynx 161
      Bay 164
      Canada 162
      canadensis 162
      rufus 164

machrina, Talpa 28
machrinus, Scalops 28
      Scalopus 28
macrotis, Corynorhinus 86
major, Equus 332
Mammalia 14
Mammals 14
Mammonteus compressus 10, 343
Mammoth 10, 335, 341
      Columbian 342, 348
      Hairy 342
      Jefferson's 343
      Roosevelt's 343
Mammut 335
      americanum 338, 341, 352
      ohioticum 338
Man 168
      American Indian 168
      Colored 168
      White 168
maniculatus, Hesperomys 236
Marmot 171, 172
Marmota 172
      monax 172
Marsupialia 18
Marten 99
      Pine 99
Martes americana 99
      pennanti 100
Mastodon 10, 334, 335, 338, 352
      americanum 338
      giganteum 338
      giganteus 338
Meadow Mouse 247, 254
          Buff-bellied 257
          Pennsylvania 254
          Prairie 257
Mearns' Chipmunk 12, 191
mearnsii, Sylvilagus 290
Measurements 8
megacephalus, Peromyscus 241
Megalonychidae 349
Megalonyx 349
      jeffersonii 350
megalotis, Corynorhinus 86
Megatherium jeffersonii 350
Men 167, 168
mephitica, Mephitis 128
Mephitinae 99
Mephitis 123
      americana 128
      avia 129
      mephitica 128

mesomelas 128, 129
nigra 127
putida 128
putorius 121
merriami, Reithrodontomys 231
mesomelas, Mephitis 128, 129
michiganensis, Calomys 236
              Peromyscus 236
Microsorex 45
       hoyi 45
Microtinae 247, 250
Microtus 254
    austerus 257
    ochrogaster 257
    pennsylvanicus 254
    scalopsoides 261
migratorius, Sciurus 203
Mink 101, 109
mink, Mustela 109
Mole 25
    Brewer's 27
    Common 28
    Hairy-tailed 26, 27
    Prairie 28
    Star-nosed 14, 34, 35
Moles, Shrews, etc. 25
monax, Arctomys 172
    Marmota 172
    Mus 172
Monkey 167
moschatus, Bos 325
    Ovibos 325
Mouse, Harvest 231
    House 274
    Jumping 276, 277
    Lemming 14, 251
    Meadow 254
    Old World 270
    Pine 259
    White-footed 231, 233
Mouse-Eared Bats 57
Mouse-like Rodents 231
Muridae 270
Murmeltier 177
Muroidae 231
Muroids, Cricetine 231
Mus 274
    agrarias 238
    bairdii 236
    bursarius 216
    decumanus 271
    humilis 231
    leucopus 238
    monax 172
    musculus 274
    norvegicus 271
    noveboracensis 238
    palustris 241

rattus 272
sylvaticus 238
volans 211
Musculus, leucopus 238
musculus, Mus 274
Musk-ox 324, 325
    United-horn 326
Muskrat 247, 262, 264, 352
Mustela 101
    allegheniensis 103
    americana 99
    canadensis 100
    cicognanii 109
    erminea 104
    mink 109
    noveboracensis 104
    pennanti 100
    pusilla 103, 104
    vison 109
Mustelidae 98
Mustelinae 99
Mylohyus 298
            nasutus 10, 299
Myotis 57
    austroriparius 62
    grisescens 63
    leibii 67
    lucifugus 60, 66
    septentrionalis 65
    sodalis 10, 66
    subulatus 62, 65
    velifer 63

Narrow-snouted Peccary 301
Nasua 5
nasutus, Dicotyles 299
    Mylohyus 299
    Tayassu 299
Neosciurus 194
Neotoma 242
    floridana 243
    illinoensis 247
    pennsylvanica 243
New York Weasel 104
niger, Sciurus 195, 204, 205
nigra, Mephitis 127
    Viverra 127
noctivagans, Lasionycteris 68
Nomenclature 8
North American Deer 307
Northern Gray Squirrel 204
    Pine Mouse 261
    Short-Tailed Shrew 53
norvegicus, Mus 271
    Rattus 271
noveboracensis, Atalapha 78
    Mus 238
    Mustela 104

Peromyscus 238
Putorius 104
Vespertilio 78
nubilis, Canis 150
nubilus, Canis 150
nuttalli, Peromyscus 241
Nycteris borealis 78
Nycticeius 83
    humeralis 84
Nyctomys 5

obscurus, Pipistrellus 71
occidentalis, Canis 150
Ochetodon humilis 231
ochrogaster, Hypudaeus 257
    Microtus 257
Odocoileus 307
    dolichopsis 313
    louisianae 311
    virginianus 307, 311, 352
ohioensis, Castoroides 230
ohioticum, Mammut 338
Old World Mouse 270
Old World Rat 270
Ondatra 262
    zibethica 264, 352
Opossum 19
    Virginia 19
Opossums, etc. 18
Oryzomys 241
    palustris 241
Otter 115, 117
Ovibos 324
    cavifrons 329
    moschatus 325
Oxen 296

Painter 158
palustris, Calomys 241
    Mus 241
    Oryzomys 241
Panther 158
Parascalops 26
    breweri 27
Parasciurus 195
Parelephas jeffersonii 10, 343
parva, Blarina 45
    Cryptotis 45
parvus, Cryptotis 45
Peccary 10, 14, 297, 299
    Ancient 301
    Gentle 297
    Long-snouted 298, 299
    Narrow-snouted 301
    Two-toed 300
Pedomys 257
Pekan 100
pennanti, Martes 100

Mustela 100
Pennsylvania Meadow Mouse 254
pennsylvanica, Neotoma 243
pennsylvanicus, Arvicola 254
    Bison 319
    Microtus 254
Perissodactyla 330
Peromyscus 233
    aureolus 241
    bairdii 236
    gossypinus 241
    leucopus 239
    megacephalus 241
    michiganensis 236
    noveboracensis 238
    nuttalli 241
personatus, Sorex 39
pheonotus, Lepus 288
Physiographic features 10
Pig 296
Pigmy Shrew 45
    Hoy's 45
pigra, Didelphis 19
pinctis, Geomys 216
Pine Marten 99
Pine Mouse 259
    Northern 261
    Southern 262
pinetorum, Arvicola 259
    Pitymys 259
    Psammomys 259
Piney 195
Pipistrellus 71
    obscurus 71
    subflavus 71
Pitymys 259
    auricularis 262
    pinetorum 259
    scalopsoides 261
Plains Bison 317
Platigonus compressus 301
Platygonus 300
    compressus 301
    vetus 301
platyrhinus, Blarina 39
Plecotus rafinesquii 86
Pleistocene American Bison 320
Pleistocene Black Bear 93
Pleistocene Coyote 150
Pleistocene Elk 307
Pleistocene Period 10
Pleistocene Virginia Deer 311
Pocket Gopher 12, 214, 215
    Illinois 216
Porcupine 14, 281, 283
Prairie Meadow Mouse 257
    Mole 28
    Squirrel 182

White-footed mouse 12, 236
Wolf 143
primaevus, Canis 156
Primates 167
primigenius, Elephas 341, 342, 343
Proboscidea 334
procerus, Ursus 93
Procyon 95
        lotor 95
Procyonidae 95
pruinosus, Arctomys 172
         Vespertilio 80
Psammomys pinetorum 259
Pteromyinae 210
Pteromys volucella 211
Puma 158
pusilla, Mustela 103, 104
pusillus, Putorius 103
putida, Chincha 128
        Mephitis 128
Putorius allegheniensis 103
         erminea 104
putorius, Mephitis 121
Putorius noveboracensis 104
         pusillus 103
putorius, Spilogale 121
Putorius vison 109

Rabbit 286, 287
Rabbit, swamp 12, 14, 293, 295
Raccoon 95
Rafinesque's Bat 83, 84
rafinesquii, Corynorhinus 86
            Plecotus 86
Rat, Black 272
     Cave 231, 242
     House 270, 271
     Old World 270
     Rice 12, 14, 241
     Wood 12, 242
Rat-like Rodents 231
Rattus 270
rattus, Mus 272
Rattus norvegicus 271
        rattus 272
rattus, Rattus 272
Red Bat 78
Red Fox 136
Red Squirrel 14
Red Squirrel, Eastern 195
Reithrodontomys 231
               lecontii 231
               merriami 231
Rhoads' Bat 62
Rice Rat 12, 14, 241
riparius, Arvicola 254
Rodentia 169
Rodents 169

Hystricomorph 281
Mouse-like 231
Rat-like 231
roosevelti, Elephas 343
Roosevelt's Mammoth 343
rufa, Felis 164
rufiventer, Sciurus 205
rufiventris, Sciurus 205
rufus, Lyncus 164
       Lynx 164
       Vespertilio 78

sapiens, Homo 168
Say's Wolf 150
Scalops aquaticus 28
        breweri 27
        canadensis 28
        machrinus 28
scalopsoides, Arvicola 261
             Microtus 261
             Pitmys 261
Scalopus 28
        aquaticus 28
        machrinus 28
Scapanus americanus 27
Scaphoceros cavifrons 329
Sciuridae 171
Sciuroidea 171
Sciuropterus volans 211
Sciurus 194
        carolinensis 199, 204
        cinereus 199
        hudsonicus 195
        leucotis 204
        loquax 195
        ludovicianus 205
        migratorius 203
        niger 195, 204, 205
        rufiventer 205
        rufiventris 205
        striatus 187
        volucella 211
        vulpinus 205
septentrionalis, Myotis 65
               Vespertilio 65
Serotine Bats 74
Short-Tailed Shrew 47
               Common 47
Shrew 37
       Bachman's 14, 43
       Carolina Short-Tailed 53
       Cinereous 14, 39
       Common 39
       Pigmy 45
       Short-tailed 47
       Small Short-tailed 45
       Smoky 44
Siffleur 177

Silver-Haired Bat 68
Skunk, Common 123
    Eastern 127
    Illinois 12, 129
    Spotted 12, 14, 119, 121
Small Short-Tailed Shrew 45
Smoky Shrew 44
sodalis, Myotis 66
Sonoran Region 12, 14
Sorex 39
    aquaticus 28
    carolinensis 53
    cinereus 39
    cristatus 35
    fumeus 44
    harlani 10
    hoyi 45
    longirostris 43
    parvus 45
    personatus 39
Soricidae 37
Southern Gray Squirrel 204
Southern Ground-hog 172
Southern Pine Mouse 262
Southern Woodchuck 172
Spermophiles 171
Spermophilus franklinii 182
            tridecemlineatus 179
Spilogale 119
Spilogale putorius 121
Spotted skunk 12, 14, 119, 121
Squirrel 171, 194
    Flying 210, 211
    Fox 205
    Gray 14, 199
    Prairie 182
    Red 14, 195
Squirrel-like Rodents 171
Star-nosed Mole 14, 34, 35
Stegodon insignis 341
stonei, Synaptomys 251
Stone's Lemming Mouse.........................251
striatus, Sciurus 187
        Tamias 187
Striped Ground-Squirrel 179
subflavus, Pipistrellus 71
        Vespertilio 71
subulatus, Myotis 62, 65
        Vespertilio 67
Swamp Rabbit 12, 14, 289, 293, 295
sylvaticus, Lepus 290
        Mus 238
Silvilagus 289
    aquaticus 295
    floridanus 290
    littoralis 295
    mearnsii 290
Symbos 326

cavifrons 329
Synaptomys 14, 251
    cooperi 251
    stonei 251

tajacu, Tayassu 297
Talpa machrina 28
Talpidae 25
Tamias 187
    fisheri 187
    griseus 191
    striatus 187
Tamiasciurus 194
Tapeti 293
Tapir 12, 14, 330
    Hays' 330
Tapiridae 330
Tapirus 330
    haysii 330
    terrestris 330
Taxidea 131
    americana 131
    taxus 131
Taxidiinae 99
taxus, Taxidea 131
    Ursus 131
Tayassu 297
    lenis 297
    nasutus 299
    tajacu 297
Tayassuidae 297
Teeth 16
terrestris, Tapirus 330
Thirteen-lined Gopher 197
        Ground Squirrel.......12, 179
Thous 143
Timber Wolf 150
Transition Zone 12, 14
tridecemlineatus, Citellus 179
        Spermophilus 179
Tropical Region 14
Trouessart's Bat 65
Two-toed Peccary 300
Type locality 9

United-horn Musk-ox 326, 329
Upper Austral Zone 12, 14
Urocyon 140
    argentatus 141
    cinereoargentatus 141
    cinereoargenteus 141
Ursidae 89
Ursus americanus 89, 93
    lotor 95
    luscus 113
    procerus 93
    taxus 131

Varying Hare 288
velifer, Myotis 63
Vespertilio austroriparius 62
          borealis 78
          cinereus 80
          fuscus 74
          gryphus 60, 66
          humeralis 84
          lucifugus 60, 65
          noctivagans 68
          noveboracensis 78
          pruinosus 80
          rufus 78
          septentrionalis 65
          subflavus .... ·71
          subulatus 67
Vespertillionidae 56
vetus, Platygonus 301
Virginia Deer 307, 352
          Opossum 19
virginiana, Dama 311
          Didelphis 19
virginianus, Cariacus 307
          Cervus 307, 311
          Odocoileus 307, 311
          Vulpes 141
vison, Lutreola 109
          Mustela 109
Viverra nigra 127
volans, Glaucomys 211
          Mus 211
          Sciuropterus 211
Voles 247
volucella, Pteromys 211
          Sciurus 211
Vulpes fulva 136
          virginianus 141
          vulpes 136

vulpinus, Sciurus 205

Wapiti 303
Waschbär 96
Weasel 101
          Bonaparte's 109
          Least 103
          New York 104
Weasels and Allies 98
Weights 8
White Man 168
White-footed Mouse 233
                    Prairie 12, 236
                    Woodland 238
White-tailed Deer 307
Wide-browed Bison 322
Wild-cat 164
Wolf 134, 143
          Dire 12, 155, 156
          Gray 150
          Prairie 143
          Say's 150
          Timber 150
Wolverine 113
Wood Rat 12, 242
Woodchuck 172
          Southern 172
Woodland White-footed Mouse 238

xanthognata, Arvicola 257
Xenarthra 349

Zapodidae 276
Zapus 276
          hudsonius 277
zibethica, Ondatra 264, 352
zibethicus, Castor 264
          Fiber 264

NATURAL SCIENCES IN AMERICA

An Arno Press Collection

Allen, J[oel] A[saph]. **The American Bisons,** Living and Extinct. 1876

Allen, Joel Asaph. **History of the North American Pinnipeds:** A Monograph of the Walruses, Sea-Lions, Sea-Bears and Seals of North America. 1880

American Natural History Studies: The Bairdian Period. 1974

American Ornithological Bibliography. 1974

Anker, Jean. **Bird Books and Bird Art.** 1938

Audubon, John James and John Bachman. **The Quadrupeds of North America.** Three vols. 1854

Baird, Spencer F[ullerton]. **Mammals of North America.** 1859

Baird, S[pencer] F[ullerton], T[homas] M. Brewer and R[obert] Ridgway. **A History of North American Birds:** Land Birds. Three vols., 1874

Baird, Spencer F[ullerton], John Cassin and George N. Lawrence. **The Birds of North America.** 1860. Two vols. in one.

Baird, S[pencer] F[ullerton], T[homas] M. Brewer, and R[obert] Ridgway. **The Water Birds of North America.** 1884. Two vols. in one.

Barton, Benjamin Smith. **Notes on the Animals of North America.** Edited, with an Introduction by Keir B. Sterling. 1792

Bendire, Charles [Emil]. **Life Histories of North American Birds** With Special Reference to Their Breeding Habits and Eggs. 1892/1895. Two vols. in one.

Bonaparte, Charles Lucian [Jules Laurent]. **American Ornithology:** Or The Natural History of Birds Inhabiting the United States, Not Given by Wilson. 1825/1828/1833. Four vols. in one.

Cameron, Jenks. **The Bureau of Biological Survey:** Its History, Activities, and Organization. 1929

Caton, John Dean. **The Antelope and Deer of America:** A Comprehensive Scientific Treatise Upon the Natural History, Including the Characteristics, Habits, Affinities, and Capacity for Domestication of the Antilocapra and Cervidae of North America. 1877

Contributions to American Systematics. 1974

Contributions to the Bibliographical Literature of American Mammals. 1974

Contributions to the History of American Natural History. 1974

Contributions to the History of American Ornithology. 1974

Cooper, J[ames] G[raham]. **Ornithology.** Volume I, Land Birds. 1870

Cope, E[dward] D[rinker]. **The Origin of the Fittest:** Essays on Evolution and **The Primary Factors of Organic Evolution.** 1887/1896. Two vols. in one.

Coues, Elliott. **Birds of the Colorado Valley.** 1878

Coues, Elliott. **Birds of the Northwest.** 1874

Coues, Elliott. **Key To North American Birds.** Two vols. 1903

Early Nineteenth-Century Studies and Surveys. 1974

Emmons, Ebenezer. **American Geology:** Containing a Statement of the Principles of the Science. 1855. Two vols. in one.

Fauna Americana. 1825-1826

Fisher, A[lbert] K[enrick]. **The Hawks and Owls of the United States in Their Relation to Agriculture.** 1893

Godman, John D. **American Natural History:** Part I — Mastology and **Rambles of a Naturalist.** 1826-28/1833. Three vols. in one.

Gregory, William King. **Evolution Emerging:** A Survey of Changing Patterns from Primeval Life to Man. Two vols. 1951

Hay, Oliver Perry. **Bibliography and Catalogue of the Fossil Vertebrata of North America.** 1902

Heilprin, Angelo. **The Geographical and Geological Distribution of Animals.** 1887

Hitchcock, Edward. **A Report on the Sandstone of the Connecticut Valley,** Especially Its Fossil Footmarks. 1858

Hubbs, Carl L., editor. **Zoogeography.** 1958

[Kessel, Edward L., editor]. **A Century of Progress in the Natural Sciences: 1853-1953.** 1955

Leidy, Joseph. **The Extinct Mammalian Fauna of Dakota and Nebraska,** Including an Account of Some Allied Forms from Other Localities, Together with a Synopsis of the Mammalian Remains of North America. 1869

Lyon, Marcus Ward, Jr. **Mammals of Indiana.** 1936

Matthew, W[illiam] D[iller]. **Climate and Evolution.** 1915

Mayr, Ernst, editor. **The Species Problem.** 1957

Mearns, Edgar Alexander. **Mammals of the Mexican Boundary of the United States.** Part I: Families Didelphiidae to Muridae. 1907

Merriam, Clinton Hart. **The Mammals of the Adirondack Region,** Northeastern New York. 1884

Nuttall, Thomas. **A Manual of the Ornithology of the United States and of Canada.** Two vols. 1832-1834

Nuttall Ornithological Club. **Bulletin of the Nuttall Ornithological Club:** A Quarterly Journal of Ornithology. 1876-1883. Eight vols. in three.

[Pennant, Thomas]. **Arctic Zoology.** 1784-1787. Two vols. in one.

Richardson, John. **Fauna Boreali-Americana;** Or the Zoology of the Northern Parts of British America, Containing Descriptions of the Objects of Natural History Collected on the Late Northern Land Expeditions Under Command of Captain Sir John Franklin, R. N. Part I: Quadrupeds. 1829

Richardson, John and William Swainson. **Fauna Boreali-Americana:** Or the Zoology of the Northern Parts of British America, Containing Descriptions of the Objects of Natural History Collected by the Late Northern Land Expeditions Under Command of Captain Sir John Franklin, R. N. Part II: The Birds. 1831

Ridgway, Robert. **Ornithology.** 1877

Selected Works By Eighteenth-Century Naturalists and Travellers. 1974

Selected Works in Nineteenth-Century North American Paleontology. 1974

Selected Works of Clinton Hart Merriam. 1974

Selected Works of Joel Asaph Allen. 1974

Selections From the Literature of American Biogeography. 1974

Seton, Ernest Thompson. **Life-Histories of Northern Animals: An Account of the Mammals of Manitoba.** Two vols. 1909

Sterling, Keir Brooks. **Last of the Naturalists:** The Career of C. Hart Merriam. 1974

Vieillot, L. P. **Histoire Naturelle Des Oiseaux de L'Amerique Septentrionale,** Contenant Un Grand Nombre D'Especes Decrites ou Figurees Pour La Premiere Fois. 1807. Two vols. in one.

Wilson, Scott B., assisted by A. H. Evans. **Aves Hawaiienses:** The Birds of the Sandwich Islands. 1890-99

Wood, Casey A., editor. **An Introduction to the Literature of Vertebrate Zoology.** 1931

Zimmer, John Todd. **Catalogue of the Edward E. Ayer Ornithological Library.** 1926